The University of Santa Clara

The University of Santa Clara

A HISTORY
1851-1977

Gerald McKevitt, S.J.

To Sodie P. Arbios —
Santa Clara 1911
Gerald McKevitt S.J.

STANFORD UNIVERSITY PRESS

Stanford, California   1979

STANFORD UNIVERSITY PRESS
Stanford, California

© *1979 by the Board of Trustees of the*
LELAND STANFORD JUNIOR UNIVERSITY
Printed in the United States of America
ISBN 0-8047-1024-4
LC 78-65396

For Mother
and in Memory of Dad

Acknowledgments

M y list of debts is long. To John W. Caughey, who first suggested the history of Jesuit education in California to me as a field of historical inquiry, and to John B. McGloin, who directed me to the Santa Clara story, I am very grateful. I also owe a debt of gratitude to Santa Clara's former president Thomas D. Terry and former academic vice-president William F. Donnelly, who jointly invited me to the university in 1975 to research and write this book. They provided unconditional cooperation and assistance.

Aid in the research for the project was freely given by several institutions in the United States and Europe, including the Bancroft Library at the University of California, Berkeley; the Henry E. Huntington Library at San Marino, California; and the California State Library in Sacramento. Portions of this book appeared in somewhat different form in articles published in the following journals: *Records of the American Catholic Historical Society of Philadelphia* (Sep.–Dec. 1974), *Southern California Quarterly* (Summer 1976), *The Pacific Historian* (Winter 1976), and *San José Studies* (Feb. 1977). I thank the editors for permitting me to quote from those articles.

I am especially grateful for the generous research assistance provided by Leo C. Cullen and Thomas A. Marshall of the Archives of the California Province of the Society of Jesus at Los Gatos, California; Edmond Lamalle and his staff at the Archivum Historicum Societatis Iesu in Rome; Renato Guidotti, archivist of the Turin Province of the Society of Jesus, Turin, Italy; the late Arthur D. Spearman of the University of Santa Clara; Francis J. Weber, archivist of the Archdiocese of Los Angeles; Lowrie J. Daly of the Pius XII Memorial Library at St. Louis University; Vincent Bellwoar of Georgetown University; and Francis Edwards, archivist of the English Province of the Society of Jesus, London. To the many persons who aided my research by consenting to be interviewed I also express my warmest appreciation.

I wish to thank those who read portions of the manuscript: Charles T. Phipps, Donald F. Crosby, Stephen A. Privett, Louis C. Rudolph, Charles J. Dirksen, Louis I. Bannan, Joseph F. Deck, and the late Edward R. A. Boland. Special thanks are due Edward D. McShane for his patience and good humor in reading in its entirety the first draft of the manuscript. I also gratefully acknowledge the assistance given in a variety of ways by Walter J. Kropp, Christine Woodward, Don Dodson, David P. Arata, Denis E. Collins, and Peggy Major. Herbert Jansen helped compile the statistical tables found in the appendixes of the book. Gigia Bjorn, Gary Gardner, Katherine Oven, and Teresa Pugh aided in preparing the Index. I owe a debt of very special gratitude to Palmer W. Pinney for his invaluable and expert assistance in editing the final version of the manuscript.

Last, and by no means least, to my family and friends who facilitated the completion of this study by their sustained interest and words of encouragement, I offer heartfelt thanks. Without their support the book would not have been realized.

G.McK.

Contents

1. Introduction   1
2. The Setting: Gold Rush California   7
3. From Franciscan Mission to Jesuit College   25
4. The Nobili Years, 1851–1856   37
5. Italy Comes to California, 1854–1861   51
6. The End of the Era of Adobe, 1861–1865   65
7. Early Student Life   79
8. Progress Amid Poverty, 1865–1880   92
9. A College in Conflict, 1880–1893   111
10. The Search for "A Broader Place," 1892–1905   130
11. Los Angeles Beckons, 1901–1911   154
12. From College to University, 1910–1917   166
13. Doughboys and Quarterbacks, 1917–1930   181
14. The House That Zach Built, 1921–1926   194
15. Fire and Sunspots, 1926–1932   214
16. The Depression Years, 1932–1940   230
17. Years of War and Years of Calm, 1941–1958   259
18. Traditions Shattered, 1958–1977   284
19. Conclusion   306

Appendixes

A: Enrollments, 325. B: Degrees Conferred, 326. C: Members of the Board of Trustees Since 1855, 329. D: Presidents and Other Officers, 331. E: Student Body Presidents, 333. F: Presidents of the Alumni Council, 334. G: Nobili and St. Clare Outstanding Student Medal Winners, 335. H: Recipients of Honorary Degrees, 337.

Notes   339
Index   374

The University of Santa Clara

I

Introduction

In today's secular world it is difficult to appreciate the extent to which religion dominated American life in the nineteenth century. The Christian churches then enjoyed remarkable cultural ascendancy. When Alexis de Tocqueville arrived in the United States in 1831, he recorded that "the religious aspect of the country was the first thing that struck my attention." "There is no country in the whole world," he said, "in which the Christian religion retains a greater influence over the souls of men than in America." He argued that by regulating domestic life, the church regulated the state. Religion, Tocqueville concluded, "is the foremost of the institutions of the country."[1]

One of the most effective instruments of the Christian influence was the denominational college. That the nation's colonial colleges were primarily religious in origin and character is well known. Harvard and Yale, for example, were established by Congregationalists; the founding of Princeton and Dartmouth can be traced to the revivalist movement of the Great Awakening in the late colonial period. What is less recognized is that almost all of the institutions of higher learning founded between the Revolutionary War and the Civil War—with the exception of certain state universities—were also established, supported, and controlled by religious groups. According to Donald G. Tewksbury, of the 182 permanent chartered colleges started in the United States before the Civil War, only 21 were state colleges. The rest (nearly 90 percent) owed their origin to religious denominations. The four permanent colleges established in California during that period were all church-related: the University of Santa Clara, the University of the Pacific, the University of San Francisco, and the Congregational-Presbyterian College of California, which became the University of California.[2]

What accounts for this remarkable multiplication of private, church-related schools? The vast size of the country, the multiplicity of religions, and the pervasive influence of laissez-faire individualism were certainly factors. The absence of a state religion or a state-controlled ministry for education that might have restrained the college-founding process was also important. When various denominational and sectarian movements sprang to life in the early nineteenth century, they fostered a nationwide proliferation of small colleges. Every sect and every denomination sponsored institutions that served to "strengthen denominational loyalty, meet denominational rivalry, and extend denominational influence."[3] As a result, by the time of the Civil War, America had become "the land of colleges."[4]

The western frontier provided an extended arena for the churches' missionary zeal. In the nineteenth century the spiritual conquest of the continent became the goal of a militant and aggressive Christianity. Worried lest traditional ideals and traditional culture perish in the wilderness, Protestant New England launched a crusade to save the West from "atheism, infidelity, the slaveholder and the Pope." As a consequence, during the period of accelerated westward migration in the 1850's the college movement gained great impetus. Sixty-six institutions opened their doors during that decade, more than twice the number established during the previous ten years. The process continued at only a slightly diminished rate until the end of the century.[5]

One of the hallmarks of the movement was overt sectarian competition. The various Protestant denominations rivaled one another for influence. They also waged a campaign against the twin evils of infidelity and Roman Catholicism. The West had to be won for the churches; it also had to be saved from the threat posed by a floodtide of foreign emigration from Catholic Europe.

Santa Clara College, founded in the 1850's, played a distinct role in the sectarian rivalry. Its success and the success of other early Jesuit colleges in the West stirred Protestant educators into action. "The main consideration to excite our fears," wrote a pamphleteer in 1856, "is the calm, shrewd, steady, systematic movement of the Jesuit order now attempting to do in California and in the Mississippi Valley what it once did in Austria; by the unobtrusive, unobserved power of the College, to subvert the principles of the Reformation, and to crush the spirit of liberty. There, Brethren, there our great battle with the Jesuit, on Western soil, is to be waged. We must build college against college."[6]

Catholics, on the other hand, were animated by worries about Protestant successes. One of the motives behind Santa Clara's founding was to offset growing Protestant influence in "Catholic" California.

Nineteenth-century churchmen associated with a particular college believed intensely in the superiority of their school and in those features that set it apart from the schools of rival sects and churches. In fact, many of the denominational colleges possessed (and still retain) traits allotting them a certain historical uniqueness. Catholic Santa Clara, for example, was in its earliest decades staffed almost exclusively by Italian-born Jesuits, and it served a student clientele that was largely of immigrant stock, especially Irish and Italian. With the passing of time and with the merging of national groups into the mainstream, such differences have greatly paled at Santa Clara, as elsewhere. Similarly, the doctrinal differences that once set Santa Clara apart from many other California colleges appear much less conspicuous in today's ecumenical age than they did in an age of theological confrontation.

"To Form and Cherish Good Habits"

The fact that the denominational colleges had much in common is suggested by their statements of purpose. The statements stand in marked contrast to the aims of the modern secular university.

The shared purpose of the nineteenth-century schools was not the imparting of useful information, but intellectual and spiritual formation. "To cultivate the heart, to form and cherish good habits, to prevent and eradicate evil ones" was the way Jesuit John Nobili described Santa Clara's goals. "A more than parental care of the morals of the pupils, no less than their intellectual improvement," was a duty "kept constantly and sacredly in view" by teachers at Santa Clara and at almost all nineteenth-century colleges.[7] A prescribed curriculum, subordinated to the institution's religious aims, constituted the course of study. Limited to a more or less fixed body of knowledge, it consisted chiefly of philosophical studies and of years of training in the Latin and Greek classics. Its overriding purpose was not vocational training, but mental discipline.[8]

If the denominational colleges shared certain convictions concerning the purpose of education, they also faced common difficulties. Chief among them was the drift of American higher education from the classical tradition toward secular and practical goals. That movement began in the second half of the nineteenth century. Its causes were many, including, especially, the rapid post-Civil War expansion of American industry. Industrial development called not simply for the preservation and transmission of knowledge, but for research to enlarge it. At the same time, American capitalism created an "almost insatiable demand" for technicians and specialists.[9]

Thus was born what Burton Bledstein has called the culture of professionalism. The American college was now made to serve the vocational needs of aspiring, career-minded, middle-class professional persons. Consequently, higher education itself began to specialize and to become more professional. New service-oriented institutions such as the land-grant colleges, state uni-

versities, commercial schools, and state teachers' colleges began to appear and
to offer vocational specialization.[10]

Defenders of orthodox college ideals—and they were not limited to
churchmen—fought the drift toward utilitarian learning. That battle, which
centered on the merits of the elective system, decided in practice the question,
"Should the American college remain predominantly religious in orientation, . . . or should it become essentially secular, serving the interest of utilitar-
ianism, social efficiency, and scholarly research?"[11] Jesuit educators, promoters
since the 1600's of the liberal arts tradition, were among the last to concede victory to the new learning.

The traditional college, clinging to its prescribed curriculum and its forma-
tive goals, was plunged into a crisis by the secularization of higher learning.
With seemingly no socially valued reason for existing, many institutions
failed. Those that survived did so by embracing electivism in whole or in
part and by modifying or abandoning their commitment to character formation. By the mid-twentieth century many Protestant colleges and universities had long since severed their denominational ties and had become completely secular. Catholic institutions, of which Santa Clara is a typical case,
were slower to conform, but animated in the late 1960's by the *aggiornamento*
of the Second Vatican Council, they began a fundamental reexamination of
their academic position. Having come to terms with other realities of the
modern secular world and wishing to meet its educational needs, they joined
the academic mainstream. They abandoned mandatory curricula, and they
made their academic standards more professional. Catholic colleges that had
long stood *in loco parentis* resigned their role as shapers of character. Whether
they too will eventually lose their religious character and succumb completely to secularization as a result, observe historians Brubacher and Rudy,
remains a "moot point for the future."[12]

The Perpetuation of Values

Though no longer a major force in higher education, the denominational
college performed a vital function in American history. In the nineteenth
century, when Tocqueville described religion as America's "foremost institution," the denominational college stood as "one of the most effective agencies
of the rapidly increasing religious forces in the country."[13] Indeed, the college
was often the first and principal means whereby the Christian churches,
Protestant as well as Catholic, established themselves in a new locality. It was
also the nucleus out of which their later influence extended. Thus Santa
Clara, in addition to overseeing the religious training of thousands of stu-

dents, also served the spiritual needs of the Catholic public in its part of California. Through the founding and supplying of parish churches, through public lectures, retreats, and other ministries, and through the influence of former students who became priests, the college contributed in a major way to the shaping of the religious history of Northern California.

The propagation of religion was not the sole purpose of the denominational college. Before the rise of secular higher learning, the multiplication of colleges like Santa Clara, especially in the West, provided not only hubs of religious influence, but also radiating centers for the "formulation and perpetuation of the fundamental elements of culture . . . on the wide front of an advancing population."[14] Whatever higher education existed in California prior to the establishment of a state university, observed John Swett, founder of California's public school system, was provided by Santa Clara and the state's other denominational colleges.[15]

With the passing of time, the denominational college slid from its position of ascendancy. Public institutions assumed the role that had once been almost exclusively that of the denominational school. But the rise of secular institutions did not spell the collapse of the general, liberal arts tradition in American higher education. Nor did the decline of the denominational college mean the disappearance of value-oriented training. Although it is easy to caricature the training's nineteenth-century forms, the concept of holistic education has proved of perennial value. That ideal, stripped of its outworn features and the narrow sectarianism of the past, survives today in many small private colleges and universities. Some of those institutions, such as the University of Santa Clara, are still church-related. They have conformed their standards of academic excellence to the norms that prevail in contemporary secular education, but their central purpose remains "the development of moral as well as intellectual values, an education of the whole person, an education constantly seeking to answer not only 'what is' but 'what should be.'"[16]

The value of such institutions lies beyond the fact that they provide an element of variety in the showcase of American higher education. They do indeed offer an educational alternative in a pluralistic society, but that alternative possesses an intrinsic worth. Furthermore, as historian Richard Hofstadter argues, that alternative has corrective value for higher education in general. Because of its practical and vocational bias, contemporary higher education has lost much of its emotional and spiritual content. Knowledge, however, is not "a mere utility," but a part of the innermost character of the human person. What is needed, Hofstadter suggests, is a "restoration of some of the spiritual content" to the curriculum of American higher education and a return to the "supremacy of the intellect as opposed to all the utilities that have crept into the educational system." Here it is that the value-oriented university, with its commitment to holistic development, provides an essential service. By striking a balance between the extremes of the old and the new systems of higher education, it not only salvages the best features of both, but it also discovers "the educational poise that society needs."[17]

2

The Setting:
Gold Rush California

"Whether it should be called a villa, a brothel, or Babylon, I am at a loss to determine." With these words Michael Accolti summed up his first confused impressions of gold rush San Francisco.[1] Even the newspapers and letters from California, whose every line he had scanned before sailing from Oregon, had not braced the well-traveled Jesuit for the brawling, bustling scenes he met when he stepped ashore from the *O. C. Raymond* on a December morning in 1849. He stood bolted to the busy waterfront in open-mouthed amazement.

Shaking off his surprise, Accolti grabbed his valise and pushed his way through the crowd. He marched toward the plank sidewalk that led into the burgeoning metropolis in pursuit of the mission that had prompted him and his traveling companion, John Nobili, to leave the rural tranquility of Oregon. The two Italian Jesuits had no idea where they were headed. The purpose of their visit was clear enough: they had come to scout the possibility of launching a Jesuit ministry in gold rush California. Although they had vague ideas of educational work, precisely what form that work might take, where it might be exercised, and what its future might be were veiled in mystery. Without money or friends or even their order's full approval, the two priests trod an unfamiliar path.

Fifteen months later they achieved the goal for which they had sailed into the Golden Gate. Their wanderings had led them through the streets of San Francisco and some forty miles beyond to the quiet cloisters of Mission Santa Clara. In response to the request of local Catholics, the two Jesuits had converted the crumbling adobe buildings of the former Franciscan mission into a school. The sign arching over the mission's front gate now read "Santa Clara College."

Although they did not appreciate the significance of their undertaking, Accolti and Nobili had founded the first institution of higher learning in California. The seed they planted has grown, and today their college is the University of Santa Clara.

The history of Santa Clara's transformation from a Franciscan mission into a Jesuit college and its gradual emergence into a modern university is complex and fascinating. Although it focuses on local events primarily, that history also reflects wider actions. As an outpost of European imperialism in the eighteenth century, Mission Santa Clara was for generations the center of Hispanic civilization in its part of California. Even after it had been reduced to a parish church in the 1830's, it remained a dominant institution in the Santa Clara Valley. It survived the ebb and flow of events in the last days of Mexican rule over California, and it witnessed the advent of the conquering *Yanqui*. In its progress from mission to university, Santa Clara mirrored more than two hundred years of California history.

The Mission

Jesuits Accolti and Nobili were latecomers to the Santa Clara area. Before the arrival of the priest-professors from Italy, Mexican Franciscans had walked the tiled corridors of Mission Santa Clara; and before the advent of the Franciscan padres, generation upon generation of Indians had lived along streams of the valley. The natives called the place Thámien, a name suggested perhaps by the groves of trees that lined the banks of the river later known as Río Guadalupe.

Thámien became Santa Clara in 1777. On January 12 of that year, after a week's march from San Francisco's Mission Dolores, a scruffy band of Spanish soldiers, their families, and a Franciscan priest appeared along the banks of the Río Guadalupe. There they hastily assembled a palisade of mud and logs. They named the mission Santa Clara in honor of St. Clare of Assisi, the girl who in the thirteenth century ran away from home at the age of eighteen to join St. Francis and who later founded the order of Poor Clare nuns. Established a few miles upstream from the shore of San Francisco Bay, whose environs it was meant to secure, Santa Clara began as the eighth link in the chain of California missions.

The mission seemed to its founders ideally placed. The vast plain surrounding the lonely outpost—its flat monotony broken by scattered groves of trees—provided plenty of pasturage and good soil for agriculture. The Río Guadalupe flowing nearby promised easy irrigation for crops of wheat, beans, and barley. Spain's ambitious colonization program required the cultural and religious conversion of the native peoples. Thus the presence of more than forty *rancherías*, or Indian villages, within a thirteen-mile radius of the mission compound also augured well for Santa Clara's future. This mission, Fray Francisco Palóu summarized, occupied perhaps "the best place in all our conquered territory."[2]

Crude stockades of mud and log soon yielded to more permanent adobe dwellings. Administered for more than thirty years by Fray José Viader and the saintly Magín Catalá (whose reputed holiness of life moved the church years later to weigh his possible canonization), Santa Clara flourished. To visitors, it seemed one of the cleanest and best regulated of all the missions.[3]

Not that there were no difficulties. Three times—twice after floods and once after an earthquake—the Franciscans moved their outpost to safer ground, thus withdrawing it almost two miles from its original site along the banks of the Río Guadalupe. But after each disaster the institution recovered and expanded. Its herds of livestock multiplied (reaching 30,922 head one year), its walls grew thicker, and increasingly more Indian villages fell under the sway of Santa Clara's far-sounding bells. At its height, the mission housed a community of nearly fifteen hundred hispanicized Indians, friars, and soldiers. No California mission recorded as many baptisms or marriages as Santa Clara—or as many deaths. European diseases struck the native population at an alarming rate. At Santa Clara, as elsewhere, births barely kept pace with burials.

By eighteenth-century standards, however, Mission Santa Clara was a success. It boasted a bountiful site and a church that Fray Junípero Serra once judged "the most beautiful yet erected in California."[4] Except for the setbacks from flood and earthquake and an occasional jurisdictional joust with the *pobladores* of nearby Pueblo San José, Franciscan rule over Mission Santa Clara continued unchallenged and unbroken for nearly sixty years.

Then in 1833, some ten years after Mexico won its independence from Spain, the Mexican legislature ordered the dissolution of the California mission system. Three years later Santa Clara became a parish church, and its valuable lands were released for other purposes. According to the decree of secularization (which was only feebly enforced), half of the property was to be divided among the mission Indians.

The mission's envied monopoly over acres of land and its tutelage of the Indian now terminated, a new cast of characters stepped upon the stage. A small staff of Mexican padres displaced the Spanish friars as custodians of Santa Clara's diminished domain. Because the mission-turned-parish remained the religious center of the Santa Clara Valley, worshipers from Pueblo San José still journeyed down the Alameda to pray at the mission church on Sundays and holy days. But the Indians, ravaged by disease and no longer protected by priestly paternalism, disappeared in increasing numbers. In their stead, new proprietors rode the tracts of the partitioned mission. A chastened Santa Clara endured the last decade of Mexican rule, short of funds and often poorly administered.

The earliest known photograph of Mission Santa Clara, probably taken in 1854. The mission cross stands in front of the church; to the left is the east wing of the mission quadrangle. The bell tower of the church has been encased in wood to prevent erosion of the adobe. Note the simple, flat façade of the church, on which frescoed designs and figures of the saints have been painted. Contrast this photo with that of the restored church on p. 318. *Courtesy: Archives, Univ. of Santa Clara.*

In 1846, the first wave of the mighty tide of Americans that would soon inundate California appeared at the gates of the mission. The vanguard was a band of families from the States recently arrived at Sutter's Fort. Seeking shelter from winter rains and from the enemy troops that patrolled the countryside during the Mexican War, they were advised by Captain John C. Frémont to set up quarters in the abandoned buildings of Santa Clara.

When the war was over, some of the newcomers refused to leave. They were convinced that the mission was now United States property and therefore subject to preemption by American citizens. Colonel Richard B. Mason, the American military governor, responding to complaints from the resident padre, visited Santa Clara and discovered that "the vineyards had been damaged, the doors and windows removed, and the immigrants in complete possession." One formidable woman squatter even announced her intention of putting in a crop of wheat by plowing up the mission orchard.[5]

The cry "Gold! Gold! Gold!" drew the full tide of settlers to California. Some of them eventually settled in the Santa Clara Valley. In the dusty fields beyond the walls of the mission, squatters laid out a town whose streets they lined with canvas tents and prefabricated frame houses imported by ship from Boston. With the rise of the new hamlet, the mission was no longer the area's sole center of settlement. But its scattered clay buildings and untended fields continued to attract enterprising villagers, intent on borrowing more than just a town name from the dilapidated and almost abandoned mission.[6]

Squatter claims to former mission tracts would pose a thorny legal problem to the Jesuits who inherited custodianship of Santa Clara a few years later. More vexing, however, would be the status of property that passed from ecclesiastical to secular jurisdiction through the agency of their immediate predecessor, Padre José Suárez del Real, the last Franciscan pastor of Santa Clara.

Suárez del Real, one of the black sheep of the California missionary fold, showed slight interest in preserving the parish during his stormy seven-year pastorate. "A man of fine appearance and very popular with the fast set," the convivial cleric centered his interests on horses, women, and local politics. Repeating the habits that had scandalized his parishioners at Monterey, California, Real arrived at Santa Clara in 1844 and lived in open concubinage with a woman whom he set up in a house across the street from the mission church.[7] Under his distracted direction, Santa Clara's decline during the 1840's continued. Real began to sell off the lots and buildings that still remained under ecclesiastical control to support himself, the parish, and his progeny in those last days of Mexican rule. With the fall of California to the

Americans, his real-estate transactions brought him further personal profit, but also increasing notoriety. Both civil and ecclesiastical authorities forbade further alienation of the property over which he was administrator, but their prohibitions had little effect.[8] Even on the eve of his hasty departure for Mexico in 1851, Real conveyed into the hands of his friend Andrés Pico the title to the mission vineyard, for which he requested, but never received, a payment of $1,000.[9]

The dissolution of Santa Clara's physical plant mirrored the decline of parish life during the troubled reigns of Suárez del Real and his equally lax predecessor, Jesús María Vásquez del Mercado. Administered by two priests whose commitment was no match for the troubled times, the religious life of the mission withered and decayed like the product of its neglected orchards. "The walls have crumbled down," a visitor reported, "and the unpruned trees have run into a tangled mass of wild shoots." The orchards of Mission Santa Clara, "looped together with the tendrils of various parasites," bore "only an abortive fruit."[10]

Catholicism in Crisis

Suárez del Real was not a typical pastor. However, the major problems that beset Santa Clara typified the troubled state of California Catholicism at mid-century. The church, shaken by "the decline of the Franciscan theocracy and the rise of liberalism," endured through the decade of the 1840's. It emerged from the Mexican War "practically leaderless and without funds" and with but a "corporal's guard" of twenty-one padres.[11] In a state of "near extinction," it was unprepared to care for the throngs of immigrants who converged on California after the American takeover in 1846, much less the thousands who came after the discovery of gold two years later.[12] Because the founding of a Jesuit college at Santa Clara was one step taken to improve the church's ability to serve its people, the difficulties of Catholicism in those transitional years should be examined.

Transformed overnight by the gold rush from a backwater Mexican province to an urbanized international mining frontier, California enjoyed a status that placed new fiscal demands upon the mission-centered church. But the church was penniless. Some Catholics entertained hopes that the recovery of the mission system and the Pious Fund would provide an economic foundation upon which the church might rebuild. In the meantime, it was futile to assert a disputed dominion over Mission Santa Clara and its sister establishments until the American courts reviewed and defined the status of mission property under American law.

Moreover, the church lacked leadership. Mexican Bishop García Diego had died in 1846, leaving the diocese of California to the interim administration of the capable but overworked Padre González Rubio. When California passed to American hands after the Mexican War, church authorities delayed naming a successor to García Diego until an American could be found to head the Anglo-dominated diocese. It was not until late 1850 that an acceptable candidate, Joseph Sadoc Alemany, O.P., a Spanish-born American citizen, arrived in California to assume the leadership of the state's racially mixed Catholic population.

One of the first problems Alemany had to solve was California's paucity of priests. In 1851 the church employed twenty-one priests to staff its twenty-six churches and to minister to an estimated forty thousand Catholics among California's suddenly swollen population of one hundred fifty thousand.[13] The number of Franciscans had dwindled to a mere handful, and the remaining Spanish-speaking clergy lacked both the numbers and the training to care for the multinational congregations that crowded their churches on Sunday mornings. The problem was aggravated at Santa Clara by the presence of Padre Suárez del Real, whose stormy pastorate made his replacement mandatory. But where could a substitute be found?

An additional crisis—one shared by both church and state—was a scarcity of schools. During the unstable and chaotic years of Mexican hegemony, formal education had been little esteemed and scarcely encouraged. Governmental weakness, constant intrigues, changes in administration, and public apathy combined to "foster a climate in which educational matters played a less than secondary role." Schooling, such as it was, centered at the missions and tended to be "simple and religious in emphasis."[14] But the population boom that accompanied the gold rush made educational reform imperative. "Here daily great numbers of Protestants and Catholics are arriving," González Rubio observed in 1849, "with no one to whom they can entrust the education of their children."[15]

González addressed but could not solve the difficulties of the church. "To preserve the Catholics in their faith, and to convert the native infidels and, most of all, to train our youth in knowledge and virtue"—these were the reasons he sought priests for his diocese. In one of his pastoral letters he termed the insufficiency of priests and teachers the "most difficult problem." He specified that "In so extensive a diocese we need at least forty missionaries," but he admitted he did not know how they might be found. California, lacking colleges and seminaries, was incapable of producing its own clergy, and Mexico could no longer supply men as it had in the past. Europe alone offered help. However, since the church in California was "entirely destitute" and without "the sources of revenue which it formerly possessed in the Mission system," Padre González revealed that he could not even pay the travel fare to California for interested European clerics. Unless the people themselves could provide the resources, there was "no prospect of relief."[16]

Eventually, several religious congregations responded to González's appeal by sending priests and nuns to California. Among them was a group of Italian Jesuits from the Pacific Northwest, whose destiny it would be to bolster the sagging fortunes of Mission Santa Clara.

The Jesuits

California was not a field of Jesuit missionary activity before 1849. The seventeenth- and eighteenth-century Jesuit missionaries, such as Eusebio Francisco Kino and Juan Salvatierra, evangelized northern Mexico and Baja California. But the Jesuits were suppressed in 1767, before the chain of missions in Baja could be extended north into Alta California. After the restoration of the Society in 1814 by Pope Pius VII, a new missionary area, promoted by the Belgian Jesuit Peter De Smet and administered from St. Louis, Missouri, was opened among the Indians of the Rocky Mountains and of the Pacific Northwest. Spanish California was beyond the boundaries of this apostolate. Mexican authorities occasionally contemplated admitting the restored order into the province. Also, William Hartnell of Monterey, California, an early settler and a naturalized Mexican citizen, indicated in 1844 that he would be "very glad indeed to see 20 or 30 Jesuits" come to California to perform religious and educational work. Nothing, however, came of either plan.[17] Dr. John McLoughlin, chief factor of the Hudson's Bay Company at Fort Vancouver, on the Columbia River, urged his Jesuit friends in Oregon to "open a communication with California," but five years passed before the Rocky Mountain Mission, finally stirred to action by the gold rush, agreed to send some of its members into California to explore the possibility of establishing a ministry.[18]

That the Jesuits finally sailed south toward the Golden Gate was largely due to the one-man promotional campaign waged by an energetic Italian priest, Michael Accolti. He was the driving spirit of the venture. Accolti had been born to provincial nobility near Bari, in southern Italy, and reared in a setting of vast green orchards, sunshine, and whitewashed houses overlooking the blue waters of the Adriatic. This setting must have influenced his character, for acquaintances testified to his pleasant, outgoing personality. His portraits, too, reveal an open face wreathed always in a smile. Schooled in Rome's prestigious Academia dei Nobili Ecclesiastici, Accolti in 1832 surprised his aristocratic family, who had apparently planned a career of ecclesiastical preferment for their young scion, by entering the Jesuits. To his family's added dismay, he later sailed from Europe with Peter De Smet to work as a missionary among the Indians of North America.[19] Because of his talent for practical matters, Accolti was soon named procurator, or business agent, for the Jesuit missions in the Northwest, whose local headquarters were in Oregon's Willamette Valley.

Though he had originally volunteered his services to the mission with enthusiasm, Accolti after five years became discouraged over the prospects of Indian evangelization and his own aptitude for that undertaking. It became his view that the Oregon Jesuits might more profitably devote themselves to a broader educational and ministerial apostolate among the white population of the Pacific Coast, a work to which Accolti was inclined both by background and by personality. As mission procurator, Accolti recognized that the scarcity of funds and of qualified workers crippled the Jesuit missionary effort in Oregon. He became convinced that spiraling operational costs—inflated chiefly by the California gold discovery—threatened to make it impossible for the missions to survive.[20]

By the summer of 1849 Accolti's attention became more focused on California (it "surpasses all imagination") than on the problem-plagued missions of Oregon. His curiosity stirred by rumors of affluence and his business acumen piqued by the contrast of California with impoverished Oregon, Accolti concluded that the solution to the Indian missions' "deplorable state of indigence and extreme distress" lay in the gold mines of Eldorado.[21] Alert to all the implications of a fast-growing society, he also developed an interest in California as the home of a permanent Jesuit apostolate.

Since March of 1849 Accolti had been receiving a steady flow of correspondence from a friend in San Francisco, John B. Brouillet, a diocesan priest from Oregon. Sent south in search of money for his indebted home diocese, Brouillet had shifted his attention to a religious ministry, instead. So numerous were the demands and so great were the spiritual needs of California as observed by Brouillet that he turned to Accolti for assistance. Brouillet urged him to use his influence to see that Jesuits came from Oregon to provide spiritual and educational assistance to California's Catholics. "The door to California lies open before you," Brouillet wrote to Accolti. In a letter from Mission Santa Clara, he informed his Jesuit friend:

The people desire you warmly and are urging you to come. Everybody is asking for a Jesuit College and here is what they put at the joint disposition of yourselves and

No pictorial record of the original interior of Mission Santa Clara has survived. This photograph shows the interior of the church as it appeared in the late nineteenth century. The large paintings of St. Patrick and St. Ignatius on either side of the altar were added during the college period. However, the reredos with its statues of the saints, standing behind the altar, and the ceiling painting on redwood slabs date from the mission period. All were destroyed in the fire of 1926. *Courtesy: Archives, Univ. of Santa Clara.*

the Sisters of Notre Dame: an entire mission, one of the finest and best equipped in the whole of California, with a magnificent church . . . on condition that a college and convent be set up there with the least possible delay. . . . Living expenses will not be higher than in Oregon and you will be able to charge stiff boarding-rates with no fear of frightening anybody; and so you are assured a gross revenue which will be of aid to you in supporting your missions in the Mountains. But above all other considerations the spiritual needs of California, the immense good to be done there, and the opportunity created by the circumstances ought to make you decide.[22]

At the same time, Brouillet submitted his plan to Padre González Rubio, in whose charge the diocese of California still remained. The Mexican approved enthusiastically and, though his material resources were few, he offered to help the Jesuits "as far as I can." González then suggested Los Angeles or Santa Barbara as a potential school site and urged that "one or two [Jesuits] come as promptly as possible to collect alms" in order that they might begin their educational work on a solid foundation.[23]

Attracted to the possibilities promised in Brouillet's letters and led on by his own curiosity, Accolti became obsessed with a desire "to go and investigate the matter on the spot."[24] There was only one obstacle standing between himself and the next ship to San Francisco: the opposition of Jesuit superiors. Mindful that Mexican church authorities had previously barred Jesuits from California and unwilling to add to the burdens of the overextended and understaffed Indian missions of Oregon by accepting new responsibilities elsewhere, leaders of the order had for several years prohibited the assignment of men to California.[25] As late as February, 1849 the Jesuit father general, John Roothaan, had ordered that "No one should be sent to California."[26]

Not easily dissuaded, Accolti countered that circumstances had changed since Roothaan's prohibition. Diocesan authorities now welcomed Jesuits; a growing Catholic population required priests; resources appeared available in California not only for educational work, but even for the indebted Indian missions of Oregon. "All that glitters is not gold," Accolti conceded. "On the other hand I think we ought not to show ourselves indifferent to . . . a project which . . . will not fail to offer considerable advantages."[27]

Convinced beyond all doubt himself, Accolti failed to fire others with his enthusiasm. Months of frustrated waiting passed, but no Jesuit administrator in either Oregon or Europe was willing to give the nod to the launching of a California apostolate.

Then, after nearly a year of what he considered "fruitless negotiations" and letter writing, his persistence overcame the opposition of the superior of the Oregon missions.[28] Father Joseph Joset, worn down by Accolti's "most warm and earnest solicitations," reluctantly authorized him and a companion to go and see what California had to offer.[29]

Accolti in "Babylon"

A fellow missionary, the Roman-born John Nobili, accompanied Accolti on the voyage to California. They had been traveling companions once before, when they sailed from Europe in 1844 with Father De Smet as recruits for the Indian missions of Oregon. After a strenuous year's ministry near Fort Vancouver, Nobili, at age thirty-three, had been assigned to a new mission called New Caledonia in extreme western Canada, today's British Columbia. For three long and difficult years Nobili ministered to the traders and trappers of the Hudson's Bay Company and to the Indian tribes who dwelt in the vast wilderness of his mission field. Sustaining wretched living conditions and spoiled food, often forced to work alone and sometimes traveling as far north as the Alaskan frontier, the small priest drove himself until his health broke under the burden.

When Nobili returned to Jesuit headquarters in Oregon in 1848, Joset was shocked by his deteriorated condition. He recognized that Nobili "was by no manner of means made to live among the Indians."[30] Despite his protests, Nobili was withdrawn from further work in New Caledonia, and the mission itself was closed. When the time came for Accolti to sail for California, Nobili was a natural choice as a companion. It was hoped that the California trip would give the frail missionary an opportunity to find a good doctor in San Francisco and to gain some rest before his return to Europe for a less strenuous assignment.

On December 3, 1849, the two travelers boarded a lumber ship bound down the Columbia River for California. Hurried on its way by strong winds, the vessel entered the Golden Gate five days later. "The next day," Accolti recorded, "we were able to set foot on the longed-for shores of what goes under the name of San Francisco, but which, whether it should be called a villa, a brothel, or Babylon, I am at a loss to determine."[31]

The real California differed from the bright picture painted by Brouillet's "glowing and very pressing letters."[32] Not only was the noise and confusion that filled the streets of the new-born city more frenetic than Accolti had imagined, but the interest in religion and education was less than he had expected. "The disorder, the brawling, the open immorality, and the reign of crime which . . . brazen-faced, triumphed on a soil not yet brought under the sway of human laws" surprised him. He even met vagabond clerics, some of them in disguise, who had descended on California from every corner of the globe in pursuit of wealth and adventure.[33] The fact that Accolti and Nobili arrived knowing no one was more distressing. Brouillet had concluded from the Jesuits' interminable delay that they had abandoned the idea of coming to California. Thus he had returned to Oregon, leaving Accolti to "open a way for myself practically alone."[34]

Consoling letters of welcome from González Rubio in Santa Barbara eventually reached Accolti. But the administrator of the diocese made no mention of transferring to the Jesuits the mission of Santa Clara.[35] Accolti, no longer sure what to expect regarding the old mission, began to travel about and investigate alternatives.

Catholics in San Francisco, Sacramento, San Jose, and Sonora suggested to Accolti that he establish a school in their communities, though none appeared able to provide the necessary financial help. Accolti recognized that his religious order would be stretching its own resources to the utmost even to found one institution. So he addressed himself to the task of deciding which city offered the best chance of success.

Though convinced that San Francisco was "the leading commercial place of California and will soon be such of the entire world," Accolti feared that the city was not "well suited for a college in view of the ebb and flow which prevails there."[36] Instead, he favored San Jose, "one of the oldest cities in California." The former pueblo recently had replaced Monterey as the capital of the state, and its inhabitants keenly desired educational facilities. Having been "cordially received" into several Irish and Spanish households in San Jose, Accolti discovered that the children of his hosts were "entirely bereft of any sort of instruction" and that their parents were eager to open schools "as soon as possible."[37] Included in his circle of acquaintances were Martin Murphy, Jr., a prominent settler, and the new American Governor, Peter Burnett. One of the "perplexing difficulties" facing both men was the education of their children.[38]

If San Jose provided friends, it also supplied foes. In the capital city the two Jesuits met bitter opposition from an unexpected quarter, a fellow priest in charge of the local parish. According to Accolti, José María Pinyero—a Spanish padre who knew "nothing about the Jesuits" except what he had read in novelist Eugène Sue's anti-Jesuit *Le Juif errant* (*The Wandering Jew*)—petitioned the San Jose town council to prohibit the proposed college on the grounds that the sons of St. Ignatius were "not suited to this country." Accolti's friends deflected the attack, but the episode left the two Italians discouraged.[39]

In fact, Accolti's companion began to doubt the wisdom of their enter-

prise. Still suffering from wretched health and now piqued by Accolti's preoccupation with the school project to the exclusion of the ministry, a worried and unhappy Nobili suggested that they sail home to Oregon. Nobili
was concerned also by the continuing absence of any approval of their mission
by officials in Rome.

Accolti was not dissuaded from his investigations. "In spite of the dis-
couragement and counsels of Father Nobili," he confided in a letter to Brouillet, "I have always continued to be patient, to wait, to try and to hope." Accolti did admit, however, that there loomed ahead a worrisome and potentially insuperable obstacle. This was Father Roothaan's silence. Without
the father general's approbation there could never arise a Jesuit school in
San Jose.[40]

Accolti continued to barrage Roothaan with long, argumentative letters
to Europe. Within a characteristic flow of emotion, the loquacious Italian
gave reason after reason for committing the Society of Jesus to California.
Paramount were the religious needs of the Catholic population who, in spite
of the preponderance of their numbers, were "in comparison the least provided for."[41] "Churches are lacking everywhere," he insisted, "and yet everybody wants them, everybody offers to put them up provided only there are
priests."[42]

Catholic educational needs formed another main theme of Accolti's letters. "With this concourse of people" from all over the world, "the number
of families goes on increasing and so there is a great host of children needing
the benefits of an education without anybody being in a position to satisfy
this need."[43] There are "no schools except those of the Protestants," Accolti
claimed, "who make every effort to show the inadequacy and sterility of Catholicism."[44] Revealing a major religious role he expected of a Jesuit school,
he concluded dramatically, "If we do not move in the matter, the Protestant
ministers are there to appropriate all the Catholic youth."[45]

Five long letters later, Accolti still had received no reply from Roothaan.
A silence of months descended upon the grand proposal. The only news
reaching him from Europe came indirectly, from his correspondents in St.
Louis, Missouri. At last a travel-worn missive arrived, announcing that the
general had appointed Accolti superior of the Oregon missions. Postmarked
1848, the letter had been mailed from Marseilles, France, approximately a
year before Accolti's departure from Oregon for California! Dismayed by
the unreliability of the mail service and discouraged by the persistent "debate and dilly-dallying" of superiors over his school scheme, Accolti sailed
for Oregon in July, 1850, to assume his new responsibilities.[46] One bright

Michael Accolti, co-founder of Santa Clara College. No photograph or portrait of John Nobili, the first president of the college, who died in 1856, has ever been found. *Courtesy: Archives, Univ. of Santa Clara.*

spot in his leaving was the realization that his new position as superior gave him leverage in advancing the cause of California. He left Father Nobili behind to await Roothaan's decision, after arranging his friend's appointment as assistant pastor at the parish church in San Jose.

Nobili thus far had evidenced little enthusiasm for the project that had consumed all of Accolti's attention during his eight months in California. In their joint effort, one man was the prime mover and the other the recruit. Though he would later shoulder with enthusiasm responsibility for the project, Nobili was at this time still reluctant. In a letter to a friend he had made it clear that he had had "no part at all, either by my actions or my counsels in these matters in which [Accolti] has engaged himself."[47]

While Accolti had been canvassing the state, seeking support for his school, Nobili had busied himself in more directly pastoral work. With the diet of Indian gruel and the howling winters of Western Canada just an unpleasant memory, his health had improved. Ironically, his ministry in San Jose found him as assistant to Padre Pinyero, the Spaniard who was said to have lobbied to keep the Jesuits out of California. Hence it was with relief that Nobili's multiple pastoral duties often required that he travel from the parish church to Mission San Jose and to other scattered congregations miles from the huge "unsightly barn" of whitewashed adobe that served as the main Catholic church in the state capital.[48] His absorption in his ministry and Rome's continued silence kept him from attempts to advance Accolti's school plan after the latter had returned to Oregon. Nonetheless, the two companions maintained a "continuous correspondence" after their separation in July. Thus Accolti was kept "minutely informed" of the situation in California and stood ready to act should a breakthrough occur.[49]

Alemany: "An Angel of Order"

The breakthrough began late in 1850, and it quickly led Nobili and Accolti to commit themselves and their order to educational work in California. In December a new bishop arrived in California to occupy the long vacant see of Monterey and to assume the leadership of the state's Catholic community. Accolti lauded with characteristic hyperbole the newcomer, Bishop Joseph Sadoc Alemany, as "an angel of order in the midst of all that chaos and confusion."[50]

Alarmed at his frontier diocese's "most miserable" condition in regard to education and convinced that without schools young people would be left "a prey to Protestantism and immorality," Alemany resolved that the Catholics must exert themselves "to open some good institutions" at once.[51] During a whirlwind tour of his diocese, he learned of Accolti's project and welcomed it as a partial remedy. On February 10, 1851, he met with Nobili in San Francisco and resurrected the proposal first broached by Brouillet two years earlier. Then the Dominican bishop offered the Jesuits the Franciscan mission at Santa Clara.[52]

The next day, Alemany penned a short letter to Accolti in Oregon, repeating the proposition he had laid out to Nobili. "I believe we should have at least two colleges in this state," he wrote, one in "the lower part of the state," to be run by the Fathers of Picpus, and another "in, or near Santa Clara." The bishop concluded:

> For this, it would not be necessary to have many Fathers to commence; yet Father Nobili alone could not probably undertake to commence it. Will you not, then, be so good as to send him one or two Fathers more? The Mission of Sta. Clara will soon be vacant, and might be transferred to your Society for that purpose. It is true that Mission has been squandered, but from all my researches upon the subject of Missions, I entertain the hope that the American Government will feel disposed to give us considerable [property]. At any rate the people of California commence to feel the necessity of education, and could no doubt, aid greatly the enterprise.[53]

Alemany demanded a prompt reply to his proposition. He was determined to open schools as quickly as possible and, equally important, he feared that the survival of Mission Santa Clara as an active parish was at stake. A replacement was needed for the wayward Padre Suárez del Real, who was reportedly packing his bags for an expedition into the Sierra Nevada to look for gold. (Bishop Alemany subsequently ordered him instead back to Franciscan headquarters in Mexico, where he became embroiled in Mexican politics and eventually left his order.)[54] Moreover, the mission property seemed in a state of siege. Even as Alemany and Nobili conferred, newspapers described the Santa Clara Valley as "bespattered with squatters," and according to one news account the mission itself had been sold at public auction.[55] Although the story proved erroneous, it underscored the embattled condition of the church's title to the mission and prodded the bishop to a swift defense. Alemany was confident that the United States Land Commission would eventually recognize the validity of his title to Mission Santa Clara. But in the interval he endeavored to protect this claim by maintaining continuous clerical representation at the mission. If the Jesuits could not accept his offer of Santa Clara, he would find others who would.

Alemany's offer left Nobili in a quandary. Reluctant to act unilaterally in so important a matter and yet fearful that waiting for a decision by mail from superiors might nullify the opportunity, Nobili decided to act on his own.

24   The Setting

After all, Accolti had recently given the nod to his accepting Santa Clara as a parish assignment in the event it was offered to him by Suárez del Real, who was laying plans to depart.[56] But Nobili went one step further by agreeing to accept the mission as a school. "With an optimism that one can only qualify as audacious," a later historian wrote, John Nobili committed himself and his order to educational work in California.[57]

The die was cast. All that remained was the ratification of the agreement. On March 4, 1851, Alemany posted from San Francisco a handwritten message to Nobili that is preserved in the University of Santa Clara Archives. In it he formally appointed the Jesuit permanent pastor of Santa Clara and administrator of "all belonging to said mission."[58] It was presumably two weeks later, on the feast of San José, patron of the nearby pueblo and Alemany's namesake, that Nobili took possession. The date was March 19, 1851. A ceremonial transferral of authority was probably also celebrated that day to coincide with a visit of the bishop himself to the mission.[59] A few days later Nobili and Suárez del Real, Santa Clara's last Franciscan, signed an inventory of mission properties, thus concluding the formalities of the transfer.

Completing the paperwork was deceptively easy; many difficult tasks lay ahead for Nobili. Precisely what he might claim as still belonging to Santa Clara and what had legitimately passed into other hands during the turbulent 1840's and the confusion that followed the American conquest of California was far from clear. Indeed, if he could have known the sum in dollars and dolors that recovery of the mission property would cost him, it is unlikely that he would have accepted Alemany's gift. In March of 1851, however, all that lay hidden from view.

3
From Franciscan Mission
to Jesuit College

"We [have] commenced it and have carried it on at a great sacrifice."
Thus Nobili recalled the opening of Santa Clara College and the
frustrations of the first year. "Had pecuniary profit been our object in its establishment," he added, the school "would have run its course and ceased to
exist many months ago."[1] If he could have foreseen the barriers that still lay in
the path of his school's progress, he might have preferred that the institution
had, in fact, ceased to be. For Santa Clara's metamorphosis from a Franciscan mission into a Jesuit college would tax Nobili's resources to the utmost.

Some of the problems that confronted the institution's first president were
those of any would-be schoolmaster in gold rush California. Others were
peculiar to the circumstances of the school's emergence from the ruins of a
moribund mission. For example, the ecclesiastical hold on the property was
exceedingly shaky. Even if the United States Land Commission eventually
approved Bishop Alemany's request for land for the Catholic Church at each
of the California mission sites, years might pass before the petition was acted
upon. Meanwhile, Nobili faced an army of competitors who challenged his
claim to nearly everything but the mission church itself. Consequently, the
bulk of his budget and a great deal of his time were spent establishing title to
the lots and adobe buildings scattered around the central mission. The land
whose title he sought is the heart of the modern campus.

An academic difficulty, one which struck down dozens of other attempts
to establish schools in California in the 1850's, was the lack of a permanent
faculty. Nobili discovered that capable teachers were scarce and that a salary
of $100 a month was often not sufficient to retain a man in a classroom. Since
his order could not then spare Jesuit teachers for California, Santa Clara
College survived for three years with a handful of lay instructors and an
occasional missionary who had been forced to leave Oregon because of poor
health or old age. A further drain upon Nobili's purse and an added challenge
to his ingenuity was the task of repairing Santa Clara's dilapidated adobe
buildings and outfitting them as classrooms.

Santa Clara as it appeared when John Nobili arrived in 1851: (1) the mission church, (2) the baptistry, (3) the cemetery, (4) the priest's house, (5) the portion of the east wing of the mission quadrangle occupied by the family of James Alexander Forbes, (6) the entrance to the vineyard, and (7) an Indian dwelling, which extended all along the east wall of the vineyard. *Courtesy: Archivum Historicum Societatis Iesu, Rome.*

The Beginning

"Wretched." That was the word Alemany used to describe the adobe hovels he handed over to the Jesuits to transform into a school.[2] The old mission had been so "plundered and reduced to the condition of a big stable" by Padre Real's negligence that Accolti conceded it formed a "poor and ugly school."[3] The mission church stood "sadly out of repair," Nobili recorded, and the few buildings attached to it "that were not either sold, bestowed or filched away, were in a condition of dismal nakedness and ruin."[4] Stripped by previous occupants, the nearly bare rooms revealed a meager inventory of some liturgical vessels and vestments, a variety of musical instruments in "good and poor condition," and a few scattered pieces of furniture. The only acquisition of value was a small library of some two hundred fifty books.[5]

Almost everything else had fallen into the hands of "swindlers and squatters." Rivals occupied the vineyard, the orchard, and the mission courtyard. In fact, the only properties securely Nobili's were the mission church, the small cemetery adjoining it on the north, and part of a wing of rooms to the south, which had served in the days of the mission as the friars' residence.[6] Nobili's control of this structure was incomplete because half of it housed the large family of James Alexander Forbes, formerly a majordomo of the mission as well as a British vice-consul for California. "I found the state of affairs

here anything but prosperous and encouraging," Nobili summarized in a letter to a friend. "In civilized St. Louis, Bardstown, or New York," he lamented,
"you can have no idea of the cheerless aspect presented by our residence for
the first few months."[7]

Postponing temporarily the task of determining his involved land rights,
Nobili set about improving the quarters over which his claim was uncontested in order to receive students as soon as possible. With a "herculean
effort," Accolti tells us, he began by cleaning the "augean stable" to which
he had fallen heir.[8] Down the lanes of the bumpy Alameda from San Jose
came horse-drawn wagons piled high and creaking under a cargo of bricks
and lumber. At considerable cost, masons and carpenters were hired to paint
buildings, replace doors and windows, and convert dank adobe cells into
acceptable classrooms and living quarters. Via steamer from San Francisco
came books and bedsteads, crates of writing paper, desks, stoves, oil lamps
and, happily, even a piano. Through Jesuit educators in the East and in Latin
America, Nobili ordered hundreds of dollars' worth of textbooks, which
could not be found in sufficient supply and variety on the West Coast. Having observed Nobili's efforts, his neighbor Forbes admitted a year later to
being "really surprised to see all the work that he has done with so little
means."[9]

Before Nobili's hasty preparations were completed, the San Francisco *Alta
California* informed its readers that "a moral and literary institution, . . . a
thing much needed in that part of the country," was about to open its doors
in Santa Clara. The course of instruction, the paper reported, would comprise
"a complete English education, together with the Spanish, French, Latin,
German and Greek languages and Music, both vocal and ornamental."[10]

In May of 1851 Nobili admitted his first pupils: a dozen boarding students
and probably a few "day scholars" as well. A later historian described the
circumstances: "With $150 in the treasury, the mission buildings, a plot of
land 120 feet by 225 feet, two secular teachers, a Kanaka cook and 'a respect-
able matron' to take care of the house and the smaller boys, the modest school
began."[11] Despite improvements, learning and lodging at Santa Clara took
place in an atmosphere devoid of superfluities and many physical refine-
ments. "We cannot lay claim to advantages we do not possess," Nobili admitted. "The fare is plain, but substantial and healthy; and the general comfort
of the pupils is as fully secured as the accommodations of the house will
admit."[12] Such was the beginning of the first permanent school in American
California.

It should be noted that Santa Clara was not the state's first chartered college. A few months after Nobili received students at the mission, a group of Methodist educators obtained a charter from the State Superior Court for the California Wesleyan College (now the University of the Pacific), to be located in the town of Santa Clara. Though instruction at California Wesleyan did not commence until May of the following year, the institution was incorporated on July 10, 1851. Santa Clara College, on the other hand, delayed incorporation until April 28, 1855, probably because Nobili was unsure of the school's future and because he lacked the $20,000 endowment required by the state. Thus California Wesleyan was the first to obtain a charter; Santa Clara was the first to begin instruction. The College of Notre Dame, now in Belmont, California, also traces its founding to 1851. Although it offered instruction beginning in August of that year, Notre Dame was not chartered until 1868, when it became the first chartered women's college in California.[13]

All three schools set out from small beginnings. Despite their titles, none was a college in the modern understanding of that term in 1851. Both Santa Clara and California Wesleyan started as preparatory schools, though they offered degrees and courses of collegiate rank within a few years. "We do not now claim for it even the name of a college," Nobili wrote of Santa Clara in early 1852, "but have looked upon it merely as a select boarding and day school—the germ only of such an institution as we would wish to make it and the wants of the community will require."[14] To a Jesuit correspondent he described it as "the foundation, *perhaps*, of a future College," adding that he hoped "before long to be able to put it on a much better footing."[15]

During the school's first brief session in 1851, only elementary instruction was offered in subjects such as reading and writing and foreign languages. A slight increase in his faculty in 1852 led Nobili to advertise courses in secondary subjects, such as algebra and geometry, indicating that the school was functioning as a combined elementary-secondary school by the end of its first full academic year.[16] Even so, younger students remained in the majority, in part because, as Nobili explained, "my accommodations for boys far advanced in years are not yet complete and for that reason I have been obliged to refuse a great many who have applied for admittance to the college." By 1853 enrollment had risen to seventy-eight students, all of whom were "over four and under eighteen years of age." It was not until the 1853–1854 session that students were enrolled on a limited scale in classes such as logic, corresponding to the freshman year in college.[17]

Santa Clara was not unusual in admitting students of tender years. According to Edward J. Power, the majority of Catholic colleges before 1850 were little more than elementary schools during their first years. George-town University, for instance, admitted boys of eight years of age if they could read and write. The University of Notre Dame accepted children of grammar-school age. St. Louis University's bulletin of 1869–1870 declared, "No student will be received under the age of ten, nor over that of sixteen, unless he is considerably advanced for his studies."[18] The admission of young students was a necessity for many colleges. In many instances, as with Santa Clara, it also reflected a philosophy of education that placed a high priority on a student's early mental and moral formation.

The Search for a Faculty

The chief obstacle to a more advanced curriculum was the lack of teachers. In 1851 Nobili acquired two part-time Jesuit assistants from Oregon who, like himself, were no longer suited for missionary work. These two, and an occasional diocesan priest, joined the small staff of laymen that Nobili had managed to assemble. But their total number remained inadequate for the diversity of courses that Nobili hoped for and that his students soon de-manded. To obtain a larger and more permanent faculty, Nobili requested help from Oregon, where Michael Accolti still served as superior of Jesuit activities on the Pacific Coast. His intense interest in the school's survival notwithstanding, Santa Clara's co-founder replied with regret that he could spare no one for assignment to California.

Nobili's search for suitable teachers remained unaided by Rome. Until late 1851 Accolti and Nobili had received no official approbation of their project from Jesuit headquarters in Europe. Accolti frequently had petitioned the general in Rome for his support of the educational work to which they already had committed the order, but because of poor communications be-tween the Pacific Coast and Europe, no reply had been received. A full year after Accolti's first appeal and four months after Nobili had launched the school at Santa Clara, the much-delayed and long-awaited response arrived.

The letter contained both good news and bad. Accolti learned with cha-grin that Rome could not accede to his request for a large-scale undertak-ing in California. Because the order was already overextended in its Indian missions scattered throughout the Pacific Northwest and because of a general shortage of men and money, Superior General John Roothaan announced that he could not afford to send additional men to California as school teach-ers: "However great is the hope of doing good, and very much good, in that country, . . . I cannot agree to houses or colleges of the Society being estab-lished there unless the Province of Spain takes upon itself the charge of furnishing subjects [Jesuits]. Father Nobili . . . can work there, and look about for teachers of elementary schools. Then, if possible, let him be given a father for companion."[19]

Accolti and Nobili were stunned. The latter immediately wrote a lengthy reply to explain that an elementary school was in fact already in operation, stressing that it was Accolti, not himself, who had made the final decision to accept the mission in California. Nobili justified his role in the affair and expressed his hope that from the modest seed they had planted at Santa Clara something grand might grow. He based his hope on the slender good news in the letter from Rome. Roothaan had left slightly ajar the door to broader educational work in California. His letter indicated that he opposed the establishment of Jesuit colleges in California *unless* the Province of Spain was willing to assume the responsibility for furnishing men. Thus, Accolti explained to a friend, "If on the one hand, the definitive answer of our Father has really broken my heart, on the other I am much comforted by the hope that perhaps the dispersed Province of Spain might assume the task of cultivating this new field" by supplying teachers for Santa Clara.[20]

Accolti's guarded optimism was traceable to recent events in Europe. Anti-clerical sentiment unleashed by the political revolutions of 1848 had nearly destroyed many Jesuit provinces. As a consequence of the identification of the Society of Jesus with opposition to nationalist movements in many countries, a number of houses and colleges of the Society had been closed and their clerical occupants driven into exile. In 1848 Father Roothaan himself had fled from Rome in disguise to avoid the wrath of republican Italians.

Jesuits from Spain had been included in the diaspora. Some had sought refuge in Latin America, while others had scattered throughout Europe. In effect, Roothaan was suggesting that these Spanish exiles be recruited for Santa Clara with a view to their formal acceptance of California as a mission field. Accolti immediately communicated with leaders of the Spanish exiles in Europe. Likewise, Nobili contacted dispersed Jesuits working in Jamaica and Chile. But the campaign failed. The Spanish had already accepted new missions elsewhere, and no other province at that time could spare men for California.

This left Nobili in charge of an institution whose faculty seemed certain to remain inadequate. "There are not yet enough teachers in the school to give it the solid reputation that it should have," Forbes complained to Accolti during the school's second year; nor were there enough to provide for "the advancement of pupils in the various branches of education."[21] Without

One of Santa Clara's early classrooms, the Philalethic Senate Debating Hall, which was located in a remodeled mission adobe known as the California Hotel. *Courtesy: Archives, Univ. of Santa Clara.*

more Jesuits who, unlike salaried laymen, would teach without recompense, it appeared unlikely that the struggling school could survive. "I fear that Father Nobili will have to quit the field," Forbes warned Accolti on another occasion, "if you do not send him some fathers to aid him in the school."[22] But for three years after Santa Clara's founding not even the energetic Accolti, who had a personal stake in the enterprise, could uncover a supply of Jesuit teachers.

Claiming a Campus

The lack of suitable academic advancement for students and the lack of an adequate faculty were not the only problems Nobili faced during Santa Clara's founding years. One of the most formidable threats concerned the ownership of mission property. Events of the 1840's had not only left the buildings and grounds of the old mission in "wretched" condition, they had also left the question of ownership in a highly confused state.

Though apparently only vaguely aware of the problem at the time of his acceptance of the mission, Nobili could not long overlook the extent of the confusion. A host of rivals challenged the ecclesiastical title to portions of Santa Clara. In most instances, several parties claimed ownership of the same piece of property, each linking his title to a different source.

There were basically five sources from which the conflicting claimants drew their demands of proprietorship. Nobili, as an agent of the local bishop of the Catholic Church, claimed title to certain properties by right of ecclesiastical presence at the mission since its founding. Other claimants, such as James Alexander Forbes, whose rancho comprised the pasture lands of the old mission, traced their titles to grants bestowed by the Mexican government in the years following mission secularization. Some men, like the prominent Thomas O. Larkin, who claimed fifteen acres of the mission pear orchard, based their claims on purchases from Pio Pico, last governor of Mexican California. Several Californios possessed lots and buildings that they had obtained through Padre Real, who had continued to dispose of mission property up to the time of his departure for Mexico. Finally, many American squatters asserted ownership on the basis of preemption.

Though he complained about their presence in his private correspondence, Nobili was not willing to wage legal battle against the army of squatters encamped in the fields surrounding the mission. By 1851 the squatters' canvas tents and frame houses constituted the village of Santa Clara. The cost in time and money required to gain possession in court would have been too great, and such aggressive action also would have aroused disagreeable opposition. Besides, most of the area preempted by the American squatters lay beyond the bounds of the central mission site. It was territory over which the church's claim to ownership, as the decision of the United States Land Commission subsequently indicated, was doubtful. Nobili's primary interest was in the buildings and small lots that fell within the central "mission block." Precisely how his rivals were evicted remains unclear, but the mission-block buildings claimed by squatters were among the first properties Nobili repossessed. Perhaps the local sheriff assisted his efforts. In any case, no records remain of Nobili's having regained them by purchase.

It proved more difficult to remove the more tenured rivals who linked their claims to sales or gifts from Padre Real. Real had been prohibited from alienating mission property at certain times by Mexican and American military, civil, and ecclesiastical authorities, but there were intervals when Mexican law allowed such sales. For this reason, if Nobili wished to establish the illegality of a transfer of property by Real, he had to prove two matters in court: that the prohibiting authority had exercised valid jurisdiction, and that each particular sale had, in fact, occurred when Real was explicitly subject to such prohibitions. Because such proof required extensive historical research and considerable expense, Nobili normally achieved his objective by the simpler expedient of purchasing a quit-claim from those with whom he contested title.

In one case, however, it was a rival who took the initiative and threatened Nobili with legal action. In late 1853 a claimant asserted proprietorship to the entire Santa Clara establishment, even the mission church, on the basis of a debt owed his family by a former missionary. This unprecedented challenge led Nobili to fear eviction from even the small portion of the mission quadrangle he occupied. However, James Alexander Forbes, who himself had a stake in the contest, came to his rescue with information establishing that the debt had been paid.[23]

Equally challenging from Nobili's point of view was the question of the validity of claims based upon grants allegedly bestowed by José Castro, military commandant of Northern California, and Governor Pio Pico during the final months of Mexican rule over California. The contest waged for ownership of the mission pear orchard reveals the importance of these grants. It also graphically illustrates the confused condition of property titles in general at Santa Clara.

The fifteen-acre orchard was claimed by four separate parties besides Nobili. Fresh fruit sold for high prices in gold rush San Francisco and the claimants were not reluctant to go to court to lay hold of this highly valued stand of pear trees. Nobili contended that the orchard was part of the core of ecclesiastical property never alienated by secularization. Hence it was his to administer by right of the transfer of Santa Clara to the Jesuits. Antonio Osio, a public official under Mexican authority, asserted, however, that the title to the plot had been bestowed upon him by José Castro in 1846. Competing with Nobili and Osio were three Americans, each with his own claim. One of the latter, John Murphy, alleged ownership through purchase of the title of an earlier claimant, a squatter. Joshua Redman, a Santa Clara county judge, and Thomas O. Larkin, former consul of the United States, each presented separate titles to the orchard on the basis of grants made by Governor Pico in 1846. After five years of tedious and costly litigation, all three of the asserted Mexican grants were declared fraudulent and/or invalid. Nobili finally emerged with uncontested title to the mission pear orchard by purchasing Murphy's squatter-based title for $1,400. Today the orchard site is occupied by Ryan Athletic Field.[24]

The only major church-affiliated attempt to secure title to Santa Clara lands in the courtroom was Bishop Alemany's suit, entered in 1853 on behalf of the Catholic Church and the mission Indians, for a square league (about seven square miles) of land at the mission. (The same claim was made at each of the twenty-one California missions.) In the absence of a grant upon which to base this ambitious demand, the United States Land Commission rejected it. In 1855 the commission did, however, grant the church title to the actual mission site at Santa Clara and to the orchards and vineyards in its immediate environs. The bishop subsequently deeded his title to the Jesuits.

The commission's judgment afforded Nobili little consolation. Pressing circumstances at Santa Clara had forced him to initiate efforts to acquire the former mission land several years before the commission rendered its decision and all appeals were exhausted. Besides, the government's confirmation of title was qualified by the stipulation that it should not affect the interests of third parties.[25] Consequently, if Nobili hoped to use the government's ruling to obtain clear and undisputed title to the sections of property that still remained encumbered, further litigation would have to be initiated. Rather than invest additional time and money in lawsuits whose outcome was never predictable, Nobili continued his practice of simply purchasing quit-claims from those with whom he disputed ownership. As a consequence of this policy of obtaining clear title to lands through out-of-court settlements, in one year alone, 1854, he increased the college's indebtedness by $26,000.[26] Thus began the major fiscal struggles from which Nobili and his successors would never be free.

His heavy expenses obliged Nobili to use novel means to satisfy his creditors in addition to the traditional expedient of borrowing money at exorbitant rates of interest. When he purchased Forbes's portion of the mission quadrangle, for example, the two men agreed that because Forbes needed building materials for the new home he was to construct and because Nobili could obtain these materials at a cheap rate, the priest would render part of the $11,000 payment in bricks and lumber. The two men also agreed that $3,000 of the debt could be met by educating Forbes's several sons at the college free of charge.[27] On another occasion Nobili attempted to purchase the small mission vineyard from Andrés Pico by a similar arrangement, but he was curtly informed that Pico had "no boy he desires to educate."[28]

Despite his usual resourcefulness in financial matters, Nobili occasionally blundered. He foolishly acquiesced in a request of Alemany and others in 1853, when he attempted to salvage a foundering school begun by the Picpus Fathers among the sand dunes near Mission Dolores in San Francisco. Nobili, persuaded by friends that the site would someday be of enormous value, purchased the two-story schoolhouse and the land upon which it stood. The venture proved disastrous. Nobili discovered that not only was his title insecure, but the recently constructed institution was heavily indebted to contractors, architects, and other creditors. Before he could extricate himself from the financial sand trap into which he had stumbled, Nobili had sunk more than $20,000 into the "School of Sorrows," as Accolti dubbed the Mission Dolores venture.[29] At the height of the crisis Nobili feared that his costly mistake would "derange my finances and ruin me."[30] Although motivated by a desire to assist the archbishop and the cause of education in San Francisco and eager to make a good investment, Nobili acted so as to squander both his manpower and financial resources at a time when both would have been more prudently invested in the struggling school at Santa Clara.

The Burden of Property

When James Alexander Forbes observed that the Jesuits began Santa Clara College burdened by "great expenses" and that its founders were hence "necessarily retarded [in] their purposes," he did not overstate the case.[31] During the five years that Nobili occupied the presidential chair, further expenses—near bankruptcy at Mission Dolores, high faculty costs, expenditures for building improvements, fees for lawsuits, and especially real estate purchases—did much to impede the development of the school and at times came near to destroying it.

In 1850, when Accolti's ambitious plans for an educational apostolate in California were still nebulous and before Bishop Alemany had offered the mission of Santa Clara, Accolti suggested that the Jesuits commence their venture by importing from New York a prefabricated schoolhouse, which could be uncrated and resurrected on a favorable site in the Far West. In retrospect, this proposal, which to an amused Peter De Smet surpassed "all former speculations on California," may have been a more prudent and less costly option than the subsequent Jesuit commitment to a school built upon the divided and disputed ground of Mission Santa Clara.[32]

Considering the thousands of dollars that Nobili and his successors poured out to rehabilitate crumbling adobe buildings and to expand the acreage of the mission campus, Joseph Riordan, historian and later president of the college, concluded that the founding fathers "would have done better financially had they never touched the ruins of Santa Clara."[33] He was probably correct. The recovery of the old mission at Jesuit expense was an act of generosity to the bishop and to the Catholic community that still worshipped there. But like many generous acts, it was not practical. Involvement in the Santa Clara site forced Nobili to direct a disproportionate amount of his straitened educational budget to real estate. It also bound his successors to a cramped and expensive-to-expand campus. A few generations later, some presidents of the college would wish to relocate or even to close the institution.

4
The Nobili Years
1851–1856

One barrier that John Nobili never was forced to hurdle was a lack of pupils. During the 1850's, requests for admission exceeded the capacity of his school's facilities. Nobili was obliged to turn away prospective pupils because he lacked the quarters and faculty to accommodate them.

That Santa Clara enjoyed immediate and broad popularity is chiefly explained by the fact that its patrons had nowhere else to go. "California now has a very large percentage of educated men, but where shall they educate their sons?" a concerned Protestant minister inquired in 1860. "A moment's reflection will suffice to show that they will not, to any considerable extent, send them five or six thousand miles from home for this purpose."[1] Unless a parent was willing to ship his children to Europe, to Hawaii, or to the East for schooling, he had to be content with California's educational resources. But apart from Protestant and Catholic institutions the state had little to offer, especially in higher education.

The arrival of American families in Mexican California spurred considerable educational advancement, but the pace of progress was less than swift. The first halting step toward education for American children had in fact been made at Santa Clara in 1846. Late that year Olive Mann Isbell, a niece of Horace Mann, the noted educator, began instructing children in one of the mission's abandoned adobe buildings. It was the first American school in California, but it lasted only two months. Such a brief life typified scores of other attempts to provide schooling. They surfaced suddenly and then disappeared with equal haste into the sea of unstable conditions and constant mobility that characterized California at mid-century. During the gold rush some public and private grammar schools appeared in San Francisco and other population centers, but these, too, usually survived no more than a term or two until the schoolmaster or the families whose children he instructed abandoned the locale for more lucrative employment at mining sites.[2] The state constitution drawn up at Monterey in 1849 provided California with a public school system, but its paper provisions were implemented slowly. When Nobili and Michael Accolti stepped ashore in San Francisco later that same year, no free public school had yet opened its doors anywhere in the state.

Financial factors retarded the evolution of California's school system. Moneys gathered from the sale of public lands, a traditional source of educational revenue, for years failed to supply an adequate school fund. The lands set aside for that purpose were sold rather quickly, but at a price that was too low to provide sufficient capital to immediately remedy the state's educational problems. Besides, until 1855 a generous portion of the revenue available was channeled into private and denominational schools. This practice guaranteed the public at least some access to education, but it delayed the emergence of a solid system of public instruction.

Despite California's generally acknowledged shortage of schools, legislators were reluctant to levy special school taxes. They argued that the drain upon the frontier state's purse for scores of other costly and more necessary public services was too great to justify burdening the population with additional taxes solely for education. Not until 1867 did California elect to shoulder a tax-supported public school system.[3]

In the meantime, decision makers contended that private and municipal resources could meet the state's educational needs. Thus in 1850 the only city in California with free public schools was San Francisco, and many of these were in fact only quasi-public, administered by religious denominations.

Elsewhere the task of educating the youth of the state, especially on the collegiate level, was left to private institutions. Chief among these were the Catholic establishments of Santa Clara College, St. Ignatius College in San Francisco, and Notre Dame College in San Jose; the Methodists' University of the Pacific in Santa Clara; and the College of California, a Congregational-Presbyterian institution in Oakland. As late as 1863 state legislators felt that these private institutions would suffice "for the kind of instruction usually imparted in a college course; it will be a good many years before the number of persons demanding a college education will be large."[4] This reliance upon private enterprise explains why California did not have a state university until the University of California was established in 1868. One observer noted that, with the exception of the Protestant and Catholic churches, "there was little general interest in the establishment of an educational system in California."[5] Whatever there was in the way of higher education, wrote John Swett, founder of California's public school system, was provided by Santa Clara and the other denominational colleges. Another educator declared in 1860 that, regarding schools, "Nothing can be expected from the State."[6]

First Students

Given the scarcity of schools, Santa Clara flourished. It accepted a great variety of students in those early years: sons of foreign consuls living in San Francisco; Mexicans and Australians; Frenchmen and native Californians; and farmers' and merchants' sons whose enterprising parents could pay the yearly charge of $350. Several families who had come to Mexican California before the American conquest had been obliged by circumstances to temporarily neglect the education of their offspring. They were among the first to send their sons to Santa Clara when it opened. They included the children and wards of such pioneers as James Alexander Forbes, Martin Murphy, Jr., Abel Stearns, Job F. Dye, William M. Keith, and Alpheus Thompson. Most of the student body, however, came from families who had arrived after the American takeover and the discovery of gold.

The college enjoyed a wide patronage among established Californians, many of whom were members of the state's landed aristocracy. Such names as Alviso, Suñol, Pinero, Berryessa, Vallejo, Estudillo, and Bandini appear on the earliest enrollment lists. A large number of young Californios attended the school during the 1850's and 1860's because of the predominance of this ethnic group in the local population. In 1852, for example, at least 45 percent of the 6,664 inhabitants of San Jose were native Californians or Mexicans.[7] Another factor was the affinity between Mexican Americans and the Catholic church at mid-century. As historian Leonard Pitt has stated, during the years of transition from Mexican to American rule, the native Californian "found it easier to retain his identity as a Catholic than as a miner, rancher, voter or naturalized citizen."[8] The fact that several of the faculty spoke Spanish must also have attracted those native Californians for whom bilingual education was a necessity. As late as 1867 Santa Clara issued a Spanish version of its yearly bulletin for the benefit of its Californio and Latin American patrons.

Despite their bonds with the established California ways of life, it is not apparent that the Santa Clara Jesuits worked to preserve the local culture of the Californios who came to them for schooling. Indeed, the opposite seems to have been the case. Young Californios (like the foreign-born faculty itself) were encouraged to adjust to the dominant Anglo-American way of doing things. Adding to the encouragement were the parents of many Spanish-speaking students, who were concerned that their sons master English and the basic subjects crucial for success and survival in the world that had burst upon them with the arrival of the Anglos.

Some students, like the future state treasurer of California, José G. Estudillo, arrived at the college speaking only Spanish. He asked his brother-in-law, William Heath Davis, to "overlook all my mistakes in writing because it is [a] very short time since I commenced to learn English."[9] To further hasten the acquisition of English, a later rule of the school required that Spanish-speaking students "should not be allowed to speak Spanish except for the 1st month after coming."[10] Hence José's cousin, Jesús María Estudillo congratulated himself the day he was able to record in his diary that "I did not speak two words in Spanish" today. His arrival at a new level of self-confidence and expertise in English was recorded the day his Dublin-born teacher assured him he recited his prose assignment "with the feeling of an Irishman."[11] Lack of funds forced twenty-year-old Jesús María Estudillo to drop out of school in 1864, before completing his education. Few Californios remained long enough to take the bachelor's degree; but neither did the majority of students who first attended the institution.

Santa Clara's Catholic label also enhanced its appeal among Anglo Catholic families, made aware of their religion not only by the Know-Nothing movement but also by vigorous California Protestantism. The value they placed on the catechism as a critical element in any educational system and their general esteem of Jesuit pedagogy ensured the initial success of Santa Clara. James Alexander Forbes, himself Jesuit educated, informed José Antonio Aguirre that the school was "the best there is in California" because faculty members "are concerned about the religious education of the students, without which there can be no true instruction."[12] Peter Burnett, former governor of California and an outspoken convert to Catholicism, sent his two teen-age sons to the school. He also served as one of the college's first lay trustees during Nobili's presidency. Martin Murphy, Jr., whose father had led his large Catholic clan from Missouri to California for religious reasons, was one of the first to have supported Accolti's educational project in 1849. He enrolled his three sons at Santa Clara. When the three boys arrived at the school they were accompanied by their private tutor from Rancho San Martín; the tutor joined Nobili's faculty.[13]

Enrollment was not restricted to Catholic students. Indeed, the Protestant response to the institution amazed its Italian priest-founders. "One half of the boarders are Protestants," teacher B. J. Reid boasted in 1852, "their parents preferring that school to any of the Protestant schools in the country."[14]

Some Protestant parents preferred to board their sons at Santa Clara College rather than to ship them to distant Hawaii or Boston simply to avoid Catholic influence. Why they preferred Santa Clara over the other schools in the state is unclear. Perhaps Santa Clara's reputation for stern discipline made it attractive to some parents. Besides, the college enjoyed considerable praise in the local press. Catholic schools in general "have an enviable reputation," one non-Catholic critic conceded, "and have thus far succeeded too well in drawing to them the children of Protestants." But, he added, "We do not regret the existence of these schools. . . . They do much good for the cause of education by provoking us to vigilance and emulation."[15] The fact that nativism never reached the level of intensity in the Far West that it manifested in other sections of the country facilitated Protestant patronage of Catholic institutions.

Moreover, anti-Catholic feeling was moderated or at least channeled by the possibilities of educational competition. The potentially destructive energies generated by the Know-Nothing phenomenon and by traditional sectarian hostilities were directed into constructive educational rivalry. Although in the long run this led to an excessive proliferation of schools, in the short run higher education in America during the pre-Civil War period, especially in the West, benefited from intense denominational competition. College foundings were seen as events in the religious campaigns waged by the various denominations for the spiritual conquest of the continent. This "struggle for territory" was reenacted on each successive frontier, including California.[16] "Vigilance and emulation" were the watchwords with which most Protestants greeted the program of the California Catholics to found schools. Protestant promoters, believing that the "wily, tireless" Jesuits were "anxious and ready to educate the youth of the state and endeavor to make their institution popular," pointed to Santa Clara's success as reason for founding the College of California in 1855. It was the precursor to the University of California.[17]

Catholics reacted in like manner to Protestant successes. Santa Clara's founding triumvirate, Joseph S. Alemany, Accolti, and Nobili, moved to establish schools as a means of combating growing Protestant influence in the one-time Catholic province. Correspondence among Santa Clara Jesuits during the 1850's reveals their determination to "counteract the bold influence" of their Methodist neighbors at the University of the Pacific. In the view of historian Louis B. Wright, sectarian rivalries such as this produced a fervor for educational supremacy among the churches in California to a degree seen on no other American frontier.[18]

The Proselytization Controversy

Religious rivalry occasionally burst the bonds of verbal restraint. In 1852, for example, a debate was waged in the press over the alleged proselytization of Protestant children in the classrooms of Santa Clara. Nobili seems not to have been embarrassed by the accusation; in fact, he welcomed the publicity the debate brought the school. The following year, however, Nobili complicated the issue by attempting to procure for underfinanced Santa Clara a portion of the public-school fund. In so doing he brought down upon himself the criticism of those who, like John Swett, resented any move that weakened California's embryonic public-school system.

Nobili based his petition for funds on an ingenuous argument. He claimed that Santa Clara was equivalently a public or "common" school because it was "open to all boys without regard to religious tenets." He also appealed to contemporary legislation that tolerated the channeling of public moneys into parochial schools. Fund sharing was, for example, used to sustain the "ward schools" of San Francisco. Nobili's request for aid was rejected by the school commissioners of Santa Clara County. Although the college gained nothing but publicity from the controversy, public education benefited. The quarrel prompted John Swett and others to rally to the support of California's underdeveloped public-school system. They opposed the consolidation of public and private schools, and the lenient laws that Nobili had sought to exploit were soon amended by the state legislature.[19]

By attempting to borrow from the public purse, Nobili unwittingly gave his critics a further motive to assert Santa Clara's dread sectarianism. Catholic schools are "full of sectarianism and nothing else," blasted one opponent. "All possible means" are employed there, he warned the public, to induce students "to conform to Roman Catholic worship."[20]

Nobili responded to this charge in 1852 by assuring the parents of prospective pupils that no students "are instructed in the principles of Catholic doctrine without the express consent of their parents." Catholics, it is true, were catechized every Sunday in the mission; but no Protestant pupil, in accordance with "a strict regulation" of the school, was allowed to attend except by express parental mandate.[21] Proselytization had exploded into a sensitive public issue. Consequently, Nobili and his staff scrupulously adhered to the regulation.

When a spokesman for the college asserted that "Catholic doctrine is never taught in the presence or hearing of Protestant pupils," he was incorrect. All students, regardless of religion, were obliged to attend religious services where Catholic doctrine naturally supplied the subjects for sermons.[22] If a parent requested that his son be excused from this exercise, Nobili answered that "attending with the rest at divine worship" remained an "indispensable rule of the institution." "Whilst principals, teachers, and most of the pupils are present at the customary worship," Nobili queried, "how could a part be permitted to be elsewhere unattended, without producing confusion and destroying all discipline?" The pupils were "entirely free in matters of religion," with the exception of this "exterior conformity to the religion of the institute."[23] Most parents were aware of the nature of the school and its regulations before they entrusted their sons to the tutelage of the Jesuits. Few, therefore, found reasons to complain.

Nobili's request for public funds and his defense of his school's religious policies produced a harvest of publicity for Santa Clara. This pleased the small but devoted faculty. The attacks "do you no harm" one teacher assured Nobili.[24] "All this cannonading against the Jesuits and the school of Santa Clara has done this establishment much good," Forbes concurred, "for now there are more scholars than there were before."[25] Even the critics conceded as much. As one protagonist observed in 1854, even "Protestants are found to believe in and praise the education of Romanish schools."[26]

Problems of a Pioneer Boarding School

One of the features that drew students to Santa Clara was its boarding facilities. If schools were rare in California in the 1850's, establishments that offered sufficient staff and accommodations to sustain a boarding school were rarer still. A San Francisco newspaper told its gold rush readers that "A parent whose business calls him away to the Atlantic States may leave with his mind perfectly at ease" if he entrusts his son to the "parental superintendence" of the directors of Santa Clara College.[27]

The management of a boarding school burdened its proprietors with a host of petty disciplinary problems more characteristic of a nursery or kindergarten than an educational establishment. But the availability of dormitories did attract students from far and wide. Although many pupils commuted daily to the college from nearby Santa Clara and San Jose, the majority were boarders from San Francisco, Sacramento, Stockton, Santa Barbara, and Los Angeles. Some came from the mining camps and mountain towns of the Sierra Nevada. A prospective scholar's admission was almost guaranteed if he appeared at the door with "sufficient bedding," an iron bedstead, and $350 a year to cover board and tuition. The school "is open to all who choose to avail themselves of its advantages," Nobili grandly announced. Each stu-

A sketch of Santa Clara in 1856 by Henry Miller. From the left are the east wing of the mission quadrangle, the mission church, and the walled cemetery. The small building with gothic windows is the brick chapel whose construction led to John Nobili's death in 1856. At the far right stands the California Hotel. This former mission building received its name in the 1840's, when it served for a few years as a wayside inn. After the college was founded, a second story was added to the inn; its rooms served as debating hall, dormitory, and classrooms. *Courtesy: Bancroft Library.*

dent upon being admitted was examined "and placed in that class for which his previous attainments may adapt him."[28]

What was it like to attend Santa Clara in the 1850's? A newly enrolled student recorded his first impressions when he arrived from San Francisco. He traveled perched on the roof of a stage coach. "We passed along the high adobe walls that guarded . . . the college grounds," he recalled. "The quaint low buildings, the red tile roofs, the old adobe church and the great wooden cross in front" were sights that impressed upon the young man's memory as his coach drew to a halt in the dusty plaza in front of the mission church. Also memorable were "the peaceful atmosphere of the place and its seclusion."[29]

Because "privations and inconveniences abounded" in the beginning, it was advisable that the new student bring with him a Spartan detachment from material comforts.[30] "The furniture and board were necessarily of a primitive kind," an early historian recorded. "The pupils slept in a loft over the school rooms, made their own beds, and helped to slaughter and cup up the cattle which supplied the table, and to make the bread needed for general use. . . . A fountain in the mission garden gave water both for cooking and washing and morning ablutions were made in the open air at all seasons."[31]

Uncomfortable students might take satisfaction in the fact that the faculty was no better off. The staff lacked rooms of their own, and for several months after their arrival at the crowded institution, two young Jesuit teachers from Italy "were in the habit of carrying their mattresses at night to any available spot, often on the verandas in the open air."[32]

If students found the diet and dormitories deficient, they viewed the school's disciplined routine with greater dislike. Nobili's promise to treat boarders with "affectionate care" undoubtedly reassured parents, but his guarantee that pupils would be "always day and night under the eye" of the faculty did not win their sons' approval.[33] To the frontier lad used to the freedom of ranch life or the excitement of San Francisco, the restraints imposed by Santa Clara's seminary-like regimen seemed oppressive.

The earliest rules dictated that older students rise at half-past five. Before breakfast at eight they attended the liturgy and spent an hour and a half preparing the day's lessons. Morning classes ran from nine until noon. After a two-hour respite for lunch and recreation, the remainder of the day, until five o'clock, was spent in the classroom. Evenings were devoted to "familiar scientific conversations" and "exercises in the languages." Free time on Wednesday and Saturday afternoons broke the study routine.[34]

Except for the twice-weekly afternoons of freedom, when "the pupils generally take a pleasant ramble accompanied by the teachers," boarders were confined to the small campus.[35] They were allowed to visit parents or friends on the first Saturday of the month provided they could return the same evening. Nobili insisted on this regulation because he considered it very important that the students should be "exposed to as few as possible distractions calculated to wean them from their books and from habits of regularity."[36]

Nobili accepted some students at the age of six, which obliged members of his staff to give them "constant supervision." The willingness of nineteenth-century schoolmasters like Nobili to do almost everything for their charges led many parents to ask for even more detailed attention. One anxious mother wrote to Nobili from Sacramento to complain that she had not heard from her son "for three months at a stretch." She instructed the priest, "If my poor boy is dead, do let me know it and if alive make him write to me at least every two weeks."[37] Another parent wrote that his two sons should be "compelled to clean their teeth every morning," and inasmuch as the younger "has the unfortunate weakness of wetting his bed from early childhood," the solicitous father hoped Nobili would "not be too severe if it should happen occasionally" at Santa Clara. Later, the same parent sent an angry missive to protest Master Frank's "practice of assisting in the kitchen operations or wait[ing] on table."[38] If the regimen at boarding school was a trying experience for the student, its maintenance was tedious for the schoolmaster.

What did students think of school life? It is easier to discover the attitude of principals and parents to early Santa Clara than that of the pupils. Some correspondence has survived, however, to reveal student views. One home-sick boy informed his mother by letter that the president "is very kind to me," but in the next breath he implored, "You must not urge it on me to remain here next year dear Ma because I cannot stand it."[39] Another young student, not without a sense of humor, began a letter to his father, "I have at least found out how I like the school." "To tell the truth," he disclosed, "I do not like this school one quarter as well as Mr. Towell's." He then proceeded to tally his complaints:

They make me go without my supper when I do that which you told me to take so much care not to do. But they are very willing to give some meat, such meat as it is, and some bread, but nothing to drink at all and no soup. The boys have to take turns to sweep out the dormitory and you have to clean the chamber pots. You are not allowed to talk loud between 6 o'clock and breakfast or to play with the boys with your hands such as hugging them. In the morning a bell rings and if it does not wake you up you have to have some water poured in your face. When you get up you make your own bed, and then go out to the pump and wash yourself. Then you go to Mass whether you like it or not, and after Mass we go to breakfast, where we find a small chunk of bread as sour as vinegar, or was when we came here first.[40]

The Search for Teachers

Though a strict discipline remained in force, the school facilities improved with each passing year. Indeed, "the liberal patronage" that the school received encouraged Nobili to render—as he put it—"increased exertions" to make the institution "worthy of the confidence of parents" and "more adapted to the great work of the education of youth."[41] But the area of greatest progress was academic. This progress occurred as a consequence of Michael Accolti's search for a Jesuit faculty.

While Nobili worked with a limited staff of laymen and priests, Accolti looked to Europe, Latin America, and the eastern United States for Jesuit teachers. In his letters he complained "at the sight of the great good there is to do and the scanty means we have" to do it. Nobili was "killing himself" in order to keep up with his many obligations. And after two years some of the students were "so advanced as to require something more" than the primary and secondary instruction that the understaffed institution was capable of providing.[42] Accolti feared that without assistance it would be impossible for the school to continue.

When he saw that his lengthy epistles to Rome were accomplishing "nothing at all," Accolti hit on another solution. In the spring of 1853, after discussing the idea with Nobili, he resolved to travel to Rome to confront the father general face to face with his arguments on behalf of the college. "You can accomplish more in one conversation," Accolti decided, "than with a hundred letters."[43]

The decision proved propitious. Accolti persuaded the Jesuits of the Province of Turin, Italy, to adopt California as a permanent mission. This agreement suddenly assured a supply of university-trained teachers for Santa Clara. Their arrival marked an epochal point in the history of the institution.

Clerical reinforcements soon began to converge on California from scattered posts of exile. The first to reach California were three young priests already in the United States: Charles Messea, Aloysius Masnata, and Anthony Maraschi. The trio arrived together in November of 1854. Maraschi remained in San Francisco, where he founded St. Ignatius College (later to become the University of San Francisco). Messea and Masnata were assigned to teach at Santa Clara. Others followed this vanguard.

Before Accolti's successful trip to Rome, Santa Clara's faculty never numbered more than ten full- or part-time teachers. By 1855, the college boasted a faculty of eighteen priests and laymen. One historian claimed it was unequalled in California "for scholarship both literary and scientific."[44] Now confident of the school's future and having obtained the required $20,000 endowment, Nobili petitioned the state for a charter of incorporation for the four-year-old institution. This was readily granted. Nobili then published the first bulletin for the newly chartered college. In it he announced that Santa Clara was prepared to offer "a thorough course of mercantile, scientific and classical studies such as are pursued in the best colleges of the Union, together with a solid moral and Christian education." The president revealed that the college possessed a library of ten thousand books, which was remarkable considering that some fifteen years later the University of California had a library of only thirteen thousand volumes.[45] However, Nobili did not describe the quality or type of Santa Clara's collection. The bulk of the holdings were probably theological tomes of interest only to the Jesuit faculty.

Santa Clara had ventured into collegiate instruction for the first time in

Thomas I. Bergin, Santa Clara's first graduate and the recipient of the first bachelor's degree awarded in California. After graduating in 1857, Bergin went on to study law in New York and later practiced in San Francisco. He was one of the first directors of Hastings School of Law. The legacy he left to his alma mater in 1915 helped to found Santa Clara's School of Law. *Courtesy: Admiral and Mrs. Walter F. Rodee.*

1853, though only on a limited scale. The acquisition of a larger faculty from Italy the following year enabled an expansion of the college curriculum. In 1857 Santa Clara College conferred its first collegiate degree, a Bachelor of Arts diploma, on Thomas I. Bergin of San Francisco. This was the first diploma granted by any institution of higher learning in California.

Nobili Felled by a Nail

Nobili attended to the school's physical growth by purchasing new properties and by rehabilitating additional mission buildings. In 1854 he obtained title to an old adobe structure known as the California Hotel, standing north of the mission church. This historic building had for generations housed the family of the majordomo of the mission. During the Mexican War, American families fled to the building in search of protection from winter weather and from Mexican troops. The building then passed into the hands of an associate of Padre Real, who operated it as a wayside inn which he dubbed the California Hotel. In 1854, Martin Murphy, Jr., purchased the building and the lot upon which it stood and sold them to the college.[46] By remodeling the old hostel and adding a second story, Nobili provided Santa Clara with an additional dormitory and eight new classrooms. The venerable structure housed generations of Santa Clara students until it collapsed during the earthquake of 1906.

Nobili next adorned the campus with its first new building, a brick chapel. While inspecting the construction of the chapel in February, 1856, he stepped on a nail. The wound seemed a trifle, and his quick recovery was expected. Eleven days later, however, Nobili suffered a serious relapse. His doctor discovered that he had contracted tetanus, "a disease both terrible and mortal." After suffering the agonizing pains of lockjaw for two days, Nobili died on March 1, 1856.[47]

With the death of Nobili, the Jesuits of Santa Clara College and California felt "deprived of their founder and their principal support." This ex-missionary, whose early reputation among his fellows owed more to his intellectual attainments than to his ability in practical matters, had proved himself a capable administrator. Paradoxically, he had first resisted Accolti's plan for an educational apostolate, though he inherited almost sole responsibility for the undertaking at Santa Clara when Accolti returned to Oregon. He therefore shares with Accolti the title of co-founder of the institution whose destiny he guided for five years. "All that we have and all that we shall have," his successor declared, "we owe to Father Nobili. He was the soul and sinew of all our labors."[48]

Nobili described the school at its inception as "the germ only of such an institution as we would wish to make it." Santa Clara had become at the time of his death a well-patronized institution with an enrollment of more than one hundred pupils.[49] Nobili had begun in 1851 with "little or no funds," and he had begged and borrowed enough to expand the modest school beyond the bounds of the church and tiny cemetery to a campus embracing nearly twenty acres of real estate and half a dozen buildings.[50] Santa Clara, though its physical accommodations were still Spartan and the instruction was seriously handicapped by debts, had prospered beyond its founders' "most sanguine expectations."[51] Its Jesuit directors were convinced by 1856 that their young college was "certainly the best in the state, by far." Their opinion was reinforced by the begrudging praise of Santa Clara's critics.[52] In an editorial describing the school at the conclusion of its third academic year, the San Francisco *Alta* concluded that it had "sustained its reputation" as California's "first educational establishment."[53]

5

Italy Comes to California
1854-1861

W hen Harvard's President Charles W. Eliot lamented in 1869 that "It is very hard to find competent professors for the University," he voiced a complaint shared by many nineteenth-century educators. "Very few Americans of eminant quality," Eliot noted, "are attracted to this profession." As a result, a characteristic of early American higher education was its reliance upon Europe for teachers.[1]

The lack of qualified American teachers, lay or clerical, posed a special challenge to the scores of Catholic colleges that sprang to life in the United States during the nineteenth century. To educate the church's mushrooming immigrant population, these institutions frequently looked to European religious congregations for help. Georgetown University, for instance, the oldest Catholic institution of higher learning in the United States, counted many European Jesuits among its early faculties. The University of Notre Dame was run by French brothers of the Congregation of the Holy Cross. According to a study by Edward J. Power, nearly 30 percent of the teachers in America's pre-Civil War Catholic colleges came from Europe.[2]

The Jesuits in particular relied heavily upon their Old World membership to sustain their educational missions in the New. Early St. Louis University was staffed by Belgian priests. French Jesuits operated Spring Hill College in Alabama and Fordham College in New York. German Jesuits, many of them exiled by Bismarck's *Kulturkampf*, founded schools from New York westward into the Mississippi Valley, including Canisius College in Buffalo and John Carroll University in Cleveland. In the Far West, Italian Jesuits from Turin manned schools in Seattle, Spokane, San Francisco, and Santa Clara. The first rector of every Jesuit college started in America before 1900 was—with only two exceptions—a foreigner.[3]

The Italian influence upon Santa Clara College did not end with the passing of its founders, John Nobili and Michael Accolti. In fact, as a consequence of the upheavals created by the Italian Risorgimento, the European character of the college became more pronounced. What Italy lost, Santa

Clara gained. In the wake of the decision taken in 1854 by the dispersed Jesuits of the Turin Province to adopt California as a mission field, the obscure frontier college was flooded with well-educated teachers from Italy. Within six years, Santa Clara's faculty increased fourfold.

The Turin Province could offer little financial support to Jesuit operations in the American West. Even the travel expenses of its recruits for America depended upon charity. Nonetheless, it was generous with its manpower. As anticlerical sentiment swept through the Italian peninsula, other Jesuit provinces also sent men. Thus refugees from Rome, Naples, Sardinia, and Sicily joined their confreres from Turin in the United States. During the fifty-five years of Turinese administration, nearly one hundred priests, brothers, and scholastics from the Turin Province and from other parts of Italy sailed for America to fill educational and missionary positions in California and the Pacific Northwest.[4] The greatest waves seem to have arrived in the 1850's and 1860's. Most spent at least some time at the college. Many taught only a year or two before being transferred elsewhere. As a result of their numbers and responsibilities, the Turinese cast a definite Italian hue upon Jesuit activities in California generally and upon the administration of Santa Clara in particular. Even after the presence of Jesuits was accepted in unified Italy, the California Mission was administered from Turin. This administration continued until 1909.

The "California Mission" is not to be confused with Santa Clara as the "mission university." The California Mission was a geographical and jurisdictional designation of the area dependent upon the Turin Province of the Society of Jesus from 1854 to 1909. Santa Clara was merely one of several institutions included in that mission. In 1909, when California's status as a mission field ended, its dependence upon Turin ceased, and the California Mission became the independent Province of California.

By 1870 Italians were a clear majority in the college's staff of fifty. With the exception of the four-year term of Burchard Villiger, a Swiss priest, Italians occupied the presidential chair for thirty-two years. For nearly half a century, Italians, with the exception of Villiger, also held the influential post of superior of the Jesuit mission in California.

What was the caliber of these exiles who for two generations directed Santa Clara's development? It was the common opinion of their non-Italian contemporaries that Italy "did not send mediocrity to California." Men like Accolti and Aloysius Varsi were regarded as gentlemen of great culture and personal charm, according to the testimony of numerous acquaintances. For their day, many of the Italians at Santa Clara also possessed impressive academic credentials. Most of them had acquired teaching experience in Europe or the United States before coming to Santa Clara; some were also trained administrators.[5] Nobili, whose studies at the Roman College had been "successful even to the point of brilliance," taught in several Jesuit schools in Italy before volunteering for missionary work in Oregon.[6] Accolti, who returned permanently to California in 1856, had studied in Rome at the prestigious Academia dei Nobili Ecclesiastici before entering the order. Nicholas Congiato, Nobili's successor, had been vice-president of the College of Nobles in Rome and then vice-president of the College of Fribourg in Switzerland; before coming to Santa Clara, he had presided over the small Jesuit college at Bardstown in Kentucky. Felix Cicaterri had been rector of the Jesuit college in Verona until revolution forced him to flee. Henry Imoda had taught in Monaco and at the College of Naples, and Paul Raffo had been professor of scripture and Hebrew at St. Beuno's in Wales. Varsi had studied mathematics at the University of Paris in preparation for a career at the Jesuit-operated Imperial Observatory in China until a change of plans sent him to America and then to Santa Clara College. Many younger men had studied in France and England; others had completed their education at Jesuit institutions in the United States.[7]

Few of the exiles were as brilliant or versatile as Joseph Bayma, mathematician, philosopher, and theoretical physicist. Bayma's *Elements of Molecular Mechanics* (London, 1866), combined with his other writings and accomplishments, earned him recognition as a pioneer in stereochemistry as well as "the foremost, intellectually, of the Jesuit body in California."[8] Though few could match Bayma's brilliance, most of the other Italians possessed a "sound academic background." "It was the ordinary education of the better classes in Europe," one historian concludes, "with extra philosophical and theological training. . . . Although by present standards this education had serious defects, in mid-nineteenth century America, and especially on the frontier, it was impressive."[9]

The Italian clerics were not without shortcomings by American standards. One Irish contemporary observed that the "manners and ideas" of the Turinese Jesuits were often "too Italian to meet the tastes of the young Republicans of the West."[10] Throughout the nineteenth century, the religion and alien ways of Italian Jesuits drew stern censures from some native Americans, who feared that their arriving "a baker's dozen weekly from Europe" was a menacing portent for California. The derisive public attacks of these critics only reinforced the clannish characteristics they found so reprehensible in the foreigners.[11]

Joseph Bayma, mathematician, philosopher, and scientist. In the nineteenth century this Italian Jesuit was the outstanding scholar on the college faculty. *Courtesy: Archives, Univ. of Santa Clara.*

A more substantial if less public criticism arose within the Catholic community itself. The strict discipline of the Turinese colleges and religious communities was not unique in and beyond Europe in the 1850's, but it became increasingly anachronistic in California as the century drew on, leading many American-born Jesuits on the Santa Clara faculty to urge a less severe regimen. The Italians' severe conservatism may have led the Jesuit General Peter Beckx to doubt the wisdom of a request by Joseph Bayma, the superior of the California Mission, for more English Jesuits for California. Beckx remarked that the English could work with the Italians only "with difficulty."[12]

The Italians' most obvious academic disadvantage was linguistic. Many of the young seminarians had received at least a few years' schooling in England or in the eastern United States before traveling to California. Some learned in time to speak English "fluently and with precision." But most, in both the pulpit and the classroom, "spoke and taught in a language not altogether English."[13] Nobili's pronunciation, for example, was said to be "not all that might be desired," although he had a facility in learning languages. Only a few California Jesuits "know English well," Father Beckx observed in 1870.[14]

The Italian Jesuits at the colleges in Santa Clara and San Francisco recognized their deficiency and succeeded in recruiting Jesuits from England, Ireland, and the Maryland and Missouri provinces who could "impart a knowledge of higher English" to their students.[15] Some of these remained in California only a few years. Others, like Edmund Young, a popular teacher of literature and debate from New England, liked what they found at Santa Clara and remained permanently.

For decades, vocations to the Jesuit order from California itself remained rare. Consequently, the Italian superiors of the California Mission undertook trips to Jesuit colleges and novitiates in the eastern United States and Europe to interest adventurous young men in educational and ministerial work in the Far West. Most of the recruits came from Europe, but occasionally there was a prized American such as Richard Gleeson, who became the thirteenth president of the college. When he proceeded west from Philadelphia to join the order in 1877, at the age of seventeen, he traveled in the company of twelve other seminarians, most of whom were European.[16]

The Ideal: A Classical Education

Though many of the Italians of Santa Clara lacked skill in English, they were not deficient in Latin and Greek. Classics constituted the humanistic core around which their own education as Jesuits had been constructed; it was this same liberal education they imparted to their students.

It was not because Latin was the language of the church or because their
schools functioned primarily to train future churchmen that the Jesuits
championed a classical education. Rather, they were convinced that the classics provided the optimum vehicle for an education that was both forma-
tive and informative. The ambitious objective of Jesuit pedagogy as formu-
lated in the *Ratio Studiorum*, or "Plan of Studies"—initiated in 1599, revised
in 1832, and echoed in the catalogs of Santa Clara College and of all Jesuit
schools into the twentieth century—was "the full and harmonious development of all those faculties that are distinctive of man."[17] In this plan, the development of the "whole man" was held up as the end and essence of education.
The Jesuit system aimed not at vocational training, as its practitioners never tired of explaining, nor did it seek the "mere accumulation of learning":
its goal was the development of the student's "faculties" and the "training
of his character."[18] "The acquisition of knowledge, though it necessarily ac-
companies any right system of education, is a secondary result of education.
Learning is an instrument of education, not its end. The end is culture, and
mental and moral development."[19]

This was the whole basis of a Jesuit institution. Its program of catechetics
strove to develop the student's moral sensitivities, and its employment of
ancient literature and the classical languages aimed to sharpen the student's
mental powers. Because their complicated syntax and idiom were "remote
from the language of the student" and because mastering them demanded
"continual attention, concentration, and accuracy," the highly inflected languages of Latin and Greek were viewed as the ideal instruments for imparting "mental discipline" and laying bare "the laws of thought and logic."[20]

To this end, approximately half of the six-year classical course at Santa
Clara (a period roughly equivalent to the modern high school) concentrated
on mastery of the rudiments and grammar of the Latin and Greek languages.
The objective was ambitious: to habituate young minds to "correct and
accurate reasoning, to close observation, to tireless industry, to keen discrimi-
nation, to vivid and lively imagination." Having acquired accuracy and facility of thought and expression, the young classicist was promoted to studies
on the collegiate level. Several years' study of philosophy and the natural
sciences (interspersed with classes in literature, history, and the modern languages) crowned the Jesuit system and stood as the goal of the long years of
"mental training."[21]

The classical curriculum was not peculiar to Jesuit schools. Most American
colleges in the mid-nineteenth century had similar programs. What made
Santa Clara and other Jesuit institutions unique was the persistent devotion
to the classical ideal long after other American schools had abandoned it in

favor of a more varied and more utilitarian schedule. The California Jesuits were "slow to capitulate" to the demands of the times, one of their members later complained. "For fifty years at least, they clung to the *Ratio* as far as circumstances permitted, which was not very far."[22] Long before the trends in twentieth-century American education forced reluctant Roman authorities to the wholesale abandonment of the classics, a combination of factors led the Jesuits of Santa Clara to compromise piecemeal their ideal of an exclusively classical training.

"The problem how to bestow the blessings of a classical education on the reluctant youth of western America," one historian wrote, was a "perplexing one."[23] In the first place, the Jesuits charged tuition. This discouraged many students from remaining at Santa Clara long enough to complete the lengthy classical course. Second, few parents requested classical training for their sons. They could neither understand its purpose nor "see in it any practical value."[24] Andrew J. Moulder, California's Superintendent of Public Instruction in the 1850's and a firm foe of the classics, expressed the attitude (as well as the misconceptions) of many when he declared: "Ours is eminently a practical age. . . . We want no pale and sickly scholars. . . . This may do for old settled communities, but will never do for California. . . . For the mere bookworm—for the Latin and Greek antiquarian—this is certainly not the country."[25]

Responding to such views, the Italians of Santa Clara in 1854 introduced a course in commercial education designed to satisfy pupils who wanted nothing more than business skills. By the mid-nineteenth century this course had become a popular alternative to Latin and Greek in many American Jesuit colleges. The business curriculum at Santa Clara was basically at the high school level, although some students of college age were also enrolled. For some Jesuits, the appearance of such a course was a regrettable abandonment of the order's humanistic and liberal arts tradition. Laments of the purists notwithstanding, the commercial course was launched in 1854, and it became popular.

In 1858 the Turinese reluctantly introduced another course of studies that was less traditional and more practical than the classical curriculum. It was euphemistically dubbed the scientific course, and it led to a Bachelor of Science degree. It might more appropriately have been entitled the nonclassical course; it was identical to the classical curriculum except for the requirement of Latin and Greek. In this revision the Santa Clara faculty was avantgarde at a time when other Jesuit institutions, even pace-setting St. Louis University, continued to require the classical languages.[26]

Though they adapted their courses to the demands of the times, the Santa

Clara Jesuits persisted in their belief that the classics were the optimum vehicle for a liberal education. To them, the ideal alumnus of the college throughout the nineteenth century was a bright young man whose personal talents and parents' purse enabled him to remain at the college long enough to master the full classical course and to graduate with the Bachelor of Arts degree. Sadly, such a student was a rarity. Of the several thousand students who studied at Santa Clara during the school's first half-century, only a small percentage enrolled in the classical course. And of these, fewer than one hundred graduated with the Bachelor of Arts diploma.[27] The Bachelor of Science degree was far more in demand.

The number of students interested in a baccalaureate of any kind remained small. The preparatory department continued to attract pupils of grammar-school age; most were content to complete their education at the secondary level. Though the Jesuit system of a unified, six-to-eight year classical course drew no sharp line between the conclusion of secondary studies and the beginning of collegiate instruction, probably a majority of the students who chose an early termination of their studies would be classified today as high-school students.

The Annual Exhibition

The classical learning of the scholarly few was proudly displayed at the annual exhibition, or commencement, which closed each academic year. In 1857, before Thomas Bergin received the Bachelor of Arts degree, he demonstrated his mastery of Greek by a public defense of the *Odyssey*. In like manner, before Delphin Delmas, a graduate destined for national legal prominence, received his degree in 1861, he was prepared to "translate into either Latin, French, or English" the twenty-four books of the *Odyssey* from the original Greek.[28] In 1864, the administrators of the college concluded that "as a token of due appreciation of the classical course," preference would be given in the future to classicists in selecting student speakers at the annual exhibition. Santa Clara's devotion to the classics was, however, surpassed in one detail by its neighbor, the University of the Pacific, where for a time candidates for degrees at commencement were presented in Latin.[29]

A typical exhibition was a two-day academic marathon, which attracted full coverage in the San Francisco press and drew large crowds of parents and spectators to the campus. Scientific lectures and experiments, dramatic productions, and musical entertainment manifesting a natural but pleasant bias in favor of Italian composers were standard features on the program.

Another favorite form of student presentation at exhibition time was debate on a controversial topic of the day. During the 1850's, when California newspapers daily reported stories of bloody duels, one Santa Clara graduation program announced an extemporaneous student debate on "duelling and suicide" to which "any one of the audience may make and urge objections." The same audience endured the dubious delight of hearing students defend theses in scholastic philosophy. Included were such propositions as, "The principle of causality is not experimental, as Mr. Hume contends, but analytical and absolutely certain," and "Felicity is the general and ultimate object of all man's volitions."[30] The exhibition began with a public examination of the pupils' learning and concluded on the second day with the distribution of prizes and diplomas.

Besides its public-relations value, the annual exhibition served a pedagogical function. It displayed an important consequence of the Jesuit method of liberal education, namely, the ability to express oneself with facility and accuracy. This was a hallmark of successful mental training.

Competition and emulation were constantly and deliberately cultivated as a stimulus to learning. "In every class in every subject and at every level competition was the rule," in all Jesuit colleges.[31] To this end, Santa Clara's school year was punctuated by a series of weekly and monthly examinations, both written and oral, in which students in every class competed for top ranking and prizes. The rivalry was keen. One student, after several days of intense preparation, recorded in 1861 that he woke up on the morning of the exam having dreamed he had just won a gold watch at a public raffle. "This is now a hard task before me," he confided to his diary on another occasion, while preparing for monthly places, "as so many of the class are trying their best to get ahead."[32] The record of monthly places was used to determine the honor of performing in the annual exhibition. The privilege of appearing publicly then and perhaps earning a prize encouraged competition. It also rewarded excellence and held up for imitation the accomplishments of talented and industrious students.

Nobili's Successors

Elaborate commencements and an idealization of the classics typified Jesuit education at Santa Clara during the five-year period of Nobili's administration and for many years thereafter. Both characteristics of the school were accepted as part of the Jesuit training that had produced generations of grateful students. But a tradition of success resists innovation. The changes in Santa Clara after Nobili centered on questions of money and buildings, not curricula. This was particularly noticeable during the lifetime of Nicholas

John M. Burnett, son of California's first American governor, Peter Burnett, was Santa Clara's second graduate. In this portrait taken in 1860 Burnett is seen wearing his commencement medals. He holds what are probably his bachelor's diploma (1858) and his master's diploma (1859). *Courtesy: Clyde Arbuckle.*

Congiato, the institution's second president. Having served administratively in Jesuit colleges in Italy, Switzerland, and Kentucky, Congiato was qualified to assume the direction of Santa Clara; but as superior of all Jesuit activities on the Pacific Coast, he was unable to give sustained attention to the affairs of the college. Distracted by poor health and by the duty of constant travel between California and the Northwest, where Jesuit missionaries were involved in the crucial and difficult role of mediating between Oregon's warring Indian and white populations, Congiato resigned his post at Santa Clara after a year to devote his full attention to troubled Oregon. In subsequent decades, he exerted much greater influence over the college as superior of the California Mission, a position he held intermittently over a thirty-year period.

During Congiato's brief presidential term, many of his duties were performed by Gregory Mengarini, who at the age of forty-five had been retired from the Indian missions and assigned to Santa Clara. Though he served as treasurer and teacher of modern languages at the school for nearly thirty years, Mengarini is remembered best for his contributions to linguistics and ethnology. In addition to his missionary memoirs, written in 1888, he compiled *A Selish or Flathead Grammar* (1861) and contributed to a two-volume *Dictionary of the Kalispel or Flathead Indian Languages* (1877). Mengarini also supplied vocabularies of several other dialects for John Wesley Powell's *Contributions to American Ethnology* (1877).[33]

Under the direction of Mengarini and Congiato, the slow-paced conversion of the mission into a school continued. The little brick chapel whose construction had occasioned Nobili's death was completed; a new study hall was begun; and alongside the California Hotel dormitory, Mengarini erected a wooden washroom for the boarders, thus ending the era of a primitive outdoor facility that had a pump, tin basins, and crude wooden benches.

Another popular addition was a swimming pool, scooped out of the old mission orchard in 1856 at the site of a hollow that had once supplied adobe for building bricks. Filled with water diverted from an artesian well and later sealed with a concrete liner, the large pool provided a welcome diversion for generations of boarding students. Santa Clarans proudly asserted that theirs was "the first college plunge on the Pacific coast."[34]

Jesuit educational theory aimed at the development of "the whole man" and of all his faculties, intellectual, moral, and physical. The swimming pool joined other places of physical exercise "as a means toward the physical development of the students."[35] With the same end in view, construction began in 1857 on a primitive gymnasium, one which could double as a college theater.

Floored with tanbark from a local mill, it provided a stage for everything from debates and dramatic productions to clandestine fights and fencing lessons.

A Fence Versus Fandangos

It was also in the 1850's that the entire campus was encircled by a wooden fence, which in time acquired great notoriety among students and alumni. In 1856 the faculty discovered that, contrary to a regulation that strictly forbade unchaperoned absences from the schoolyard, some boarders were secretly slipping into town. The administration quickly surrounded the school grounds with a high wooden fence to frustrate these flights from academe. Although the barrier was not as insuperable as intended, its presence provoked resentment. It also produced endless hours of diversion at alumni banquets during the course of the next half-century, where the retelling of adventurous escapes over the college wall provided hilarious entertainment.

The existence of the fence was justifiable. It deterred younger pupils, some of them seven years old, from roaming at will, and it controlled the immature pranks of older students who needed (the faculty believed) close supervision. The fence also sheltered the little academic community from "bad neighbors." Included in this category was *la favorita* of Padre Real, whose house and lot were purchased by the college for $700 sometime after Nobili died. According to Accolti, more than one of the old adobe buildings in the vicinity of the former mission had become houses of "evil commerce" where the "gravest scandals and prostitutions" are "committed, so to speak, right before our very eyes."[36]

The large public plaza opposite the mission church was another place of low character. Bull-and-bear fights had been staged there in Nobili's day, until he persuaded the local populace to find other forms of Sunday entertainment. The plaza could be a dangerous place. Teacher B. J. Reid recorded in his diary on January 5, 1852, that "a lot of drunken Spaniards and Indians had got into a quarrel last night in which one man was killed and one badly wounded. The dead man was found this morning lying in the mustard, stabbed and gashed in a horrid manner. . . . There is great excitement and the general feeling is to hang the murderers if they can find them."[37]

Candalaria's Fandango House stood almost directly in front of the college gate. This crumbling adobe structure had once been part of the mission and had served in the 1820's as a temporary church while the mission was being rebuilt. The structure now operated as a loud and lively dance hall and gambling den—and worse, if Accolti's dark intimations are to be believed.

This turn-of-the-century photograph presents the college swimming pool. In 1856 the pool had been scooped out of a hollow in the mission orchard, near present-day Ryan Field, which had once supplied adobe for mission building. Santa Clarans claimed it was the first college plunge in the West. It may also have been the first artificial outdoor swimming pool in California. *Courtesy: Archives, Univ. of Santa Clara.*

When the possibility of ridding the college of this colorful neighbor arose in 1860, the president bought it for $800 and a few years later razed it to the ground. The foundation stones of the hall that once shook to the stomping of dancing feet and the squeal of crude violins now lie buried beneath the green lawn and spreading cedars that front St. Joseph's Hall.

Financial Crisis

The turnover among administrators at early Santa Clara was frequent. Having surrendered the actual administration of the school into Mengarini's hands some months prior, Congiato officially resigned the presidency in 1857. He was replaced by Felix Cicaterri, a one-time rector of the Jesuit college in Verona. Cicaterri's four years at Santa Clara were devoted to attempting to resolve the school's accumulating financial woes. At Nobili's death, the college was weighed down with a debt of more than $61,000, a sum roughly equivalent to ten times that amount in today's currency. On this indebtedness an interest of $6,620 was paid annually.[38] Cicaterri fell heir to this debt and to debts occasioned by recent construction projects. He inherited the task of finishing the several structures that his predecessors' poverty had left uncompleted. A gymnasium, for example, whose foundations had been laid in 1857 was not finished until early in 1859.

To satisfy his creditors and to meet the current costs of the college, Cicaterri borrowed money at the exorbitant rate of 1½ percent interest per month. In 1859 benefactors in Mexico surprised him with an unexpected gift of $1,100. Although this contribution helped defray the $3,500 operating loss incurred during the 1857–1858 academic year, it did little to retire Santa Clara's increasingly worrisome debt.[39] By December, 1859, resources were so low that two priests were sent begging to Mexico and Central America. Two years later they returned with only $1,000.[40] With no source of increased income and no means of lowering the mounting deficit in sight, Santa Clara had come on hard times.

6
The End of
the Era of Adobe
1861–1865

W as it because of Rome's displeasure with Santa Clara's mounting financial difficulties that Felix Cicaterri was removed from the presidency of the college in 1861? There may have been other reasons, but early in that year an official Roman visitor examining American Jesuit houses analyzed the condition of the California Mission and decided that certain changes were "imperatively needed."[1] Shortly thereafter, San Francisco newspapers announced that Cicaterri had departed "on the last steamer for St. Louis."[2] Burchard Villiger arrived a few months later from Maryland to assume the leadership of the western Jesuits and the presidency of Santa Clara.

It should be noted that all of the college's administrators ostensibly were selected by the school's board of trustees. However, this body, composed almost entirely of Jesuits, merely ratified appointments antecedently determined by Jesuit superiors. Moreover, because the same man always occupied both the presidency of the college and the rectorship of the resident religious community, the administration of the school was completely Jesuit-controlled. In addition, the order was totally responsible for both staffing and financing.

What was the role of the local archbishop in the governance of the college? Because of the great autonomy that ecclesiastical law grants to religious orders, his influence was never great. Institutions founded by exempt orders like the Society of Jesus are controlled by the orders themselves rather than by diocesan authorities. Thus the archbishop of San Francisco, in whose diocese Santa Clara College was situated, was never directly involved in the internal day-to-day administration of the college merely by virtue of his office. That is not to say that his influence as leader of the Catholics within his diocese was insignificant. Indeed, as occasional disagreements between the college and the chancery office showed, the archbishop was not reluctant to make his views known when he felt some aspect of college public policy was not in the general best interest of the diocese. Such instances were rare, but the episcopal will usually prevailed when they arose.

The archbishop of San Francisco enjoyed a special relationship with the college owing to the circumstances of its origin. Archbishop Joseph S. Alemany was, after all, Santa Clara's co-founder; he also served for a brief time on its first board of trustees. Even after handing over Mission Santa Clara to the Jesuits, the archbishop retained legal title to some key mission properties. (Not until 1926 did his successor at that time, Archbishop Edward J. Hanna, finally relinquish whatever right he still had to the mission site.) But essentially it was the Society of Jesus, not the archbishop, who controlled and financed Santa Clara College.

At the pyramid of Jesuit authority stood the superior general of the order, in Rome. In descending order of importance beneath him were the provincial of the Turin Province (also resident in Italy), the superior of the California Mission, and finally the rector-president of the college. The constitutions and rules of the Jesuit order spelled out in precise detail the jurisdictions of each official. All major appointments, all major building projects, and all important innovations required the explicit approbation of the general in Rome. Most decisions of lesser importance had to be approved by the Italian provincial and by the superior of the California Mission.

From a secular and a practical point of view, this system had obvious shortcomings as well as advantages. Given the hierarchy of jurisdictions, the opinion of the president might be disregarded; or, accommodations to local circumstance might be sacrificed to the principle of Roman uniformity. But this same centralized system enabled the Jesuit order to shift personnel and resources around the world with remarkable facility. The system contributed greatly to Santa Clara's success; the college assuredly would have failed had it been forced to rely solely on local resources and manpower.

Villiger Takes Charge

When they directed Burchard Villiger to the Far West, the superiors of the order gave the college the most progressive and imaginative of its early presidents. The only non-Italian to head the institution during its first thirty years, this Swiss-born priest had, like many of his Italian fellows, fled to America after the revolutions of 1848 began to rock Europe. Before his assignment to California, Villiger had served as president of two Jesuit colleges in the East and as provincial of the Maryland Province. He was, therefore, a man of considerable administrative experience. By the time he completed his presidency in 1865, he had totally transformed Santa Clara.

California itself was undergoing a metamorphosis when he arrived. The society that Villiger encountered was not the swashbuckling, gaudy Eldorado that had greeted John Nobili a decade earlier. The California of the gold rush frontier was becoming a more settled and stable society; the youthful exuberance of the 1850's was slowly being transformed into the mature adulthood of the 1870's. "Californians," writes Kevin Starr, "were becoming more and more conscious of the fact that they were developing what they hoped could pass for a civilization."[3]

The state's citizens expressed their new-found aspirations in a variety of forms. The handsome Victorian mansions that began to crown San Francisco's Nob Hill symbolized the desire to build a more permanent and a more admirable society. When John Swett, a young San Francisco schoolmaster, became state superintendent of schools in 1862, he admonished his fellow Californians for having erected more elegant prisons and courthouses than schools. Stirred to action by Swett's earnest campaigning, legislators approved a system of tax-supported public education for the state. California's isolation from the outside world was also coming to an end. As the tracks of the Union Pacific inched closer and closer to their transcontinental rendezvous with the Central Pacific at Promontory, Utah, everyone recognized that California stood on the threshold of a new era.

This was the society that Burchard Villiger met in 1861. He was delighted by the novelty he encountered upon his arrival in May of that year. The drums of the Civil War had not yet sounded on the peaceful shores of the Pacific, and the climate of the Santa Clara Valley was a pleasant contrast to the heat and humidity of Baltimore. His new home was "a paradise" of "perpetual verdure," he wrote to friends in the East, and everything was "beautiful and pleasant."[4] Villiger was pleased also by the warm welcome he received. When the coach carrying him from San Francisco finally drew to a stop at the college gate, the entire student body and faculty was assembled to greet him, including a corps of musket-bearing student cadets who stood at rigid attention as the new president stepped from the stage and as the college band struck up a tune in his honor.

There was only one discordant note. Santa Clara College proved more primitive than the well-traveled Villiger had expected. He was shocked at the row of ugly squat adobe buildings that constituted his frontier college. "You could scarcely see it above the plank fence" he remarked in disbelief.[5] Despite the best efforts of his predecessors, the appearance of the former mission had improved little in ten years.

The new president was more disturbed to discover that during the past decade the faculty had retired only one fifth of the $60,000 debt amassed in establishing the school. With $48,000 still outstanding and "no stable income or investment as yet to live upon," the Jesuits "in their poverty" were scarcely able to pay the interest on their debt. They were "totally unable" to diminish its principal. The only thing to their credit was the high reputation their school enjoyed. But even that was bound to be lost unless their financial problems could be solved.[6]

As it turned out, events beyond Villiger's control came to the rescue. While pondering the school's troubled state, he learned that the Southern Pacific planned to extend its rail line from San Francisco to San Jose. The project had been considered as early as 1851 and pushed by promoters in San Jose, but when Cornelius Vanderbilt withdrew his support it collapsed. Another group of tycoons had resurrected the idea a few years later as a means of increasing real-estate values in south San Francisco, but with the arrival of hard times the plan was again consigned to limbo. With the return of prosperity in the 1860's, however, the rail link between the two Bay cities was finally carried to completion. San Jose suddenly enjoyed a prosperity that it had not experienced since its brief reign as state capital. Real-estate values soared and building construction boomed.

It was expected that the little town of Santa Clara—which Accolti described in 1863 as "nothing more than a village"—would share in the prosperity. Villiger was convinced that the arrival of rail transportation also augured well for the future of the college, especially since a terminal was planned within a few blocks of the campus. In the completion of the San Francisco-San Jose line the new president discerned a solution to Santa Clara's problems, which he presented to the faculty. "I said to the Fathers," he recalled later, " 'You will never be able to pay the interest nor the principal unless you run into more debt. You must show yourself above the fence, show yourself to the world and strike their senses with a decent appearance.' "[7]

A year later, construction began on a massive new faculty residence and office building. Now for the first time the college raised its head above its "humble adobe home."[8] For economy's sake, the foundation of the new structure rested upon the former residence of the Franciscan missionaries, its ground floor retaining roughly "the same old adobe walls, reinforced with heavy beams and rafters."[9] But the new wooden building, with its Italianate facade and long balustrades, rose four stories above the mission gardens, and across its handsome white front an inscription in gold letters two feet high proclaimed, "Santa Clara College." The hall was capped with a lofty tower from which, a student suggested, "no prettier view of the Valley could be

many faces of Mission Santa Clara. *Above*, the mission church as it appeared when the college was
ed. *Below*, the church as it appeared after an Italianate façade of wood with two matching towers was
ver its original adobe front in 1861. The mission cross, seen at the far right in both photographs,
es the same position today. *Courtesy: Archives, Univ. of Santa Clara.*

had."[10] "In those days," Villiger himself boasted, "it was a grand, magnificent affair": "It created astonishment not only in Santa Clara, but throughout all California, because just at that time the railroad was finished . . . and the passengers seeing the College from the railroad cried out with surprise: 'we did not know we had such an establishment in this country.' "[11]

Santa Clara's passage from an era of one-story adobe to one of ornate wooden buildings was quickened by the rise of other structures. After crowning the eastern side of the old mission courtyard with the multistoried hall, Villiger next set carpenters to work remodeling the row of rooms that made up the western side. Once again the original adobe walls were retained, and once again heavy beams and rafters were added for reinforcement. When the work was completed, the western wing (today's Adobe Lodge) boasted a second story. Built of wood, it housed the college infirmary, private apartments for resident lay teachers, and an elegant, wood-paneled college library. The library section was capped by a high mansard roof.

But the transformation still was not complete. The adobe façade of the old mission church desperately needed repair if it, too, was to conform to the college's new image. Instead of mere facelifting, however, the historic church was subjected to radical surgery. Over the simple, mission-style church front of 1822, workers imposed a new façade in classical lines, complete with cornices, cupolas, false quoins, and two matching bell towers where one had stood before. The drastically altered mission church conformed in style and design to the rest of the renovations.

Science at Santa Clara

Another addition to the campus was a three-story Science Building that Villiger erected to provide lecture halls and laboratories for the science department, as well as a new dormitory on the topmost floor for the younger students. Santa Clara's interest in science antedated the appearance of this building. To make their curriculum more relevant to the needs of mid-century California, the faculty had in the 1850's invested heavily in scientific equipment and chemical and mineral collections. The college had been founded partly as a consequence of the gold rush, and it continued to serve a population whose economic lifeblood was Sierra gold and Comstock silver. Santa Clara already had gained "credit and renown," Villiger noted upon his arrival, in the field of mineral analysis.[12] After a chemistry laboratory was constructed in the new Science Building during his presidency, it was reported that "assaying and chemical analyses are daily practiced by the more advanced students with the aid of a five-flued smelting furnace, two cupelling furnaces, and a complete stock of chemical glassware, and utensils of every description."[13] A priest newly arrived from Italy, Joseph Neri, was director of the department. Trained in chemistry and physics, Neri had studied mineral analysis under professional assayers in gold rush San Francisco before putting his knowledge to work in the chemistry laboratory of the college. There he supported his department with income from assays performed for miners. Neri let no opportunities slip by. When a former student traveled to Virginia City in 1864, for example, the enterprising professor asked him to distribute Neri's "circular letters amongst the presidents and superintendents of the principal mines of the Territory." His promotional efforts met with success, for Neri performed as many as six hundred assays a year.[14]

But it was not merely to perform assays or to train assayers for the West's booming mining industry that Santa Clara developed its science department. Reflecting both the nineteenth century's lively interest in science and the Jesuits' traditional liberal arts curriculum, the department existed chiefly to round out the education of students enrolled in either the classical or the scientific course. Even classicists, it was reasoned, needed heavy doses of chemistry, physics, and mathematics.

For this reason the college purchased an impressive collection of minerals, biological specimens, and expensive scientific instruments. At a cost of nearly ten thousand dollars, a wide assortment of minerals, along with "a complete philosophical [scientific] and chemical apparatus," was imported from La Maison Eloffe in Paris in the 1850's. Each year, clipper ships carried in their holds the "latest inventions" from Europe and the eastern United States for Santa Clara College, thus enabling the school to "keep pace with the progress of science."[15]

Visitors were frequently astonished to find a frontier college "on the shore of the North Pacific" in possession of a laboratory and museum so well supplied. A visitor from Scotland who passed through in 1860 was surprised when the door of the college's "philosophical cabinet" was opened to reveal a display of more than five hundred reagents. He was even more impressed by a collection of "the most recent inventions from Europe," including electrical instruments manufactured by Rumkhoff, a Duboscq telescope, Faraday's electromagnetic machine, and "the most modern arrangement for producing electric light." Describing himself as enlightened by his findings, the visitor concluded his account with effusive praise for the college's ability to educate students "according to the needs of the age in which we live." A few years later a caller from San Francisco expressed surprise at finding what he described as the only copy in America of a famous European apparatus "for the

Students learned to assay gold and silver in this chemistry laboratory. *Courtesy: Archives, Univ. of Santa Clara.*

liquefaction of gases." He also discovered a collection of "Gassiot's tubes," used in "exhibiting the electric light in different gases, of which there is but one other set in the United States."[16] Accounts such as these found their way into the press. They advertised Santa Clara and encouraged the steady growth of student applications.

Complementing its investment in laboratories and instruments, the school added several science teachers to the staff during the 1850's and 1860's. All were Jesuits from Italy. The first to arrive was Charles Messea, who founded the science department and supervised the purchase of the college's impressive treasury of instruments and minerals. During the 1860's Messea was joined by three other young clerics. Anthony Cichi, whose reputation as a chemist and mineral analyst led to his being consulted frequently by mining firms, taught both at Santa Clara College and at St. Ignatius in San Francisco. Aloysius Varsi, a former student of mathematics and physics at the University of Paris, joined the Santa Clara staff in 1864. He had taught briefly at

Boston College and at Georgetown before coming west to teach physics and chemistry. Joseph Neri, mentioned earlier, was a well-known specialist in spectroscopy and electricity as well as in ore analysis. He, like Cichi, alternated his teaching between Santa Clara and St. Ignatius in San Francisco, where he was the first to introduce electrical lighting to the city streets. In 1876, as his contribution to the city's celebration of the American centennial, Neri amazed San Franciscans by illuminating Market Street in front of the Jesuit college with "arc lights of his own invention." Neri's career as inventor, teacher, and public lecturer, according to a study by Mel Gorman, made his name "a by-word in science in California" in the nineteenth century.[17]

Expansion in the 1860's

The publicity and reputation that Santa Clara garnered from its investment in scientific undertakings was one of the factors contributing to its growth during the Civil War years. Another was the increased capacity of the classrooms and dormitories resulting from Villiger's ambitious building program. During the 1863–1864 session more than two hundred students attended, twice the enrollment attained ten years prior. Of these students, 80 percent boarded at the college.

The railroad, too, played a part in Santa Clara's development. Previously the campus could be reached from San Francisco only "by stage over dusty roads in summer and muddy ones in winter or by steamer from the little port of Alviso."[18] When the driving of the last spike in the peninsula line was celebrated on January 16, 1864, Villiger declared a school holiday in order that the student body and faculty could add their shouts to the "booming of the cannon" and the "hurrahs of the citizens" of San Jose that greeted the first wood-burning locomotive as it pulled into the city from San Francisco.[19] The college naturally profited from both the improvement in transportation and the general economic prosperity that the Santa Clara Valley enjoyed when the rail line was completed. Moreover, passengers could not help notice the school's handsome high-towered buildings as the train passed through the valley. President Villiger acknowledged that the railroad contributed not a little to spreading "the rumor and fame" of Santa Clara College "all over the land."[20]

The Civil War

The Civil War, which coincided with Villiger's term of office, had little impact on the campus. It was only by means of "a narrow escape" that Villiger had slipped out of riot-torn Baltimore in April, 1861, just as the great conflict was beginning, to travel to California. Upon his arrival he discovered that in contrast with embattled Maryland, "Here things are pretty quiet so far and we hope there will be no disturbance." There was always the fear that "political matters might gradually create trouble in California," he wrote, but "whether it will break out, the Lord knows."[21]

Early in the Civil War, the Confederacy contemplated capturing California, and later on Confederate sympathizers promoted the state's withdrawal from the Union and the formation of an independent western republic. The majority of Californians remained loyal, however, and the flames of war never spread to the distant Pacific shores. Nonetheless, activities of the pro-Southern faction of the Democratic Party did create an atmosphere of tension and instability in California throughout the war years. The college could not remain aloof from the war's controversies and impassioned debates.

Anti-Catholics, "reasoning from the analogy of the Jesuits' history in Europe," warned Californians that "it cannot be doubted" that these same "political ecclesiastics" were playing an "important part" in the national conflict.[22] But apparently few citizens heeded these alarmists. More persons might have doubted the Jesuits' Union loyalties had they known that the Santa Clara College safe contained $3,000 in Confederate bonds. (Some of the bonds are still preserved in the university archives, mute testimony to their short-lived negotiability even among pro-Southern Californians.) Had the faculty's loyalty been put to the test on account of their Confederate currency, however, they could have jesuitically revealed a reserve of an equal amount of Federal greenbacks.

The closest the California Jesuit body came to direct involvement in the Civil War occurred through the actions of a Santa Clara faculty member. At the outbreak of hostilities, Father Joseph Bixio traveled east to serve as a chaplain to the troops. Serving in Virginia and West Virginia, his work brought him into contact with both Confederate and Union armies. Bixio's unique ministry among both rebel and Federal soldiers led to a brief arraignment before General William Tecumseh Sherman; it also earned him a romantic but unmerited reputation as a spy.[23]

Student interest in the distant battles found an outlet in the Santa Clara Cadet Corps, which had been organized in 1856. Military drill companies were common in schools of the day, and the Santa Clara corps grew in popularity during the war, especially after the student armory received from Governor Leland Stanford in Sacramento "forty stand of Minnie Rifles, with accoutrements and side-arms and camp and garrison equipage necessary to forty men."[24] Thus military drill and target practice became part of the Cadet

Corps regimen. During their periodic full-dress parades down the tree-lined Alameda to San Jose, these student soldiers were "the observed of all and the envy of the young," although one envious younger classmate facetiously dubbed them "invincibles in peace, and invisibles in war."[25]

The diary of a student who attended the college during the war years indicates that newspaper coverage of the progress of the conflict and the oratory of California's pro-Unionist Thomas Starr King did not escape local notice. But apart from the "great excitement" the diarist recorded when Savannah fell to the Federal Army, the highlight of his interest centered on his own speech, prepared for delivery in class. It was entitled "Union Forever."[26] One of the last official acts of Villiger's presidency and the last one to concern the Civil War occurred in 1865, when the college staged a public drama to raise funds for wounded soldiers.

Tuition Troubles

One consequence of Santa Clara's increased popularity was a shift in its clientele. Although statistical data concerning the students' socioeconomic backgrounds are not available, there is some evidence suggesting that the college's middle-class students were increasingly replaced in the 1860's by the sons of the wealthy. It was becoming more expensive to attend Santa Clara. In 1859 the school raised its fees from $350 to $400, a sum that the Athertons, the Temples, and the Herefords, as well as James C. Flood of Comstock fame, could easily afford for their sons' education. But because of the $400 for room, board, and tuition that a year's attendance at the school now required and because the financially straitened college could afford few scholarships, students from middle-class and lower-class homes sometimes could not attend.

Villiger applauded this development. The patronage of Santa Clara by the sons of "three Governors and rich farmers and rich merchants of San Francisco," he contended, "kept up the fame of the College" and enabled the faculty to "live decently." More significantly, it enabled him to keep up payments on the enormous debt resulting from his building program.[27]

Archbishop Alemany disagreed. After inviting the Jesuits to Santa Clara and handing over to them "considerable property" so that "a good solid Christian education" would be "almost within the reach of all," Alemany felt disappointment. "Very, very few of my Catholic people can avail themselves" of Santa Clara's services, he complained, because of the "high, too high prices of the College." As a consequence, he said, he found himself "forced to beg from door to door to make other provisions to have the young educated."[28]

The Jesuits were not unsympathetic to the archbishop's complaint. When

Swiss-born Jesuit Burchard Villiger was the college's fourth president. Shocked at the "long, tumble-down line" of dilapidated adobe buildings that greeted him upon his arrival at Santa Clara in 1861, Villiger transformed the campus during his three-year term. *Courtesy: Archives, Univ. of Santa Clara.*

first founded, the order endeavored to provide not merely inexpensive but gratuitous instruction in all its schools. In the United States, however, the absence of a wealthy Catholic population capable of endowing institutions made implementation of this ideal impossible. Tuition-free education was offered briefly at St. Ignatius College in San Francisco in the late nineteenth century, but the experiment was struck off as financially impractical. The contributed services of the Jesuit faculty did decrease student costs, but this unusual form of endowment did not offset routine expenses.[29]

In the 1860's, extensive building programs at St. Ignatius College and at Santa Clara caused costs to soar.[30] To get money for building during the Civil War, Villiger was obliged to borrow funds at incredibly steep rates, reaching as high as 16 percent per year.[31] Given their pinched finances and their commitment to maintain two schools, the Jesuits were not inclined to cut off their main source of revenue, income from Santa Clara. After "serious consultations" regarding Archbishop Alemany's complaint, Villiger and his advisers announced in 1861 that tuition and room and board would be cut back to $350—but no further.

The archbishop was not pleased with this action. He believed that the charge was still excessive, and he began to look elsewhere for a solution to his educational problem. Thus it was that Saint Mary's College, Santa Clara's future rival on the athletic field, was founded in San Francisco in 1863, after Alemany invited the Christian Brothers into his diocese to establish schools available to a wider spectrum of the Catholic population. The archbishop permitted a few of his seminarians to continue to attend Santa Clara, but he remained convinced that the Jesuits "keep many away" from their schools "because they charge too much tuition."[32] Though the decision lessened the Jesuits' old friendship with Alemany, Villiger claims that they "kept mouse-still, and went on gloriously." But if the truth were told, they also looked to the future with anxiety, waiting to see what effect the founding of Saint Mary's, whose annual charge was only $175, would have on Santa Clara's enrollment.[33]

Villiger's Departure

Villiger resigned the presidency of Santa Clara in 1865 to assume the same office at the newly constructed St. Ignatius College in San Francisco. A year later, owing to conflict with Alemany over the canonical status of the Jesuits' church in that city, Villiger resigned his new post. In 1866 he bade California good-bye and returned permanently to the East.

With Villiger's departure, Santa Clara lost one of its best early administrators. By replacing the "long tumble-down line of adobe rooms" that had "shocked" him on his arrival, Villiger had, in effect, reestablished the college.[34] So striking was the impression made by the Villiger campuses, both at Santa Clara and in San Francisco, that the editor of a usually hostile San Francisco periodical concluded in 1864 that "the Jesuits have the most prosperous and populous educational institutions in California." Their holdings were worth "millions of dollars," he estimated, "constantly augmented" by "far-seeing speculators and the most accomplished of financiers."[35]

At this early date, the two Jesuit colleges may indeed have been the "most prosperous and populous" in the state. But their combined valuation hardly totaled the"millions" stated in the periodical. When John Swett visited the Santa Clara campus in 1865 and estimated its worth to be "at least $300,000 or $400,000," his first figure was more accurate.[36] Nor could Villiger—to say nothing of Nobili and other of Villiger's predecessors—be accurately described as "the most accomplished of financiers." Indeed, Villiger was unable to pay for the impressive structures he erected. When he departed Santa Clara, he left behind a huge debt whose reduction became the chief worry and concern of his successor.

But by his program of building, Villiger laid the foundation for the prosperity that Santa Clara came to enjoy in the following decades. He increased the school's burden of debt, but he also increased its enrollment. When he arrived in 1861, the student body numbered some one hundred thirty boarders and day students; before he left in 1865, the campus housed a total student population of nearly two hundred. One early chronicler concluded that Villiger was a man who "measured by the possibilities and probabilities of the future, not by the limitations of the present."[37]

7
Early Student Life

The imparting of knowledge was recognized as a necessary and proper aim of colleges in mid-nineteenth century America, but not as their chief aim. That was mental and moral improvement. When the president of Carleton College, a small Congregationalist school in Minnesota, declared in 1887 that "the grand aim of every teacher" since the time of Socrates had been "the building of character," most American educators—including the Jesuits of Santa Clara—would have agreed. Although this viewpoint came under increasing criticism in the following decades, many small denominational colleges continued to uphold the formation of morally and religiously upright students as their primary goal.

Character building required a controlled environment. From the day a young man entered college until the day he departed, his life was regimented. The extreme detail with which a student's conduct was supervised is revealed by the regulations of the colleges of that era. Harvard's rules, for example, prohibited any student from leaving the campus on Sundays without special permission. These rules filled eight pages of fine print. Columbia's student manual devoted two full pages to "a description of proper deportment during the daily compulsory chapel exercises." At most colleges, each student's room was subject to unannounced faculty inspection. To discipline-minded educators, the social life of the college was no less important than its intellectual activity. Closely-supervised dormitories were just as central to the institution's main pedagogical purpose as were its classrooms. The typical mid-nineteenth century American college was, writes Laurence Veysey, "a disciplinary citadel."[1]

"Not so Stringent as West Point"

From its founding, Santa Clara functioned primarily as a boarding school. Students who would commute daily to class were admitted; at times they constituted as much as one third of the student body. But they never enjoyed the institution's full focus of attention. That the college developed as a boarding school was a consequence of circumstances as well as design. The school's relatively isolated location in a state with a widely scattered population required that housing be provided if the school hoped to secure students. Indeed, the availability of boarding facilities greatly contributed to the school's initial success.

Dormitories at the college also reflected the institution's educational design. Dedicated to developing "the whole man," the school through its boarding facilities provided unique opportunities for directing students' moral and intellectual formation. Through continuous daily contact and close supervision, the faculty sought to instill "habits of order and discipline" that would produce "perfect scholars and gentlemen." To assure good habits, the faculty reared their boarders under a regime of strict control. This was not untypical for the age, since most nineteenth-century colleges closely resembled seminaries. But students at Santa Clara were kept on an exceptionally tight rein. Co-founder Accolti boastfully contrasted the "exact compliance with the rules of discipline" at his school with the "unlimited liberty" allowed in other California colleges. And yet, though more strict than most, discipline at Santa Clara was "of course not so stringent as that enforced at West Point," he once remarked![2]

In order that their ambitious program succeed, the Jesuits preferred to accept students at an early age. If the goals of the classical course were to be attained, for example, it was best to begin instruction in the classical languages while the mind was young and sufficiently pliable to memorize rules of syntax and the rudiments of Latin grammar. Likewise, it was desirable to introduce a pupil to habits of moral self-control early, before he could form opposing patterns of behavior that would reject the imposition of restraints as oppressive. "There is no use," Accolti said, "in sending boys to a well-conducted and disciplined Seminary of learning at seventeen, eighteen or nineteen, when they have already drunk in large draughts the poisonous cup of forbidden indulgences [and] know no other rule of living but that of wild and unrestrained self-will." "Young men at that age, with such dispositions," he warned, will look upon the college as a house of correction or as a state prison. Regulations of "the most reasonable and mild discipline" will appear unbearable, and the students will fast become "restless and spiteful, make themselves unhappy, and cause a great deal of trouble." "To try to put learning in the heads of such youths is almost as useless as to pour water into a bottomless cask."[3]

On the other hand, younger lads were an entirely different case. Their minds were less infected by "contaminating influences," and they were more apt to be curbed under the yoke of discipline. "Their hearts being more inclined to love their tutors and look up to them in everything, as substitutes for their own parents, . . . the chances of success in the course of their literary, mental and moral education must naturally be more hopeful and encouraging both to the tutors and the pupils." Thus Accolti was happy to report in 1864 that two thirds of the boarders at Santa Clara were still less than fourteen years old.[4]

Rules and Regulations

What was it like to be a student at nineteenth-century Santa Clara? One aspect of school life frequently neglected in histories of education is the student's reaction to the educational experience. Every autumn a reading of the regulations of the college to the assembled student body inaugurated the academic year at Santa Clara. This lengthy list of caveats, which was subsequently posted in a prominent position in each study hall, spelled out in precise detail the do's and don't's of the institution's "most reasonable and mild discipline."[5]

The least reasonable regulation from the students' point of view was the one that confined them to the campus. Boarders were forbidden outside the front gates unless accompanied by a faculty chaperone. Nor could they go home for visits of any length, except at Christmastime. Even students whose parents lived in the vicinity of the college were prohibited from visiting home more than once a month, and they were required to return before dark.[6] The rule was enforced during the day by the high wooden fence that enclosed the entire campus and at night by a watchman and his dogs who patrolled the darkened yard to keep students within and prowlers without.

This isolation had several justifications. In the faculty's mind, it facilitated intellectual growth by separating students from all distractions that might "wean them from their books and habits of regularity."[7] Accolti said flatly that some diversions were "essentially incompatible" with learning. "You cannot put together in the same mind mathematics and sweethearts, calculus and billet-doux, study and courtship." Eventually, one will "drive away the other."[8]

It was also hoped that confinement would promote moral growth by shielding the young from the world's corrupting influences. At the same time, confinement facilitated the faculty's efforts to instill habits of restraint and moral self-discipline that would enable students to resist the "dangers of every degree" to which they would be exposed after leaving the protective halls of alma mater.[9] "Once outside these college walls," a commencement speaker warned the graduates of 1872, "you will find before you a thousand tempting avenues whose course is downward and whose destination is ruin."[10]

Even indirect communication with the outside world fell to the scrutiny of tutors. Correspondence was "subject to the inspection of the President," and "books, pictures and the like" not approved were liable to confiscation.[11] Nor were boarders allowed to seek the help of day scholars to evade these barriers. For a further regulation—very difficult to enforce—warned that day scholars were "strictly forbidden" to take "charge of any commission what-soever that may be entrusted to or requested from them by any of the Board-ers." Smuggling "papers, books, messages or anything else" into the college invited punishment. Forbidden liaisons between boarders and commuters were further frustrated by restricting the day scholars to their own section of the school yard. When dismissed from class at five o'clock, the commuters were not free to "remain and play" with the boarders without permission.[12]

Additional rules governed student behavior. Open use of tobacco "in any shape" was "positively forbidden." The possession of "ardent spirits," the condition of drunkenness, or even "entering grogshops" provided grounds for dismissal. "Seductive conversations" or "causing general disturbances" in the dormitories or study halls brought the same penalty. "Secret societies," a universal bugbear for Catholics of all ages at this period, were not tolerated. Parents were urged to allot their sons no more than twenty-five cents a week for spending money, a custom borrowed from Jesuit colleges in the East. Silence was to be kept in the dormitories before morning prayers and after night prayers, as well as in the dining room, where there was reading during meals at table.[13] Though these customs were echoes of the seminary, the reading material selected for student edification was not exclusively monas-tic. Sometimes it included entertainment, such as passages from a popular biography of Daniel Boone.[14]

Other directives illustrate the grossness of the age. In 1865, teachers were urged to check in their pupils "the habit of chewing [tobacco] in school" and "spitting on the floor."[15] Another directive forbade "all sorts of arms, such as guns, pistols, etc." These were to be deposited in the office of the president for safekeeping.[16] Younger students were pleased with the rule that restricted their use of the hot-water bathtub to one evening a week.[17]

To the faculty belonged continuing responsibility for the close and con-stant supervision that was calculated to foster mental and moral formation. Nobili had assured parents that their sons would be "always day and night under the eye" of their tutors, and his successors sustained the founder's

The class of 1898 interrupts study to pose for an informal photo. From left to right: Francis Gaffey (a graduate of 1899); Francis Hennessy; Charles Graham; Elmer Westlake, holding a book; Thomas Norton; Leo Sandino; Michael Griffith; Edward Ramer; Henry Guglielmetti; Eugene Breen; and James Galvin. The aged Jesuit in the right background may be Father Cichi. *Courtesy: Archives, Univ. of Santa Clara.*

promise. The purpose of surveillance was not "mere bodily presence" or "the discovery and punishment of faults." Rather, by studying closely "the individual character" of their pupils, the faculty could cultivate "the better nature of the boys" through a "kind but firm discipline."[18] Even the physical layout of the campus—closely grouped buildings surrounded by a fence—promoted this purpose.

Round-the-clock prefecting placed a burden upon the faculty, both lay and clerical. They were not only obliged to spend most of their waking and sleeping hours in their charges' company, but they were subjected to similarly petty restrictions. "Let us keep our rules," one president exhorted the staff, "and the boys will keep theirs."[19] Lay professors and Jesuits alike were told they were not free to leave the college without previously having obtained permission. Jesuits were constantly reminded that "they have [never] done enough when the hour of their employment has expired," inasmuch as the school depended upon them to implement its program of prefecting and character formation. Thus they were urged to ever greater self-sacrifice and "more devotedness."[20] It is no wonder that the teacher was "as anxious as his charges to enjoy the escape from the humdrum of continuous confinement."[21]

Compensations

If the school's tightly controlled atmosphere appears oppressive today, it seemed less so to nineteenth-century students. A regimen of restraint was common in the home as well as in the classroom. In fact, "adult life—all life—was governed by such codes, explicit or implicit," writes Laurence Veysey. "Similar restraints upon behavior existed in law offices and business firms and indeed in nations as a whole; to impose them in colleges was merely to be realistic." "Forced to work hard," advocates of discipline argued, "the student would acquire a liking for hard work."[22] Discipline was universally regarded as a hallmark of good pedagogy. "Indeed, discipline is itself the great educational process," the United States Bureau of Education advised in 1881.[23]

Despite the relentless supervision and restrictions of their school days, graduates of Santa Clara displayed a devoted attachment to their alma mater and to their former tutors. Often the "old boys," as even the most recent alumni were called, returned to the college for debating club reunions, religious retreats, or participation in undergraduate dramatic productions. "If at this moment I was asked, 'Would you like to go back to Santa Clara?' " a student forced to leave for lack of funds recorded in his diary in 1864, "I would not hesitate for a moment, but would this very day start."[24]

Student life was not without some variation. The monotony of regimentation was broken by numerous holidays. In addition to Sunday and Thursday, the appointed vacation days at Santa Clara, the academic calendar was interrupted by numerous religious feast days and national holidays. Chaperones were readily available for off-campus excursions on such occasions because at other times the faculty felt "restricted to the confines of the college grounds with almost the same rigid ruling as the students themselves."[25]

The most common form of holiday recreation was a hike or picnic, which drew together all the members of the academic community. Even under the scrutinizing eyes of prefects, these Thursday outings were very popular with the students. "Plenty of champagne, cake, and every other thing we could wish" was the fare at a picnic, and for entertainment there were quadrilles danced "under the shade of an alder tree."[26] Supervising picnics was a challenge to the prefects, who faced "the inconvenience of having the boys that drive to Picnics in buggies, scatter over the country out of sight" of their guardians.[27]

Many of the prohibitions listed in the school catalog were more stringent in print than in practice. Moreover, disciplinary practice was less strict under some presidents. Traditionally, students of college age were supervised less and allowed certain privileges, which mitigated the rigors of boarding school life. The stern prohibition against smoking, for example, applied primarily to the grammar- and high-school students. The college students were free to indulge their taste for tobacco as long as they did not do so in "an ostensible manner."[28] A smoking room was set aside where they enjoyed after-dinner cigars and cigarettes in private, shielded from the envious and admiring gaze of their younger fellows.

The official regulations tying students to the campus often were relaxed. In addition to the Thursday outings, teachers and students attended lectures, circuses, public celebrations, and other events as they occurred in San Jose and the neighboring colleges. Occasionally, unsupervised excursions were permitted. In the 1860's a trusted student could withdraw his rifle from the gun room and spend Thursday hunting small game in the grainfields and marshes along the Guadalupe River. That evening his bag of game would be prepared by the kitchen and served in the refectory to the hunter and to those who shared his table.[29] By the time a student had reached the age of nineteen, other diversions became attractive. Thursday was spent calling on girl friends at the local women's colleges.[30]

Athletic competition was a major diversion from the tedium of boarding-school life. It gradually replaced hikes and picnics as the most popular recreation. Handball and especially baseball were the favorite sports. Each division within the school produced at least one baseball team, and by 1874 the populous second division boasted five. "Baseball went on forever at Santa Clara," recalled one student. Winter rains merely postponed the playing long enough for the clay schoolyard to dry out.[31] At first, rivalry was restricted to intramural games, but soon the school began to play against teams from local towns and neighboring colleges. By the 1890's, baseball had assumed such importance in the eyes of the administration that an out-of-town game

Athletic competition provided an escape from the tedium of boarding-school life. Baseball was the favorite sport in the nineteenth century. Seated in the center with top hat and cane is Jesuit Edmund Young, teacher and founder of Santa Clara's Literary Congress debating society. *Courtesy: Archives, Univ. of Santa Clara.*

justified overnight absences from the campus for student players. Baseball was also one of the few events that excused a student from Thursday or Sunday afternoon study hall.[32]

Escapes and Insubordination

Despite these distractions and diversions, a student at the college felt confined and restricted. Neither the perpetual round of baseball games nor the program of hikes and picnics could exhaust his stored-up energy or relieve the strain of his disciplined daily life. "How the boys could tolerate it is beyond our present day comprehension," a teacher of a later generation wrote, "but the truth of the matter is that they did not tolerate it."[33] Occasional rebellion was inevitable. Though Santa Clara never experienced the riots and violence that shook some American college campuses in the nineteenth century, restive students in the mission school certainly were known to display their defiance.

Flight from supervision was the most common form of defiance. The obstacle of the fence was "highly successful in confining, if not refining the inmates," one former student notes, and yet "many of us clandestinely clambered over it."[34] "In the morning Josselin and I stole out of the College," a boarder confided to his diary in 1863. "We had an excellent time by ourselves as there was no prefect on duty." "After smoking to our heart's content," the fugitives returned undetected to the enclosed yard.[35] Student ingenuity and determination conquered the ten-foot fence with ease.

Prefects were constantly on the alert for minor disturbances in order to "nip the evil in the bud." They were informed by veteran teachers that "the secret of success is the foreseeing and preventing of trouble." They were told to take care, for example, that the various "gangs" do not get themselves admitted to the college infirmary at the same time "by simulating sickness."[36] And the prefect on duty in the students' dining room was in dread of those nights when the lights failed. Pancakes, potatoes, and whatever other foods were on the table were hurled through the darkness, covering walls, ceiling, and the students themselves. Frankfurters and oranges were periodically smuggled into the dormitories for similar "revelry by night."[37]

The most serious student rebellion occurred in the first-division dormitory in the fall of 1875. According to the president's account, the senior boarders had begun to show "signs of insubordination" shortly after returning to school from summer vacation. Then, one night in October, a disturbance broke out that the shocked faculty later described as "serious" and even "tragic."[38] Precisely what happened is uncertain, but the major result of a "skillful and well-laid plot of a few malcontents" was that two Jesuits assigned to serve as prefects in the dormitory were suddenly surrounded, seized, and tied to their beds. The jubilant students then "climbed through the window to liberty and license."[39]

The captive clerics were released before long, presumably within hours, but they felt humiliated at having been seized. There is no evidence that they were physically harmed, although it was recorded that they "suffered for a long time from the effects of that trying ordeal."[40] One was a French priest, Francis Veyret, whose earlier requests for reassignment from dormitory duty because of his age and temperament had gone unheeded.[41] The other, Angelo Coltelli, was an inexperienced twenty-five-year-old seminarian recently arrived from Italy. The dormitory uprising proved such a traumatic event in his sheltered life that an account of the episode occupied a major portion of his obituary when he died thirty years later![42]

Aloysius Varsi, who was president at the time, met this unprecedented rebellion against the "wise and strict rule" of the college with swift and timely vigor. "I checked it at once," he boasted to a newspaper reporter, "by the expulsion of twenty of them." As a result, he added, "never have students conducted themselves as well as they do now." "Pruning the tree at the proper season," the president explained, "insures the Physical as well as the Moral health of the body." This philosophy of discipline, a like-minded journalist added, is "the true cause of the success of this noble College."[43]

"Spare the Rod"

The "Regulations for Students of Santa Clara College" stipulated that "causing general disturbances" in the dormitories was punishable by expulsion. It also warned that other breaches of discipline, such as drunkenness or overnight absences from the college without leave, also merited dismissal. Privately, however, Jesuit superiors urged administrators to exercise restraint in invoking the ultimate punishment. "The dismissal of troublesome boys, if not for immorality," they were told, "should not be resorted to but very cautiously." After all, "Troublesome boys will always be found in any college."[44]

For most offenses less drastic punishments were prescribed, such as "standing in the refectory," removal from student offices, confinement to one's room or to the campus, and "the reading of a public apology."[45]

The most common penalty was the assignment of lines to be committed to memory or to writing. Soon after its inauguration in 1856, this penalty became known as "Letter A" because of the letter over the door of the classroom where the penalty was performed. Here, on Thursday and Sunday afternoons, while their classmates played baseball outside, "delinquents in studies and discipline made reparation for their shortcomings." The names of the "culprits with the aggregate number of lines" had been read out in the dining room at the preceding noon meal "to refresh poor memories and take away the excuse that they had not heard the punishments."[46]

At times, "Letter A" challenged the ingenuity of prefect and pupil alike. Teachers were advised to keep on hand new texts for memorization and not to "give lines always out of some ordinary books" since it had been discovered that "some pupils know such books by heart."[47] At a later date, when the potentially worthwhile task of memorization had been replaced by the mindless and monotonous punishment of writing over and over a few assigned lines, one student devised an instrument "whereby one could hold two pencils and write two lines simultaneously," thus freeing himself more quickly from his obligation.[48]

In 1875, the year of the surprise rebellion in the first-division dormitory, "Letter A" became more elaborate by the introduction of the "1,000 line system." According to the new plan (eventually proven unsatisfactory), a student who accumulated "the fatal number" of 1,000 lines for committing certain major offenses was automatically subject to dismissal.[49]

Jesuit administrators were not oblivious to the dangers of excessive discipline. They admonished the faculty to "be mild" and not to exaggerate "the number of lines" given.[50] If a teacher is imprudent in imposing punishments, Varsi warned, the boys "become disgusted" and "parents complain that we do not give their boys a fair trial and that we fail in our duty of trying to form the character of the boys." A "boy sometimes appeals for justice" when unfairly penalized, the president warned, "and it must be given him."[51]

His attitude reflected the school's policy regarding corporal punishment also. Though common in schools of the nineteenth century, physical chastisement was rare at Santa Clara. If resorted to, it was applied only to the palms of the hands of the youngest students, "whose intellect and conscience responded best to such primitive methods."[52] Prefects were informed by the president that they must not strike a boy.[53] "No matter how repulsive they may seem to you," the "boys are entitled to respect."[54] "Let us keep our temper and control ourselves" and "the correction will have a better effect."[55] Teach by example and gain the esteem and affection of your pupils, the faculty was told, because more can be accomplished by exciting a spirit of emulation than by punishment.[56]

The Role of Religion

"True education must be suited to a man as such and therefore must aim at perfecting all that is proper to a rational being." Thus a college publication summarized the philosophy of education at Santa Clara. "Intellect, body and soul, all must receive their share of development."[57] In their dedication to the development of "the whole man," the Jesuits' pedagogical purposes matched those of most schools of the day. What made the Jesuit schools different were the specifically Catholic elements in their programs of moral formation.

These elements had motivated the foundation of the college. "The great end and purpose of our teaching," an official visitor from Italy reminded the faculty in 1869, "is the catechism." The secular sciences were merely "a means of attaining the teaching of the science of God."[58]

Curiously, in spite of the priority of spiritual formation, until late in the nineteenth century few classes were devoted to formal religious instruction. Occasionally, the president would gather the student body on Saturday morning for a lecture on a general religious topic.[59] But during the school's

The regimentation of student life was broken by numerous holidays. Pictured here is a President's Day celebration on April 29, 1905. The athletic fields were at that time located in front of the college, between Alviso Street and The Alameda. In the background stands the Jesuit faculty residence, the mission church, and, at the far right, the so-called Ship. *Courtesy: Archives, Univ. of Santa Clara.*

first decades the catechism was taught only once a week, on Sunday after-noon for an hour.[60] This schedule did not necessarily reflect the fact that half of the student body were not Catholic.[61] More likely it illustrated the fact that at Santa Clara—as at any Jesuit school—there were means besides the catechism to implant religious values.

The entire school year was pervaded by exercises indirectly instructive in religion. Moral values were stressed by speakers at the annual commence-ment, and Catholic doctrines were put forward in sermons during Mass. Every school day began in the chapel, where the student body assembled, each member in his assigned place, for morning prayers; the day concluded in like manner in the evening. On Saturdays the rosary was recited in common.

All students were obliged to attend divine service daily, during which they were expected to "peruse a book appropriate to the time and place." It was recommended that Catholic students "approach the Sacrament of Penance at least once a month, and endeavor to be worthy to receive Holy Communion as often."[62] Disregard of this "recommendation" sometimes produced appalling results. It is recorded that on occasion students were dismissed "for not approaching [the] Sacraments."[63]

Catholic students were also expected to make an annual three-day retreat. Often a guest Jesuit was invited to the retreat to give the customary series of devotional lectures whereby "a reckoning is made in matters spiritual."[64] Non-Catholics were not obliged to attend, but the only other option was to remain in class. A faculty member reported in 1885 that "every Protestant but two, and even a Jew" had made the school retreat that year. Within a decade of the school's founding, the annual retreat had become so popular that alumni returned to "retire within the college" for three days of spiritual renewal and self-examination.[65]

Then there were sodalities. First established in 1855 for "the cultivation of virtue," sodalities had a membership restricted to students "distinguished among their comrades for their exemplary conduct." Through the influence of this elite group it was hoped that "a gentlemanly and Christian spirit" might pervade the entire student body. Individual sodalities were formed for the three divisions of boarders and for the senior and junior day scholars. That the sodalities possessed a special library and meeting hall for weekly conclaves and devotional exercises testifies to their importance.[66]

Daily contact with Jesuit teachers was also expected to influence the students' religious development. No professor should allow himself to be satisfied with merely teaching, the faculty were told; even in conversation with students, each teacher should strive to promote piety as well as study and to improve the students' conduct through good example. "Let every one pray every day for the success of all." "We must make it our purpose to do in school as much good as possible."[67] Lofty counsel indeed, but judging from the frequency and apparent sincerity with which it was offered, essential for the success of the educational venture at Santa Clara.

8

Progress Amid Poverty
1865–1880

The decade and a half following the end of the Civil War was a bright period in the school's history. The money that Burchard Villiger had channeled into dormitories, scientific apparatus, classrooms, and other educational facilities was now returning dividends. Little difficulty was encountered in attracting students. An unprecedented burst of attendance in 1875 pushed the size of the student body to 275, the largest enrollment recorded by the institution in the nineteenth century. One third of the students were enrolled in the collegiate division; the remainder attended the college's preparatory and high-school departments.

The curriculum supplied a range of courses to satisfy various student ambitions. With the expansion of the mercantile curriculum in 1877, the three departments (commercial, scientific, and classical) reached their fullest development ever. The offerings listed in the catalog for 1871, however, still reflected the school's liberal arts orientation:

Theology, Philosophy, Chemistry, Physics, Mathematics, Mineralogy, Classics, Oratory, Literature, French, German, Italian, and Spanish, Architectural, Mechanical, Landscape, and Figure Drawing, Dancing, Dramatic Action and Delivery, Military Drill.
Practical Schools of Telegraphy, Photography, Surveying, and Printing; Daily assays of native ores, in a thoroughly fitted laboratory; one of the most complete cabinets of apparatus in the United States; several libraries, a brass band; the finest collection of printed music possessed by an American college.

In 1871, Santa Clara could claim "the largest number of Professors and Tutors connected with any institution on the Pacific Coast." Its general liberal arts education, resting on the three pillars of science, philosophy, and the classics, was offered by a faculty as qualified as any in the state. The day was not far distant when the balance of achievements would begin to shift in favor of other institutions, but until a decade after the Civil War, Santa Clara held its own in general reputation and student enrollment.[1]

It faced few rivals. Stanford University had not yet opened its doors. Santa Clara's next-door neighbor, the University of the Pacific, had come upon hard times and, in hopes of forestalling complete collapse, was in the process of abandoning its Santa Clara campus in favor of a site nearer to San Jose. The University of California at Berkeley, that future colossus whose size and accomplishments would far overshadow the Lilliputian mission school, had just begun to grow. When it opened its doors in 1869, Berkeley enrolled a mere 50 students. Four years later it reported a total enrollment of 185 and a graduating class of only 12 seniors.[2]

The stingy budgets accorded public education on the college level and especially on the high-school level left the task of educating young Californians largely to private institutions. This fact partially accounts for Santa Clara's growth in the 1870's. It also helps explain why in 1868 the student body of the Catholic college was half Protestant. The only discordant note in Santa Clara's modest symphony of success was the persistent knock of creditors at the front door.

The note was a familiar one to Villiger's successor, Aloysius Masnata, a Genoese priest. It was recorded that this fifth president of the college had "little to do" apart from diminishing the debts of his predecessors. Given the size of the debts (nearly $99,000), the scarcity of benefactors for Santa Clara, and the rate of interest due on the principal (as high as 12 percent), Masnata's success in paring nearly $28,000 from the total by the time he left office after three years was no small accomplishment.[3]

Shy and unable to speak English well, Masnata was replaced in 1868 by a Jesuit whose personality and skill in dealing with outsiders suited him for administering the affairs of the financially troubled institution. This man was Aloysius Varsi.

The Varsi Administration

Like his contemporaries, the thirty-eight-year-old Varsi had led a checkered career before immigrating to California. Born of provincial nobility in Sardinia, he joined the Jesuits of Turin Province, but fled Italy following the disturbances of 1848. After studies in exile in Belgium, his "more than ordinary talents" led him to the University of Paris and to preparation for a career as a missionary-scientist in China. A change of plans sent him west instead of east, first to Georgetown University in Washington, D.C., and then in 1864 to California to teach physics and mathematics at Santa Clara College. Three years later Varsi became president. Occupying that office for a nine-year term, Varsi served longer than any other president in the history of Santa Clara until Father Patrick Donohoe one hundred years later.[4]

Despite the college's heavy debt, Varsi began a new construction project immediately upon taking office. The spur to this activity seems to have been the imminent completion of the transcontinental railroad. The linking of East and West by rail (an event that would occur in 1869) was expected to have profound effects on California. It would not only boost the state's standard of living to a new level, but it would present every type of local institution with the challenge of Eastern competition after two decades of relative isolation. Even in the field of education the railroad would have a clear impact. Overnight it would become easy for young Californians to travel east for their schooling. And by flooding the state with imported material luxuries, the transcontinental line was likely to make the public less inclined to tolerate the primitive educational facilities of an earlier time. In view of the fact that, as one of the faculty once put it, "the American public is apt to judge the efficiency of an educational institution by its exterior," Varsi in 1868 made timely plans to improve the campus and thus to preserve the school's clientele.[5]

The Ship

In 1868 Varsi drew up plans for an edifice that would house both a dormitory and a college theater. It was dubbed the Ship by later generations because, according to one story, its eighty huge beams were held in place like ship beams, by dovetailing and wooden pegs instead of by nails. According to another story, the name resulted from the "multitudinous storms" through which the venerable structure and its occupants passed over the years.[6] The first floor of the Ship contained a vast, 130-bed dormitory, along with an adjoining area of water closets and a washroom "where every boy has a distinct faucet [and] basin."[7]

The college, having lost Nobili's brick chapel to a shifting of the San Andreas Fault two years earlier, assured its patrons that the new student residence was earthquake proof. Temblors were a frequent occurrence in the Santa Clara Valley. Vibrations generated by the San Andreas and Hayward faults had influenced Santa Clara's architectural history since the founding days of the mission. Teacher B. J. Reid vividly described a quake that struck in 1852: "The earth was not jarred or shaken merely, but actually *moved* as though it possessed life and muscle. The motion was from West to East and back again, and resembled the twitching of a horse's flesh when he feels himself annoyed by a fly. Father Nobili ran out of the house crossing himself and

Aloysius Varsi, president of the college from 1868 to 1876. *Courtesy: Archives, Univ. of Santa Clara.*

gathered all the boys around him in the front yard."[8] A later slipping of the fault in 1864 had created pandemonium in the dormitories. Some terrified students had bolted for the windows, a witness recalled, while others remained "almost paralyzed, not knowing what to do." Still others, "thinking that their last end had come," began to invoke divine assistance.[9] No one was killed, but the experience was one that Varsi did not wish repeated. By careful construction he hoped that his flexible wooden structure could ride out the periodic quakes.

The building's most striking feature was its second-floor theater. It had a decorated drop curtain, fourteen sets of scenery of "considerable merit," and elaborate gaslight chandeliers. The *Alta California* described the new auditorium as "larger and handsomer than any thespian temple in San Francisco" and noted that the theater's 3,000 seats were "such as have lately been introduced into some of our street cars."[10]

The new hall was inaugurated in a ceremony calculated to promote patronage and financial support. The speaker was John T. Doyle, prominent jurist and collector of Californiana. He traced the history of Santa Clara's development and concluded with an appeal for support of California schools. "Let us agree to educate our youth at home" rather than on the East Coast, urged Doyle, thus acknowledging the competition in education ushered in by the completion of the transcontinental railroad. "Let us build up and encourage institutions of learning, here, at our own doors" and not "publish our belief in their inferiority by sending our boys abroad."[11]

Santa Clara's enrollment did not decline. In fact, the exceptional increase to 275 pupils in 1875 necessitated a new division of the student body. Students had theretofore been segregated into two age groups. Now a third was formed, comprising approximately fifty students. The new preparatory division, with its own playground, classrooms, study hall, and dormitory, was established to isolate the youngest pupils from the older junior and senior divisions. Though the Jesuit system of education drew no sharp line between secondary and collegiate instruction, the junior and senior divisions were roughly equivalent to the modern high school and college. In 1875 perhaps one half of the students were enrolled in the junior division, one third in the senior division, and the remaining one sixth in the preparatory department.[12] Insufficient records make it impossible to determine the exact enrollment in each of the three groupings. The quest for accuracy is further frustrated by the Jesuit practice of promoting a student to a higher class in a given subject as soon as he had mastered the subject as taught in a lower class. Thus a student might be assigned to study Latin in the junior division, but his proficiency in Greek would enable him to enroll in a senior-division Greek course.

Financing Private Education

Though Santa Clara easily attracted students during the 1870's, its discreet requests for financial assistance fell on deaf ears. A Jesuit chronicler ascribed the problem to the school's affluent appearance: "People looked at the magnificent [new theater] building and imagined the College was rich."[13] This interpretation was probably correct but incomplete, for it appears that the institution exercised neither vigor nor imagination to acquire funds. Another decade would pass before Santa Clara administrators attempted anything even remotely resembling a modern fund drive.

Meanwhile, the debt grew. Santa Clara's liabilities were small compared to those carried by its sister establishment in San Francisco, St. Ignatius College. Yet its deficit was large enough to be Varsi's chief preoccupation during his nine years in office. "Totally discouraged" at times, the young administrator frequently voiced "great apprehensions for the future of the College." Account books reveal that three years after he had completed construction of the Ship, Santa Clara was $118,000 in the red—a sum comparable to more than $1 million today.[14]

No evidence suggests that Varsi was a much better fund raiser than his predecessors. But he was resourceful in other ways. Like those who preceded him, Varsi managed to obtain an occasional interest-free loan from friends of the college—not an insignificant achievement, inasmuch as some creditors still demanded as high as 12 percent annual interest on their loans. Despite the cost of building improvements, Varsi was able to bring the debt down to $98,700 by the time he left office in 1876.[15]

One means of augmenting income and of reducing operating costs was agricultural production. Since Nobili's day, the Jesuit faculty had helped save money by supplying the boarding-school table with produce raised by themselves. In addition to growing food crops, the Italian fathers gave special attention to viniculture, a natural consequence of their European background. They had inherited a small vineyard from their Franciscan predecessors. This plot, which measured less than an acre, had been tripled in size to provide more altar wine soon after Mission Santa Clara was acquired by the Jesuits.

Under Varsi's direction, the college in 1871 purchased a tract of land near Cupertino, on the western edge of the Santa Clara Valley, to augment wine production. Villa Maria, as the farm came to be known, served not only as an investment, but also as a vacation spot for the faculty and students. On those critical occasions when an epidemic of smallpox or dreaded influenza struck the campus, the villa also functioned as a handy quarantine camp for the sick.

The Italians' taste for wine sometimes made them the butt of sarcastic humor. From the pens of their ever-vigilant critics came portraits of vine-tending, drunken clerics, who daily consumed gallons of claret and port.[16] Such scurrilous descriptions in the nativist press did not deter the faculty from their palatable and profitable enterprise.

Most of the wine produced from the college vineyards was used for sacramental purposes and for domestic consumption. (The older students, if their parents consented, were allowed a glass of wine with meals.) Even so, the money from wine sales augmented the college income by an average of several thousand dollars annually, and one year yielded a record $10,000.[17] By the late 1880's, its vineyards were considered "one of the main resources" of Santa Clara.[18]

The California Jesuits expanded production in the 1880's by founding a novitiate and winery in the foothills of Los Gatos, a few miles south of Santa Clara. There the order purchased property that included a vineyard. Under the direction of Brother Louis Olivier, a Frenchman, the vineyard was improved with cuttings from France. Los Gatos became the new center of Jesuit winemaking in California. The novitiate was independent of Santa Clara College, and the income from the novitiate's winery paid for the training and education of the Jesuit seminarians of the California Mission.[19]

The college attempted to control its debt by economic self-sufficiency. A visitor in 1870 described the enclosed twelve-acre campus, with its clustered workshops, classrooms, and orchards, as "a village more than a mere institution for educational purposes." A dairy on the periphery of the campus supplied butter and milk. Hogs and several types of fowl provided meat. From the campus vineyard came "the wine and brandy with which the numerous guests of the College are regaled on public occasions." A stand of forty mission olive trees produced a sufficiency of oil, a staple of the Italian diet, and nearby orchards and gardens supplied the dining room with fresh fruit and vegetables.

Santa Clara's image as a self-sustained country village was completed by a tailor shop, a cobbler shop, a machine shop, a carpenter shop, a blacksmith shop, an apothecary store, and even a printing office, where "Father Bosco not only prints the catalogues, programmes, tickets and circular letters of invitation, but actually turns out sheet music."[20]

The custodians of this extensive enterprise were a staff of nearly twenty-five Jesuit brothers. Men of varied vocational and educational backgrounds, they performed the tasks of infirmarian, night watchman, cook, and milkman, as well as being craftsmen and growers. Their services freed the priests for ministerial and teaching activities, and minimized the school's need for paid employees. One Italian brother, Bartholomew Tortore, a professional artist before becoming a Jesuit, taught painting and drawing at the college for twenty-five years; his works still decorate Adobe Lodge on the campus and churches in several parts of the country. Though few Jesuit brothers occupied the classroom, they were responsible to no small degree for the survival of the school during its periods of financial stress.

The college apothecary shop supplied an unusual source of educational revenue. The store was administered by the school infirmarian, Brother John Baptist Boggio, who had acquired his medical knowledge from French army doctors during warfare in Algeria. So popular were Boggio's medical and pharmaceutical ministrations that he acquired a wide clientele beyond the college walls.[21] Account books for 1873 reveal that his apothecary store grossed $900 a month. The pharmacy continued to provide the college with revenue until the end of the century, although the school's attending physician, H. H. Warburton, and some of the faculty strongly discouraged Boggio's uncredentialed medicine making.[22]

Extracurricular "Eloquentia"

One of the purposes of the new college theater was to promote debating and dramatic activities. *Eloquentia perfecta*, or the cultivation of style, was integral to Jesuit tradition. Because poise in word and manner and the ability to speak and write correctly reflected a disciplined and educated mind, literary and debating societies were of first importance in the extracurriculum of the typical Jesuit school.

Debating was officially introduced at Santa Clara in 1856, when Michael Accolti organized the Philalethic Debating Society. According to its constitution, the aim of the society was "to accustom its members, by means of literary discussions, to speak with ease and fluency on useful and interesting subjects, avoiding everything of sectarian tendency." Among the subjects debated during the first year were "Whether the emigration of the Chinese to California is beneficial or detrimental to the interests of the state" and "Whether the gold mines are more conducive to the progress of California than agriculture."[23]

The Santa Clara College campus as it appeared in the late nineteenth century: (1) the mission cross, said to date from Santa Clara's founding in 1777, which still stands today; (2) the mission church, with its remodeled façade dating from the 1860's, which was destroyed by fire in 1926; (3) the faculty residence erected by Burchard Villiger during the Civil War and destroyed by fire in 1909 (its ground floor rested on the east wing of the original mission quadrangle); (4) the adobe wall that was once the southern periphery of the mission courtyard; (5) the west wing of the mission quadrangle, to which Villiger added a second story whose high mansard roof at the south end covered the college library (this wing, today's Adobe Lodge, was restored to its original one-story form after the fire of 1926); (6) the college vineyards, the site where the Varsi Library was built in 1931; (7) St. Joseph's shrine, near the site of Ricard Observatory today; (8) the Commercial Building erected by President Aloysius Brunengo in 1877; (9) Villiger's high-towered Science Building, dating from the 1860's (together with the Commercial Building, razed in the 1920's to provide space for Nobili Hall); (10) the building that housed the students' dining room on the ground floor; (11) the students' chapel, built by President Robert Kenna in 1885 and destroyed when the mission burned in 1926; (12) the California Hotel, a mission building that provided classrooms soon after the founding of the college (the earthquake of 1906 necessitated its dismantlement); (13) the Ship, built by President Aloysius Varsi, which contained a dormitory on its ground floor and a theater on its second and which survived until 1962; (14) the baseball diamond. *Courtesy: Archives, Univ. of Santa Clara.*

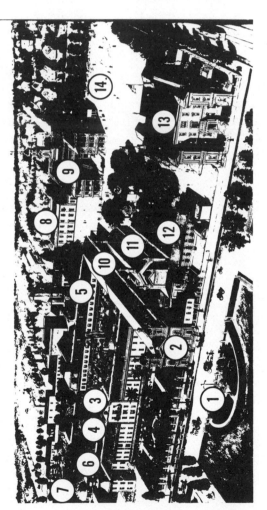

Forensics at Santa Clara received its greatest boost in 1861 with the arrival of Edmund Young from the Maryland Province. Sent west to aid the Turinese with their English curriculum, this New England Jesuit taught rhetoric and directed the school's literary activity for the next thirty years. As a youth Young had worked as a page in the United States Senate. Thus he later conceived of the idea of forming a student debating society patterned on the national Congress. "By making our work our play," as one student put it later, Young's innovation succeeded famously.[24] The Literary Congress not only enabled the students to "enjoy all the advantages offered by debating societies," but also to "acquire a knowledge of parliamentary law and the manner in which legislative bodies are conducted."[25] Yale in 1896 and Harvard in 1901, allegedly in imitation of Santa Clara's organization, established similar congresses to supplement their forensic programs.[26]

Alumni praised Young's highly popular pedagogy and attributed to it their ability to rise "in any gathering" and "express clearly [their] views on any question of the day." It was their skill in public speaking, one graduate claimed, "that made the sons of Santa Clara stand forth pre-eminent in the public life of our State."[27]

One of the most gifted of these was Delphin Delmas. He graduated from the classical course in 1862, received his master's degree the following year, and then finished his studies in law at Yale. A well-known criminal lawyer, Delmas achieved nationwide publicity in his conduct of the defense of Harry K. Thaw in the latter's first trial for the murder of Stanford White. A public speaker of considerable popularity, Delmas was also active in Democratic Party politics. Another prominent student debater, James F. Smith, graduated in 1877 and subsequently became Associate Chief Justice of the Supreme Court of the Philippines and later Governor General.

Valentine and Charles McClatchy, sons of the California newspaper pioneer, developed their powers of expression under Young's tutelage. Charles later became editor of the *Sacramento Bee* and founder of the Modesto and Fresno branches of the family-owned group of newspapers. Other students attained positions of political prominence. Stephen M. White, who received medals as a student debater both at Santa Clara and at St. Ignatius College, entered the United States Senate in 1893 after a successful career in California state politics. White is best remembered for his victory over Collis P. Huntington and the Southern Pacific Railroad in the battle over whether the city of Los Angeles would build its harbor at Santa Monica, an inferior site monopolized by the Southern Pacific, or at San Pedro, a better site preferred by White and by the residents of the city.

The theater that Varsi built stimulated dramatic activities as well as debating. Theatrical performances perfected the carefully taught art of the spoken word. They also provided students a welcome outlet during the era before athletics began to dominate extracurricular collegiate life. Religious and historical themes were popular, and the plays of Shakespeare appeared with frequency on the college stage. Declamatory pieces, dialogues, farces, and one-act plays written and staged by the students were also standard theatrical fare. Though careers in public entertainment were a more powerful attraction to graduates of a later era, some Santa Clara students of this period achieved minor prominence in the theater. Playwright Clay Greene attended Santa Clara until the University of California opened its doors in 1869. Greene became closely associated with the college in later years when he wrote *The Mission Play of Santa Clara* and *The Passion Play of Santa Clara*. John T. Malone, lawyer, writer, and actor, graduated from the college's classical course in 1871.

Music was another popular activity. Father Joseph Caredda organized the Santa Clara college band in 1855, under the title of the Cecilian Society, for the purpose of adding "solemnity to the celebration of Religious, National and Literary Festivals."[28] Several other Santa Clara teachers were trained in music, and it was customary for faculty and students to perform together at Santa Clara's many musical entertainments. Part-time teachers were retained to offer private lessons in voice or instrumentation.

The Santa Clara College Press

Journalism suffered a retarded development in most nineteenth-century Catholic colleges. Deterred by the high cost of printing and fearful of the rebellion that might attend student efforts at publishing, these institutions generally tolerated only the printing of religious material.[29]

Santa Clara stands as an exception to the pattern. Old account books reveal that as early as 1866 the college possessed a hand-powered Gordon Press, which it had purchased for $412.75. That same year the school began printing its annual prospectus, or catalog. Supervised by Father Bosco and run by a layman who worked with an occasional assistant and with student typesetters, the Santa Clara College printing office received top billing when visitors were hosted to tours of the campus. From it issued not only the yearly catalog, but prayer books, leaflets, the student literary magazine, programs, music, and even paper currency used in the commercial department's "Santa Clara College Bank." Charles Warren Stoddard's poem *Pedro de Alvarado*, which the poet read at the annual meeting of the students' Philhistorian Society in 1881, is also listed among the Santa Clara imprints.[30]

Two books by members of the Jesuit faculty were published on campus:

The printing office of the Santa Clara College Press in 1878. The Press operated until the end of the century, when the presses and type were sold to a local newspaper. *Courtesy: Archives, Univ. of Santa Clara*.

Michael Shallo's *Lessons in Scholastic Philosophy* and a Greek grammar by Gregory Leggio. A later chronicler of the college undoubtedly was correct when he boasted that Leggio's work was "the first book of its kind to be printed on the Pacific Coast."[31]

An unusual imprint was the *Reglamento para el Gobierno de la Provincia de Californias*, published in 1874 by the California Historical Society. The society, which had been founded on the campus three years before, commissioned the college to print the document as the organization's second publication. All but 6 of the 150 copies produced were believed lost to fire, the original Mexican document was destroyed in 1906, and hence the few extant copies of the *Reglamento* are the rarest and most valuable of the Santa Clara College Press publications.[32]

One of the press's regular publications was the college's monthly literary magazine, *The Owl*. Begun by the students in 1869, *The Owl* was for the first fifteen issues printed by the firms of Edward Bosqui and of A. L. Bancroft, but all the remaining issues (1871–1875) were printed on campus. The magazine's title was not a classical reference to the bird of wisdom but an allusion to night study. When their rhetoric class was dismissed one winter evening in 1869 just as the stars began to appear, the student editors—"conning our books of lore in the night"—likened themselves to the owls that inhabited the campus neighborhood.[33] Hence the title of their magazine. It was not the first collegiate publication in California, as its editors claimed. But *The Owl* was among the first; it appeared only a few months after the *College Echo* of the University of California.

The Owl was described as a "magazine devoted to mental improvement," and its well-polished and carefully constructed sentences reflect the "intense classical studies" of the college.[34] Unfortunately, the little journal was shortlived. "To our surprise," its editors announced in the October issue of 1875, *The Owl* faced "sudden death."[35] Readers were left in the dark concerning the cause of the passing, but the minutes of the meetings of the president and his advisers show that student apathy combined with the retirements of the campus printer and the magazine's faculty moderator contributed to the decision to terminate *The Owl*. Thus, after a six-year span, the pioneer student magazine expired, not to be revived for another fifty years.[36]

Nativism Revived

In some respects, relations between the college and the community at large appeared little changed during the post–Civil War period. For example, the sustained influx of European priests continued to inflame local nativists, whose indelicate accusations and carping criticisms, in turn, increased the faculty's sensitivity to opposition. In 1876 the town council of Santa Clara decided to abandon the old public plaza directly in front of the mission church, which Villiger had given to the town some years earlier for a public park, in favor of another location. Later, when it was rumored that "a Chinatown or something worse" might occupy the site, college officials ascribed the plan to "narrow minds" and "the bigotry of narrow hearts." The Jesuits were as appalled at the thought of a Chinese ghetto facing the campus as they had been by the offensive fandango house of an earlier decade, and they felt that the plaza should automatically revert to its former owners. The crisis was solved when Joseph Donohoe, a San Francisco banker and dry-goods merchant, presented the college with a gift of $6,050 with which to repurchase the property from the town.[37]

Nativist opposition was more easily identifiable in other instances. On two occasions, banners bearing the inscription "No More Jesuits Wanted" appeared in political parades in the streets of San Francisco.[38] "A Jesuit cannot be a good citizen in any country estranged from Rome," warned one polemicist. Jesuits will "sow sedition amongst our people and another bloody war will be the result . . . we are nursing a horde of vipers in our bosoms who will sting us yet." These "villains" must be made to "respect our laws."[39] Another critic summed up his hatred for "monkish orders" by declaring that the Jesuits were "enemies to civil and religious liberties."[40]

The reasons for the nativist phenomenon in American history are multiple and complex. It suffices here to observe that nativism occurred in an age that, as Robert D. Cross puts it, "found the melting pot a suitable metaphor of the process of acculturation." The flood of immigrants that poured into the United States by the millions from Europe in the late nineteenth century caused many nativists to fear the subversion of American institutions. Thus to be recognizably foreign was to be unfit for citizenship. The black robed priests of Santa Clara, with their heavy Italian accents and egregious Italian manners, appeared dangerously alien and hopelessly unassimilable.[41]

One focus of anticlerical feeling was the faculty's outspoken and rigidly conservative stand on the controversial public-school question. The Santa Clara Jesuits appear to have given no support to California's slowly evolving system of public schools. Quite the contrary. Michael Accolti, a man of normally liberal views, maintained that the "dreadful machinery" of public education would "subvert all morality" and introduce "indifferentism and infidelity" into "the very bosom of Christian families."[42] A San Francisco Jesuit promised that Catholic education would live to see the burial of the public system. Father Joseph Bayma, prominent Santa Clara professor, once predicted that "godless" secular education, if left to do its "unwholesome work," would turn the United States into "a huge mass of corruption" within ten years.[43] An occasional speaker at the college, Zachariah Montgomery, conservative Catholic layman and author of *Poison Drops in the Federal Senate* warned that educational legislation was "an opening wedge toward 'state absolutism.' "[44]

That the Jesuits should look upon secular education as incomplete because it failed to provide religious training is understandable in light of their own tradition. But their denunciation of the system as "godless" and worse was unfortunate. Their fears probably benefited public education in the long run. The Catholic attack caused many Protestants to abandon any idea of establishing systems of parochial schools of their own and led them to rally instead to the defense of the beleaguered public system.[45]

But peaceful breezes also wafted through the campus during the 1870's. During Varsi's administration efforts were made to engage the institution more intimately with the non-Catholic world beyond the walls of the campus. Santa Clara in 1876 bestowed its first honorary degree. The recipient was a non-Catholic, the man sometimes referred to as the father of western science, George Davidson, professor of geodesy and astronomy and later regent of the University of California.[46]

Another potential link between the college and the academic community at large—which was never fully exploited—was the founding of the Historical Society of California in 1871. Formation of this organization was the result of the address delivered by John T. Doyle at the dedication of the Ship the previous year. Doyle was both a collector of early Californiana and an expert in litigation concerning California land claims. Reflecting on the Jesuit role in the history of Baja California and on the order's pioneer educational work in American California, he suggested that the faculty and friends of Santa Clara sponsor the formation of a society to "collect, preserve, and from time to time make public the interesting records of our early colonial history."[47] In direct response to his proposal the society was established, with Doyle and Varsi serving on the board of trustees. Its first meeting, held at Santa Clara on June 6, 1871, was presided over by Michael Accolti, the oldest pioneer present. From San Francisco, Hubert Howe Bancroft extended to the members the free use of his magnificent library.[48] The following year the twenty-five-member organization again held its annual meeting at the college on commencement day. Little is known of the society's activities in the next decade. Its chief contributions to California historiography were its publication in four volumes of Palóu's *Noticias de la Nueva California*, printed by Edward Bosqui of San Francisco, and its publication of the *Reglamento para el Gobierno de la Provincia de Californias*, which, as noted earlier, was printed by the Santa Clara College Press.

By 1883 the Historical Society of California was considered defunct. With the passing of this association, whose activities and membership had been closely affiliated with the college, Santa Clara let slip an opportunity to exercise a leadership role in preserving the history of the state and in promoting historical scholarship. The society was, however, reorganized in 1886 at the University of California, with Varsi and Doyle again serving as trustees.[49] Today this active organization maintains research facilities in San Francisco and in Los Angeles.

Commerce Versus the Classics

Aloysius Varsi remained as president of the college through 1876, the year of the national centenary and the school's twenty-fifth anniversary. In December of that year, he ended his nine-year term and handed the reins of government to Aloysius Brunengo, who presided over the institution for the next three years. Looking more like a prosperous businessman than the teacher of philosophy that he was, Brunengo was responsible for the expansion of Santa Clara's commercial course.

Throughout the United States after the Civil War, commercial training had emerged as a very popular alternative to a classical education. The demand for the inclusion of more practical subjects in the typical high-school and college curricula was so strong that Jesuit institutions, strongholds of the classical tradition, accepted the necessity of expanding their course offerings. In 1862, because of its popularity and because of the financial advantages it brought, commercial education was officially conceded a place in the curricula. Recognition came in the form of a uniform national policy that established guidelines for those American Jesuit colleges that had already established commercial courses or that contemplated doing so.[50]

Santa Clara had offered courses in commercial subjects since 1854 for students who preferred "limiting themselves to the common branches of a business education." The commercial course included no instruction in the classics, nor did it enjoy collegiate rank. Not until the early twentieth century was the commercial course given college status in most Jesuit institutions. Its curriculum included bookkeeping, mathematics, algebra, geometry, English grammar, and rhetoric, Spanish, French, political science, and American jurisprudence.[51] Students finishing the three-year program received only a certificate of completion.

Brunengo's decision to expand the school's commercial course and to construct a special building for the purpose encountered some faculty opposition. The promotion of mere vocational training seemed not only a betrayal of hallowed Jesuit educational practice, but an odious compromise with American materialism. The commercial course may be "greatly suited to the temperament and training of Americans, who from their very cradle are engaged in the accumulation of money," complained one unhappy European, but it is "very foreign to our [Jesuit] customs, by which boys are educated in the study of the humanities and natural sciences."[52] Even Varsi, in his new position as superior of the California Mission, wrote to Rome urging the father general to use his influence to effect the "abolition" of this unwelcome innovation.[53]

Brunengo's embrace of relevancy nonetheless prevailed. During the summer of 1877, a new Commercial Building arose on the campus alongside Villiger's Science Hall. Built of wood and brick at a cost of $10,000, the controversial structure contained two stories. The first provided classrooms. The

The commercial department in 1878. Santa Clara College provided its business students with a classroom that was intended to be "the commercial world in miniature." *Courtesy: Archives, Univ. of Santa Clara.*

second housed two large halls equipped with extensive pedagogical apparatus designed to instruct young students in the theory and functioning of nineteenth-century American capitalism.

The two halls resembled elaborate reproductions of typical business offices of the period. The purpose of their unique construction was explained in the college bulletin. "As it not infrequently happens that young men, after having studied bookeeping for years, are yet much embarrassed in its application to business transactions," the Commercial Building was established to obviate the problem by recreating "as faithfully as possible" the commercial world "in miniature." By training students to conduct "all the ordinary routine business of bankers, brokers, merchants, and clerks in elegantly appointed offices in every way resembling the business houses in cities," the commercial faculty hoped that graduates would leave the college "thoroughly acquainted with the intricacies peculiar to each branch of business."[54]

A post office, an express office, a bank, and other alcoves designed to represent the more important lines of mercantile activity were ranged along the walls. Even a "tribunal of commerce" was included, arranged in the fashion of a typical courtroom, for "the adjustment of cases by legal procedure." The atmosphere of authenticity in which the future clerk or capitalist might learn his trade was enhanced by a telegraph line, connected with other college buildings, "whence as if from abroad, a Board of Brokers receives regular Financial and Stock reports." But the ultimate touch of realism was provided by the college press. It supplied a flow of bills of "commercial currency" that served as cash for student transactions.[55] Because few Jesuits qualified, several laymen instructed students in this miniature commercial world.

Lay Faculty

Reliance upon lay instructors was traditional at Santa Clara. According to instructions Nobili received from the Jesuit general in 1851, it was the original intention that Santa Clara be manned almost exclusively by lay teachers, with only Nobili and a Jesuit companion acting as directors. Bernard J. Reid and William Bulkley, who were among several lay persons on the teaching staff during the first year, worked closely with Nobili to get the school started.[56]

The lay role also was traditional within the board of trustees. In 1856, a year after the school had obtained its charter, the board contained one-third lay members, including former governor Peter Burnett, who had helped draft the college's original articles of incorporation. But once the Turin Province committed itself to work in California, the ratio of lay to religious teachers dropped dramatically, and both the faculty and board of trustees soon became dominated by Jesuits.

In the 1870's lay persons remained on the faculty, but they taught courses for which most of the available Jesuit teachers were unqualified. These included courses in bookkeeping, music, dancing, fencing, and subjects in the school's preparatory department. In 1880, the lay faculty numbered only half a dozen members.

The reasons for the relatively few lay teachers were primarily economic rather than philosophical or religious. The school was perennially short of revenue; if a Jesuit could fill a particular vacancy he, rather than a salaried layman, inevitably would be hired. Not until the college reached university status in 1912 and expanded its curricula to embrace schools of law and engineering did lay teachers at Santa Clara reach numerical parity with the Jesuit faculty.

9
A College in Conflict
1880-1893

Santa Clara commenced its fourth decade with a new president, Father John Pinasco. At the completion of a four-year term as president of St. Ignatius College in San Francisco in 1880, Pinasco packed his bags and caught a southbound train to Santa Clara to administer the mission campus. His three-year regime at Santa Clara was burdened with a drop in enrollment, which hampered the Genoese priest's attempts to balance the school's account books.[1] Enrollment later improved, but Santa Clara remained in difficult circumstances. Beset by heavy debts and distracted by conflicts among the faculty over curriculum and student discipline, the college struggled through the last decades of the nineteenth century.

Joseph Bayma

If it was not the best of times, it was not the worst, either. There were bright spots to illuminate the dark days of the debt-ridden 1880's. One of these was the arrival of Father Joseph Bayma, Santa Clara's most gifted faculty member in the nineteenth century. A giant of a man both physically and intellectually, Bayma enjoyed a reputation in academic circles that had been established long before President Pinasco welcomed him to Santa Clara. Thirty years earlier, as a young priest, he had taught theology at the Jesuits' Roman College. He had also helped write a three-volume commentary on the order's famous *Ratio Studiorum*, or *Plan of Study*, which was published in 1852. Soon after, he was named rector of a diocesan seminary in Bertinoro, Italy, which he directed until political turmoil in the Piedmont forced him and his confreres to flee to France. In 1859 Bayma received a teaching position as professor of philosophy at the Jesuit College of Stonyhurst in England. Among his students were John Pinasco and many other Jesuit scholastics from Italy who had come to England to resume the studies that political upheaval in their homeland had interrupted.[2]

During his eleven-year sojourn at Stonyhurst, Bayma produced the works upon which his reputation chiefly rested. Earlier in his career the versatile scholar had written a book on ascetical theology, *De Studio Religiosae Perfectionis*. It enjoyed considerable popularity and was translated into several languages. While in England he published *Realis Philosophiae*, a controversial three-volume philosophical study in which he attempted to reconcile the metaphysics of St. Thomas Aquinas with the physics of the nineteenth century. His interest also turned to scientific questions. In 1863 he read a paper before the Royal Society of London, which he expanded into a volume published three years later, *The Elements of Molecular Mechanics*. In this book and in subsequent papers, Bayma developed the hypothesis that the ultimate unit of physical reality was not the Daltonian atom, but "a large number of simple, unextended, quasi-material, primary point-particles" of force.

Though Bayma's concepts of molecular configuration did not prove of lasting scientific value, a modern evaluation of his work by Professor Mel Gorman of the University of San Francisco credits it as notable in other respects. Considering the fact that his was "a lone effort, carried out in the quiet of a college in the English countryside, isolated from the centres of scientific thought," Bayma produced a "remarkable synthesis."[3] He was primarily a philosopher and mathematician, according to Gorman. In contemporary terms, he was a theoretical physicist. He also was a pioneer in the evolution of stereochemistry. By combining a "synthesis of the atoms of Boscovich and the chemical equivalents of Regnault," he produced "a self-consistent system of atomic and molecular shapes" at a time when "very few scientists were thinking three dimensionally."[4]

A few years after the appearance of *The Elements of Molecular Mechanics* and *Realis Philosophiae*, Bayma's scientific speculations suddenly were broken off by a change in assignment. He was sent by Jesuit superiors to California. The occasion for the transfer was not scientific inquiry, but theological controversy: the orthodoxy of some of Bayma's writings had fallen under ecclesiastical suspicion in Rome. This circumstance—and the fact that the brilliant priest possessed two qualities which the California Mission sorely needed, fluency in English and proven skill as an administrator—led to his new immigration. He was told to quit England and "aid with his talents and counsel" the Turinese mission in California. In 1869 a reluctant but obedient Joseph Bayma sailed from Liverpool for San Francisco to assume the presidency of St. Ignatius College.[5] As president, Bayma showed his keen interest in science by expanding the school's laboratories and lecture halls. He assembled a collection of scientific apparatus that some accounts praised as "second to none" in the nation.[6]

The reason for Bayma's transfer to Santa Clara in 1880 was poor health. Arriving at his new post at the age of sixty-five, he soon recovered and spent the remaining twelve years of his life in productive writing and teaching. Even while in Europe, Bayma's career as a writer and speculative thinker had suffered at the hands of ecclesiastical censors. The full impact of that censorship was not felt, however, until he reached America. From 1873 to 1875 Bayma had written a lengthy series of articles that appeared in *The Catholic World*. In these articles he had attempted to explain in philosophical and scientific terms the Catholic doctrine of the transubstantiation of the eucharist. In 1875 his explanation was branded "untenable" by the Holy Office. A few years later the strict interpretation accorded Leo XIII's encyclical *Aeterni Patris*, which aimed at restoring Thomism in Catholic philosophical circles, further doomed Bayma's hypotheses.[7] Thus he was forced to abandon his attempt to reconcile science and scholasticism.

Bayma did not, however, surrender his pen. Age and experience seem to have made him more conservative but no less productive in writing on a variety of subjects. In addition to highly critical essays on evolution and on the public-school question, he published five textbooks on mathematics during the 1880's. Bayma also delivered lectures in theology to diocesan seminarians, and he taught mathematics and ethics at Santa Clara until his death in 1892.[8]

One other noteworthy event of Pinasco's short term was the organization of an Alumni Association, a proceeding undoubtedly borrowed from St. Ignatius College, where President Robert Kenna had formed a similar group two months prior.[9] The annual gathering of the Philhistorian Debating Society, for which many alumni assembled at Santa Clara on April 27, 1881, provided the occasion for the association's first meeting. The association strove to give alumni opportunities to meet socially and particularly to exercise their penchant for public speaking. Because alumni always returned to the campus as speakers at the annual commencement, the first night of the commencement exercises emerged as the traditional date of a gathering at which alumni might "renew the bonds of affection."[10]

Unlike its modern counterpart, the Alumni Association at its inception apparently did not serve a financial function within the college. There is no evidence that President Pinasco even discreetly invited the assembled alumni to ease the burden of debt under which the institution struggled. Pinasco's successor was more imaginative, and his modest effort to elicit building funds from the association a few years later heralded the beginning of a resourceful approach to educational financing.

First American President

In the summer of 1883 Robert Kenna replaced Pinasco as president. Born in Mississippi to an Irish father and American mother, Kenna had traveled west to California with his parents in 1849. He studied in San Francisco and later served for a year as secretary to Archbishop Alemany. In 1865 Kenna sailed to Ireland to attend college, but two years later sickness forced him to abandon his European study plans. Upon his return to California at the age of twenty-three, he enrolled at Santa Clara. A year later he joined the Jesuits.

Because of his poor health, Kenna was allowed to do his entire eleven years of seminary studies at the college. Later, as a priest, most of his assignments were at Santa Clara. He served as pastor of the mission church, then as vice-president of the college, and finally twice as president, from 1883 to 1888 and from 1899 to 1905. With the exception of Father Joseph Caredda, "no one was more closely identified with the College" up to 1912 than was Robert Kenna.[11]

At the completion of his theological studies at Santa Clara in 1880, he was sent to St. Ignatius College to become that school's first non-Italian president since Villiger. His skill in public relations explains the assignment to this difficult and important post only one year after his ordination. Jesuit superiors had amassed a million-dollar debt in the construction of the new San Francisco campus, and they hoped that their prominent American protégé's familiarity with wealthy and influential persons in the city might rescue St. Ignatius from its financial crisis.

Although he was able to make only the slightest dent in St. Ignatius' enormous indebtedness during his short term of office, Kenna's appointment to Santa Clara three years later reflected similar expectations. The mission school's burden of debt was, however, considerably lighter. Kenna did not disappoint those who placed their hopes in him. By dramatically wiping out most of Santa Clara's deficit, he gained a lasting reputation in Jesuit circles as an effective fund-raiser. He began his term in 1883 with a debt of $93,000 and saw it shrink to $14,000 when he left office five years later.

Kenna's discovery of benefactors only partially explains his success. The revenue from wine sales also helped him reduce the college's debt. Heavy winter rains threatened to destroy the college vineyards at the Villa Maria for several years running, but the harvest for 1886 yielded 22,000 gallons, which were sold for more than $10,000.[12] Under Kenna's direction the vineyards, which by now constituted "one of the main resources" of the school, were constantly improved.[13] The president and his consultors in 1884 had decided to expand the Villa Maria vineyards, but they debated the wisdom of hiring Chinese to do the work. The Jesuits of San Francisco had recently clashed with labor leader Denis Kearney over the use of bricks manufactured by Chinese workers in the construction of the new St. Ignatius College. Consequently, Kenna and his advisers now proceeded with caution. Finally, however, the consultors decided that cheap Chinese labor could be employed to plant the new vineyards.[14]

Another factor responsible for the school's improved financial condition was a marked increase in enrollment. The downward drift of Pinasco's term was reversed, and by 1885 the student body had again climbed to 260 students. Because 195 of these were boarders, the largest number in the school's history, the capacity of the college's facilities was taxed "to its utmost."[15]

Why the upswing in registration? In part, it reflected a nationwide climb in college enrollments. It also reflected the increased patronage that Santa Clara in particular received from Mexico and Latin America. (In 1894 administrators debated whether to publish a catalog in Spanish, as had been done in the 1860's, for circulation to Mexico.[16]) Patronage from California was aided by the state's recovery from the prolonged effects of the panic of 1873 and the sudden passage into the boom times of the 1880's. This meant that more parents were able to afford tuition at Santa Clara. They had reason to enroll their sons in the school's second division: there was a continuing paucity of public high schools in the state. In what has been called a "shortsighted show of democracy," the California constitutional convention of 1878 had redirected the bulk of the state's educational revenue to elementary schools. As a result, California found itself in the incongruous position of possessing "a relatively vigorous system of elementary and higher education without a steady steppingstone between the two."[17] Until corrected by legislation at the end of the century, the gap was bridged by high-school departments or preparatory departments of colleges such as Santa Clara.

More Buildings

Financial stringencies and admonitions from his superiors to economize prevented Kenna from pushing enrollment further upward by increasing classroom space and dormitories. He did succeed, however, in remodeling the old mission church. Soon after taking office, Kenna proposed that the deteriorating condition of the church required either its renovation or complete replacement. At the time, Californians had not yet turned their attention to mission preservation. In the late 1870's painters had begun to pro-

The interior of the mission church as it appeared at the end of the nineteenth century, after several remodelings. The altar, reredos, and sanctuary-ceiling painting date from the mission period. But walls of wood replaced the original adobe walls in the body of the church, thus widening the interior. An attempt was made to preserve the original designs painted on adobe by copying them on the walls and ceiling of the remodeled church. *Courtesy: Archives, Univ. of Santa Clara.*

voke romantic interest in the decaying missions as artistic subjects, but it was not until the turn of the century that the public was aroused to the notion of historical restoration. In the meantime, man and nature conspired to distort the appearance of many of the venerable structures.

Before Kenna's coming the church at Santa Clara had been encased in wood to prevent its collapse, but it still seemed "far from solid." Not only was the ceiling "in danger of falling," but the long narrow building was considered "by no means healthy" and ill-suited to the needs of the enlarged parish congregation it served.[18] Lack of funds and disagreement as to the best means of remodeling the church postponed modernization for more than a year, but in 1885 the workmen's hammers finally struck, and the old adobe walls returned to dust. Then new walls of wood were erected and decorated to resemble the destroyed adobe. For the sum of $7,000 the mission church was renovated almost beyond recognition.[19]

Kenna also inaugurated a campaign in 1885 to construct a new students' chapel of brick to replace the temporary wooden chapel erected after the earthquake of 1868 had destroyed Nobili's brick building. To raise the required $35,000, Kenna tried methods of financing shunned by his predecessors. Writing as the first former student to become president, Kenna petitioned the alumni for money to erect the new church as a memorial to "the boys who honored the College from the year 1851 to the year 1885."[20] It was the first attempt at a fund drive in the history of the school. The campaign netted enough funds to begin construction within a year, but after that the alumni's enthusiasm was not sufficient to allow completion of the Memorial Chapel as the "gem" that Kenna had planned. Though functional, the chapel for several years afterward had an interior that revealed portions of unpainted concrete and bare bricks. The chapel was "an eyesore to the College," "a heartsore to its author," and a silent testimonial to the school's enduring shortage of funds.[21]

During Kenna's incumbency the Jesuit novitiate was removed from campus. Since the founding of the California Mission nearly forty years earlier, young Jesuits had received their training at Santa Clara. Although the separation of the seminary from the campus had been under consideration for a decade, it was not until Kenna had reduced the college debt that the plan became a reality. In 1888 the Jesuit scholastics, juniors as well as novices, along with their teachers, moved into their new quarters at the Sacred Heart Novitiate in the isolated foothills of Los Gatos. The Jesuit philosophy students were transferred that same year from Santa Clara to St. Ignatius College.

The Old World Versus the New

The influence of the college's first American president was not limited to finances and buildings. Kenna also emerged during his first term as spokesman for the liberal side in a domestic squabble between Jesuit traditionalists and advocates of change within the California Mission. The same basic conflict occurred in other areas of the country as well, as native elements in the American Catholic Church grew in numbers and made their influence

A College in Conflict

felt. In California the conflict aligned Italian and American clerics on opposite sides. The basic question was: Should we break from the European mold into which the order's work in the United States has become fixed?

It was the conviction of many Jesuits that the California Mission had outgrown its mission status and that its old-world practices and customs were no longer suited to the American scene. That California should continue to be administered by a provincial thousands of miles away in Europe seemed increasingly irritating and in fact unnecessary. Native priests began to argue for jurisdictional independence and a severance of California's historic ties with the Turin Province. Autonomy was granted in 1909 through the creation of the province of California, but during the three decades preceding that innovation, the debate between the Old World and the New continued to rage in California Jesuitdom.

The case against Italian rule was stated in 1897 by the superior of the California Mission, Father John Frieden, himself European-born. The Turinese provincials "simply do not and cannot appreciate the true nature of affairs in the United States, and particularly in California," he stated bluntly. He attributed the failure to general ignorance of the country and its customs. "Our being united to the Province of Turin is no help to this Mission; on the contrary, it proves an impediment—it hampers us."[22] There were echoes of Frieden's criticisms. "I am not blind to the work of the older fathers, nor ungrateful for all they have done," explained Joseph Riordan, Santa Clara's president in 1895, but because circumstances have changed, "the policy that was admirable years ago may not be admirable now." "I expect very little" from the California Mission, he concluded, "until it has its own autonomy."[23]

The Italian faction disagreed. This group, which included many who were elderly and no longer capable of the flexibility they had demonstrated as young men adapting to the needs of a missionary country, fought the drift toward autonomy. They also resisted the innovations advanced by the young "revolutionists." Some complained when younger men (usually Americans) were appointed to positions of authority in the colleges. The cause of these complaints was the liberalization that the Italian faction knew would follow. Some even feared the eventual "Americanization" of the order itself.[24]

What were the repercussions of this intramural controversy for Santa Clara? The immediate point at issue was usually the strict application of the norms of the *Ratio Studiorum*, which had for centuries governed the pedagogy of all Jesuit institutions. The debate about these norms focused both on the extent to which the classics should continue to hold a position of honor in the Santa Clara curriculum and on the degree to which traditional concepts of student discipline should be retained. The movement to alter or abandon such long-cherished practices did not attain its objectives without trial and testing. Because Jesuit leaders in Europe resisted innovation abroad and because conservatives often continued to occupy the post of superior of the California Mission, the full adaptation of Santa Clara to the American scene was accompanied by decades of acrimony.

The first sign of conflict at Santa Clara surfaced in 1883, when Rome returned the sixty-year-old Sardinian Nicholas Congiato to the superiorship of the California Mission for a third term. His first tenure of office had been thirty years earlier. He was destined to direct all Jesuit activities in California for another five years. Congiato's insistence on traditional Jesuit education and his attempt to turn the clock back at Santa Clara quickly established his conservative reputation among his younger confreres.[25]

As soon as he returned to office Congiato ordered President Kenna to assemble his faculty for a special consultation. An agenda prepared in advance was handed to the president. Displeased with the relaxation of the rules of student discipline at Santa Clara in recent years Congiato called for a restoration of the old order. Would it be possible, Congiato queried, "to no longer grant to students the freedom of leaving the College without prefects," as had been the practice in the past? Second, could the old custom of having "reading at table for the students" be revived? Third, would it be expedient to require all students to attend Mass daily?[26]

Thrown open for frank debate to "nearly all the fathers," Congiato's proposals were roundly rejected. Only two faculty members felt student liberties ought to be "more restricted"; the remainder urged that nothing be changed lest the students "think the College is a prison." The restoration of refectory reading was likewise resisted because of its "many inconveniences." The "unanimous response" to the suggestion regarding enforced worship was that students should be "persuaded, if possible" to attend daily Mass, but not "compelled."[27]

The strongly negative response to his suggestions persuaded Congiato not to press them for the moment. Kenna, emboldened by the show of faculty support, encouraged the expansion of student freedom. Students were now granted "the privilege of going once a month, and alone, to the city of San Jose, where they may remain the whole day." The only conditions were parental approval and, as one student recalled, that "our conduct had been good."[28] Attendance at weekday Mass continued to be left to the individual student's discretion. In the refectory, conversation (rather than reading) re-mained common practice. And older boarders were still allowed to smoke after meals—a practice that Congiato and other old-timers viewed as gravely injurious to both the health and morals of young men.[29]

Kenna's allowances did not long pass unchallenged. Alarmed not only by the increase of student freedom, but also by Kenna's apparent indifference to the classics, Congiato moved to restore the old order. Since his earlier at-tempt to reinstate discipline by democratic methods had failed, Congiato now sought redress by the more traditional expedient of laying his com-plaint before the superior general in Rome.

In contrast with Nobili's day, when poor communications with Europe had made frequent intervention by distant Roman superiors in the ad-ministration of the college difficult, the late nineteenth century, with its steamships and steam locomotives, allowed the superior general to have timely knowledge of the everyday affairs of the order's far-flung global com-mitments. Speedier communication encouraged the general's tendency to govern all Jesuit activities, regardless of place, according to European norms, thereby delaying the Americanization of the order's schools in the United States. Thus, in response to Congiato's representations, a displeased Father General Anton Anderledy sent word across the Atlantic that Kenna's abuse of allowing boarding students to "go out alone" must cease.[30]

Kenna refused to surrender the issue without presenting his side of the argument. He explained to the European superior that allowing students to leave a campus unchaperoned was "very common in all our Colleges in the United States." He also observed that inasmuch as both parents and students attached "no little importance" to the practice, it could not be easily with-drawn. In response, Anderley washed his hands of the debate by inform-ing Congiato that it was left to the latter's "prudence to examine the matter with your consultors and make a decision." In the end, Congiato's point of view prevailed. Thus a few years later he informed the general that the sit-uation at Santa Clara was much improved: Kenna had been ordered to end all the controversial abuses.[31]

The Classics in Conflict

At the same time Kenna was attacked for laxity in discipline, he came under fire for allowing observance of the *Ratio Studiorum* itself to decline. Especially disturbing to traditionalists was the waning of devotion to the classics. The impact of the nationwide shift from the traditional curriculum to a more vocational one had already been felt at the college. The problem of

Four venerable Jesuits gather in the mission garden beside the adobe wall, *ca.* 1893. From left to right: Thomas P. Leonard, Charles E. Messea, John Pinasco, and Joseph Caredda. *Courtesy: Archives, Univ. of Santa Clara.*

promoting the classics was not, however, confined to Santa Clara. Statistics reveal that of the nearly six thousand students attending Jesuit colleges across the United States at this time, less than 2 percent graduated with the Bachelor of Arts degree in the classics. American higher education, partially in response to the country's rapid industrial development, was moving increasingly away from the classical tradition. The new pattern in education, notes historian Laurence Veysey, was "in the direction of concessions to the utilitarian type of demand for reform." There were at Santa Clara some but relatively few concessions to the demand for service-oriented courses. The only major exception was the commercial program, which was, however, not of collegiate status. When Kenna attempted to make more concessions he was prevented from doing so.[32]

That Latin and Greek were becoming less and less popular at the college is clear from complaints voiced by several contemporary Jesuits. Students are not disposed to "receive that education which we are ready and desirous to give," one California Jesuit admitted in 1884. Many pupils came from poor Irish working-class families, seeking only sufficient knowledge to give them a start in life. Because they are "too anxious to finish their college course when it ought to be only beginning," the Jesuit observed, a lengthy and expensive commitment on their part to classical training was out of the question. Teachers did what they could to promote the *Ratio Studiorum* and the study of Latin and Greek by "discouraging, as far as prudence permits," the commercial course. But to follow traditional methods "as strictly as we would wish" was "impossible" in California. Eventually, as Catholics rose in the social scale, a demand for a more solid and serious education would naturally spring up, the Jesuit predicted. In the meantime, however, administrators must proceed cautiously when trying to raise the standard of education, for in precipitate action "there is the risk of seeing our classrooms emptied, and our work strangled instead of being strengthened."[33]

Such cautious counsels, however, did not impress Nicholas Congiato. Writing to the superior general in 1884, he dramatically announced that the classics had been "almost abandoned by everyone."[34]

Though the details of Congiato's charge remain unknown, his complaint, which placed the blame squarely on Kenna's shoulders, found a sympathetic ear in Rome. Do not let Kenna "act contrary to the Institute and introduce novelty," Anderledy advised. "Let your reverence be assured that if he does not do what he is supposed to do, you take the means you judge opportune."[35] In a separate letter, Anderledy urged Kenna to do everything he could to elevate the study of Latin and Greek, especially among the Jesuit scholastics still on campus.

Facing the authority of the superior general, Kenna had no choice but to comply. He complained that Congiato's report lacked accuracy, but he also promised to rehabilitate the classics. Six months later the president and his consultants agreed that the obligation of studying Latin should be imposed on all the students.[36] Privately, however, Kenna continued to lobby with superiors for an adaptation of the classical curriculum to the needs of American education.

Despite Kenna's wish to liberalize requirements, defenders of the classics soon scored their greatest victory. In 1887 the college catalog announced that henceforth academic degrees would be granted only to students who enrolled in the classical course and passed examinations in Latin and Greek. In other words, the Bachelor of Science and the Master of Science degrees were thrown out. The new norms did not apply to students currently enrolled, nor was the commercial course affected by the changes.

This was a startling about-face. The scientific course had enjoyed much greater popularity than the difficult classical program. Between the years 1857, when the college bestowed its first diploma, and 1891, when the last Bachelor of Science degrees were granted, Santa Clara had conferred the science diploma 171 times. By contrast, only 44 students had qualified during that same period for the classical diploma.

Declining student interest in classical studies undoubtedly contributed to this mandatory restoration. Horrified at the prospect of the complete collapse of the cherished classical curriculum, Jesuit superiors tried to save by regulation what could not be preserved by popular demand. They also took advantage of the current high enrollment at Santa Clara. They supposed that their rigorous innovation could be accomplished without a drastic diminution in attendance. This was a misjudgment. Both at Santa Clara and at St. Ignatius College, where the new norm also applied, there was a slight decline in enrollments.[37]

The example of more rigorous standards at California's other institutions of higher learning may also have contributed to the new degree requirements. For the restoration of the classics did improve the quality of Santa Clara's diploma. Even the study of scientific subjects was enhanced because the classical degree "embraced the scientific in all its fullness, and superadded to it the culture imparted by the classical studies of Latin and Greek."[38] Moreover, by 1892 an extra year's study in the areas of science, philosophy, and literature was added to the requirements for the new bachelor's degree. As a result, the number of courses that previously had earned a Master of Arts degree now sufficed only for the baccalaureate. The requirements for the Bachelor of Arts degree now included examinations in Latin, Greek, and

English literature, as well as courses in logic, metaphysics, trigonometry, analytical geometry, physics, organic and inorganic chemistry, calculus, geology, ethics, and natural-right philosophy.[39]

Thus, while on the one hand eliminating degrees in science, the college also refashioned its curriculum to satisfy the growing demand for more courses in the physical sciences and the liberal arts as part of a rigorous program. Like most Catholic colleges in the United States, Santa Clara still adhered to the theory that mental discipline was the purpose of higher education and that "the classics are the best mind-formers."[40]

The "Ratio" Reinforced

Soon after Kenna's administration it became clear that devotion to traditional goals and methods of education was not restricted to European clerics. John Pinasco returned to Santa Clara for a second term as president in 1888, and a year later the college received a visitor-general delegated by Rome to examine the state of Jesuit affairs in California.

The man selected for the visitation was an American, Rudolph Meyer. As provincial of the Missouri Province and earlier as president of St. Louis University, Meyer had fought against all departure from Jesuit tradition. He had earned a reputation for an inflexibility that had "frozen the mid-western Jesuits in a European educational posture." Empowered to change "anything [that] should need amendment or correction," the visitor-general arrived in California determined to restore a more faithful observance of the *Ratio Studiorum* and a "uniformity" from which "no one should be allowed to wander in the future."[41]

In the *memoriale* that he left after his visit Meyer ordered that "first place" was to be given to the study of Latin and Greek. Disregarding the question of faculty versatility, he also urged that the old practice prescribed in the *Ratio* of having one teacher instruct a given group of students in all their subjects should be restored. The commercial course also met Meyer's disfavor. "If the Commercial Course is necessary," he directed, "then the reasons must be explained to Father General."[42] A flurry of correspondence between California and Rome subsequently concluded that the course might be retained, but only on the conditions that it not "disturb" or "destroy" the implementation of the *Ratio* and that it allow its students to spend some time studying letters and rhetoric as well.[43]

Meyer left detailed instructions in the matter of student discipline. He required that more stringent rules regarding the use of tobacco be drawn up, rules that could not be "violated with impunity" or with "the connivance" of the prefects. He ordered that reading at table be restored and that all students be required to attend Mass daily "if possible." Meyer during his stay instructed President Pinasco to cancel an Easter vacation that had been promised to the student body because it broke with tradition.[44]

The burdens placed on the Jesuit faculty by the visitor-general were hardly less onerous than those imposed upon the students. Pinasco was reminded that Jesuit legislation required that he confer with his consultors every time he planned an extraordinary purchase in excess of $30; for purchases beyond $100, he should seek permission from the provincial residing in Turin, Italy, through the mediation of the superior of the California Mission. For the sake of "piety," the newspaper reading of the fathers was restricted to one daily journal and two Catholic publications a week. Scholastics on the faculty were allowed "Catholic papers" as long as they dealt solely with "Catholic matters" and "assiduously avoided political questions."[45] Though the extent and fidelity with which Meyer's stringent instructions were followed remains subject to interpretation, the repressive character of the directives is clear.

Challenge from Within

The last decades of the nineteenth century ushered in a period of challenge both for Santa Clara College and for the California Mission itself. Educational practices whose efficacy and value had been taken for granted for generations were becoming increasingly impractical. And yet too few Jesuits perceived either the necessity for change or the manner in which change might be accomplished within the context of their educational tradition.

More readily apparent was the fact that the material and manpower of the Mission had become unequal to the heavy demands placed upon them.[46] Administrators of the handsome new San Francisco college labored to make payments on the school's crushing debt; the interest alone amounted to nearly $35,000 per year.[47] On the other hand, Santa Clara bore little debt by the time Kenna left office in 1888, but it was encumbered with an increasingly outdated campus, whose wooden buildings stood in constant need of repair. Because reserve funds were lacking, new construction seemed imprudent.

More serious was the California Mission's lack of personnel. "Our greatest obstacle," one member declared in 1884, is "want of subjects." Death depleted the ranks annually; few men from the West came forward as replacements. Vocations to the order remained "rare in this part of the world."[48] Eager to increase the number of its novices, the Mission continued for a long time to accept applicants from the East and from abroad and to follow a

A panoramic view of the interior of Santa Clara's mission gardens as they appeared in the late nineteenth century. The gardens, which occupied the former mission quadrangle, are said to have been laid out by Joseph Bayma in the 1880's. Grape trellises crisscrossed the gardens during the time of Italian hegemony. Later the vines were replaced with less bothersome wisteria. In the background stands the remodeled mission church, and to the right is the Jesuit faculty residence. *Courtesy: Archives, Univ. of Santa Clara.*

liberal policy of admission. This policy, however, earned the Mission a reputation in Jesuit circles for admitting candidates unacceptable elsewhere. Superiors frequently admonished the Californians to employ more stringent standards in assessing the qualifications of those seeking entrance to their Los
Gatos novitiate.[49] Regardless, the new seminary gradually began to fill. But
the new members faced a decade of training and education before becoming available for permanent assignment in the schools. Consequently, their
number offered no immediate solution to the Mission's pressing manpower
problem.

In the meantime, a working force of approximately a hundred men maintained the Mission's two schools.[50] Their accomplishments were rather remarkable. Some fifty Jesuits, of whom only half were teachers or administrators,
resided at St. Ignatius College. Their school had an enrollment of more than
seven hundred students in 1884, qualifying it as the largest Jesuit school in
the United States.[51] Though Santa Clara's student body was only one third
as large, it required a staff of almost equal size because it housed resident students. During the same period a short-lived classical school, which had developed out of the Jesuit parish in San Jose, required an additional ten men.

The California Mission was also heavily committed to the pastoral ministry. Since Nobili's time Jesuits had maintained both the Santa Clara mission
church and St. Joseph's parish in San Jose. In subsequent decades nearly a
score of additional parishes were either founded or staffed by the Jesuits of
the college. Though they chiefly served the Santa Clara Valley, priests from
the college also ranged as far north as San Mateo (near San Francisco) and
westward through the mountains to Boulder Creek and beyond to Half
Moon Bay on the Pacific Coast. During the Civil War, men from Santa
Clara journeyed into Arizona Territory for pastoral and educational work.
By the 1880's the only obstacle preventing the permanent establishment
of Jesuit houses in the Southwest and Nevada was lack of personnel.[52]

Because the Mission's reach had overextended its grasp, neither Santa
Clara College nor St. Ignatius College could be run as efficiently as desired.
Finding men to fill positions each term, one man confessed, "is not always an
easy task."[53] The structure of the Jesuit order made it possible to shift faculty
from one school to the other with an ease that other institutions might envy,
but it also resulted in teachers sometimes being assigned to offer instruction
in subjects for which they were not adequately trained. Reflecting on the
difficult schedules that the faculties of the two colleges constantly faced, one
young teacher yearned for the day when each Jesuit could be given "the time
necessary to make himself a perfect master in his special branch."[54]

Younger teachers in particular were often both undertrained and over-worked. In that part of their training known as regency, Jesuit scholastics traditionally served a brief term as prefects or teachers in one of the order's schools. The seminarians were not expected to be assigned to the task before they had acquired sufficient academic preparation. Nor were they expected to be retained at a school for an unreasonable length of time. Because of Santa Clara's shortage of personnel, however, it became common practice to keep minimally trained scholastics at the school for as long as seven years.

During the 1860's, scholastic John Pinasco was employed at the college for eight years for the simple reason that "he could not be spared."[55] Thirty years later, when Pinasco returned to Santa Clara as president, even admonitions from Rome had failed to end the abuse of excessively long regencies. Owing to "the strained condition of the College for want of professors in the clasical departments," in 1892 three scholastics who should have departed for studies in Europe that year were retained at the school for a seventh year of teaching.[56] This practice satisfied the immediate teaching requirements of the two institutions, but it undercut the quality of the Mission's faculties in the future. Not only did a young man's religious formation suffer, but if he was assigned prefecting and teaching in the lower grades his intellectual development suffered, too. The practice was, in short, a total perversion of the purpose of regency.[57]

Manpower limitations also affected the administration of the college by restricting governing power to a few individuals. In a process which later came to be known as "musical chairs" or "the trapeze," a small group of men with administrative ability shuffled back and forth from one executive post to another in the California Mission. As a result, most of Santa Clara's presidents during the nineteenth century also served in the same capacity, though at different times, at St. Ignatius College. Because no other qualified administrators could be found, two presidents, Kenna and Pinasco, were even summoned back to Santa Clara for second terms. And Nicholas Congiato served three terms as mission superior.

Challenge from Without

External events as well as troubles from within put the college to the test in the last decades of the century. "We are in competition with State educational institutions," a California Jesuit conceded in 1884. That year, after fifteen years of unspectacular growth, the University of California changed its admissions policy. Following the example of the University of Michigan, it adopted an accrediting system according to which high-school students

were admitted to the university without examination. Thereafter, enrollments at Berkeley began to climb swiftly. Attracting students was not the
only competitive problem of which the California Jesuit complained in 1884.
Not only must the order's teaching compare favorably with that offered in
the public schools, but its manner of financing its unendowed institutions
must "first and foremost be made to pay expenses."[58]

An even greater rival than the University of California appeared in 1891
in the form of Stanford University, whose immense campus was located a
short distance from Santa Clara. Commencing with a total capital reported
to be almost $30 million, the West's newest and most impressive institution
of higher learning forced all of the state's educational establishments, public
as well as private, to take notice. Even Berkeley, whose highest enrollment
thus far had been 332, stood by in amazement when Stanford's registration
climbed to 1,100 three years after the university opened its doors.[59]

Stanford's shadow fell across Santa Clara. Franklin Hichborn, a student at
the college in the 1890's and later a prominent California reform journalist,
recalled that Stanford "drew heavily" upon both Santa Clara and the University of the Pacific for its first students. Hard-pressed by Santa Clara's tuition, Hichborn himself left the college in 1892 and joined the crowd which
"drifted off toward Stanford" where "no tuition or other charges except for
books and materials were exacted" and "even the syllabi were free."[60] As increasing numbers of students from the University of the Pacific transferred
to Stanford and to Berkeley, that institution, too, was plunged into "the darkest period" of its existence.[61] In 1893, Santa Clara's own registration dropped
to 185 students, the lowest figure since the Civil War.

Competition alone, however, did not explain the college's decline in enrollment. The economic depression that struck the East with full force in
1893 had begun to make its influence felt in the West five years earlier. The
drop in prices and the collapse of the spectacular California real-estate boom
in 1888 coincided with the beginning of Santa Clara's drop in registration.
Thus both financial depression and institutional rivalry combined to end on
a black note the modest prosperity that the college had enjoyed under Kenna
during the boom of the 1880's. For Pinasco's successor, some serious questions regarding Santa Clara's future awaited solution.

10

The Search for "A Broader Place"
1892–1905

During the nineteenth century, colleges multiplied in the United States at an astounding rate. By the end of the century they expired with equal rapidity. "Colleges rise up like mushrooms in our luxurious soil," President Lindsley of the University of Nashville once observed. "They are duly lauded and puffed for a day, and then they sink to be heard of no more." The exact number of institutions that flourished and faded in the course of the nation's history is not known. According to a survey made by Donald G. Tewksbury, of 516 colleges founded outside of New England before the Civil War, only 104 proved permanent. On the average, then, about 80 percent failed. This high mortality rate, Tewksbury concluded, was "one of the striking aspects of the college movement in this country."

What accounts for the great number of casualties? The haste with which they were erected doomed many schools to quick oblivion. The lives of others were cut short by the selection of a poor site, by financial disaster, or by natural catastrophe. Some colleges were undermined by interdenominational competition or by intercommunity rivalry. Internal dissension sealed the fate of others.[1]

Neither Santa Clara nor California's other early colleges were immune to these maladies. Of some forty church-related seminaries, academies, and colleges begun in the state before the Civil War, only five still survive as colleges and universities. These are Santa Clara; California Wesleyan College, now the University of the Pacific; the College of Notre Dame; the College of California, today's University of California at Berkeley; and St. Ignatius College, now the University of San Francisco. Santa Clara is among the survivors, but in the late nineteenth century it came close to joining the casualty list.[2]

Crisis Years

The depression sparked by the panic of 1893 presented Joseph W. Riordan, president of the college from 1893 until 1899, with the "most serious crisis" Santa Clara had faced since its founding years.[3] Falling enrollment and the loss of tuition revenue upon which the school urgently depended was only one facet of the challenge. Though visitors continued to comment on the college's "imposing appearance," the new president recognized that antiquated buildings and a dearth of decent classrooms made it impossible for Santa Clara "to compete with the best Colleges of the country for pupils."[4]

"We sadly need better accommodations," Kenna admitted in 1900. "Other institutions are so much better appointed that we suffer by comparison."[5] *Rough*, *impecunious*, and *austere* were the words a student used to describe the turn-of-the-century campus. The school had developed haphazardly over fifty years, "without reference to any plan at all," and hence the task of constructing a unified campus and "up-to-date College buildings" out of the existing architectural chaos seemed to Riordan "a hopeless task." So grim had the situation become that one Jesuit official concluded that it was "not impossible that Santa Clara would have to be closed."[6]

Not only were its classrooms and dormitories inadequate, but its site now seemed ill-suited to Santa Clara's needs. The proper appearance of the college was compromised by the "poverty" of the town of Santa Clara. The business district abutted on the campus, and the attendant heavy taxes constituted "a steady drain on resources."[7]

The town also seemed beset with dangers that made it an unhealthy environment for students. "With saloons at our very door," the Jesuits felt obliged to restrict the measure of liberty they granted their students, though the old policy of confinement was becoming more and more difficult to enforce. Robert Kenna had increased the boarders' freedom slightly, but older students still resented the college fence. Even "the best boys" told me, President Riordan recalled, that "to see boards, boards, boards for weeks at a time" was "the hardest thing for them to bear." Incarceration not only made student life irksome, it also burdened the faculty with the task of constant prefecting. Santa Clara's reputation as a prison, Riordan observed, deterred some very desirable boys from seeking education within its walls. And yet the fence and the unpopular restraints seemed a necessary evil at the school's site.[8]

Thus, the possibility of transferring the college to a more suitable location was seriously reviewed. Several administrators before Riordan had suggested that the school required a larger campus. In 1893 his predecessor, John Pinasco, had suggested that the school move "some place near San Jose." "My own term of office" of six years, Riordan declared, "proved to me plainly that a broader Santa Clara needed a broader place."[9] From a discussion with his consultors on the desirability of a site near Santa Cruz, two points of agreement emerged: the boarders deserved something better, and the question of relocation should be postponed until the effects of the current economic depression had passed. In the meantime, temporary repairs continued to be made on existing buildings.[10]

Opposition from Kenna

Riordan's conviction that the college should abandon the campus it had occupied for half a century was not shared by all of his fellow Jesuits. But Riordan expected that his successor would carry on to completion the program for removal he had envisioned. He was, therefore, annoyed when Robert Kenna returned to the presidency in 1899 and "immediately set himself to work to undo what I had done." After only one month of his rectorship had elapsed, including only two weeks of school, Kenna called a general meeting of the priests of the college to consider the question of removal. Making no secret of his own wishes in the matter, Kenna proposed that new Santa Clara buildings should go up on the old site. Because Kenna had erected a new chapel at Santa Clara during his first term, his opposition to removal was spitefully ascribed by Riordan to the fact that "he could scarcely be expected to be anxious to undo" his previous work.[11]

Kenna admitted that the narrowness of the existing grounds at Santa Clara, cut through by city streets, constituted a serious obstacle to remaining. Nevertheless, if it was at all possible, he was determined to keep the pioneer college at its historic location. It soon appeared he had succeeded. Kenna persuaded Jesuit superiors that the territory of the college in Santa Clara could be expanded easily and for the right price and that the magistrates of the town were willing to close some of the public thoroughfares that inconveniently dissected the campus. "I have fought to keep the College in Santa Clara upon the old sacred site hallowed by so many glorious memories," the president jubilantly reported after persuading Jesuit superiors of the feasibility of obtaining more property, and "I hope and believe that I have been successful." Assuring alumni and townspeople that Santa Clara was neither "a moribund college" nor "a croaker," Kenna warned that his success would ultimately "depend upon my ability to raise funds sufficient to secure more land right here."[12] Gearing his appeal for financial support to historical sentiment and to publicity generated by the school's impending fiftieth anniversary, Kenna, along with his faculty, waited to see how many alumni and friends shared his nostalgia for the old site and to what extent they would translate their devotion into dollars.

Santa Clara completed its first half-century in 1901. The event was celebrated in grand style by a two-day civic celebration in the town of Santa

Clara in March and by four days of festivities at the college in June. Parades, banquets, and baseball games drew thousands of visitors to the campus in June and earned welcome coverage in the press. A religious drama, *Nazareth*, was written for the occasion by playwright Clay Greene. So large was the audience that flocked to see the drama that special trains were scheduled to carry the crowds from San Jose and San Francisco. Archbishop Patrick W. Riordan and well-known alumni such as Charles McClatchy and Delphin Delmas delivered lengthy panegyrics on the accomplishments of "California's oldest educational institution." While praising the past, the speakers also tactfully reminded their audiences of "the necessity of college improvements" if the future were to be equally glorious.[13]

When the applause died down and the last train departed, the college had little besides publicity to show for its efforts. "There was a great glitter of golden sentiments and words," former president Riordan caustically observed, "but a conspicuous absence of anything else golden."[14] "Even small gifts are oftentimes an incalculable help," a spokesman had pleaded; and these were all the college received.[15]

The failure of the golden-jubilee fund appeal was attributable to several causes. Not the least of these was the fact that the college, though it had matriculated several thousand students in the course of fifty years, could count fewer than three hundred college graduates among its alumni. Of these graduates, only a limited number were capable of large benefactions. In addition to the scarcity of alumni of either college or high-school level to whom it could turn for support, Santa Clara's financial appeal itself was poorly executed. Still uninitiated in the techniques of effective fund raising, the college had naively assumed that a sentimental review of the past glories of alma mater and a vague declaration of need would suffice to stimulate benefaction. By refusing to issue a financial statement demonstrating graphically its economic plight and the extent of its future requirements, Santa Clara lost a unique opportunity to convince the public of its serious need for assistance. Failure to communicate frankly and effectively led many persons to assume that the college was wealthy.

The result of the disappointing search for funds was a renewed Jesuit debate on moving the school. Lack of financial support for sustaining the old mission campus persuaded authorities that the wiser option was to reconstruct the college on broader and less expensive ground. It was remarked that the collapse of the very promises of help from friends to enlarge Santa Clara may have been a sign of the will of God that the college should move. So Father General Luis Martín piously suggested to the superior of the California

Mission. Besides, Martín added optimistically, a more suitable place much further removed from Santa Clara and the other houses of the Mission would not only improve the college, but would also make it easier to assign Jesuits to it.[16]

Reluctantly, Kenna agreed to abandon the mission site—especially, so the story goes, when a smallpox epidemic struck the area, underscoring the dangers of an urban location.[17] The search for a new site commenced once again. In 1902 "200 acres and $500,000" were offered as an inducement to transfer the college to Sacramento. Though the bid was eventually rejected, the pros and cons of the proposition were debated by the Junior Dramatic Society, with the affirmative team arguing for acceptance because the land and money constituted "the only real generous offer" made to help Santa Clara out of its difficulties since its appeal at the time of the Golden Jubilee the year before.[18] Finally, after considering several alternatives, President Kenna announced to an alumni gathering in San Francisco on June 7, 1904, that Santa Clara's "need of larger grounds and better environments generally" had led to the purchase of 414 acres near Mountain View. This "magnificent piece of property," which was obtained for $36,000, was located in an undeveloped portion of the Santa Clara Valley some eight miles northwest of the mission campus. Additional parcels of land later were bought until the college possessed more than 600 acres of rolling countryside. Boasting a panoramic view of the Santa Clara Valley and San Francisco Bay beyond, the Loyola tract, as it was called in honor of the Jesuit founder, seemed an ideal location for the new Santa Clara.[19]

The site was determined, but the challenging task of designing a campus and erecting buildings remained. Kenna immediately set about organizing the machinery for a promotional campaign to "secure the funds necessary for the great work."[20] But only a year remained of Kenna's term of office, and responsibility for starting the new campus transferred in 1905 to his successor, Father Richard Gleeson. Financing the removal to Mountain View was to be the central theme of Gleeson's five-year administration.

Kenna Makes His Mark

Not all of Kenna's energies were absorbed by the question of Santa Clara's site or by the routine tasks of education. The six years of his second administration proved to be a period of great activity as he plunged himself and the institution into a series of undertakings unthought of by many of his semicloistered European predecessors.

Kenna lent his name and personal influence to the conservationist campaign that resulted in the creation near Santa Cruz of California's first state park. He also frequently addressed off-campus groups. When he spoke before the Methodist student body of the University of the Pacific in 1903, the local press described it as "an event such as this valley has never known before" and hoped it augured an "era of good feelings" between Catholics and Protestants.[21] Kenna also succeeded in drawing to Santa Clara an impressive host of visitors and guests. Irish poet William Butler Yeats lectured at the college theater in 1904, as did Douglas Hyde, leader of the Gaelic revival. Kenna arranged for President William McKinley to visit the school during his tour of the state in 1901, though the event was canceled at the last minute by the illness of the president's wife.

Two years later President Theodore Roosevelt came to Santa Clara. After delivering a "vigorous, manly" address at the San Jose railway station, Roosevelt was accompanied down the spectator-lined Alameda by an escort of Rough Riders and horse-drawn carriages. Roosevelt was received by Kenna and town officials in front of the mission church to the sound of screaming mill whistles, pealing church bells, and "Hail Columbia" played by the college band. There he addressed a crowd of townspeople and students before traveling to Santa Cruz to see the redwood grove that Kenna's efforts had helped preserve as a park.[22]

Kenna was also energetic in bestowing honorary degrees upon college benefactors and upon alumni who had brought recognition to the college through their accomplishments in various fields. During the period when the progressive movement was beginning to take form in California, he publicly honored two former students who had helped uncover political graft in Boss Abraham Reuf's San Francisco: Franklin Hichborn, investigative journalist for the *Sacramento Bee* and Charles McClatchy, the paper's editor. James D. Phelan, Santa Clara benefactor and reform mayor of San Francisco, and Delphin Delmas, alumnus and by now the most celebrated criminal lawyer in the United States, both were awarded similar diplomas in 1903.

"Marconi of the West"?

In the 1800's, Joseph Neri, Anthony Cichi, Charles Messea, and Joseph Bayma had earned recognition for the college by their scientific work. In the early twentieth century, a lay professor, John Montgomery, and a Jesuit priest, Father Richard Bell, built upon that tradition through their pioneering work in aviation and radio broadcasting.

Bell was the lesser known of the pair. While studying theology in Rome in the early 1890's, he had become interested in Guglielmo Marconi's experiments in wireless telegraphy. When he returned to America in 1898, Bell brought with him to California a copy of Marconi's recently published account of his early findings and, on a small scale, began duplicating Marconi's laboratory work in San Francisco. There is no evidence, however, that Bell produced the first wireless communication on the West Coast, as has been claimed frequently by his admirers. News of Marconi's breakthrough had reached the United States before Bell's return from Europe, although many who heard of it doubted his mysterious manner of plucking messages out of thin air. In 1899 a team of San Franciscans reproduced Marconi's method of communicating by radio waves and demonstrated its usefulness by sending a message in Morse code from a lightship anchored outside the Golden Gate to the Cliff House on the San Francisco shore. This was the first wireless message broadcast on the West Coast and the first ship-to-shore wireless transmission in the United States. A month later Marconi himself came to America and repeated many of his experiments, thus convincing skeptics of the possibilities of wireless telegraphy. Soon amateurs everywhere were imitating his pioneering feats, and wireless stations began to appear on lightships and lighthouses on both coasts.

Bell helped to popularize the new device by his experiments, inventions, and lectures at Santa Clara. Though he had dabbled in the field as early as 1898, it was not until 1903, according to his own testimony, that he began serious work on wireless communication. In that year he and John Montgomery succeeded in transmitting a message from a hilltop at Villa Maria to the college tower, a distance of seven miles. Soon afterward, the Jesuit began lecturing to packed houses on the subject of wireless transmission, illustrating his talks with live telegraphic communications to the college from Los Gatos or San Francisco.[23]

Bell also was interested in the problem of voice transmission by radio waves. According to one account, Bell succeeded as early as 1904 in establishing voice communication by speaking over the wireless with Charles D. Herrold, San Jose radio pioneer.[24] That he talked frequently by radio with Herrold, who in 1909 formed the first radio broadcasting station in the United States, is probable; but that he and Herrold transmitted the first spoken words in the West, as has frequently been claimed at Santa Clara, has never been conclusively proven. Credit for that accomplishment is usually given to wireless operators broadcasting from Roosevelt's Great White Fleet when it steamed into San Francisco Bay in 1908. Popular tradition has also attributed several inventions to Bell's creative genius. However, the only invention that he ever patented was a radio signaling device in 1928, late in his career. Bell's significance seems limited chiefly to the influence he wielded in local radio circles and to his role in making Marconi's invention known to the public. In 1933, when the famous inventor visited California, he came to Santa Clara, inspected Bell's former laboratory, and met with the aged priest, whom enthusiastic campus admirers had long since dubbed "the Marconi of the West."[25]

Montgomery and His "Aeroplanes"

More significant contributions to science were made by John J. Montgomery, an aviation pioneer who attended Santa Clara for a year and graduated from St. Ignatius College in 1879. As a boy he was preoccupied with "the problem of aerial navigation." After his graduation, Montgomery moved to his family's ranch in San Diego, where he pursued research in the subject that fascinated him beyond everything else. Convinced that the secret to flight lay in unraveling the principle of the bird's flight, Montgomery decided to follow the construction of the bird's wing in making his aircraft, and thus he discovered the lifting power of the curved-surface wing.[26] Though the Wright brothers are correctly credited with the greatest breakthrough in aviation because theirs was the world's first powered flight, Montgomery demonstrated the basic possibilities of flying two decades before Kitty Hawk. On August 20, 1883, at Otay Mesa, south of San Diego, he flew a glider whose wings were designed in imitation of those of a seagull. The craft traveled a distance of perhaps three hundred feet. It was the first time an American had flown a heavier-than-air machine.

Montgomery was then twenty-five years old. According to aviation historian Tom Crouch, if he had continued his pioneering glider experimentation, he might have played a main role in aviation history. For reasons that are unclear, however, after 1886 his interest shifted from flying to fruitless speculative studies on the theory of flight. By 1893 he had summarized his ideas in a paper that he read to the Aeronautical Conference in Chicago at the World's Fair. He also had published a few articles on the subject of flying that attracted the attention of other flight enthusiasts around the country, including Octave Chanute, inventor and early aviation authority. But Montgomery's speculations received a cold reception in the scientific community.[27] Frustrated by this rejection, he turned instead to teaching.

In 1896 Montgomery came to Santa Clara, whose laboratories he had been using intermittently for several years. During his years at the college, his interest in actual flying was rekindled. By 1905 he no longer depended upon horses or hills to launch one of his gliders. Instead he employed a more dangerous method. Montgomery hired a balloonist to lift the machine thousands of feet in the air. Then the suspended craft was cut loose, and a professional stuntman named Daniel Maloney guided the craft in flight.

The first public demonstration of this technique took place at the college on April 29, 1905. Convinced that Professor Montgomery's discovery was "the greatest invention of the age," authorities cooperated to "make the first exhibition a grand affair."[28] A school holiday, President's Day, was set aside for the demonstration, and a throng of more than one thousand spectators and reporters gathered in the campus vineyard to watch the launching of Montgomery's red and white glider, *The Santa Clara*. Released from its moorings, the giant balloon to which *The Santa Clara* was tethered soared rapidly upward until it looked like a basketball high in the sky. Then, at an elevation of some four thousand feet, the dangling glider was cut loose from the balloon, and aviator Maloney, "clad in red tights and hanging on to it for dear life," skillfully guided the frail craft on its soaring, silent course. For twenty minutes the glider swept earthward, rose and fell in response to signals from the controls, tacked in different directions, and finally, its altitude spent, coasted to a rest on the exact landing spot designated before the flight. The altitude reached by *The Santa Clara* and the degree of control demonstrated by Maloney broke all previous records.[29]

. The next morning newspapers from San Francisco to New York headlined the event. "Sails on aeroplane as bird in flight," announced the *San Francisco Examiner*. "This is the first machine upon which any man has ever been able actually to fly in the bird fashion." The article exclaimed that the imagination "runs riot" in contemplating the possibilities of aerial navigation.[30] Expert reaction to the 1905 flight was equally enthusiastic. It was the most daring feat ever attempted, Octave Chanute, benefactor and counsel of the Wright brothers, is alleged to have said. Alexander Graham Bell, who had studied and experimented with the problem of flying, later declared that "all subsequent attempts in aviation must begin with the Montgomery machine."[31] For the first time in history, Victor Lougheed said, man had solved the one great problem of aerial navigation, the challenge of controlling flight while maintaining equilibrium. Lougheed, an early aeronautical engineer and half-brother of the founder of Lockheed Aircraft, evaluated the 1905 flight as "the greatest single advance" in the history of aviation.[32] In retrospect, such accolades seem excessive. Historians of aviation, viewing Montgomery's work from a broader perspective, attach a more modest sig-

John J. Montgomery, standing to the right in a bowler hat, prepares his glider, *The Santa Clara*, for flight in 1905. Pilot Dan Maloney takes his position at the controls. Both Montgomery and Maloney were killed during later aviation experiments. *Courtesy: Archives, Univ. of Santa Clara.*

nificance to it. Despite the publicity that the turn-of-the-century glider experiments generated, Montgomery did not regain the position of leadership he had briefly enjoyed earlier in his career. His bold glider flights were overshadowed by the experiments of the Wright brothers, who had made their historic motor-propelled flight at Kitty Hawk in 1903.

Disaster befell Montgomery's later efforts. Three months after the much-acclaimed flight of *The Santa Clara*, the glider broke a strut in mid-air, and pilot Maloney plunged to his death. Six years later Montgomery himself was killed in a freak accident while he was testing another craft. At the time of his death, aviation had advanced far beyond glider experiments. Powered airplanes were already flying—not in mere feet, as in the case of the Wrights' first flight—but in miles. In 1911, the year John Montgomery died, the first cross-country flight in American history had occurred, though it took months to complete.

Despite his stubborn, lifelong disdain for the problems of powered flight, and despite the exaggerated claims sometimes made for him by local enthusiasts, Montgomery deserves a niche in early aviation's hall of fame. That he was the first person in America to fly a heavier-than-air machine seems certain. (Others had accomplished the feat in Europe before Montgomery's 1883 flight.) His development of some of the principles of aerodynamics helped in a modest way to lay the foundation of modern aviation. Montgomery did not invent the curved wing, but he did demonstrate the lifting power of the curve and its use in maintaining flight equilibrium. Nor did he invent wing warping, but he made effective use of this wing shape in his earlier gliders. According to his biographer, Arthur Spearman, Montgomery was the first to use the word *aeroplane* to refer to the entire flying craft. Even after Kitty Hawk, the Wrights and others were still using the term *flying machine*. Montgomery's appelation was adopted by the press soon after the 1905 flight at Santa Clara.

Montgomery's standing as a pioneer of early aviation has received some of the attention it deserves. Monuments now mark the sites of several of his early flights. A school has been named for him in Chula Vista, California, and an airport in San Diego. One of his later gliders, *The Evergreen*, is preserved at the Smithsonian Institution. And in 1946 Hollywood paid Montgomery its ultimate tribute. Columbia Pictures produced a full-length film of the aviator's life, *Gallant Journey*.

"Save the Redwoods"

While Montgomery's gliders advanced the science of flight, other Santa Clarans were pioneering in another twentieth-century movement, the cause of conservation. A former student in the high-school department, Andrew P. Hill, played the leading role in the creation of California's first state park. In this campaign he was aided by his former classmate, the president of Santa Clara, Robert Kenna.

In 1900 Hill, who worked as an artist and photographer in San Jose, was commissioned by a London magazine to photograph California redwoods. When the owner of a grove of ancient trees near Big Basin, a forest site south of San Jose, refused to cooperate and even demanded his negatives, Hill grew angry. And when he learned of a plan to fell the trees for lumber, he became deeply concerned over the fate of the redwood forest. Hill, fearing that lumber companies and private owners would soon destroy other stands of trees, conceived of the idea of preserving the area as a public park. A few months after his encounter at the redwoods, the Sempervirens Club was

A hot-air balloon lifts aloft John J. Montgomery's glider and pilot Dan Maloney in San Jose in 1905. *Courtesy: Archives, Univ. of Santa Clara.*

born. With the support of Stanford University, the University of California, and Santa Clara College, its members launched a campaign to form Big Basin Park and to save the redwoods from the ax and saw.[33]

President Kenna, whom Hill had known since his student days at the college in the 1860's, was recruited for the campaign. Kenna was one of the leading spirits of the movement, Hill recalled later, and many times it was he who directed the fight. The task of persuading the California legislature to approve appropriations for a state park proved difficult. It was here that Kenna's influence was crucial, for not only were many private interests opposed to the plan, but the expenditure of public funds for such a purpose was unprecedented. In 1901 Hill, representing the Sempervirens Club at the state capitol, managed to get the bill out of committee and onto the floor of the assembly, but he could not obtain $50,000 required by a lumber company as a first-payment guarantee toward moving their mill in case the legislature agreed to purchase the land. In desperate need of funds to meet the deadline, Hill rushed south on an evening train in search of assistance. When President David Starr Jordan of Stanford could not help, Hill turned to Kenna. Before the night was over, the Jesuit had not only persuaded his nephew, San Francisco Mayor James Phelan, to provide the guarantee, but he committed himself to go to Sacramento to speak on behalf of the bill. "We marshalled all our forces," Hill recalled, "and he addressed the senate, conferred with members of both houses, and the bill was passed. The governor signed the bill and Father Kenna became one of the first park commissioners."[34]

Though the legislature appropriated $250,000 to purchase the redwood lands, several battles remained for Hill and his associates. In the months that followed, Kenna continued to advertise the needs of the park, often turning for help to Charles McClatchy, who lent timely support through the columns of the *Sacramento Bee*. Other duties obliged Kenna to resign his appointment in 1903, but successive presidents of the college served on the California Redwood Park Commission until the board was absorbed into the State Park Commission in 1927.

Student Activities: Communication

The regard with which eloquence was held in the classical course of studies at Santa Clara assured a high degree of dramatic and literary activity among students in the early twentieth century, as it had in the nineteenth. In 1902 a new periodical appeared. Unlike its literary predecessor, *The Owl*, the new magazine functioned as a chronicle of current events as well as a showcase for student compositions. The new periodical was entitled *The Redwood* in honor of the part the college had played in the campaign to save the red-woods of the nearby Santa Cruz mountains. The family spirit that prevailed at the small college was shown by the weekend camping trips made by the periodical's student staff, President Kenna, and Andrew P. Hill into the Big Basin wilderness.

The Redwood reflected the concerns of the day, both within and without the college. In its pages students expressed their views on such varied topics as the engineering of the recently opened Panama Canal, "atheistic" secular education, California mission architecture, the Ku Klux Klan, Professor Montgomery's "aeroplane," and "that grandiloquent siren of the American Federation of Labor," Samuel Gompers.[35] In 1910, through the efforts of Jesuit moderator Cornelius Deeney, the magazine scored a minor literary coup by its publication of an article on the life of the late Henry Harland by his widow. Harland was the popular editor of *The Yellow Book*, a colleague of Aubrey Beardsley, and a friend of Henry James.[36] *The Redwood*'s days as a literary magazine ended in 1922, and its title was appropriated by the university yearbook.

Play writing was popular among students and faculty. Jesuit D. J. Kavanagh's *Henry Garnett* was enacted on the stage of the Ship, and so were the dramas of Professor Charles D. South, whose *Santiago* also played before audiences in San Jose and San Francisco. Student playwright Martin Merle produced several popular one-act plays before he graduated with a Master of Arts degree in 1906. The young author's most successful production was *The Light Eternal*, which first appeared on campus in 1905, then toured the West Coast with a professional troupe, and finally was staged in New York by Henry Miller. The first of several performances of Merle's *The Mission Play of Santa Clara*, which dealt with the secularization of the mission, appeared on campus in 1913. Several students who later attained professional prominence made their dramatic debuts in Merle's campus productions, including Desmond Gallagher, John Ivancovich, and screenwriter George Beaumont. Actor Edmund Lowe began his theatrical career at Santa Clara. He earned a bachelor's degree in 1910 and a Master of Arts diploma a year later.[37]

"Long Hair and Bruised Limbs"

Athletics, which enjoyed a spectacular rise in popularity in American colleges and universities at the end of the century, competed with dramatics for student attention. Soon after Rutgers and Princeton played the first intercollegiate football game in 1869, the sport found favor with undergraduates everywhere. Begun as a soccerlike game with improvised rules, football evolved rapidly as Harvard, Yale, and other eastern schools each contributed new features to the sport. Before the turn of the century, football had also become the rage in California. In the 1890's it made its debut at Santa Clara. "It is a game full of dangers," exclaimed one professor upon witnessing his first game—in fact, "too dangerous and hence unfit for our students."[38]

Despite the fears of some of the faculty, in 1895 a delegation of students, "ambitious of wearing long hair and nursing bruised limbs," extracted from President Riordan qualified recognition of the game. Always interested in athletics, Riordan intended to limit the sport to intramural contests, but within a year persuasive students had scheduled Santa Clara's first game with an outside club, a team from Santa Cruz. Playing in a hay field near the mission pear orchard, the college eleven was overwhelmed by the opponents—"worsted by an inferior team who knew more about the game," an interested Jesuit observed.[39] The following autumn the college team obtained a coach, Dr. Fred Gerlach, an alumnus who had returned to California from the University of Pennsylvania, where he had been a varsity player. In the years that followed, the school's schedule was expanded to include games with teams from Stanford, Berkeley, and St. Mary's College.

Competition had not yet produced the practice of granting athletic scholarships, and consequently coaches were obliged to recruit their players from the student body by promoting the advantages of participation. Besides appealing to the traditional dictum *mens sana in corpore sano*, advocates of football boasted that the sport was capable of raising the tone of the institution and imparting a "healthy moral spirit." Such arguments were persuasive; a fifth of Santa Clara's small student body, about fifty students, turned out for the team. To critics who charged that the sport was brutal and no game for a gentleman, *The Redwood* replied that if played according to the recognized rules there was not one thing a player could do on the gridiron that he could not do without shame before his mother.[40]

Student enthusiasm notwithstanding, the faculty began to worry that the increased frequency of outside games was harmful to the students' academic and religious development. Their misgivings reflected growing national concern over the merits of the sport. Evidence was mounting that it was injurious not only to study, but also to health. Mass plays, hurdling, and flying tackles left the college gridirons of America littered with injured players. The 1904 season ended with twenty-one players dead and more than two hundred wounded. That year *The Nation* and *The New York Times* launched a national campaign against football brutality.[41]

A local tragedy caused Santa Clara to join the boycott. In 1905, after a game between two public high-school teams on the Santa Clara field resulted in the death of a player, the administration decided that football should be suppressed. The president announced that until the brutal features of the game were eliminated and until the faculty could conscientiously allow students "confided to our care by loving parents" to enter competition without "such dreadful danger to life and limb," Santa Clara would do away with football.[42]

During football's hiatus, a "safer and less strenuous" new game known as basketball began to be played at the college. The sport seemed too tame, however, and failed to spark much student enthusiasm. Consequently in 1907 Santa Clara followed the example of Stanford and the University of California and took up rugby in place of the outlawed American football. The English game continued to be played until 1919, when student and alumni pressure succeeded in restoring football.[43]

Neither rugby nor football replaced baseball as Santa Clara's favorite sport. In fact, baseball soared to a new zenith of popularity at the turn of the century—testimony perhaps to the continued presence of the high board fence that forced students to seek their entertainment within the college walls. The passion and skill with which the game was pursued at Santa Clara was indicated by the large number of campus players recruited each year, not only by California and Pacific Coast teams, but by the American and National leagues as well. Charles Graham played professionally for several West Coast teams after graduating from Santa Clara in 1898, and later he became co-owner of the San Francisco Seals with Charles Strub, another Santa Clara Bronco baseballer. Harry Wolter of the class of '06 played for the Cincinnati, New York, and Chicago teams before going to Stanford as baseball coach. The talented "Prince" Hal Chase played briefly with the college nine before joining the New York Yankees and later the Cincinnati Reds. Once acknowledged as the best first baseman in baseball, Chase left the major leagues in disgrace in 1919, when he was accused of betting and bribery. Arthur Shafer, who signed with the New York Giants in 1907; Justin Fitzgerald, Yankee outfielder; Philadelphia Athletics pitcher Barry Hardin; and Robert Keefe, who pitched for both the New York Americans and Cincinnati Reds, all began their careers on the Santa Clara College diamond.

The rules that governed baseball and all collegiate sports at the turn of the century hardly could be described as rigorous. An agreement between Santa Clara and St. Mary's around 1909 reveals the laxity prevailing in intercollegiate athletics up to that time. The accord, as reported by the press, laid down new norms for eligibility in all major sports. "In order to outwit the wily busher, who would register during September and then lay off until the click of the bat awoke him in the spring, the agreement declares any student not in regular attendance during October, November, and December ineligible to compete."

To discourage the recruitment of "ringers," "deadheads," and "baseball bums" who traveled from team to collegiate team, the two schools agreed that no student who at any time during the college year played on a team other than those representing his own college would be allowed to compete in any collegiate contest. Moreover, no student would be eligible to compete for more than six years, nor would he participate in any sport if he were taking fewer than three hours of college work daily.[44]

A Catholic College

While preparing for the day when it could transfer to its new campus in the foothills of Mountain View, the college experienced other, more subtle transformations. The increase in the number of colleges and universities in California in the late nineteenth century had influenced the decision to move. Comparing its antiquated and cramped facilities with those of such institutions as Stanford and Berkeley, Santa Clara had felt compelled to fashion a new campus to attract more students. But the rise in the number of schools produced other effects, too. One of the most important was that Santa Clara became both numerically and ideologically more Catholic.

In its earlier period the college had not gone out of its way to call attention to its religious affiliation. Everyone recognized that the school was run by the Jesuits and that moral training was one of its chief aims. Hence there was little reason to advertise the college as a Catholic institution. Moreover, the school was sustained by a large number of Protestant pupils. During Varsi's administration, half of the student body was non-Catholic. Though some Jesuits feared that contact between non-Catholic and Catholic students worked "to the possible detriment of the latter in faith and morals," they privately admitted that "were it not for the Protestants we could not support ourselves."[45]

With the dramatic rise of secular education the situation was altered. The growing number of private and public colleges greatly increased the options available to Californians desiring a college education. Inevitably, the number of Protestant pupils at Santa Clara shrank to a minority— though the shift was not sudden. Moreover, as American higher education abandoned its purpose of character formation and replaced the liberal arts curriculum with more utilitarian training, traditional institutions like Santa Clara were put on the defensive. The college was now forced to outline in stronger detail those features that distinguished it from other schools of higher learning. The prospect of losing hundreds of Catholic youth to secular education encouraged Santa Clara and other Catholic institutions to stress the value of moral training, to define their Catholic aims more explicitly, and to seek patronage on this basis. Thus by 1911 the Jesuit provincial advised the president of the college that "great care" was to be taken in admitting students and that "the number of non-Catholic students should be kept down."[46]

Forces other than academic ones led to a stronger emphasis on religion. A new rash of nativism in the 1890's contributed to a sense of self-consciousness among Catholics throughout the United States. A product of old-fashioned bigotry and of new-found alarm at the recent flood of immigrants, the American Protective Association sprang to life in the midwest and quickly extended its influence westward. In San Jose the "loudly enthusiastic" reception accorded alleged ex-priests and runaway nuns by local supporters of the A.P.A. soon pushed Catholics into retreat. Public debates over the dubious loyalty of "the Pope's Irish" produced "bitter" memories among Santa Clara Valley Catholics. The Spanish-American War and the emotional opportunities it afforded finally focused national interest away from religious denunciations.[47]

The war provided Catholics with a special opportunity to prove their loyalty. Contemporary literature gives the impression that Catholics could not rush to the warships fast enough when hostilities erupted between the bellicose United States and enfeebled Spain. "How many A.P.A. regiments have gone to fight for Uncle Sam?" the St. Joseph's Church bulletin of San Jose demanded rhetorically. Thousands of Catholics rushed to Cuba and the Philippines at the start, the newsletter bragged; "the Navy is full of Catholics" and Catholic blood has "flowed freely." The San Francisco *Monitor* boasted that a Catholic had fired the first shot of the war.[48]

Jesuit pastors kept their congregations informed of the activities of the Santa Clara alumni who were engaged in the Philippine campaign. The careers of Joseph McQuade and William D. McKinnon, both chaplains, were carefully chronicled. (After the war, McKinnon remained in the Philippines to organize the municipal school system of Manila according to the American pattern; he was joined by several younger alumni who sailed across the Pacific to teach school.) But the man who did the most to boost the Catholics' sense of patriotic pride was James F. Smith of the class of 1877. Smith commanded the First California Regiment of Volunteers. After the conquest he became a member of the Philippine Commission, and he was appointed Governor General of the Islands in 1906. He subsequently became a Federal judge in Washington, D. C.

Church Versus State

The Catholics' feeling of being different was also fostered by the educational policies of the American Catholic hierarchy. The church had always insisted on the importance of religious instruction, but as nonsectarian public education came of age in the United States, the emphasis became more forceful. To Archbishop George Montgomery of San Francisco, a frequent speaker at the college, exclusion of "the religious element" in education was equivalent to "teaching sectarianism in its worst form, namely: Agnosticism."[49] This fear, coupled with the hostility many Catholics perceived in their environment, led the American bishops to exert a Herculean effort to construct a separate Catholic school system. Most of this energy was directed toward building parochial schools, but church leaders, with varying degrees of success, also discouraged Catholic students from pursuing undergraduate studies at secular institutions. "In a land where men talk infidelity," Archbishop Riordan instructed a congregation in San Jose, youngsters must be "secured by . . . proper educational safeguards."[50]

Spokesmen at Santa Clara College were no less partial. The incompleteness of any system of instruction that disregarded religious questions and moral training was the repeated theme of the college's fiftieth anniversary celebration in 1901. Speaker after speaker stepped to the podium to inveigh against secular education and to praise the contrasting advantages of the Santa Clara system. Secular education is deficient, Archbishop Riordan complained, and it "perverts or uproots the sources of the spiritual life which is the basis of character." "The tendency of every school of learning which is not religious," he warned, "is necessarily towards Atheism or Agnosticism." Alumnus Charles McClatchy, with a vividness of style which must have gratified his former mentors, decried "that so-called 'Higher Education' [that] polishes the mind and leaves the heart to take care of itself; an education that pampers the intellect and maroons the conscience; an education that while pretending to teach all the wonders of botany, all the marvels of astronomy—leaves it to a debatable question whether blind Materialism did not preside at the birth of a flower and uncalculating Chance swing God's vesper lamps in the heavens." "No such 'Higher Education,' " he assured his audience, "will ever taint the teaching of Santa Clara College."[51]

"Save the Redwoods." Robert Kenna (fifth from the left, in a broad-brimmed hat and resting on a cane) and Andrew P. Hill (standing at the extreme right and sporting a goatee) gather with conservationist friends at the base of the "Santa Clara Tree" in Big Basin Park. *Courtesy: Archives, Univ. of Santa Clara.*

In private many Jesuits were even more critical of the increasingly power-ful "oligarchy" of secular education. The neutrality of such a system could be tolerated, but not its open opposition to traditional Christian principles. That the lecture halls of state universities had gradually become pulpits for "anti-Catholic tirades" and "bitterly hostile" attacks on "revealed religion" was the Jesuits' frequent complaint. From once being merely nonsectarian, one Jesuit argued, state institutions "have in the process of time become pos-itively anti-Christian." Catholic mentors were using every means at their command, another declared, to dissuade young Catholics from attending such institutions, where "the study of atheistic systems of philosophy" and "the materialistic theory of biology" puts students "in the imminent dan-ger of having their faith unsettled or destroyed."[52]

Some Jesuits by 1903 were convinced that the University of California at Berkeley had become openly "hostile to our graduates." That year, under the reforming direction of President Benjamin Ide Wheeler, new entrance requirements for Berkeley's professional schools of law and medicine were established. They included courses in "evolutionary philosophy" and courses in biology that were anathema in Catholic institutions. The Santa Clara faculty, expecting that the effect of Wheeler's reforms would be to stan-dardize undergraduate training in California, feared that the new norms would necessarily shut their graduates out of the schools of law and medi-cine, which many Santa Clara students had entered in recent years.[53]

Biological evolution was one of the chief bugbears of Catholic intellec-tuals, who believed that Darwin's theory could topple the faith of intellec-tually immature students. (Catholic institutions were not alone in opposing the teaching of the controversial subject. Evolution was also an unacceptable topic of instruction in 1880 at such institutions as Princeton, Williams, La-fayette, and Amherst.) But it was a sad judgment of the Jesuit system that after years of intense philosophical and theological study graduates could not cope with unorthodox questions. Who was at fault? One California Jesuit suggested the answer when he admitted quite candidly to Roman superiors in 1900 that if the "circumstances of the times" had gradually pushed the classics into a secondary position in American education, "the progress of knowledge" had also "discredited" the metaphysics taught in many Catholic colleges. Though persuaded that Jesuit professors as a group were "at least the equal in learning and culture to any in the United States," he maintained that many of his fellow philosophers were "second or third rate men who are employed in this position because they seem to have little aptitude for anything else." Moreover, they often knew "little or nothing of natural science or modern philosophy." Catholic philosophy "may be an inestimable blessing" if it is well presented, but if it is poorly taught it is "an unmitigated curse."[54]

Such frank admissions were rare and confined to the private forum. Besides, most Catholic educators, including the critical Jesuit cited above, remained convinced of the fundamental superiority of their system of education, its shortcomings notwithstanding. Thus it was imperative that Catholics continue to receive the traditional training.

Despite clerical counsels, however, many Catholic parents found attractive reasons for enrolling their offspring in the state's several secular institutions. When Archbishop Riordan of San Francisco, in recognition of this fact, established a Newman center at Berkeley, many California Jesuits were keenly disappointed. They regarded his action as an untimely compromise of principles and a slap in the face of Catholic institutions. The Jesuits' view of the persistent drift of Catholic students toward non-Catholic schools, combined with their view of the dangers and shortcomings in the secular philosophy of education, led them to plan the establishment of separate professional schools of their own.

No "Haphazard Knowledge"

Santa Clara's growing estrangement from the new directions taken by secular education showed in other areas as well. While arguing for the inclusion of religious training in the educational process, spokesmen for the college also boasted that their institution remained one of the few in the state where a student could pursue a broad, classical course of studies. Electivism received a chilly reception at the mission school.

The period from 1870 to 1910 was the heyday of curricular laissez-faire in American education. Large numbers of colleges and universities, following in the footsteps of Harvard, abandoned a tightly structured curriculum in favor of the elective system. But Santa Clara, like most Jesuit schools, spurned specialization through elective courses as a "mere gathering of haphazard knowledge." The school held fast to the conviction that a broad, classical training constitutes the best undergraduate course of studies.

From its earliest days, however, the college had been forced by public demand to provide a few optional courses in the fine arts, modern languages, and commerce. But such concessions were few and granted to students of the classics only "with the proviso" that the core classical curriculum would be "in no wise tampered with."[55] By 1907 electivism had made greater inroads as specialized courses in journalism, elementary law, architecture, civil engineering, and premedicine were offered for the first time. These offerings remained modest, both because the institution could not yet afford to hire the specialists required and because the administrators and faculty were still unwilling to compromise their classical curriculum further.[56]

The Santa Clara catalog for 1906 stated the case against electivism. For the most part the curriculum, especially in the lower classes, is prescribed, the bulletin explained. The prescription is justified because no one can profitably specialize without a foundation on which to do so. "As to the character of this foundation, in all humility, we deem ourselves better judges than the pupils, howsoever gifted, who may come to us."[57] The college's opposition to the Harvard plan stemmed from the value placed on a full liberal arts curriculum by Jesuit tradition. This conviction was not an exclusive Jesuit concern. Other contemporary educators opposed the tendency to reduce undergraduate education to the acquisition of professional skills. According to Santa Clara's classicists, development of a student's intellectual and spiritual faculties by means of a "well graded curriculum" was still as important an object of the educational process as the imparting of knowledge itself.[58]

But the college was not blind to the social and vocational needs of its students. Jesuit pedagogy, while maturing students' faculties and fixing their habits, also sought to build a "firm, broad, solid and substantial foundation on which to erect the superstructure of particular callings."[59] But the emphasis at Santa Clara was on the broad rather than on the particular. Having acquired a certain degree of general culture, the student was then "in a pretty good condition to take up the study of a profession or a postgraduate course in a special study at a secular institution."[60] This was, in fact, the plan followed with considerable success by many students who, after completing their undergraduate studies at Santa Clara, pursued careers in law or medicine elsewhere.

When James F. Twohy, a graduate of the class of 1907, left Santa Clara to enroll in graduate studies at Harvard, his classical training aroused the interest of his professors. Impressed with the breadth of the young westerner's knowledge and with the range of subjects he had studied, the colorful Charles Townsend Copeland one day hailed his protégé into the office of President Charles Eliot for the purpose of a demonstration. Having often debated with Eliot the virtues of electivism, Copeland was eager to illustrate the validity of his arguments in favor of a structured curriculum. President Eliot quickly perceived the thrust of Copeland's tactic and inquired of Twohy, "You mean, young man, that you never had an elective at Santa Clara?" "Not exactly," Twohy replied, "one of the fathers told us, 'We offer you one elective here at Santa Clara: you can either take what we offer or leave!'"[61] Apparently, Twohy benefited from a strict academic diet of the classics, for he enjoyed a highly successful career in business and banking in the Pacific Northwest. During the Great Depression, President Franklin D. Roosevelt appointed him regional director of the Home Owners' Loan Corporation, which eventually helped refinance one of every five mortgaged private urban dwellings in America. In 1939 he was named Governor of the Federal Home Loan Bank system.

The time would shortly arrive when Santa Clara could no longer withstand the deluge of specialized subjects that the elective curriculum and the birth of new academic disciplines precipitated. In the meantime, though, the school resisted the floodtide. After all, the careers of turn-of-the-century graduates like James F. Twohy demonstrated that the traditional system was still capable of producing creditable results.

II
Los Angeles Beckons
1901–1911

As a consequence of the decision made in 1901 to rebuild Santa Clara College in the foothills of Mountain View, fund raising once again absorbed the administration's attention. During his last year as president, Robert Kenna launched a campaign to raise the initial $250,000 required to finance the move.[1] When his final term of office drew to a close in 1905, Kenna passed on responsibility for the drive to his successor, Father Richard Gleeson, who proceeded to tour the Far West, appealing to alumni and friends for support. Working as a team, the new president and Kenna also visited colleges in the East in search of practical advice and ideas before drawing up architectural plans for the new campus.

This campaign to build a "greater Santa Clara" commenced auspiciously with several large donations. From James D. Phelan, alumnus of St. Ignatius College, and from Andrew J. Welch, whose sons attended Santa Clara, came gifts of $10,000. Mrs. Bertha Welch of San Francisco pledged $50,000 toward the construction of the college's first building, a students' chapel, and Archbishop Riordan promised the lands owned by the archdiocese adjacent to the college tract "as a gift toward building the new Santa Clara College."[2]

Additional donations as well as income derived from the sale of property soon made it possible for Gleeson to discharge the debt on the 600 acre site. The land was graded and roads laid out. A "first-class dairy and creamery" was built on a section of the tract in order to provide the college with additional income. The extension of electric car lines to Loyola Corners, as the college station was named in honor of the projected campus, also augured well. Linked by rail with San Jose, Los Gatos, Menlo Park, and Palo Alto, the new Santa Clara looked forward to "a goodly number of day scholars" in addition to the expected four hundred boarding students.[3]

Earthquake and Fire

Nature, however, upset those plans. On the morning of April 18, 1906, the head prefect recorded in his logbook that "about 5:15 a terrific earthquake struck the College." "Thanks be to God no one [was] hurt," he hastily noted, and apart from the collapse of the old adobe California Hotel that housed the debating congress, "comparatively little harm was done."[4] The tremor turned statues in the college chapel by an angle of 130 degrees, but the building itself still stood. In nearby San Jose, roofs caved in and church steeples tumbled to the ground, causing thousands of dollars of damage. But the most tragic aftermath of the quake was at Agnew State Hospital for the Insane, where more than one hundred employees and patients, including many patients shackled to their beds, lay dead or dying in the rubble. Scores of Santa Clara students rushed to the hospital to help clear the debris and remove the victims from the ruins.[5]

That evening most of the students, too terrified to remain inside the buildings, dragged their beds from the dormitories to the safety of the baseball diamond. "Spread out across that northern sky," one witness later recalled, "was an aurora that heralded a terrible dawn of ruin and disaster. San Francisco was burning! With that red glow as a background, rolling its giant canopy of glare across the sky, we at Santa Clara held eight o'clock benediction in the yard."[6]

Similar disasters have played a notable role in the history of American higher education. Fire and flood, for example, contributed significantly to the high mortality rate of the many colleges founded during the nineteenth century. "It is amazing," writes historian Donald G. Tewksbury, "to discover the large number that met their fate through the working of natural catastrophes." Although earthquakes were chiefly a California phenomenon, destruction by fire was a common occurrence. Because of their inadequate resources, many colleges could not afford reconstruction after such a disaster.[7]

The great San Francisco holocaust changed the course of Santa Clara's history. Though the temblor of 1906 dealt more gently with the college than with other educational institutions located along the San Andreas Fault, the destruction of San Francisco weighed heavily on Santa Clara's plans for relocation. St. Ignatius College, whose million-dollar construction debt had been finally liquidated only a few years before, now lay in ruins. (Its senior class came down to Santa Clara to complete their last year.) Because the California Mission resolved to resurrect St. Ignatius from the ashes, the support that Santa Clara had counted on from Jesuit resources was now to be shared with the destitute and destroyed San Francisco school. Even worse, many of the promises of financial aid from laymen—aid that was essential for the new campus—had disappeared in the flames and smoke of the April holocaust. Losses sustained by the college's San Francisco benefactors forced them to withhold their pledges until their properties and incomes could be restored.

President Gleeson had hoped to begin construction in the spring of 1908,

After the earthquake of April 18, 1906, frightened Santa Clara students moved their beds outdoors to sleep in safety. This photograph shows beds spread out on the baseball diamond, which was located at the corner of Lafayette and Franklin streets. The three-story Science Building at the far right is on the site of the present Nobili Hall. *Courtesy: Archives, Univ. of Santa Clara.*

but it became apparent that removal to the tract in Mountain View would have to be postponed until the advent of "a more opportune time."[8] Three years after the San Francisco fire and earthquake, the future campus of Santa Clara remained open fields where herds of dairy cattle grazed.

Disaster struck again in 1909. On December 23, flames from a defective flue set fire to the wooden buildings in which administrative offices and the Jesuit community were housed and razed it nearly to the ground, leaving only the thick walls of adobe on the ground floor. The Jesuit community was suddenly homeless; the administration lost offices and records. Even the blueprints for the campus at Loyola were destroyed in the flames that en-veloped the president's office, a portent perhaps of greater disappointment to come. Because the dormitories and classroom buildings escaped the blaze, instruction resumed on schedule after the Christmas recess, but the Jesuits had to lodge in private homes in the neighborhood. In view of the impending change of campuses, everyone agreed it was preferable to undergo for awhile "the inconveniences of dispersion, great as they were," than to waste money on the construction of new quarters.

Dislocation of the faculty did force President Gleeson to "hurry along" with the development of Loyola Corners.[9] Reflecting on the sudden turn of events, his assistant, Robert Kenna, concluded that the recent misfortune might not be "an unmixed evil" after all, if it proved to be an occasion of beginning work on "the Greater Santa Clara College."[10] Accordingly, Gleeson intensified the campaign to move the school as soon as possible. Two weeks after the fire, on January 10, 1910, he and his staff met with a committee of alumni in San Francisco "to devise ways and means for raising funds for the new college." It was decided to begin construction within four months if sufficient cash could be raised.[11]

Despite the urgency of the appeal, the committee's goal proved impossible to attain.[12] The pledges collected fell far short of $250,000, the amount determined in 1904 as necessary to begin construction. With hopes dashed by the collapse of the emergency drive and by six years of fruitless waiting, Jesuit superiors reluctantly decided to abandon the long-contemplated plans for moving Santa Clara to Loyola Corners.

For Richard Gleeson the decision caused great disappointment, but before the summer was over he was removed from office and spared the humiliation of having to announce the failure of the project that had been his responsibility for five years. On July 31, 1910, the presidency of the college passed to Father James P. Morrissey, a very able thirty-eight-year-old member of the faculty.

Three months after taking office, Morrissey made public the results of the recent decision. "We could not build at Loyola without a very large sum of ready money," he explained candidly. Because this could not be obtained without shouldering a large, burdensome debt, there was no alternative but to abandon the plans for relocation. To friends who had donated funds, Morrissey promised that their gifts would be returned if they so wished.[13] Since the Loyola site had never enjoyed the unanimous approval of the faculty and alumni, the announcement was greeted with relief in some quarters. Having washed his hands of Loyola Corners, the energetic young president next turned to the task of broadening the territory of the cramped mission campus and erecting new buildings for which he had already acquired permission.[14]

The Lure of Los Angeles

While Morrissey plunged into plans to renovate, other developments raised again the possibility of finding a new site for the college. Loyola Corners was definitely eliminated, but it appeared that Santa Clara might relocate in Los Angeles. The sequence of events tempting the school southward began in 1908.

Jesuit superiors were attracted by the recent growth and promise of Southern California. They were eager to gain a foothold in Los Angeles. Forestalled for some time by the opposition of the Los Angeles clergy, the quiet plea of Jesuit administrators to "find a place for us" was finally answered in the summer of 1908. Bishop James T. Conaty offered Father George de la Motte, superior of the Jesuit California Mission, a parish in Santa Barbara. Though "not wishing [precisely] that place," de la Motte accepted Our Lady of Sorrows parish in hopes that this beginning would enable his successor to establish the Society of Jesus in Los Angeles itself. A few years later, when Herman J. Goller, first provincial of the newly created California Province, visited Conaty and reminded him "how pleased we would be to get into the city," the bishop put him off: the time was not yet ripe. "Have patience," he counseled the Jesuit, "and all will come out right."[15] As it turned out, the bishop had more in mind for the Jesuits than a parish ministry in Santa Barbara.

Conaty had concluded a less-than-successful term as rector of the Catholic University of America before assuming the administration of the Monterey–Los Angeles diocese in 1902. According to his biographer, Francis J. Weber, he was determined to redeem his Washington failure by founding a center of Catholic higher education on the West Coast. The "ideal launching pad for plummeting the Church into the lofty atmosphere of graduate studies" was Saint Vincent's College, since 1865 the leading Catholic school in Southern California. But the Vincentian fathers who ran the college resisted the prelate's proddings. They were unwilling to assume the indebtedness implicit in Conaty's ambitious plans to convert the institution into a full-fledged university. To break this educational logjam between himself and the Vincentians, Conaty introduced the Jesuits into his diocese, first by establishing them in the Santa Barbara parish and next by letting it be known that he favored their opening a school in San Diego or Pasadena. Strongly resentful of the bishop's pressure tactics and aware that Southern California

Richard Bell inspects the ruins after a fire in 1909 destroyed the Jesuit faculty residence built
during the Civil War. The old mission adobe upon which that building had been constructed
is visible; the ruins were later razed to make way for St. Joseph's Hall. The twin towers of the
mission church stand in the background. *Courtesy: Archives, Univ. of Santa Clara.*

could not support two similar institutions, the Vincentians responded in
1910 by giving notice of their complete retirement from educational work
in California. With the chief obstacle to his educational master plan removed,
the bishop turned to the Jesuits.[16]

Sometime in July, 1910, Bishop Conaty summoned Father Kenna, now
pastor of the Jesuit church in Santa Barbara, to the cathedral in Los Angeles.
There, Kenna records, he "broke to me the great news which came like a
bolt out of the clear sky": the Vincentians and the bishop wished the Jesuits
to accept the administration of Saint Vincent's College.[17]

Kenna immediately rushed north to confer with the California provincial, who was then hospitalized in Oakland. After a hasty bedside consultation with Kenna and other advisers, Goller sent word to the bishop of Los

Angeles that he could count on the Jesuits to fill within a year the vacuum left by the Vincentians. Goller died three months later at the age of forty-four. On his successor fell the thorny practical problem of implementing the promise to Conaty.

James A. Rockliff, a former missionary to Japan who had only recently arrived in California from New York, became provincial of the California Province on November 18, 1910. Though a stranger to the province and to its resources, Rockliff quickly perceived that Goller's "hurried and hasty" commitment to educational work on the collegiate level in Los Angeles posed a serious dilemma.[18] On the one hand, Rockliff wished to honor the virtual contract his predecessor had made with Conaty—especially because the father general himself had urged him to comply if possible with the bishop's request. On the other hand, the number of Jesuit teachers available at that time and in the near future clearly did not warrant opening a third college in California. Furthermore, acceptance of new responsibilities could not be supported by province funds. All the money the province can raise, Rockliff declared, was needed for the construction of a new scholasticate.[19]

What was to be done? After wrestling with the dilemma for several weeks, Rockliff decided that perhaps "the best means of redeeming Goller's promise" was the transfer of Santa Clara College to Los Angeles.[20] After all, Loyola Corners had been abandoned only a few months prior and the construction of new buildings on the mission campus had not yet begun. To facilitate the transfer and to ease the demand for personnel, Rockliff also pondered the possibility of abandoning Santa Clara's troublesome boarding department, which imposed "a heavy strain on our teachers and prefects" and was more and more difficult to maintain satisfactorily.[21] Relocation offered additional advantages, including an opportunity to escape from the shadow of "the two celebrated institutions," the University of California and Stanford University, alongside of which Santa Clara appeared "ridiculous."[22] A new site also held financial attractions for both Santa Clara and its sister institution, St. Ignatius College. Their proximity made it necessary for both colleges to recruit from more or less the same territory and to appeal to the same benefactors for funds. Consequently, separation promised benefits for both.[23]

The strongest argument against relocation was the powerful pull of tradition. Though the mission campus had fallen on hard times, it was nonetheless "hallowed" with "the great memories of the past" for the California Jesuits, especially those who had made the school their life's work. It was for this reason that the same faculty who had resisted Santa Clara's removal to Loyola Corners could be counted on to oppose the transfer to Los Angeles.[24]

Weighing the Pros and Cons

In early December, 1910, the provincial summoned Morrissey to his office in Spokane to discuss the proposal. Wishing to test widely the waters of Jesuit opinion, Rockliff also drew up a lengthy questionnaire that was distributed to nearly thirty-five priests of the province as a help to the provincial and his consultors in making the final decision. In the meantime, Rockliff instructed Morrissey to postpone construction of a new administration building planned for Santa Clara.[25]

The responses to Rockliff's query understandably were varied. Morrissey claimed no personal feeling in the matter, but he warned that it would be absolutely impossible to retain Santa Clara and to administer a college in Los Angeles at the same time. "We certainly are not in a position to take up a new college," he warned, because "we have so few men that we can scarcely struggle on as we are." "If we wish Santa Clara," he advised, "let the obvious conclusion be drawn and Los Angeles be regretfully refused. If we wish Los Angeles, let us be willing to make the necessary sacrifice" of Santa Clara.[26]

Two former presidents of the college, Fathers Kenna and Riordan, embraced the proposal with enthusiasm. The only arguments for remaining at the mission campus are "purely sentimental," Kenna declared. With "a hundred ties too deep and strong for words to express," Santa Clara's elder statesman admitted that "perhaps no one has as much reason as myself" to regret "leaving this old sainted ground." However, in light of "the tremendous advantages" offered by Los Angeles, "I without the least reservations say go, and go at once."[27] Joseph Riordan, historian and long-time advocate of a better campus, agreed. After all, Santa Clara College "had its birth not in what was planned freely," but under circumstances "determined by necessity and poverty." "Why bind the future to the past?"[28]

The possibility of converting the relocated institution from a boarding college to a day college appealed to not a few Jesuits. "Those who have been at any time associated with Santa Clara College," a former teacher wrote, "should well know how many [prefects] are needed to carry on the work, what a terrible drain it is on our men, how much energy expended, and how little, comparatively little, the return."[29] The provincial himself had admitted that boarding schools are used by not a few parents and looked upon by many students as a sort of reformatory school for young gentlemen.[30]

Termination of the boarding department would not only relieve teachers of the odium of doing police work as prefects, another man suggested, but it would also enable the college to divert to other purposes the money used to construct dormitories.[31]

Though at first professing indifference, President Morrissey ultimately revealed his dislike for the college's troublesome boarding department and his inclination towards Los Angeles. Predicting "nothing but darkness and gloom" for Santa Clara's future as a boarding college, Morrissey concluded that "not to use the present opportunity offered of gracefully relinquishing our boarding department . . . would be a mistake."[32] George de la Motte, former superior of the California Mission, emphatically agreed. Boarding colleges in general, especially at that time, were productive of little good, he advised the provincial, and they were "a great drawback" to young Jesuits assigned as prefects. "If the opportunity offers to suppress one, let us take it by all means."[33]

Other Jesuits strongly disagreed. "Why destroy the oldest and most renowned college we have?" Richard Bell demanded angrily.[34] "It is unreasonable to think of doing away with a well established boarding college," another wrote. He pointed out that Santa Clara was known all over California, and its influence, through its graduates, had made the Jesuits favorably known in all the various counties of the state.[35]

Several opponents of the proposal felt it had yet to be proved that boarding colleges are "an impossibility" and "the moribund institutions that some make them out to be."[36] Others conceded problems at Santa Clara, but suggested solutions. One blamed the alleged "failures" on maladministration; another blamed the college's outdated dormitories; a third felt that the admission of too many Protestant pupils and "dead-head" athletes lay at the root of the school's disciplinary problems.[37]

The view that competition from Stanford and the University of California had a harmful effect was also challenged. "I happen to know that the professors at Stanford entertain a high esteem for Santa Clara," one priest maintained, "and I cannot see that the reputation of the dear old College suffers from the proximity of Stanford."[38] Proximity to the great universities should promote emulation, another suggested. As for competition, it was considered to be out of the question because "serious Catholic parents," desiring a sound education, will still send their children to us for that purpose.[39] Others who questioned the proposal to move recognized that better-endowed institutions challenged Santa Clara, but they doubted that flight to

Los Angeles would provide a permanent solution. In time, a state university would come to Southern California, too, one priest predicted, "and unless you have built up a substantial institution, the New Santa Clara will go the way of the old."[40]

Finally, several Jesuits deplored the province's constant vacillation over Santa Clara's fate. "These changes of heart are not at all edifying," one pointed out.[41] The collapse of plans for Loyola Corners was humiliation enough, another suggested. "What will people think of us?" he wanted to know, if, after Morrissey had already announced plans to rebuild the mission campus, the plans are changed again?[42] The college treasurer agreed:

> After all our talk and collecting for a new and better Santa Clara College—after the newspaper notoriety the project has been given—after calling on the Town Board to close the streets for us—after buying a square block for more suitable grounds—after drawing two sets of plans, and all but setting the day for the breaking of ground, I don't see how we can hold up our heads before the people and tell them that we have decided to go bag and baggage to Los Angeles.[43]

The Final Decision

The divergence of Jesuit opinion expressed in the survey provided no definite mandate. Eighteen of the priests polled favored removal to Los Angeles, whereas sixteen advised that the college remain at its present site. It was significant, however, that among those who counseled transferring the institution were several Jesuits, including Morrissey and two ex-presidents, with long administrative or teaching experience at the college.

On the eve of the crucial consultation, President Morrissey rushed a last-minute appeal to the provincial, urging that he make the "necessary sacrifice" the next day by rejecting either Santa Clara or Los Angeles. He begged Rockliff not to attempt to occupy both places. It would be "simply ridiculous" to take up educational work in Los Angeles—even beginning on a small scale—and to retain Santa Clara at the same time, Morrissey warned. "We are stretching almost to the snapping point to eke out an existence with the colleges we now have."[44]

The following morning, March 22, 1911, Rockliff gathered his board of advisers in San Jose for the final decision. As their first item of business, the assembled Jesuits debated whether the full Vincentian college with all its debts should be accepted, as Father Goller had promised, or whether the province should begin its work with merely a high school. Thus it was taken for granted that the Society of Jesus would establish itself in Los Angeles; only the mode was debated. In view of the lack of teachers and the lack of money, it was decided to start an "incipient college" by first establishing a high school.

There followed a discussion of five day's duration regarding the fate of Santa Clara. In the discussion, "all the letters in favor of suppressing Santa Clara" in order to make "a better beginning in Los Angeles" were read. Finally, the consultors unanimously agreed to keep the college open. Thus the compromise solution that Morrissey had dreaded now became a reality.[45]

Only the briefest record remains of that fateful March consultation, and hence it is difficult to decide what arguments counted the most in the two decisions. The decision to establish a high school in Los Angeles is more easily explained. In light of Goller's commitment to Conaty, the urging of the father general, and the publicity given in the press to the expected transfer of Saint Vincent's to the Jesuits, it was inevitable that some form of educational work in Los Angeles would be approved.

Why Santa Clara was not closed is less clear. The lack of strong popular support for transferring the historic school southward, especially among the faculty, undoubtedly was a factor in the deliberations. Nonetheless, maintaining Santa Clara meant that the problem of overextension would plague the province for decades to come.[46] Rockliff later claimed that Archbishop Riordan's refusal to give "the requisite consent" to withdrawing the college from his diocese helped forestall its closing.[47] However, the sole reason recorded in the minutes of the San Jose consultation was that "a boarding school is necessary for the good of the province."[48] Though two thirds of the Jesuits polled had expressed dissatisfaction with precisely that feature of Santa Clara, the consultors evidently agreed with those who argued that better accommodations would remedy the problem.[49] A boarding school may be regarded as an evil, one of the consultors concluded, "but it is a necessary evil if we wish to extend the benefit of our education" throughout the state and beyond "to well-to-do families which do not happen to reside in the large cities." "Santa Clara has been a success in the past," he observed, and "it can be a success in the future," although "some reforms may be needed in its discipline."[50]

Would the decision have been different had Herman Goller lived? Perhaps. Having championed the long-awaited opening in Los Angeles and having been "not much in favor of boarding schools," Goller, by the force of his own personality and conviction, might have brought about a different result. To preserve his commitment to Conaty he might have ignored the opposition, closed Santa Clara, and transferred its staff southward.[51] In retrospect, all that is certain is that with his passing the movement to shift the Jesuit college to Los Angeles lost its chief advocate and principal architect.

The Aftermath

Whatever the reasons for the decision, its results proved less than satisfactory to all concerned. When Rockliff declared his unwillingness to accept the heavily indebted Vincentian campus in downtown Los Angeles, conflict erupted between him and Bishop Conaty over the selection of a new site for the school. Further confusion ensued when the Jesuits, contrary to an earlier agreement but acting on the advice of their attorney, refused to incorporate under the old name of Saint Vincent's College. After months of often bitter negotiations between Jesuits, bishop, and Vincentians, the new institution, eventually known as Loyola, opened its doors in the fall of 1911. But it was hardly the great Catholic center of higher education that Conaty, by his maladroit ouster of the Vincentians, had expected to create for his diocese. Nor did the new institution provide the "perfect continuity" with Saint Vincent's College that the Vincentians and their alumni had expected.[52] The old campus of the college was abandoned and a new site selected. Forced by a shortage of personnel to suspend all collegiate courses for three years, the Jesuits inaugurated their new endeavor as a high school with a staff of seven teachers.[53]

Even the Jesuits were not happy with the arrangement. Not only was Loyola for several years after its opening "beset with difficulties," but, as several Jesuits had predicted, its needs placed troublesome demands upon the meager resources of the California Province.[54] Despite Morrissey's warning that Santa Clara was already "struggling along with an inadequate staff," that school and St. Ignatius College both had to sacrifice teachers for work in Los Angeles.[55] The new institution also had harmful effects on the quality of education provided by all three schools. For decades to come, the extended demands for manpower and money would limit the province's ability to properly prepare its men for careers in college teaching. Consequently, though the California Province by 1911 had satisfied its longstanding wish to gain an apostolic foothold in Los Angeles, it paid a steep price for it.

12

From College to University
1910–1917

After nearly twenty years' debate over the college's future, in 1911 the California Jesuits committed themselves once again to the rebuilding of Santa Clara. The burden of transforming the institution from its "present wretched condition" into the long-contemplated "New Santa Clara" was shouldered by one of the province's promising young priests, James P. Morrissey.[1]

Morrissey was no stranger to the mission school. Born in nearby Santa Cruz, he attended the college, and he was graduated with honors in 1891. A month after commencement he entered the novitiate at Los Gatos. Eleven years later, garbed in clerical black, Jesuit seminarian Morrissey returned to the campus as a member of the faculty. Impressed by the affable young man's talents and maturity "beyond his years," President Kenna, a breaker of molds, appointed him prefect of studies and discipline, a vice-presidential post hitherto always held by a priest.[2] Although the appointment antagonized traditionalists among the faculty, the thirty-year-old seminarian proved popular, and he met his duties to Kenna's satisfaction. In 1904 Morrissey sailed to Holland for the theology studies that constituted the final stage of his Jesuit training.

Five years later, Morrissey was back at Santa Clara, fresh from a successful course of studies in Europe and full of enthusiasm. He was shocked at the deterioration of the college during his years abroad. Furthermore, he was puzzled by President Gleeson's inactivity, for Morrissey "saw at a glance what needed to be done" to modernize the campus, the course of studies, and student discipline. He found a sympathetic ear in Herman Goller, recently appointed provincial of the California Province and "a young man of ambitions" similar to Morrissey himself. Morrissey's complaints were thought to have occasioned Gleeson's removal from office a year later, though Gleeson's failure as a fundraiser may also have led to his replacement.[3] On July 31, 1910, Morrissey was named rector-president of the college.

Concrete Replaces Wood

Morrissey had been disappointed at the decision to maintain the college in Santa Clara rather than transferring it to Los Angeles. Once the decision was made, however, he moved ahead with plans to rebuild the school and to carry out the province's plan of transforming it into a university.

The first task was the physical rehabilitation of the campus. This undertaking was made somewhat easier by an act of the trustees of the town of Santa Clara who, to "keep the grand old institution here on the site of its founding," agreed to close Alviso Street, which had for years divided the campus in two.[4] The college thus possessed a twenty-three-acre block of property for its new buildings.

After the failure of the drive to move the college to Loyola Corners, only two benefactors had demanded their money be returned, and hence some funds were available to begin building immediately.[5] On March 31, 1911, Morrissey signed a contract to begin construction of a new administration building, the first in a series of twelve structures his ambitious master plan envisioned. As soon as the school term ended, building materials were transported directly onto the campus by a spur track laid out by the Southern Pacific Railroad from its nearby mainline depot. Within a year the task was completed. At a cost of $105,000, the college boasted a new Administration Building (the present St. Joseph's Hall), designed to house both the Jesuit faculty and administrative offices.[6]

Morrissey then unveiled plans for a second structure, a three-story building containing classrooms on the ground floor and dormitories on the second and third stories. It was to rise on the site of the old California Hotel, whose adobe walls had fallen in the earthquake of 1906. Because his cash reserve was depleted, Morrissey's latest proposal was carefully scrutinized by the province consultors.[7] After obtaining a generous loan from a benefactor of the college, Morrissey was granted permission to spend $95,000 to erect Senior Hall (O'Connor Hall today).[8]

Thus, after barely more than a year in office, President Morrissey had greatly altered the face of the campus. Built of reinforced concrete and described by engineers as being "as imperishable and as everlasting as modern science and experience could make them," the two new structures stood in sharp contrast to the timeworn edifices of brick and wood that occupied the rest of the college grounds. Planted on opposite sides of the mission church —which was itself slated for eventual replacement—Morrissey's matching halls formed the eastern flank of a great quadrangle around which, according

The construction of St. Joseph's Hall in 1911 signaled the long-delayed modernization of the Santa Clara campus. Building materials were transported to the site by a spur railroad track, shown in the foreground. Soon after the building program began, the fence that had for generations enclosed the campus (a portion of it is pictured at the far left) was torn down. *Courtesy: Archives, Univ. of Santa Clara.*

to his grand design, a new library, chapel, observatory, gymnasium, and other buildings would rise. The "arched colonnades and red-tiled roof" of each of the new halls contributed to the handsome "mission" architectural style that set a precedent for all of the buildings erected on the Santa Clara campus during the next half-century.[9]

End of the Era of the Fence

While walls of concrete rose across the campus at the new president's command, barriers of another type came down. It was the conviction of Morrissey and several other Jesuits with experience at the college that the oppressive duties entailed in maintaining Santa Clara's traditional student discipline cried out for correction.[10] The stringent norms whereby students were kept day and night under the thumb of prefects seemed to many Jesuits no longer compatible with "the growing spirit of freedom"—as one of them put it—manifested by "liberty-loving American youth."[11] Moreover, the enforcement of the customary regimen constituted a terrible drain on the faculty, and was also a source of serious intellectual, physical, and religious detriment to the young scholastics assigned to the college as prefects.[12] Indeed, it was precisely because continuous enforcement of discipline had become so intolerable that Morrissey and like-minded Jesuits had welcomed the opportunity to close the school and its troublesome boarding department and to escape to a new beginning in Los Angeles. When this option vanished, the president turned to the implementation of reforms.

Morrissey caused life in the dormitories to improve somewhat by providing better accommodations. In place of the old study halls, which had been customarily employed to keep "the students' noses in the books" and to forestall "rebellion" during nonclass hours, the new dormitory floors offered private rooms for collegiate students. Gone without replacement was the ancient "rising bell" hanging near the refectory door, whose clanging had summoned students from sleep every morning and had sent them on their daily rounds. Even the replacement of the primitive outdoor facilities with modern toilets and running water in the new Senior Hall (today's O'Connor Hall) was seen as a step toward restoring order to the physical and intellectual chaos that had reigned before.[13] The construction of more modern facilities also was calculated to improve discipline by attracting to the college "a better class of boys."[14]

The most dramatic sign of the new era of reform was the razing of the high board fence that had encircled the campus since 1856. It was removed in the process of erecting the building now known as St. Joseph's Hall. The passing of this ancient bulwark was greeted with "shock" and alarm by many of the aging Italians still in residence. Some of the old guard predicted that a complete deterioration in discipline and school spirit would follow. "With the fences gone," the students gloried in the "relief," a younger Jesuit recorded, and they did not commit the crimes prophesied by the old-timers, nor did they lose the family spirit, "so highly extolled when behind the fences." In fact, "the spirit of the student body became cooperative in the highest degree."[15]

The students rejoiced. For with the collapse of the wooden ramparts fell also many of the regulations that had for generations been more effective than the fence itself in curtailing student interaction with the world beyond the campus. New policies regulating student conduct now appeared. Although not as liberal as the norms enforced at other institutions, they allowed Santa Clara to move slowly into the twentieth century. For example, the school catalog issued in 1912 announced that, in addition to the customary Christmas recess, vacations "at the discretion of the President" could now be granted at Thanksgiving and at Eastertime.[16] Older students were occasionally given permission to go out "even at night"; and for the first time in the history of the school a formal dance was celebrated within the college confines.[17] Though the distinction between day scholar and boarder continued, the well-defined line that had separated one group from the other began to disappear as an effort was made to treat the two groups with the same respect.[18]

Academic Renewal

The academic changes Morrissey effected to transform the college into Santa Clara University were of greater significance for the institution's future. As a starting point toward realizing "more strict and more stringent" academic standards, the school subjected applicants for admission to a more "judicious selection."[19] In place of a vague request for "satisfactory recommendations" from another college or school, Santa Clara now required candidates to pass entrance examinations and to have completed a regular four-year high-school course.[20] Having promised to make "an earnest effort" to meet the "pressing need" for financial aid for talented but needy students, the school in 1912 announced its first perpetual scholarship.[21]

As a second step in the transition of Santa Clara from a "nondescript" institution with "an infant school on one end and degrees at the other" (as one Jesuit described it), Morrissey emphasized college-level programs. He quickly terminated the preacademic department.[22] After 1911, students of junior-high-school age, who had previously been allowed to board at the college while attending classes at an off-campus school, were no longer admitted. However, another ten years would pass before finances would permit the high school's transfer to a separate campus. In the meantime, the distinction between secondary and collegiate instruction was sharpened.

New directions in American education had prepared the way for Morrissey's third step. The appearance of schools of professional education had forced the generality of American high schools and undergraduate colleges to train students in a greater variety of subjects. Santa Clara, like most Catholic institutions with a classical tradition, was slow to provide such curricular specialization, especially in view of the high cost of multiplying courses and hiring additional teachers. But the change had become inevitable. As more and more of its graduates sought admission to professional schools that required four years of standard college work, including undergraduate preparation in a given field of specialization, Santa Clara had been obliged to conform increasingly to the standards of the contemporary academic world. The changes in undergraduate programs had affected the preparatory department because the college had found it necessary to shift some of its traditional subject matter to the secondary level to make way for professional requirements.[23]

Thus Santa Clara in 1902 had broken up its integrated five-year course of classical studies. The curriculum had been reorganized so that the secondary and collegiate departments were each expanded into a separate four-year program. The classical collegiate designations "humanities," "poetry," "rhetoric," and "philosophy" had ceded for the first time to the American titles of "freshman," "sophomore," "junior," and "senior."

In 1907 the school had introduced a modest number of professional offerings for undergraduates. Students might elect courses in law, engineering, journalism, or premedicine. Though mental development and broad cultural training still were regarded as "the ideal manner of procedure," the college had acknowledged further the demands for specialization that an expanding American capitalism had thrust upon the schools.

Morrissey now initiated the third step, a distinct increase in professional courses. In 1912 the school announced that because many students were disinclined to "base their professional studies" upon a "broad and solid" liberal arts foundation and because other institutions offered them "facilities for taking up professional studies on the completion of a standard high school course," Santa Clara would henceforth make its curriculum more oriented to the professions.[24]

The undergraduate courses in law, engineering, journalism, and premedicine were expanded. The Bachelor of Science degree, discontinued since 1891, was reintroduced, enabling students in the newly organized College of General Science to substitute modern languages and literature for Latin and Greek and to choose electives from the college's broadened course offerings. Even students enrolled in the classical course were allowed an occasional elective. However, the core of the traditional Jesuit liberal arts curriculum was preserved inasmuch as courses in philosophy and religion continued to be required for all students.

A College of Engineering was established. It offered courses leading to the degree of bachelor of civil, mechanical, electrical, or industrial engineering, but the size of the staff and the quality of the laboratories did not yet make it outstanding.[25] A short-lived College of Architecture also appeared in 1912, and a College of Agriculture went into the planning stage, where it remained.

The founding of an Institute of Law, proposed by many Jesuits for a long time as a counter to the growing influence of state schools in that field, was accomplished in 1912. It began to attract many of the college's graduates. Some of Santa Clara's most prominent alumni were lawyers and judges, and it was hoped that their support would help to sustain the new institute. It was further hoped that the institute would develop great influence because of the ever-increasing popularity of law among career-minded graduates.

The new institute was relatively inexpensive to establish. Unlike engineering or medicine, law required few items of investment besides the library and the faculty, the latter being recruited from local attorneys and judges, most of them alumni who agreed to serve as part-time teachers. As was true of most Catholic institutions, law also was accepted because it complemented the college's humanistic orientation and concern for ethical issues. The institute began on a reduced scale by offering a two-year course of night study, open to both college graduates and students who had completed two years of undergraduate schooling.

From College to University

President Morrissey's goal was to create in the West "a great Catholic University."[26] To this end he raised entrance standards, stressed college-level work, and expanded the curriculum from an exclusively classical course to include undergraduate programs in engineering, architecture, and law as well as an improved premedical course. Although the only degree of graduate level that Santa Clara offered was the Master of Arts diploma and

"The Smoking Room Gang." Tobacco, once a forbidden indulgence, was permitted by the turn of the century. George Sedgley, the mustachioed director of the commercial department, stands at far right. *Courtesy: Archives, Univ. of Santa Clara.*

although the new undergraduate colleges were still of doubtful university caliber, Morrissey felt that the reorganization of the curriculum now justified Santa Clara's assuming the title of university.

The occasion for celebrating the change was the commencement of June, 1912, which also witnessed the official opening of the school's two new halls. The months of promotional work and travel by which Morrissey prepared for the event proved that the president recognized the value of public relations. The celebration generated extensive publicity in the press and drew thousands of guests to the campus, where they witnessed the day's highlight, a series of elaborate historical tableaux. Taking as their theme "the passing of the old and the coming of the new," the tableaux presented costumed actors who portrayed Santa Clara's evolution during 135 years, beginning with a parade celebrating the establishment of the Spanish mission in 1777 and including a representation of Nobili's founding of the college in 1851. The colorful presentation culminated in the inauguration of the university and the distribution of diplomas to the class of 1912, the last class to graduate from Santa Clara College.[27]

Though the celebration devoted much attention to Santa Clara's past sixty-one years of "solid achievement" as a college, President Morrissey admitted that his own interest turned "with instinctive choice" not to the past, but to the future. Having struggled against considerable odds to bring about the day of celebration, Morrissey knew that more than sentiment was needed to sustain the school's new commitments and its future growth. "The future is what makes an active human life worth living," he declared. "The past in no human life, however brilliant it may have been, is provocative of man's best energies." Santa Clara, in Morrissey's view, must now forget the past. "The University of Santa Clara is not conducted on the ideas prevailing fifty years, or even ten years ago. Though the principles of Christian philosophy and pedagogy will always be fundamentally the same," he concluded, for the sake of progress the Jesuits must "give to their students whatever is best in modern methods and facilities."[28]

Morrissey's Downfall

Morrissey's strong advocacy of change and his initial success in revitalizing Santa Clara did not prevent tragic consequences for himself. Students cheered the passing of Santa Clara's "Dickens-type school buildings and customs." They recognized the attractive personal qualities that the energetic young president brought to his office, and they felt "great admiration and strong affection" for him.[29] Young members of the faculty, too, were enthusiastic in their praise: "We who worked under him," recalled a Jesuit scholastic from the high-school department, "all loved him for his character, respected his intelligence," and "marveled at his industry." But there were others who resented his innovations. For the older members of the Jesuit faculty, "most of them European by origin and most of them in their dotage," according to a young member, Morrissey's style of governance, his sudden reforms in college discipline, and indeed "his every move" burst upon them like a "bombshell."[30]

From the very start of his administration complaints began to mount. Some of the faculty were convinced that the new president alone was responsible for the proposal to transfer Santa Clara to Los Angeles, and they resented his willingness to close the school.[31] But the zeal with which he subsequently launched the college upon the path of reform and loosened traditional discipline caused the greatest alarm. Before long, letters inundated the father general in Rome, Franz Wernz, condemning both Morrissey's innovations and his style of governance.[32]

The complaints were as varied as they were multiple, but they all protested Morrissey's break with the customary Jesuit way of doing things. Some of the old guard grumbled that Morrissey made all his decisions by himself and avoided consultation. His constant travels up and down the state, organizing alumni clubs and soliciting funds, brought more criticism. The liberty he granted himself and the freedom he allowed his assistants, including the normally sequestered scholastics, were further shocks. Also, it was alleged, he had spoken ill of Archbishop Riordan, a serious transgression in the minds of many obedience-oriented sons of St. Ignatius.[33]

The conflict between the president and his small band of letter-writing critics intensified during Morrissey's second year in office. By the spring of 1913, the complaints received in Rome about his administration caused the father general to issue a stern warning: Morrissey was to govern Santa Clara "according to our laws, not his."[34]

These and other difficulties afflicted young Morrissey's sensitivity. "I personally should find it too hard to go another year such as this has been," he informed the provincial after less than a year in office. "At times the anxiety has been such that I felt on the verge of a break-down."[35] In Father Rockliff, provincial of the California Province, Morrissey seems to have found little support or sympathy. Rockliff had only recently arrived in California from the Far East and knew "little or nothing of the Province" and "much less" of its men. It was claimed later that he gave more credence to Morrissey's critics than he did to Morrissey.[36]

During the next two years Morrissey's anxiety gradually turned to repugnance for his work. The "unpleasant" (his word) tasks he had to perform pushed him into deep depression. Life at Santa Clara was still, as the dean of the College of Engineering put it, "a battle of wits between faculty and students." Running the problem-plagued boarding school and trying to transform it overnight into a full-fledged university gradually drove Morrissey to the breaking point. He offered "several times" to resign, and early in 1913 he informed the Jesuit general that "it is impossible for me to continue." He strongly requested reassignment.[37] In late May, 1913, word came from Rome that Morrissey was to be replaced.[38] He remained at Santa Clara until graduation, preparing for the transfer of authority to his successor. Then, amid a whirl of rumors and accusations, Morrissey said goodbye to the campus that, at no small cost to himself, he had revitalized.

In the years that followed James Morrissey passed unhappily from one minor post to another in Jesuit parishes in California and the East. Finally, after severing all relations with his former acquaintances and with his health shattered by the traumatic experiences at Santa Clara, he left the Jesuit order. The complex chain of events leading to Morrissey's eventual collapse and his own role in that tragedy remain unclear, but in the judgment of contemporaries the principal cause was the opposition of his fellow Jesuits. "Santa Clara was ready for his innovations," one of his young admirers sadly concluded years later, "but the 'elder statesmen' were not."[39] Morrissey himself offered the same explanation a few years later in reference to his departure from the Jesuits: "I had disagreed with the educational policies of the Order in a very emphatic manner and endeavored to bring about what I deemed essential changes in it."[40]

Father Thornton's Reaction

It was ironic that the man sent to replace Morrissey in 1913 had confided privately to him a few years earlier that if Santa Clara was maintained as a boarding school, "no rector will ever go there without a sore pain in his heart."[41] Confronted with a student riot within months of his arrival and an influenza epidemic at his departure three years later, Father Walter Thornton's apprehensions proved well founded. The "corpulent and austere" former master of novices discovered additional reasons to lament his assignment soon after his arrival.[42]

Thornton's first worry appeared in the form of a $237,000 debt that he inherited from his predecessor's costly development program. Overwhelmed with bills, having no money allotted to pay them, and finding only $200 in the university vault, Thornton described his first months at Santa Clara as "exceedingly difficult." At his direction the university undertook heavy borrowing to keep its creditors at bay. His campaign to reduce spending led Thronton to reexamine some of the academic programs that Morrissey had created. Worried how he would pay for all the courses now advertised in the bulletin, especially the expensive offerings in mechanical and electrical engineering, the new president hit upon a simple if drastic solution. Thornton explained to Father Wernz, the Jesuit general in Rome:

My first object was to eliminate expenses that were useless. This I did by dismissing four secular teachers who were not needed, thereby saving $3,170 per year [and] by discharging a number of workmen who were not absolutely needed. I have stopped all building and refused to carry out the plans of my predecessor which I considered impossible in our present financial condition.[43]

As a result of strict budgeting, Santa Clara was all but debt-free by the time Thornton vacated the presidential chair five years later. His budgeting was aided by the fact that during his term the university fell heir to several large benefactions. Always quick to blame his financial woes on the "tangled" affairs of his predecessor, Thornton was slow to acknowledge that Morrissey's administration was largely responsible for many of the gifts that seemed to appear fortuitously during his own troubled tenure.

Thornton was also unsympathetic to certain of Morrissey's academic innovations. The classical course had suffered under his predecessor's neglect, he complained, and "the other courses have been made attractive and easier of accomplishment." Greek was almost eliminated, he informed his superiors, and Latin amounted to little. The new president intended to redress the balance.[44]

In addition, Thornton made efforts to return student behavior to the more traditional and familiar path from which it had been allowed to stray during Morrissey's rule. This endeavor was not always successful. A student revolt erupted in November, 1913. Angry because the new president had curtailed a number of privileges they had formerly enjoyed, one hundred students refused one evening to attend compulsory chapel.

To the keen embarrassment of the administration, Bay Area newspapers carried headline accounts of the strike. "Singing and giving the college yells," the student rebels gathered in front of the senior dormitory and then, their courage bolstered by the absence of the president and the prefect of discipline, the group "still singing" marched to the city park, where they held a mass meeting to protest the strict regulations governing their conduct. Some spirited members of the group proposed they cap their night of protest and revelry by seizing a nearby tram car and running it on "a personally conducted tour of San Jose." More prudent views prevailed, however, and eventually all the protesters returned to the campus for less adventurous hell raising before retiring for the night. A few days later seven students, including two star players from the varsity rugby team, were suspended from school. Milder punishments were handed out to lesser offenders.[45]

Directions of Change

Although stricter discipline prevailed for a time in the aftermath of the rebellion, it was impossible to restore the nineteenth-century code of student behavior that Morrissey's reforms had overturned. Academically too, despite reappraisals and cutbacks, old molds had been irreparably broken. What Morrissey had begun, neither Thornton nor his successors could undo. However, a continuing scarcity of resources placed severe restrictions upon their ability to build upon the foundations Morrissey had laid. The beginnings he had realized during his brief three-year reign were not abandoned,

President James P. Morrissey, who modernized the university but whose three years in office had tr
consequences for his own well-being. *Courtesy: Archives, Univ. of Santa Clara.*

but decades after his departure Santa Clara was still a long way from the "great Catholic university" he had tried to create overnight.

Santa Clara's transition from a college to a university, in the full sense of that term, would inevitably and necessarily be slow. "To maintain the University according to the university methods introduced by Father Morrissey and accepted by his successors," one Jesuit contemporary observed, "taxed the resources of the institution to the utmost."[46] Thornton's cutbacks underscored the problem. George Sullivan, dean of the College of Engineering, recalled the conditions prevailing in his department upon his arrival in 1912. Because the university "did not have the money to properly equip the laboratories or to hire enough teachers," the dean was obliged to teach "as many as twenty-eight hours per week," and although classes were small, the other faculty members carried nearly as heavy a load.[47] Conditions were no better in the Institute of Law. For years it functioned as a night school only. Most of the faculty were lawyers from San Jose, many of them alumni who maintained their legal practices during the day and generously offered their services to Santa Clara as teachers at night. Another twenty years would pass before *any* college of the university boasted a professor who held a Ph.D.

Whether Morrissey, if his health had enabled him to remain at the helm, could have done any better than his immediate successors in molding Santa Clara into a full-fledged university is problematic. No matter who occupied the presidential chair, the institution's penury imposed strict limits on any administrator's ambition. The Jesuit order frowned on deficit spending, and without surplus funds it was difficult if not impossible to hire faculty educated in the best graduate schools, to implement innovative academic programs, to expand curricula, or to build well-equipped libraries and laboratories.

The conservatism of the Jesuit leadership also slowed Santa Clara's evolution. Not only was the order too impoverished to hire qualified laymen in sufficient numbers, but it also was unwilling to train its own men for university positions. When the superior of the California Jesuits in 1908 hesitatingly discussed with Father General Franz Wernz the possibility of sending "some of our young men to state universities" to equip them for teaching in Jesuit colleges and universities, Wernz found the plan unacceptable. The Californians readily acquiesced in his reasoning: It would be inconsistent to send Jesuits to "state or atheistic" universities "when we are at the same time using every means at our command to deter Catholic boys or young laymen from going to the same places of learning."[48]

Thus the proposal was dropped. For decades thereafter, superiors steadfastly refused to countenance graduate studies at the best universities for cloister-bound Jesuits, a policy that no one—except a few discredited visionaries like Morrissey—questioned.[49] Not until the 1930's did the California Province send its men to state universities for graduate training and higher degrees to prepare them for careers in teaching and administration.

The historic decision of 1911 to develop three institutions of higher learning frustrated Santa Clara's premature grasp at university honors. The limited reservoir of Jesuit manpower and money retarded the evolution of all three schools. The setbacks suffered by Loyola College in Los Angeles (the former St. Vincent's) have already been described. By 1915 the troubles sustained by the two northern schools, Santa Clara and St. Ignatius, led one Jesuit to urge a merger. Why such a drastic solution? Its aim was to do away with the burden of providing "a double staff" of the higher faculties and to end "the existing absurdity" of two Jesuit institutions—"universities in name only"—within fifty miles of each other.[50]

No one dared to disturb the time-hallowed status quo, however, and each school stubbornly continued to get by as best it could. Consequently the sudden transformation begun by Morrissey required decades to accomplish.

His innovations were not wasted. They were his legacy to Santa Clara, his dream and ideal passed on to those successors with the vision and courage to pursue them. In gadfly fashion, Morrissey introduced the institution to university methods and committed it to goals more in conformity with the directions being taken by contemporary American higher education. He gave Santa Clara new purpose, and he deserves remembrance as one of the university's pivotal presidents.

13
Doughboys and Quarterbacks
1917–1930

Local issues yielded suddenly and dramatically in 1917 to larger concerns. "We are in a great world war," the campus magazine announced, "in fact, the greatest that has ever come to pass."[1] On April 6, 1917, President Woodrow Wilson obtained a declaration of a state of war from Congress. The European war now had become a world war.

Seven days after Congress passed its historic resolution, President Walter Thornton and the board of trustees offered the U.S. War Department the use of "our entire facilities"—halls, classrooms, laboratories, and grounds—for the purpose of training troops. While awaiting the reply from Washington, Santa Clara hastily transformed the entire student body into a cadet corps. Throughout the spring, military drill was part of the daily routine.[2] Everyone was enthusiastic and eager to do his part in the "war to end war."

"Lafayette, We Are Here"

In Europe that summer, Colonel Charles Stanton, a former Santa Clara student, uttered the phrase that became the rallying slogan for American forces. Sometimes mistakenly attributed to General Pershing, the words were spoken by Stanton on the Fourth of July, 1917, when Pershing asked him to address the crowds that had welcomed the American troops to Paris. The American Expeditionary Force, appearing in the French capital for the first time, was participating in the ceremonial laying of a wreath at the tomb of Lafayette. Standing beneath a statue of the famous French nobleman, Stanton announced dramatically to France and to the world the entry of American troops into the conflict: "Lafayette, we are here."[3] Before the war drew to its bloody conclusion, hundreds of other Santa Clarans would join Stanton in the great campaign that President Wilson had declared because "The world must be made safe for democracy."

To students returning to Santa Clara in the autumn of 1917, the campus was remarkably different. The War Department had established on campus an infantry unit within the Reserve Offiers' Training Corps. Captain Joseph

Donovan, a West Point graduate and the head of the university's civil engineering department, was called back to Santa Clara from active duty at Fort
Douglas, Utah, to head the unit. At the time the unit was believed to offer
the only ROTC program provided by any institution of higher learning in
the West. The program enabled students to receive military training while
completing their studies. Later, if conscripted, they would enter the Army
as commissioned officers.

January 20, 1918, was "the day chosen to proclaim . . . to the world at
large," as one student put it, what had already been in effect at Santa Clara for
months. The ROTC was officially inaugurated, and Santa Clara University
became "a strictly military institution." The occasion called for a special
oration, and alumnus Delphin Delmas addressed the student body, faculty,
and guests that night in the university theater. If any persons in the crowd
entertained secret doubts concerning the justification of American participation in the crusade from which hitherto "we have done everything in our
power to keep aloof," Delmas put their minds at ease. "The war in which our
country is engaged is a just war, just by every standard of human and divine
justice, just, just and a thousand times just." For the students, he had special
advice: "And remember, young men, why you are in war, why you are going
to participate in this war. You will answer me that as good Americans it is
sufficient to know that your country wills it, and that what she demands can
not be but right; but right or wrong, not yours to question why, yours but to
do, aye, and if need be, die."[4]

Registering at the university that autumn resembled military enlistment.
The school had become a training camp. Santa Clara is "the only institution
of university standing in the Western Department whose cadets live in barracks and are under constant military discipline," reported an official Army
visitor.[5] Uniforms and arms had been distributed to the student body, and
daily drill and military lectures were listed in the regular curriculum. For
boarding students, the "brazen blast of the bugle" regulated all activities, beginning with reveille in the morning and ending with taps at night. "The
dear Government has stepped in and routs us out even an hour earlier,"
one student complained. Meals, class changes, and chapel time were all announced by the bugle, and so was the dismissal of afternoon classes, after
which the entire student body assembled for drill and maneuvers.[6] The university's soldier-students were moved from their private rooms in O'Connor Hall to barracklike quarters in the building known as the Ship. The private lodgings were turned over to the high-school department, to the delight
of the new occupants.

"All the world rings with war," a student wrote in 1918. "It is in the air, in our buttonholes, pinned on our lapels and penned in the periodicals." A special section of the university magazine contained the latest letters received from former students, now doughboys abroad, detailing their impressions of army life, their days in the Atlantic crossing, and their experiences on the front and expressing their inevitable nostalgia for news of home and the campus. When a Canadian war hero visited the university to share "what he saw and what he helped to do [and] what he suffered while a prisoner among the Germans," for two hours he kept the student body spellbound. When the militarized routine of campus life grew tedious, students thought of bleeding Belgium and the hardships sustained by distant companions in the trenches "over there."[7]

Caught up in a sense of adventure and convinced that they were sharing the sufferings of the war, most students welcomed the interruptions of campus routine. Some even found unexpected advantages in their new way of life. Wearing uniforms had an advantage, one student discovered, that "I feel confident in saying . . . was never intended by the Government, but which strongly appeals to us" of the ROTC. "Garbed alike, from a distance we look alike," he explained, "a fact not to be entirely disregarded or lightly sneezed at when there is a watchful Prefect to be taken into consideration. Formerly, when slipping out into town at forbidden time, we . . . would pull our hat over our eyes so as not to be detected. . . . But now that we all look like twin brothers, we can scarcely be distinguished at a few hundred feet, the more so when the shades of night are our allies."[8]

In time, however, the novelty of military life began to wear thin. By the spring of 1918 the spirit of adventure yielded to concern and uncertainty with regard to the future. The draft replaced volunteer enlistment, and students became conscious of the possibility of a call to the front. By April, one of every three college men at Santa Clara had gone to war. As the fighting intensified, the War Department unveiled its plan to convert the ROTC program into the Students' Army Training Corps. Participants in the new plan, though assigned to a SATC unit on their home campus, were fully incorporated into the Army.

"One can never tell what changes a few months will bring," the student editor of The Redwood observed in 1918, and "it is probably not long that we shall be together." "Almost every day, it seems, some old familiar face" is missed and "we're told, 'he's gone to join the colors.' " Old pals are being taken away one by one, the editor sighed, and "when you feel all alone and you look around for sympathy and consolation, only to find your friends have disappeared—then it is that you feel discouraged." That, he summarized, is "pretty much the way we are now at Santa Clara."[9]

This atmosphere of pessimistic uncertainty was intensified in the fall, when an epidemic of influenza swept through the university. Part of a worldwide pestilence that eventually felled more Americans than did German bullets (the virus left more than half a million dead in the United States alone), the epidemic hit the university neighborhood in early October, 1918. All the day students were sent home immediately, and the boarders were ordered not to go outside the campus if at all possible. But the contagion spread. Finally, Captain Donovan, in the name of the War Department, commanded that the mission church be closed to the public until further notice. "No student [is] allowed to leave [the] premises. Sentinels [have been] stationed at all exits on our grounds." No one could enter the campus confines unless it was absolutely necessary.[10]

Five days after it first appeared in Santa Clara the influenza struck with full force. It "came on us with a rush today," a Jesuit noted on October 23, as forty students fell suddenly ill. Within a few days two students were dead and scores of others were hospitalized.[11] In San Jose and in San Francisco, the wearing of gauze masks was prescribed by law. The masks could be removed in public only under penalty of jail and fine. The measure was ineffectual. Hospitals continued to fill to overflowing, and graves could not be dug fast enough to receive the dead.

Then in November the double scourge of pestilence and war dramatically ended. On November 11 the early morning stillness of the town of Santa Clara was broken by the sounds of tolling church bells and blowing whistles: the German Kaiser had fled to Holland and the armistice had been signed. Three days later the quarantine under which the university had been placed was lifted. The city of San Jose "went wild as citizens threw off their gauze masks and cheered. The battle was over on both fronts and they had survived."[12]

Return to "Normalcy"

After weeks of concern about influenza and after more than a year of military discipline and rule, university life returned to its normal routine. With the lifting of the influenza quarantine, classes resumed. Gone were the gauze masks and the sentinels at the campus gates. Two weeks after the armistice a telegram from the War Department informed university authorities that demobilization of the campus SATC unit would be carried out immediately. More than one hundred soldier-students sent by the Army to the university turned in their uniforms and departed. Colonel Donovan's staff bade Santa Clara good-bye.

Homeward bound, June, 1914. Students prepare to load their trunks on a horse-drawn wagon behind O'Connor Hall dormitory for transport to the railroad station before returning home for the summer. *Courtesy: Archives, Univ. of Santa Clara.*

Returning students found the campus much as it had been before the war. The familiar cassock-clad Jesuits once again were in full control of the school—except for President Walter Thornton. With the passing of the wartime crisis he received a new assignment, and he handed the reins of government to a younger Jesuit, Timothy Murphy.

Although most Americans preferred to forget the war as soon as possible, the conflict had left a legacy of knowledge about foreign enmities not easily dismissed. It had also given a new perspective to some prewar issues that continued to be debated at home and abroad. One of these was the question of Irish independence. Given new encouragement by the postwar emphasis on the principle of national self-determination, the movement to gain home rule for Ireland stirred sympathetic feelings at the university. Since Kenna's time, poets and politicians from that troubled island had been received warmly by the Irish Catholics who constituted a large percentage of the faculty and student body. In the years after World War I, when the movement reached a fever pitch, the university threw its full support into the campaign for Irish independence.

At a public rally held at the university in March, 1920, President Murphy subscribed $1,000 toward the drive for Irish freedom. "It is against being England's vassal that Ireland is objecting," the president declared in a "spirited address" in which he castigated England, who at this moment "all but controls the United States."[13] When independence became a reality in 1921, Santa Clara rallied with other Irish-Americans in support of the new Free State. During the spring term almost the entire student body joined together to form the Kevin Barry Branch of the "American Association for the Recognition of the Irish Republic." It was named for the eighteen-year-old IRA volunteer and medical student from the Jesuits' Dublin College who had been recently court-martialed and hanged for his role in a Sinn Fein raid against British troops. A huge rally in support of American recognition of Eire was held in the university theater on April 8, 1921. After the colorful Father Peter Yorke of San Francisco had delivered a fiery oration on "The Cause," Santa Clara students performed a three-act play showing "the repressive measures taken by the British Crown forces against the Irish."[14]

Football

Some of Santa Clara's "fighting Irish" exuberance was channeled into athletics, which came to play an increasingly prominent role in collegiate life in the postwar era. Even before World War I, intercollegiate competition had been gaining in importance at Santa Clara. Fielding a team was now considered a requisite for keeping "pace with the position attained by becoming a University."[15]

Not long after football was outlawed at Santa Clara in 1905, rugby became the favorite contact sport. A few years after the introduction of the game in 1907, Santa Clara began playing the University of Southern California, Stanford University, and the University of California, Berkeley. In 1913 Santa Clara produced two players for an all-American team that played against New Zealand. When Stanford broke off athletic relations with Berkeley in 1914, Santa Clara at once took advantage of the opportunity and slipped into the breach left by the Bears. For the next five years, one sportswriter recalled, "Stanford and Santa Clara were booked as the big collegiate rivals of the northern part of the State." And "as long as Stanford played rugby football, so long did Santa Clara."[16] Sports fans by 1916 were congratulating the mission school for having placed itself "in the big University caliber in so short a time."[17] Several Santa Clarans played on the world championship team that the United States sent to the Olympic Games in Antwerp in 1920. The university also was represented four years later at the Paris Olympics, where the American team once again captured the gold medal and world rugby honors.

After World War I interest began to shift from rugby to American football. The game had evolved considerably in ten years, and many of the dangerous features that had led to its abolition by numerous colleges and universities had been eliminated. As a major offensive maneuver the forward pass replaced the mass formation, in which a convoy of blockers surrounded the ball carrier before the play began. The need to gain ten yards in four downs was substituted for five in three. The game gradually opened up, and the rough mass play that had characterized early competition became a thing of the past. When Stanford, Santa Clara's major rival in rugby, once again took up football, Santa Clara followed suit.

Sports competition was resumed with vigor at the end of the war. In the spring of 1919, the *San Francisco Call* announced a new era of athletics at Santa Clara. The administration had issued an ultimatum that in the future every student must participate in some form of athletics.[18] That autumn the university's newly hired football coach, Robert Harmon, began teaching the rudiments of the game to the 125 students who turned out for the first practice. Hungry for matches, the fledgling team would play anybody, anywhere. "Wanted, by the Santa Clarans," one sportswriter advertised, "a game of American football with any aggregation."[19]

Though still weak, the team scheduled games with Stanford, California, and Nevada. When Santa Clara played its first home game against Stanford's varsity in 1920, local merchants agreed to "solidly stand behind the University" by closing shop and joining the ten thousand fans who gathered on the mission campus to watch the spectacle. Santa Clara lost, twenty-one to seven. Win or lose, the *Santa Clara Journal* declared on another occasion, the bleachers would always be filled to capacity for any game on the local gridiron because "Santa Clara has no other factor that more widely advertises the town" than university football.[20] On the campus "the assembled studentry eats, drinks, sleeps, studies and dreams football."[21]

As suddenly as it had taken up the game two years before, Santa Clara dropped it in April, 1921, and cut back its general athletic program. Displaying one of those periodic rejections that would characterize its on-again, off-again relationship with intercolleeiate football, the university announced that the sport was becoming incompatible with sound academics. The administration claimed that students were obsessed with the game to the exclusion of all else.

"Intercollegiate athletics have reached a point where undue prominence is demanded," President Murphy announced to the press in defense of his decision to ban the game. Sports, he argued, have overshadowed the real purpose for which a student enters an institution of learning, and serious application to studies has become a sideshow of the main attraction. "Which shall prevail," he demanded rhetorically, "athletic prowess or classroom effort?" Studies must come first, he answered; athletics at best are only of secondary importance. Murphy admitted that some of Santa Clara's best players were no longer in school, but he denied that "we 'quit' because our 'stars' have left us." The reason they have gone, he claimed, is because, being unsatisfactory students, they were asked to withdraw. Their study or conduct standards made their presence undesirable. In the future Santa Clara "shall endeavor to establish a better balance between scholastic and athletic effort."[22]

Murphy's stand met with resounding praise from some quarters. "All honor then to Santa Clara where brains once more are to be considered as more important than muscle," declared a Sacramento newspaper. Murphy "has dared to do something which a lot of other university presidents in this country would like to do if they dared," suggested another newspaper; the president has felt the school slipping and "has thrown on the emergency brake with a bang."[23]

But gloom settled over the campus following Murphy's announcement. Local alumni were particularly disappointed. Many sports fans "are of the opinion that the Santa Clara faculty has made a big mistake," one columnist stated bluntly. After all, he queried, what else was there to do at the mission school, if not play football? "Athletics, especially to an institution like Santa Clara, are the life of the college. They offer the one big diversion from the ordinary run of school life to such a college . . . where there are no women and the celebrations that go with that article."[24]

A few months later Santa Clara fans found reason to hope that football might make its regular autumnal return after all. Word went out during the summer that there would be a change of presidents at Santa Clara because of Murphy's failing health, and hence there arose the possibility that his successor might reverse the ban. In July, Father Zacheus Maher was named pres-

ident. Amenable to any project that placed the university in the public eye
and that made money, young Maher also believed that "one thing which
the war has taught [us] is the essential value of physical training." All those
interested in athletics, one sports columnist now wrote, looked to the new
president for a resumption of athletics on a much larger scale than before.[25]
They were not disappointed, though Maher took steps to prevent athletic
opportunism.

After conferring with his advisers over the summer, Maher decided to
sustain Murphy's already announced reforms and to outlaw abuses of recent
years. "Future athletic policy," he and his consultors concluded privately,
"will be that no privileges be given athletes." Transfers and "ringers," players
who were not fully enrolled or who had already completed their years of
eligibility at other schools, would be disallowed. Athletes must enter the
university as bona fide students and "contribute a part of their tuition," they
decreed. Hoping that the excesses represented by ringers might be discouraged further by drawing upon the university's own high school graduates for
future college players, the administration agreed to hire a coach who could
put together a good team.[26]

How "good football" could be made compatible with "good academics"
—the two horns of the constantly recurring dilemma at the small school—
remained to be seen. But in September, Maher announced this news to a delighted student body: "There will be a football team at Santa Clara this year
and moreover the university will not be without a representative in the college conference. There will not be a strong schedule, as our energy at present will be directed towards building up a team for the coming years."[27]

The Broncos Versus the Gaels

After Maher had given them one victory, football enthusiasts crusaded for
another: the resumption of athletic competition with St. Mary's College. In
1912 the two Catholic institutions had severed athletic relations, each accus-
ing the other of allowing ringers to strengthen its football lineup. Convinced
that neither school had "a monopoly on that particular aspect of intercollegiate sports" and persuaded that both had much to gain by renewing their
old rivalry, the sports editor of the San Francisco Call launched a campaign
to end the ten-year rift. He rallied alumni of both institutions to lobby for
the same end.

"To bring out the best in athletics, a natural rival is absolutely necessary,"
the Call declared. "Every college in America has a natural rival" and Santa
Clara's is St. Mary's, "as every alumnus of Santa Clara will tell you." Their

ancient baseball competition, their proximity, the fact that both institutions were Catholic and that both because of their size were excluded from the Pacific Coast Conference—all contributed to the naturalness of the rivalry. Dollar-conscious administrators were reminded that renewed competition promised to be a moneymaker. The drawing power of an annual Bronco-Gael game would produce revenue for building "magnificent stadiums," the *Call* maintained, and it would help support athletics "as they should be supported at any red-blooded American school." The paper concluded: "If Santa Clara and St. Mary's are not going to resume relations, they had better eliminate all pretense at engaging in intercollegiate athletics and play checkers and ping-pong among themselves and not embarrass their alumni by trying to compete with teams which would not give either of the universities a good workout."[28]

Under pressure from the press, the alumni, and the public, administrators of both schools yielded. In 1922 Santa Clara and St. Mary's agreed to forget their old differences and renew relations. A three-year contract was drawn up and a list of terms agreed to. Observers predicted that the Santa Clara-St. Mary's game would be one of the gridiron classics of the Pacific Coast, second only to the California-Stanford contest.[29]

Relations had scarcely been restored when a new wrangle erupted. On the eve of the first game of the resurrected rivalry, St. Mary's coach "Slip" Madigan accused Santa Clara of sheltering two ineligible players from Notre Dame. Though not infrequently guilty himself of recruiting wandering performers, wily Madigan, according to a St. Mary's football historian, "exploited the issue for all the publicity he could garner."[30] Having thus sidelined two of Santa Clara's star players, Madigan led his squad to a 9 to 7 victory over the demoralized mission team on Thanksgiving Day, 1922. Not long afterward, six members of the twenty-three-man Santa Clara varsity quietly withdrew from the university. Their stay had been brief; all had first enrolled only three months before, just in time for the beginning of the football season. The same week that witnessed the exodus of these varsity players also saw the beginning of a search for a new football coach.

Santa Clara—St. Mary's competition easily survived the revelations and setbacks of the 1922 season, however. Dubbed the "Little Big Game," the annual football clash grew in popularity. It was usually played in San Francisco's Kezar Stadium because neither school had a large stadium of its own. This traditionally hard-fought contest—which frequently generated rumors of a renewed split between the schools—became a favorite of San Francisco fans. At a time before professional competition became popular in the Bay Area, the Little Big Game was that city's football classic.

Santa Clara versus Stanford in rugby, 1916. James Winston of Santa Clara, tackled by a Stanford back, is in the act of passing the ball to Rudy Scholz, on the far right. The mission team won the game, twenty-eight to five. *Courtesy: Archives, Univ. of Santa Clara.*

In the view of the local Catholic press, attendance at the Little Big Game became "an obligation for the faithful," a St. Mary's sports historian notes. One publication gave ten reasons why devout Catholics should be present for the contest in 1924. First on the list was the fact that "the game has the unqualified support of His Grace," Archbishop Edward Hanna. Additional motives included the reminder that Santa Clara and St. Mary's were Catholic and the fact that income received from the game would further Catholic education.[31] It was owing to a mistake on the part of some Catholics, one religious journal declared, that the stands were not filled to capacity for that year's contest. The editor assured his readership "that as a Catholic American citizen you and I can indeed feel proud" of the Little Big Game.[32]

Thus throughout the twenties Santa Clara shared with the rest of America the craze for college football. Raccoon coats, college yells, bonfire rallies, and pregame raids upon rival campuses became essential elements of autumn at the school. It traditionally fell to the College of Engineering to construct the towering bonfire that illuminated the nighttime "monster rally" held before every important game. Built of railroad ties piled several stories high, the bonfire structure typically was shaped to resemble some feature of the rival school's campus. The ultimate pregame caper was to infiltrate the campus of the opposing team before their rally, put their bonfire prematurely to the torch, and escape undiscovered and unscarred while flames shot hundreds of feet into the night sky. Participants in such antics not infrequently paid for their fun, as in 1922, when one Santa Clara student was felled and seriously injured by a St. Mary's student wielding a "large flashlight as a shilalah."[33]

Alumni frequently outdid students in their devotion to King Football. At Santa Clara as elsewhere the game became the focus and center of the alumni activity. "All talks will be confined entirely to athletics, particularly to football," one Alumni Association official assured his fellows in 1923, when sending out invitations to a banquet.[34] Under the direction of Father Edmund Ryan—for whom the university's athletic field was later named—alumni chapters and football attendance grew hand-in-hand in the 1920's.

Having already selected school colors by adapting the red and white of its baseball uniforms to its football jerseys, the student body in 1923 began to look about for another piece of pigskin paraphernalia—a mascot or an athletic symbol. They settled on an animal that was seen around the old mission in an earlier time. "The bronco is a native western piece of dynamite" that aptly symbolizes the mission school and its athletic aspirations, declared its Jesuit originator, Hubert Flynn, "not too large, it is true, but hard as nails and always game to the core."[35]

The hiring of one of Knute Rockne's former stars as head football coach in 1925 revealed an ever-growing commitment to the game. Under the tutelage of young Adam Walsh, who had captained the Notre Dame squad only one year before, Santa Clara's offense adopted the famous Notre Dame shift, in which the backs moved to the left or right just before the snap of the ball.

Football competition was still limited chiefly to California teams, especially other "independents" such as St. Mary's, St. Ignatius, and the College of the Pacific. In 1925 Santa Clara scheduled a postseason intersectional game with Hawaii for the first time. In each year the Pacific Coast Conference squads conceded the university a few contests, sometimes with unexpected results. It was reported in 1927 that "while his team was playing an 'unimportant' game" with Santa Clara, Stanford coach Glenn "Pop" Warner "betook himself over to Berkeley to scout the Bears," thus signaling publicly his disdain for the mission squad and its Notre Dame shift. Upon his return Warner "had to grin at the gibes of the entire press box when it was announced that the Broncos had walloped his team," thirteen to six.[36] It was in part because of his skillful defensive play during the clash with Stanford that Santa Clara tackle Roderick Chisholm was later nominated to all-American honors. Stanford took revenge the following year, winning thirty-one to zero. But in 1929, when Santa Clara surprisingly repeated its earlier margin of victory, scoring thirteen points to Stanford's seven, campus pride knew no bounds. "Pop thought twice this time and decided to remain on the Farm," the Santa Clara student newspaper gloated, "and what he saw was what he missed two years ago."[37] Opponents now recognized that despite the fact that its student body numbered fewer than five hundred, Santa Clara could produce a team to be reckoned with.

Such experiences were novel and thrilling for a small Catholic college like Santa Clara. But the mission campus was not alone in its new-found enthusiasm for intercollegiate sport. The period between world wars was the heyday of football in Catholic colleges everywhere. During the 1920's Notre Dame's gridiron success demonstrated to these institutions the advantages of football as a source of publicity and profit. For small, little-known schools like Santa Clara the benefits that flowed from ardent athleticism were difficult to resist.

One need not look far to discover why Catholic colleges and universities such as Fordham, Georgetown, Detroit, St. Mary's, and Santa Clara sought football fame, especially during the 1930's. "Although their exploits were described by sportswriters rather than educational journalists," notes historian Edward J. Power, these schools were catapulted to national prominence by football. Before World War II ended intercollegiate competition, football would make the name of Santa Clara—hitherto known only in Catholic circles in the West—recognized from coast to coast. Football also possessed a marvelous capacity for welding alumni together and motivating them to rally in support of the institution. Last but by no means least, football "allowed Catholic colleges to rid themselves of the deep feelings of inferiority" that plagued them through much of their history.[38]

14

The House That Zach Built

1921–1926

When thirty-nine-year-old Father Zacheus Maher strode into the office of the rector-president of Santa Clara in July, 1921, the university gained one of its most energetic chief executives. "Zach" Maher, as he was known by his confreres, began a long career as a Jesuit administrator during his tenure of five years at Santa Clara. In those years he manifested qualities that the order then prized in its superiors. Though in later years the manner in which he wielded religious authority was sharply criticized as rigid and dictatorial, his brusqueness was still inchoative in the 1920's. As Santa Clara's seventeenth president, young Zach Maher was developing his administrative muscles.

Maher's role in the restoration of football has been described in the preceding chapter. Determined to make Santa Clara worthy of the university title it had appropriated in 1912, Maher picked up the mantle that had fallen from the shoulders of James P. Morrissey. He resurrected the building plans that had been all but forgotten for a decade. A dynamo of energy and ambition, Maher transformed the face of the university as no president had since the days of Burchard Villiger.

All Front and No Back

Santa Clara, whose antiquated condition had led the California Jesuits to consider closing the school at the turn of the century, was still described as "a sorry sight" twenty-five years later. Morrissey had left behind two handsome structures of reinforced concrete, but his grand design for rebuilding the campus in its entirety had been buried amid the bills and bank notes he bequeathed to those who succeeded him. Visitors noticed how Morrissey's two buildings stood forth in vivid contrast to the motley array of red brick and decaying wood behind them.

"The university is all front and no back," said one observer. The two newer structures were frontage buildings that flanked the mission church. Before them stretched two weed-choked acres of playing field; behind them, in the rear of the campus, stood "a row of tumbling down" buildings of Civil

War vintage. Some of these outdated edifices still served as classrooms and dormitories. "Not only are the buildings leaky and poorly ventilated and heated," Maher pointed out, but in the case of the old Science Hall "the rear of the building is supported by a heavy beam to keep it from toppling over" onto Lafayette Street.[1] Skirting this structure was a topsy-turvy row of service buildings that drew from the pen of one of the faculty the following description:

There was no such thing as harmony. They had come into existence as the need of the moment demanded, and to the moment's need only, did they respond. Each stood in its own individuality—square, oblong, high, low—anywhere about the yard. Boiler house, laundry, store rooms, rooms for workmen looked at though they had been dropped and where they had been dropped had taken root.[2]

Maher was determined to uproot this collection of antiquities. The university cannot struggle along in its present dilapidated condition, he announced in 1922. "It must rebuild, or else close its doors." If the ever-increasing numbers of students who sought admission were to be accommodated, replacement of the fast-decaying buildings with modern structures was imperative. We "cannot meet the needs and opportunities of 1922 with the buildings and equipment of 1852."[3] Six months after coming to office, Maher launched a vigorous campaign to advertise the university's plight and to generate funds.

The drive to replace "the sorry array of shacks which disgrace the Santa Clara campus," as Maher dramatically termed the older buildings, was directed first and foremost to the university's alumni. Because communication with large numbers of alumni required a more extended Alumni Association, one of the new president's early priorities was a drive for membership, a task that had already been inaugurated by President Murphy. Every means that could be thought of to locate the institution's scattered alumni was now employed. Old catalogs and records were gone over diligently, finally producing—incredibly, for the first time—a full and complete roster of former students.[4]

There followed the tedious task of organizing alumni chapters in towns and cities up and down the state, a work that fell largely to Father Edmund Ryan. His work was effective. As their contribution to the rebuilding of their alma mater, the alumni assumed responsibility for replacing the old Science Hall. The new structure would be named Alumni Science Hall.

At Maher's suggestion, the association also took steps to establish a permanent endowment for the university. Apart from the so-called living endowment provided by the contributed services of the Jesuit faculty, Santa Clara possessed no income-producing capital. Such a fund might be started if alumni contributed a fixed amount each year toward the accumulation of an investment reserve. After investigating a plan found successful at other schools, the association decided instead to ask each contributor to apply a fixed sum as the premium of an endowment insurance policy.[5] "The procedure is simple," Maher explained to a friend. "It is to ask each alumnus and friend of the University to insure his life on an endowment policy and to have the University named as beneficiary—the amount to be paid to the University at the end of the endowment period or at prior death."[6] Starting with an empty purse in 1924, this unique project was expected to produce an endowment of $2 million at the time of the university's centenary in 1951.[7]

"My College—Everybody's College"

The appeal for funds was not limited solely to former students, as had been the practice whenever money was needed in the past. Proceeding on the premise that "the present plight of the University is due largely to the fact that the public permits it," Maher looked beyond the alumni, and for the first time in its long history the university turned to the general public for funds. To advertise the school's need, Maher took the unprecedented step of inviting local civic and business leaders to Santa Clara for Sunday luncheon and for afternoon tours of the campus. After pointing out the decayed condition of many of the classrooms to his guests, Maher, with the aid of a stereopticon, unveiled his grand design for renewal.[8] Taking as his theme "Your College—My College—Everybody's College," Maher drove home the message that Santa Clara served the general public. "The University is open to all, regardless of religious affiliation, financial condition or racial extraction."

Maher also labored to impress upon his hearers the blessings showered upon the community by the "elevating force" of an institution like Santa Clara. A university stands for law and order, or for the fundamental philosophy that is obedience to the law, he reassured audiences made nervous by red scares, labor strikes, and bomb-throwing radicals; and it is "the biggest bulwark against sovietism, anarchism, bolshevism, against everything that threatens law and order." In typically florid language, Maher argued that a university "brings out the finest in man and makes him a real protector of womanhood, finding in her not a toy, but a companion and an inspiration." In sum, the uplifting presence of an institution like Santa Clara meant "more to a community than could be measured in words."[9] But all this would be lost if the Santa Clara Valley's only remaining pioneer college was forced to close its doors. (The College of the Pacific had by then decided to move to Stockton.) "Who is to blame?" he queried. "The responsibility rests with the public, with you."[10]

In his appeal Maher cited more practical reasons for supporting "Your College—My College—Everybody's College." "Quite apart from any humanitarian motive or educational interest or matter of civic pride" there were economic considerations: "Our campaign offers an out-and-out investment to the businessman and to the community." The university spends half a million or more dollars annually in this locale, he reminded business leaders. This money would be lost to the merchants of the area if the university should close. That the expansion for which he asked support would bring economic advantages to the cities of San Jose and Santa Clara was obvious, for "every dollar we receive will go directly to the building fund." Provided they could be secured locally, all the required construction materials would be purchased in the area, and local labor would be used in the construction. "More buildings for Santa Clara mean much for San Jose," he summarized. "The community reaps the benefits."[11]

Having publicized the "absolute and crying necessity" of new buildings, in the spring of 1922 Maher launched a short but intense fund drive.[12] Its hallmark was heavy advertising and appeals directed both to alumni and to the general public. The most concentrated period of the campaign occurred in late April, when the organizers hoped to raise $500,000 in twelve days. Counting heavily on the fact that "nearly every home now has liberty bonds, victory bonds, or war savings certificates" that "have served the government as they were intended to do, and now are collectible," leaders of the drive were optimistic. "If $500,000 is not realized in this campaign," prospective donors were assured, your contribution "will be returned to you."[13] Public endorsements and promises of support poured in from local merchants' associations and from alumni. California Governor William Stephens promised to visit the campus in May, when the campaign would conclude with a homecoming, a production of *The Mission Play of Santa Clara* by alumnus Martin Merle, and a centennial celebration of "great detail and splendor," the likes of which "has never been attempted here since the foundation of the mission."[14]

The great campaign was directed from general headquarters in the Bank of Italy building in San Jose. The student body participated by sponsoring dances and other activities aimed at raising money for a new gymnasium. Special campaign announcements under a letterhead reading, "$500,000 in Twelve Days," were printed, as were thousands of pledge cards and window

Senator James D. Phelan, benefactor of Santa Clara, and Zacheus Maher, president of the university from 1921 to 1926. *Courtesy: Archives, Univ. of Santa Clara.*

decals proclaiming in red, white, and blue letters: "I'm for rebuilding Santa Clara U." Every potential benefactor received a brochure explaining the purpose of the drive and how its success would lead to incalculable benefits. At the height of the campaign, full-page advertisements appeared in the local press, promising work for the workingman and business for the businessman if the drive succeeded.[15]

Comic relief, albeit unintentional, was probably provided by young Maher's dramatic but sometimes inflated appeals for help. Despite an intense personal interest in the techniques of modern advertising, which he studied assiduously, Maher had a proclivity for purple prose that probably interfered with his salesmanship. The university is "rotting into ruins" he declared once. On another occasion, to a perhaps startled audience, he announced that he could no longer treat the university "as fodder and permit it to rot." "Human life is in the balance," he exclaimed dramatically in reference to the university's outdated classrooms and dormitories, which he described as "old fire-traps," "disease-breeders," and "sirens of death." Such histrionics, while not consoling to the parents whose sons still occupied the "fire-traps" and "disease-breeders," did generate interest and drew attention to Maher's drive to prevent Santa Clara "from crumbling into decay and disease."[16]

"How We Failed"

Despite the fanfare, bombast, and costly promotion, the drive did not attain its goal. "A few have already given liberally," Maher noted in mid-April, even before the intensive appeal began; but, he warned, "their money will have to be returned" unless more funds were forthcoming in the last days of the campaign. Those funds never appeared.[17]

Having set a goal of $500,000, Maher could not hesitate in saying when the drive drew to its finale, "Frankly, we have not raised that amount." The school had received only about $100,000, chiefly in the form of promissory notes—and of that sum "not a little" was "still outstanding in pledges" a year after the campaign ended. Nor was the endowment drive successful. The idea was right, Maher insisted, but because it was novel it met with indifference. Four years later, only ten alumni had invested in the endowment insurance plan.[18] Of the twelve thousand window decals proclaiming "I'm for rebuilding Santa Clara U.," that had been distributed, "about twelve" were displayed, one chagrined campaigner claimed at the end of the drive. This campaigner also had kept a scrapbook that he titled, "The Drive, or How We Failed to Raise $500,000 in 1922."[19]

Why did the university's first public appeal meet with such a cold response? Maher believed that there were many causes, but that two were primary. The first was "lack of commercial instinct on the part of San Jose merchants." The prosperity of the Coolidge years and the general availability of money notwithstanding, Maher's economic arguments had obviously left most businessmen unconvinced. The second cause of the drive's collapse in Maher's view was "religious prejudice injected into the campaign at the height of our endeavor."[20] That a wave of anti-Catholic sentiment swept through the country during the twenties is historical record, as illustrated by the activities of the Ku Klux Klan and the national presidential campaign of 1928. But to what extent that general movement was felt in the Santa Clara Valley and to what degree it undermined the university's fund appeal of 1922 remains unclear.

Whatever the causes, Maher's picture of Santa Clara as "everybody's college" failed to win a response from the local citizenry. The popular image of the university probably was still too narrowly sectarian in the 1920's to elicit lively interest from the public at large. Nonetheless, the fact that Maher's campaign occurred at all pointed to the passing of old animosities and inhibitions. The invisible walls surrounding the institution were crumbling. But the campaign's failure demonstrated how much remained to be done before the area's inhabitants looked upon Santa Clara as "their" college and as a community asset worthy of enthusiastic support. Indicative of the school's long isolation from the community was the disclosure by some members of the Santa Clara Chamber of Commerce that until their invitation to the campus for one of Maher's Sunday luncheon-tours, they had never visited the institution.

Nor did the fund appeal elicit strong support from the Catholic community. One might hope for a great benefactor, one of the Jesuit faculty complained, "but somehow, as far as Catholic institutions of learning are concerned, a Founder in the full sense of the word has been hitherto a dream." When the administration lamented the absence of persons who "feared not to trust the future" and who would not merely "stand back" and "demand to see something," it implicitly acknowledged that some potential donors doubted Santa Clara's worth as an investment. Not impressed with dreams and promises of its future greatness, they looked for some concrete evidence of its present stature.[21]

The collapse of the fund drive confirmed the reservations and hesitancies of those who hung back, as Senator James Phelan observed. Phelan, a benefactor of the school, was annoyed when the much-trumpeted appeal fell short of its quota. He reminded Maher that the purpose of the campaign had been "to put the college structurally upon its feet, and not continue the patching process." Yet the campaign's failure made permanent financial support less likely than ever. "It seems to me that Santa Clara is very unfortunate in its efforts to raise funds," he concluded, but people want some assurance that their contribution will "serve an adequate purpose."[22]

The number of persons of wealth like Phelan to whom the university could turn for assistance was limited. Besides, their generosity was divided among numerous other institutions. Nor were the alumni, the financial backbone of any private school, a source of much economic assistance. Even after the reorganization and expansion of the Alumni Association, Santa Clara had remarkably few former students to call upon. In 1921 the association's renewed membership list contained only 1,200 names.

In retrospect, it is easy to criticize the fund-raising techniques of early administrators like Maher. They failed to produce frank statements of financial need, to rely upon professional solicitors, and to manage better their resources. But considering the narrow limits within which they worked, they may be admired for their audacity.

The Builder

With the collapse of his much-publicized campaign, Maher faced a dilemma. On the one hand, he felt "compelled" to replace "the old wooden buildings" on the "verge of collapse" with modern classrooms in order to secure future enrollment. And yet all possibilities of replacement were circumscribed by a lack of cash.[23] Though obliged to economize at every turn, Maher went ahead with plans to build. By the time he left office a few years later, six new mission-style buildings had risen above the palm-lined campus, and two others lay on the drawing boards. Having averaged two new structures a year, the resourceful young administrator had at the end of his term been dubbed "the builder" by his admirers.

Maher's renewal of the campus began in September, 1923. After the felling of classrooms and dormitories erected in the 1860's, modernization was realized with the appearance of Maher's first monument, Alumni Science Hall. Construction of Kenna Hall followed immediately. The largest building on campus, this three-story hall provided the university's high-school department with its own dormitory, classrooms, and offices for the first time since the school's founding.[24] Before Maher vacated the presidential chair in

1926, he further enriched the campus with a gymnasium, an infirmary, an engineering laboratory, and a new service building. To his successor he bequeathed plans for a new library and an observatory.

If the fund drive of 1922 had fallen far short of its goal of $500,000 how did the university pay for an expansion program that, when completed, carried a price tag of almost $1 million? The feat was not achieved by going into debt. When he decreed that new buildings must be put up, Maher, probably acting on orders from Jesuit superiors, also stipulated that they be paid for as they were erected. If the money could not be raised, the buildings could not be built—a prudent decision in view of the depression that followed a few years later. The administration could claim in 1926 that all the new buildings had been erected "without borrowing." Every dollar received from donors has its equivalent in the buildings themselves, fund raisers boasted. "Not a dollar has gone to pay interest." The only encumbered structure was Alumni Science Hall, whose debt the Alumni Association had pledged to liquidate.[25] But who paid for the other buildings?

One major source of funds was the sale of property purchased by previous administrations. When Senator James Phelan threatened to take back his contribution to the 1922 drive unless the university realized its goal of $500,000, "either by contribution, I may add, or by the sale of property," he was in effect reminding Maher that Santa Clara owned land that could be converted into cash. Maher responded to the senator's thinly veiled ultimatum with the assurance that "since my appointment, I have put every square inch of real estate on the market, and to date have moved seven distinct parcels." To prove the earnestness of his purpose, the president parted with the university's most valuable asset, the 600-acre tract known as Loyola Corners, acquired twenty years earlier when the college was considering relocation to Mountain View. These beautiful rolling hills were sold to land developers in 1926. The $250,000 received from the sale enabled the university's building program to be carried forward without further interruption, most of the money paying for Kenna Hall.[26]

A few bequests helped finance other projects. A gift received some years earlier for the purpose of building a law school was quietly diverted by Maher into more urgent needs, thereby solving one problem at the cost of creating embarrassment for his successors when they were called upon to explain the financial legerdemain. An inheritance from the estate of Dr. George Seifert, alumnus and longtime resident college physician, paid for a new gymnasium that included a swimming pool, built in 1923. A gift from

Miss Catherine Donohoe provided a new infirmary, a structure whose need had been apparent since the influenza epidemic in 1919.

Gifts, the liquidation of real-estate holdings, and Maher's "pay as you go" building policy were largely responsible for the renewal of the campus in the 1920's. But another element in the renewal was Maher's careful "husbanding of resources" through extreme economizing in construction costs. This sometimes resulted in buildings of inferior quality; plans were trimmed down and modified to fit the slender measurements of the presidential purse. Maher had his hopes set on a new university theater, for example, but he had to be satisfied with remodeling the old Ship, which some considered "so decrepit that it could not be made whole." As a result, that venerable edifice was propped up and remodeled to provide forty more years of shaky but colorful service. Fire regulations occasioned the building's coup de grace in 1962.[27] When wreckers razed the ancient Commercial Building to make way for new construction, they salvaged its bricks and other materials. These were incorporated into the walls of the Montgomery Laboratories and the Seifert Gymnasium. Thus both structures were products of resourceful cost cutting. The swimming pool around which the gymnasium rose was the pride of the faculty and students of the College of Engineering, who were responsible for its design, heating, and filter systems. For other professional aid, the university frequently depended upon contractors, lawyers, and architects who offered assistance free or at reduced rates.

Symbolic of Santa Clara's impecuniosity and of its president's determination was the sight of Maher, conspicuous in his black clerical garb, rummaging through secondhand shops for plumbing fixtures and bargains. The pinch of poverty and the need for judicious economizing were also concerns of Maher's successor, Cornelius McCoy. The latter once explained to librarian Edward Boland the circumstances under which McCoy had built the university's new library in 1931:

I am going to let you in on a secret. There was no architect engaged for the Varsi Library. Father Gianera and I worked out the rather simple floor plan. Mr. Miller had an engineer draw up a set of blueprints. They were approved and work commenced. Remember, the furnished building cost only $52,000, all the cash we had on hand and all we were authorized in Rome to spend.[28]

Boys in Knickerbockers

The construction of six new buildings in quick succession transformed the face of the campus. For the first time the university looked like the sort of school its title proclaimed, and for the first time the faculty saw their life's work in a setting that suggested genuine higher education.

A factor in Santa Clara's institutional maturity and the attendant growth in morale was the separation of the university from its preparatory school. In 1924 the high school moved into separate quarters in the recently completed Kenna Hall on the southern periphery of the campus. Soon afterward a more radical change was accomplished. The high school was given its own identity by transferring it to an off-campus site.

Reasons for dividing the two institutions were as numerous as they were obvious. As late as 1915 there were 350 colleges and universities in the United States that still retained "prep" schools, but such arrangements were becoming increasingly anachronistic. Thus, even though the university claimed afterward that it was "the only Catholic college for boys west of Omaha that has territorially separated its high school from the college department," the fact is that for decades the tendency in American education had been to divide, both logistically and academically, collegiate from preparatory training.[29] For that reason alone its prep school had been a source of embarrassment from the day Santa Clara appropriated the title of university. Discomfited by the knowledge that "the outside world views such an arrangement as not merely detracting from the dignity of a university, but even as destructive of its title to the name," the faculty resented "the intolerable anomaly of a University frequented by boys in knickerbockers."[30]

The coexistence did not make recruitment easier, nor did it boost university enrollment. One Jesuit high-school teacher reported that many prospective college students refused to go to a school where they would have to associate with boys just out of grade school and suffer a stricter discipline because of the "preps" on the campus. In sum, students and faculty alike "resented the presence of the younger element."[31]

Running a high school in the shadow of a university brought trials for the preparatory department as well. "We forget that we are not conducting a reform school," one exasperated high-school teacher complained around 1924. Restive "preps" posed as college students and demanded the same privileges and freedoms enjoyed by their elders and, when these were not conceded, grew discontent. Expulsions from the high school were frequent, the general state of discipline was described as one of disorder, and enrollment slipped. For the advantage of both institutions, separation as soon as possible seemed imperative. Relocation of the high school in Belmont or Burlingame was discussed, but for financial reasons just as quickly forgotten. "Everybody felt that something had to be done," one Jesuit summarized, but because

In 1924 a ceremony marked the laying of the cornerstone of Kenna Hall, which served briefly as headquarters for Santa Clara's preparatory school. The Alameda is shown in the background, and beyond it is the Eberhard Tannery. *Courtesy: Archives, Univ. of Santa Clara.*

"more pressing needs pushed this particular problem out of the field of practical questions," for years nothing changed.[32]

But with each passing semester additional motives for a permanent solution impressed themselves upon administrators. Future growth was a major concern. In 1924 Santa Clara's total enrollment stood at 455 students. Of these, 289 were collegians and 166 were high-school pupils. Although miniscule by most standards, the total represented an unprecedented increase over previous years. "With every prospect of the continuance of this enlargement" as a consequence of the recent campus renovation, President Maher set his sights on a future university enrollment of 500.[33] But as long as the high school continued to share the university facilities, even that modest objective remained beyond reach.

Then there was a special financial consideration. The specter of new state taxes in 1925 increased Maher's dissatisfaction with the status quo. Exemptions that the university previously had enjoyed were threatened by the possibility of new revenues being levied against grammar- and high-school properties. Maher expected the tax to go into effect in March of the following year. That Santa Clara's host of new buildings might suddenly become a financial liability now seemed possible. The only escape from the prospective high-school tax was removal of the preparatory department to another location where the assessment would not be as high.

That autumn a solution to the decades-old dilemma suddenly materialized. Having abandoned its historic home in San Jose to build a new campus in Stockton, the College of the Pacific put its former grounds up for sale. Situated midway between the towns of Santa Clara and San Jose, this site, known as College Park, contained everything needed by a boarding school —dormitories, a dining hall, classrooms, a gymnasium, and playing fields. That some of the buildings were of the same Victorian vintage as the shacks that President Maher was tearing down on his own campus was not a source of concern. True, seventeen-acre College Park campus was not in good condition. Because the College of the Pacific's move to Stockton had stretched out over a two-year period, some of its classrooms had long stood vacant and unoccupied. But Maher felt that a few weeks of intensive work would suffice to bring it to a satisfactory condition again. Besides, there was little time to weigh the pros and cons of purchasing College Park. Anxious lest the title to the site slip through his grasp and worried about the tax threat that hung over the university, President Maher recognized that it was an "opportunity which made quick action imperative."[34]

After a hasty conference with his advisers, during which it was agreed to presume the permission of the Roman superior general and Archbishop Hanna of San Francisco, Maher decided to buy the old Methodist campus. A few days later, on September 17, he jubilantly informed the Jesuit provincial: "The deed is done, and yesterday we paid a deposit of $5,000 on the College of the Pacific to be purchased at a cost of $77,500." Though forced to part with a piece of coastal property in Santa Cruz County in order to gain the necessary cash, Maher through the transaction ended the longstanding problem of the high school. "We are solving a serious housing problem for ourselves," Maher explained to the press. "Next year would have found us unable to take care of all our students, without this change." The separation of the high school from the university was, he concluded with characteristic hyperbole, from all points of view "a consummation devoutly wished since the very inception of Santa Clara College."[35]

Eager to "be in there before the first Monday of March, 1926, so as to avoid the heavy tax that would otherwise be levied on us here at the University site," Maher pushed ahead the practical details of relocation. On Saturday noon, December 19, 1925, the Santa Clara "preps" took their last meal in the university refectory. After nearly seventy-five years on the mission campus, the high school was transferred to its new home in College Park, where it initiated classes after Christmas vacation.[36]

"Left to Die a Natural Death"

When the last truckload of high-school materials left Kenna Hall and departed in a cloud of dust down the Alameda, Maher was rid of an embarrassing obstacle to progress. But the high school faced a less roseate future. It had inherited "an old set of buildings that needed constant care and attention." Burdened with mounting repair and construction costs, the faculty looked back with nostalgia at their former home, and they complained that the high school had been "cast adrift without any visible means of support except tuition." Some Jesuits predicted that the severance from the university signaled the death knell for the high school. They likened its condition at College Park, near the Southern Pacific Depot, to that of an unwanted babe abandoned by its hardhearted parent alongside the railroad tracks. Maher, it was said, believed that the day of boarding schools was over. He had decided to cut the strings and "let the High School die a natural death."[37]

The so-called abandoned baby soon began to wail and complain loudly. Its piercing protest disturbed Father Maher's labors at the university and was eventually heard in distant Rome. The crisis peaked in January, 1926, when Maher presented the high school with a statement of debt for the new site. The price of the transfer to College Park, including building and renovation costs and the debt on the property itself, was around $150,000. It was a small sum in terms of today's inflated education costs, but in 1926 it was an awesome, unwelcome burden. Who was to pay? The administration of the high school laid the crucial question before Joseph Piet, the California provincial: Is the high school "to assume the whole burden, or is the University to assume a portion of it?"[38]

When it was proposed that the university share in the payment, Maher protested vigorously. He did not see the justice of the claim. When the removal of the high school was first considered there was no question of its receiving any financial assistance from the university. He insisted that the university had no obligations whatsoever to the high school, that the latter could easily meet its debt and its current expenses out of its own income, and that it was precisely because it was judged that the high school could support itself that the shift had been made in the first place. Besides, he concluded, "No matter what the actual purchase of the College Park was, the High School had been given a $200,000 plant; better in a thousand ways than the home it had at Santa Clara."[39]

Whether College Park was superior in a thousand ways depended on one's point of view. Certainly the new campus was better than the "shacks" that the high school had occupied for decades before Maher's modernization. But the high-school staff, recalling the new quarters they had enjoyed for a short time in Kenna Hall, found the discarded campus of the College of the Pacific decidedly inferior. At Santa Clara, the high school had been well housed and free of debt. That a "mother should send her daughter away from her without any *viaticum* [traveling money] for her journey," concluded Father Francis Dillon, superior of the high school, was "unfair."[40]

In his appeals to superiors about how the debt should be settled, Dillon resurrected a few arguments from the past:

On the property possessed by Santa Clara University, the High School has in justice an equal claim with the College. A survey of the past seventy-five years would, I think, show that the High School was more efficient in building up this property than the College. The College had urged the removal of the High School. In justice, therefore, it should receive one-half of this property before taking its departure.[41]

Such a settlement would, of course, have destroyed the university. Consequently, Dillon suggested a less drastic solution: "The least" the university could do would be "to assume the debt on the present site and put the buildings in repair." He asked that the university assume responsibility for a third, or $50,000, of the cost of reestablishing the school.[42]

The quarrel was referred to the Jesuit general for solution, and Father Wlodimir Ledochowski decided that Dillon's request was "reasonable and just." In 1927 he directed the university to accept a third of the indebtedness of its former high school. Thus the quarrel passed into history.[43] But it had been bitter. Some Jesuits joked that at the division of the assets, even the encyclopedias were partitioned, the university receiving volumes A to L and the high school, M to Z.

The struggle to partition the debt was by no means the last challenge faced by the high school. For several years after the transfer to College Park those who predicted the school's demise could readily support their prognostication. Although the university grew stronger as a consequence of the surgery that separated it from the prep school, the latter's state of health steadily worsened. While enrollment decreased, the deficits increased. When the student body dropped to 168 pupils in September, 1929, the principal, Father James Hayes, informed the provincial that "so far as I can see now, we have reached the end of our string."

A close scrutiny of the ills that plagued the high school and of its prospects for recovery was initiated. "What has happened this year" is part of an orderly process of decline that has been under way for seven or eight years, even on the mission campus, the principal admitted. But the "short-sighted and unjustifiable" administrative policies at College Park had hastened the high school's disintegration, he claimed.[44]

The onset of the Great Depression, bad bookkeeping, faulty teaching methods, poor publicity, and the competition of rival Catholic high schools all served to explain the institution's failing health. And the miserable condition of the campus was an extreme handicap. "We have reached the point where we are practically bankrupt," the principal concluded in 1930. "All things considered," the school "should be closed." Some of the faculty agreed and suggested that the campus be turned over to the California Province as a theologate. Others revived the dream of escaping to a new site somewhere north on the Peninsula. But more sober minds recognized that "Nothing short of a moral miracle would put us in a position to buy land and erect buildings elsewhere."[45]

The thinness of the school's pocketbook prevented any immediate decision. Then in 1931 registration began to creep slowly upward. Three years later a new crisis of independence occurred when it was urged that the school's title, "Bellarmine College Preparatory," adopted in 1928, be abandoned and the University of Santa Clara's "name of golden opportunity" be restored. Advocates of the change argued that "Bellarmine" was "too hard to pronounce" and that it was a source of many parodies on the football field from rival schools' rooting sections. But those who believed that the high school had been moved to College Park "to die under the former name 'Santa Clara'" protested strenuously.[46] Hence the title of Bellarmine was retained. Under this name the years of crisis gradually yielded to better times.

On the eve of World War II enrollment mounted to 349, and in the postwar period Bellarmine experienced a boom in applications. The high school's growth continued. By 1976, 125 years after its founding at Santa Clara, the school boasted an enrollment of more than 1,200 students. With nearly 99 percent of its graduates moving on to higher education and with about 80 percent of its seniors qualifying for participation in California's State Scholarship Program, Bellarmine was not only the oldest, but also one of the state's leading college preparatory schools. Testimony to the school's enduring link with the mission campus was the fact that more Bellarmine graduates chose Santa Clara for their collegiate studies than any other college or university.[47]

University Academics

If removal of the high school and the rebuilding of the campus lent a greater sense of self-respect and dignity to the university, other innovations improved the curriculum. Under the direction of the dean of faculties, Father William Lonergan, the law course was temporarily expanded into a four-year program; the premedical curriculum, which had been dropped during the war years, was reestablished; and the gradual rehabilitation of the traditional Bachelor of Arts course with its "strict classical requisites" was begun.[48] In order to meet the growing demand for trained businessmen, President Maher announced plans in 1923 to open a College of Commerce and Finance. In the late 1920's business colleges became the most popular type of professional school in Catholic higher education. By 1930 Santa Clara's was one of twenty such schools in the United States.[49] One of the principal features of the Jesuit-supervised business school was a comprehensive course in philosophy, to give students "a fundamental education along with business training."[50]

The first step to bring Santa Clara into conformity with ever more demanding national norms was taken in 1926, when negotiations were begun in Berkeley for the accreditation of the university. This first quest for accreditation convinced Maher how "much . . . we must do in proper teacher preparation." Despite the shortcoming, the Jesuit Educational Association kept on urging work toward accreditation with both regional and national groups upon Santa Clara and its other member schools wherever practicable and possible. At the same time it insisted that an institution "once accredited should live up to its requirements, not only in letter but in spirit." Jesuits themselves, however, sometimes worked at cross purposes. In 1926, when Maher was in the midst of the first difficult accreditation visit by Berkeley, a man who had been judged unqualified to teach high-school chemistry at Loyola College was promoted by the California provincial to teach the same subject at Santa Clara. Despite such domestic difficulties, Santa Clara complied with the urgings of the Jesuit Educational Association and, six years later, was approved by the Northwest Association.[51]

Santa Clara's library was housed during the Civil War on the second floor of the Adobe Lodge. The library was transferred to St. Joseph's Hall after that building was completed. The paintings, statues, and many of the books pictured here are today preserved in Orradre Library. *Courtesy: Archives, Univ. of Santa Clara.*

Although buildings rather than books were the administration's chief concern during these years, the tradition of research by such faculty pioneers as Neri, Bayma, and Montgomery continued. Reflecting diverse interests, the publications produced by the Santa Clara faculty included *McClellan* by James Havelock Campbell, a lengthy study vindicating the military career of General George B. McClellan. Father Jerome Ricard's *Sunspot*, a monthly peridical begun in 1915 to deal with meteorology and solar observation, continued to roll off the press. In 1928 Jesuit Richard Bell patented a radio signaling device, capping four decades of research in wireless telegraphy. More conventional clerical concerns were expressed in Father Joseph Sasia's *Future Life* and in a two-volume edition of W. Devivier's *Christian Apologetics*, which served for years as a textbook at Santa Clara and at other Catholic colleges.

Father Michael Shallo's *Lessons in Scholastic Philosophy* appeared in its sixth edition in 1926.

From the prolific pen of the scholarly Jesuit Henry Woods, ethician, university librarian, and classicist, issued scores of articles on as many subjects. His interests ran from political philosophy to trade unionism; from vernacular liturgy (a means of "tickling emotions") to contraception ("grievous from every point of view"). In addition to his host of articles, Woods authored several books, including *Augustine and Evolution* and a philosophy text, *The First Book of Ethics*. Woods's poems in English verse and in Latin hexameters, written on the occasion of the Virgilian bimillenium, were published in special editions by Grabhorn Press and by John Henry Nash.

While the faculty did its work Maher did his. The impact of his forceful personality was felt at Santa Clara in ways other than fundraising and building construction. In public relations he patterned his administration on the example of his more outgoing and active predecessors, Kenna and Morrissey. He appreciated the importance of involving the university in the mainstream of community affairs. Unlike most other presidents, past and future, whose off-campus public appearances were few and restricted to Catholic gatherings, Maher was always ready to deliver a speech or boost a civic event. His "whole-hearted desire to serve" was the object of admiration from outsiders, and his final departure from the university in 1926 prompted encomiums from the press for his having played so large a part in shaping community life in the Santa Clara Valley.[52]

Despite his predilection for rhetorical gimmicks—of perhaps because of it—Maher was a popular and effective orator. Often called upon as a guest speaker, he discussed topical issues, especially those affecting Catholics. Like many Catholic leaders, Maher was frank in his opposition to Prohibition. He conceded that the law must be respected and obeyed until it was taken off the statute books, but he was convinced that "It is impossible to legislate this nation dry." When Maher told a San Francisco group in 1921 that "The keeping of the law is a moral thing, but the law will not be kept if it is not itself moral," he provided local newspapers with additional ammunition for their editorials urging repeal of the Eighteenth Amendment.[53]

On the question of the compatibility of Catholicism with "the American ideal"—a subject whose urgency was keenly felt by many Catholics in the 1920's—Maher had much to say. His defense of Catholic education was both forceful and frequent. "I assert fearlessly, there is no stronger, no more trustworthy support of our country and its institutions than our Catholic universities." In a talk to the student body of the College of the Pacific, he summed

up aphoristically his view of the end and purpose of education: the formation of "not merely clever men, not merely good men, but clever men who
are good and good men who are clever."[54]

Despite his willingness to participate in outside activities and to represent
the university in community affairs, Maher was not a crypto-ecumenist rac-
ing ahead of his time; nor was he a breaker of educational molds. Tradition-
alist to the core, he lamented deviations from hallowed past practices in Catholic education and rejected the arguments of those demanding that Catholic
schools follow secular standards. Toward the end of his tenure Maher outlined the fundamental differences in educational philosophy that distinguished
Santa Clara where "the whole atmosphere of every course must be religious
[and] the background out of which it is taught must be Catholic"—from its
secular counterparts. "No Catholic college poses as a competitor to its neighboring or to any secular university, whether state or private," he declared in
1926. The secular theory of education "is entirely distinct" from the principles that gave rise to Catholic colleges, and should the latter "ever cease to
be predominantly Catholic in their principles and their policies, then they
would have lost the reason for their existence." He concluded with reference
to secular schools:

They proceed on the principle that there can be true education apart from religion;
we, on the principle that there can be no true education apart from religion . . . and let
us be frank to state that if our inspiration were the same as theirs, we should close our
Catholic colleges tomorrow and stop a duplication of men and money in what
would then be a bootless effort to rival them in material equipment.[55]

Maher rose rapidly on the ladder of Jesuit authority after his departure
from the university. He served as provincial of the California Province in the
early thirties, and he was subsequently appointed assistant to Wlodimir Ledochowski, superior general of the order. When Ledochowski died in 1942 and
wartime conditions prevented the election of a successor, Maher emerged
as supreme authority in the American Assistancy. From his headquarters
at Saint Andrew-on-Hudson, New York, Santa Clara's former president
reigned for four years as the powerful overseer of all Jesuit activities in the
United States. Thus Maher's vigorous presence continued to be felt by the university long after his farewell in 1926.

15
Fire and Sunspots
1926–1932

"Santa Clara will never be a large university." Such was the view expressed in 1926 by Father Cornelius McCoy in a press interview after his appointment as president. To reporters visiting the campus as it began its seventy-fifth year, he predicted with assurance that "We will never have more than a thousand students." At the time he spoke, three hundred young men constituted the entire student body.[1] Young women were not yet considered for enrollment. "It is mannish," McCoy confessed to a lady journalist, "but we haven't a woman in the whole place."[2]

Another thirty years would pass before the question of coeducation was seriously considered at Santa Clara. And not until 1937 would enrollment surpass five hundred, the goal set by Zacheus Maher after the removal of the university's prep school in 1925. Santa Clara's expectations were modest. When President McCoy erected a new four-story dormitory (Nobili Hall) in 1930 the criticism from some of the faculty regarding the ambition of the project persuaded him that the building would not see full occupancy for years, and hence he left unfinished the hall's upper story.

The university's low enrollment was deliberate policy. "Santa Clara believes that its greatest usefulness in the field of education can be achieved by functioning well as a small university."[3] McCoy wanted a school where students could "live and work together" and "know one another." He encouraged the "family spirit and close contact, pupil with pupil, . . . and pupil with professor" as characteristics that made Santa Clara "unique."[4] "We mean to limit ourselves deliberately to our purpose, our circumstances and the type of school we are conducting," wrote Jesuit Edward Shipsey, a teacher of English and an ardent advocate of smallness. "The purposes we have in mind in this type of school would be defeated," said Shipsey, by expansion of courses or of the student body.[5]

What were Santa Clara's purposes? Basically, they were the same as they had been for the past seventy-five years. Though he did not want a "churchy" institution, McCoy, like his predecessors, saw the formation of "men who combined education with character" as the goal of the university;

or, as the bulletin now put it, "to mold men after the model of the Man-God." The integration of religion with the study of science and the arts was still the school's raison d'etre. The president justified Santa Clara's existence with the "fourfold conviction that purely secular education promotes spiritual illiteracy, foments social anarchy, menaces moral righteousness and hampers the very intellectual life which it pretends to foster and enlarge." He regretted that Prohibition and the automobile had introduced into American life "evils that did not exist before," but he was confident that "these evils can be corrected with education along the lines of morality." To this end, the study of philosophy was required of all students, and Catholics (85 percent of the student body) were obliged to complete one unit of theology every semester.[6]

For admission to Santa Clara, freshmen candidates were expected to have completed a regular four-year high-school course. No grade requirements were specified, but applicants were required to pass an entrance examination in subjects equivalent to fifteen standard high-school units. The University of California increasingly determined what these subjects would be.[7] Santa Clara offered only one full-time scholarship in 1926. Consequently, admission was limited to students of middle-class and upper-middle-class background who could afford the $100 tuition and the $250 boarding fee required each semester.

Santa Clara's small size and its carefully focused objectives were reflected in its academic program. Forty-four full- and part-time professors, none of whom held an earned Ph.D., constituted the entire faculty.[8] The undergraduate curriculum weighed heavily in favor of the College of Arts, which, a Jesuit spokesman declared, "is the core of the University." Because, "mental training," as contrasted with "the mere imparting of information," was looked upon as "the prime function and the chief justification of the University's existence," all candidates for a degree in that college were expected to major in scholastic philosophy.[9] Minors were allowed in English, history, mathematics, classics, modern languages, education, law, and political science. Not until 1931 were arts students given a choice of additional majors in English, history, economics, and political science. The arts diploma remained the exclusive and sole prize of students who, in addition to the other prescribed studies, completed six years of Latin. In 1932 Greek was once again required for the Bachelor of Arts degree.

Students whose interests inclined toward more practical or professional training might enroll in the premedical course or in the "general science" program offered by the College of Arts. Undergraduate diplomas could also be earned in the College of Law and the College of Business Administration,

The Mission Play of Santa Clara, written by alumnus Martin V. Merle, was a melodramatic account of life at the mission in the last days of Mexican rule. The play was frequently produced on the stage of the university theater in the Ship in the 1920's and 1930's. *Courtesy: Archives, Univ. of Santa Clara.*

which offered majors in management, finance, and accounting. A bachelor's degree in mechanical, electrical, or civil engineering could be earned in the College of Engineering, which, the catalog noted, was "under the moral guidance of the Jesuit fathers"—a pointed reminder that engineers, too, were expected to take substantial doses of philosophy and theology.

The Mission Fire

If Father McCoy strove to keep Santa Clara moving along the familiar path it had trod for the past seventy-five years, it was also his intention to continue Maher's building program. During McCoy's tenure, Nobili Hall and the Varsi Library were erected, and work on the Ricard Observatory was completed. Included in McCoy's construction agenda were plans to restore the century-old mission church, which repeated remodelings had left disfigured and, from the outside, scarcely recognizable as a California mission. "I want to restore it along the old lines," the new president announced in 1926, "because it is the central and focal point of the campus."[10] Although the ancient structure had for generations served as a parish church, McCoy looked forward to its long-awaited conversion to a university chapel.[11]

The plan to restore Mission Santa Clara became an urgent necessity three months after McCoy first proposed it. Early in the morning of October 25, 1926, the cry of "Fire!" swept through the campus. The mission church was burning. By the time the blaze was extinguished, the historic building was a heap of ruins and ashes.

Apparently ignited by faulty wiring, the conflagration had broken out in the north tower that had been added to the church in the 1860's. Flames were creeping along the wooden molding of the nave before they were noticed by a priest just finishing his seven o'clock mass. A frantic tolling of bells spread the alarm across the campus, and within minutes sleepy students rushed to help the faculty fight the advancing flames with garden hoses and water buckets. Yellow tongues of fire were already curling from the top of the right tower when the first fire truck arrived. The old edifice was doomed.

Quick action prevented the destruction of many of the historic artifacts within the burning building, as students braving smoke and flame rushed into the mission and emerged with statues, paintings, and liturgical vessels under their arms. But Agustín Dávila's ceiling painting and the brightly colored reredos that had survived a sea voyage from Mexico in 1802 were lost forever, as were many documents and relics housed in the office of the pastor of the church.[12]

Destruction was not limited to the mission church. Before the holocaust was halted, it had swept to the remodeled western wing of the mission quadrangle, which contained the student and faculty dining rooms and the former library. Damage from flame and water was so extensive that this area, known today as the Adobe Lodge, had to be restored to the one-story form of its mission days. The students' chapel that adjoined the mission church on the north, though built of brick, was also destroyed.

Toward the end of the day the fire burnt itself out. Little remained of California's eighth mission but scattered stands of blackened adobe looming like lonely sentinels over a sea of smoking coals and rubble. The flames had consumed most of the church's Victorian façade, exposing for the first time in decades the remnants of the mission's original adobe entrance. Toward the rear of the church, all traces of the beautiful sanctuary had disappeared forever. Where the main altar once stood there remained only a pile of stones and scorched bricks.

The flames had not spared the three mission bells. When the belfry caught fire they plummeted into the blaze below, and it seemed a foregone conclusion that the bells of Charles IV of Spain, bells whose music had resounded through the Santa Clara Valley since the founding days of the mission, were silenced forever. Two of the trinity of bells were discovered in the debris, ruined and incapable of ringing again. A third, cast in San Blas, Mexico, in 1798 survived the crash from the tower and the furnace below. Carefully extracted from its resting place amid the coals by student fire fighters, the huge bronze bell was cooled and slung upon a scaffold of railroad ties hastily erected for that purpose. That evening at precisely 8:30 the tolling of the De Profundis for the dead, an ancient custom of the mission continued by the university, occurred once more. The somber tones rang across the mission gardens as they had for more than a hundred years.

"As It Was Originally"

Even before the smoke cleared away, President McCoy announced plans to rebuild the church as quickly as possible. The mission will rise again, he promised in reply to scores of telegrams of sympathy that poured into his office in the wake of the disaster. Within two weeks of the fire, the president met in San Francisco with a committee of alumni and concerned citizens to organize a fund drive to restore the vanished landmark. To the "friends of history, art and romance" an appeal was issued a few months later for help in rebuilding Santa Clara's "ancient temple of enchantment," as a publicity brochure now idealized the mission. Californians' romantic infatuation with "the grand old days of Spanish dons and donnas [sic]," "picturesque padres," and "humble Indians" having reached new heights in those years, the campaign to restore the mission met with instant success. Construction began in 1927, and a year later the work was essentially done, although final details of decoration continued to be added piecemeal for the next few years as funds and gifts for special projects became available.[13]

The motto of the restoration campaign promised, "As it was originally—so it will be." That the church which had gone up in flames was a gross disfigurement of the mission of 1825 was widely recognized, and hence participants in the rebuilding project welcomed the opportunity to return Santa Clara to its original form. Despite the best of intentions, liberties were taken in the reconstruction. They resulted in a less than perfect restoration, as is apparent from even a cursory comparison of the present mission with others in the California chain that still retain their early characteristics.

As in earlier remodelings, the long, narrow body of the church was sacrificed in favor of a wider design, this time reflecting the building's new function as a university chapel. Adaptations were also made in decorative motifs and coloring. In place of the pigments of crimson and yellow that early visitors indicate once dominated the decor of the mission interior, the restorers of 1928 introduced subdued pastel hues.[14] There being no pictorial representations of the inside of the original mission, much of the reconstruction was based upon photographs of the interior of the church as remodeled in 1885. That remodeling included adaptations of some of the original wall decorations, as well as certain nineteenth-century "improvements" that had acquired the hallowed patina of "tradition" and hence were incorporated into the restoration of 1928. The earlier remodeling, together with the aesthetics of religious devotion at the time of restoration, explains why the primitive simplicity of Santa Clara's early mission church was marred by "embellishments of a garish Victorian cast."[15]

On the other hand, some authentic elements of mission art and architecture were integrated into the reconstructed landmark. Perhaps the most striking artistic features of the original church were the primitive painting that covered the sanctuary ceiling and the ancient reredos behind the main altar, brought by ship from Mexico. Both of these treasures were destroyed in the fire of 1926. Through a careful study of old photographs, skilled craftsmen directed by Harry Downie succeeded in reproducing these and other relics. Today, copies of the painting, the reredos, and the mission's first pulpit occupy the same position in the restored church as they did in the original. Together with the statues and other artifacts of the mission era that were rescued from the flames, they help to recall the atmosphere of the old Mission Santa Clara.

The restorers of 1928 also intended that the exterior of the resurrected edifice should reflect the appearance of the church of 1825. Once again, however, certain features of the original mission were adapted to twentieth-century taste. Surviving written accounts and photographs of the façade of the first church reveal a crude, flat surface of whitewashed adobe, upon which were painted primitive figures and designs. According to the accounts, the paintings were done in bright cinnabar and yellow. (The woodwork of the bell tower was once painted green!)[16] The reconstructed façade of monochrome concrete is a modern interpretation in bold relief of those same flat frescoes. In place of the paintings of the patron saints, the mission today has niches containing wooden statutes—handcrafted in Oberammergau, Germany—of St. Clare, St. John the Baptist, and St. Francis of Assisi.

A special authenticity was given the restored edifice by the thousands of tiles covering its roof. Manufactured at the mission in crude wooden molds (not on the thighs of Indian maidens, as popular legend would have it), these ancient *tejas* had graced the roof of the original mission one hundred years earlier; some are believed even to date back to the church of 1790. They had survived because after their removal in 1868 and their replacement with wooden shingles, the tiles had been used to roof the barns of the college ranch. When the mission was restored in 1928, the weathered old tiles were gathered from the scattered outbuildings and returned to their place of origin atop the mission church.[17]

No detail of Santa Clara's restoration stirred as much public interest as the return of the mission bells. The one that survived the fire when pulled from the smoking embers by students was put back into use. Another was melted beyond recovery in the flames, and a substitute bell was made in 1928. The third, which cracked in the fire, was melted down and then recast. All three were installed in the restored bell tower. A fourth clarion was added in 1929, a gift to Santa Clara from King Alfonso XIII of Spain.

The story of this last bell and its journey to California evoked much publicity. Through the mediation of Luis Rodés, a Spanish Jesuit who had recently visited the university, President McCoy proposed that the king replace one of the bells that had been given to Mission Santa Clara a century and a half before by his ancestor, Charles IV. Strictly speaking, the proposed gift would be an addition to the original trio rather than a replacement because the pair destroyed by the fire had already been restored. The romantic tradition of the bells required, however, that the king replace one of those destroyed.

After an exchange of telegrams across the Atlantic, King Alfonso announced that he "accepted with great pleasure the task of replacing the bell that was destroyed during the fire" with another "worthy of its predecessor."[18] Cast in the royal artillery foundry, the new bell was shipped to California and placed in the mission bell tower. The king's gift was accompanied by the same condition as that first imposed by Charles IV, that it toll daily at the Angelus.

The bell was dedicated on Columbus Day, 1929, with a formal ceremony, plus a lengthy pageant, a parade, and impressive airplane stunts and maneuvers in the sky over the mission. After the ceremony—which was attended by members of the San Francisco consular corps and included numerous

Early in the morning of October 25, 1926, Santa Clara's old mission church, which had stood for more than a century, was destroyed by flames. The building was replaced three years later. *Courtesy: Archives, Univ. of Santa Clara.*

orations and a reading of a message from President Herbert Hoover—the King Alfonso Bell was hoisted into place. The tolling of the heavy steel bell three years after the holocaust concluded the restoration of Mission Santa Clara.

The Padre of the Rains

Among the several new buildings that appeared on the mission campus in the 1920's, none had a more colorful history than the Ricard Observatory. Erected in 1928, the monument memorialized the long and colorful career of Jerome Sixtus Ricard, Jesuit astronomer and meteorologist.

This French-born priest, who came to California in 1872 as a Jesuit novice, had little formal training for the vocation in weather forecasting that he manifested during his long tenure at Santa Clara. Apart from one summer-session course at Johns Hopkins and another at Creighton University, Ricard was mostly self-taught. Appointed to teach philosophy and mathematics at Santa Clara in 1891, Ricard soon persuaded the administration to purchase an eight-inch refracting telescope from an abandoned Methodist college at Napa, California, for $1,000. The college paid half the price and San Francisco foundry owner Peter Donahue donated the remainder.[19] With the aid of this telescope and other meteorological instruments, Ricard made the systematic solar observations that were the foundation for his theory of weather prognostication.

Comparing disturbances on the surface of the sun with climatic conditions on earth, he inferred a causal relationship between sunspots and terrestrial weather. Ricard proposed that "whenever a solar disturbance, in the shape of a spot or facula, . . . stands in a given position, there is a storm on the earth in a given position." For terrestrial weather to be affected, the spot must cross the solar meridian in one of four critical points.[20] Hence when a solar disturbance travels to a point three days distant from the western limb, or rim, of the sun, a storm front appears on the Pacific Coast. "It is not always accompanied by rain or snow," Ricard explained, "but a pronounced disturbance is invariable." Fine weather, on the other hand, seems to follow in the same general area when a sunspot passes *behind* the western solar limb. How this apparently causal relationship might be explained, Ricard did not know; but he became convinced that because of its observable regularity, "henceforth no rational being dare deny that the sun, through its changes, is making our weather changes."[21]

After six years of observing, calculating, and record keeping, Ricard began making long-range weather forecasts in 1907. He put forth weekly and then monthly predictions. This he did at a time when most forecasters, including the U.S. Weather Bureau, limited their weather news to a few days' notice. According to conventional methods, changes in weather could be detected only after a rise or fall in atmospheric pressure had registered on the barometer. Ricard maintained that by making certain calculations based on the position of sunspots facing the earth, he could with fair accuracy anticipate those barometric changes. He believed that this information enabled him to forecast the weather much further ahead than the ordinary weatherman.[22]

Ricard's claims attracted keen attention. In an agricultural region of uncertain and often meager precipitation, foreknowledge of the weather is a pearl beyond price. California agriculture, owing to its phenomenal growth after the turn of the century and to the state's seasonal rainfall patterns, depended upon prudent allocation of water. So did the state's burgeoning metropolitan centers, San Francisco and Los Angeles. Consequently, during the years when the development of the Owens Valley Project, the construction of the Hetch Hetchy diversion, and the fights over water jurisdiction in Southern California were producing banner headlines, Ricard's meteorological theories were studied and respected. Newspapers began printing the weather forecasts of the "Padre of the Rains," as he was named by a San Francisco journalist. In 1915 Ricard began circulating *The Sunspot*, a monthly review dedicated to his weather projections and to articles of general meteorological interest. Before long, weather-conscious farmers, athletic promoters, and even Hollywood movie makers began calling Santa Clara's observatory for the latest word on the weather.[23]

Others scoffed at Ricard's unorthodox claims. Although farmers in California's Central Valley and in the land to the south swore by the accuracy of his forecasts, Ricard's peers in the scientific world questioned his unconventional hypotheses. Some contradicted them outright. W. W. Campbell of the Lick Observatory, arguing that the impact of solar disturbances upon changes in the earth's atmosphere was not as great as Ricard believed, doubted that individual disturbances on the sun could effect, directly and simultaneously, short-period weather changes on the Pacific Coast. But Ricard was adamant. Sunspots not only influence the weather, he insisted, but they do so more than anything else. Four thousand spots and fourteen years of uninterrupted observations, he declared, proved the truth of his theory "beyond the shadow of a doubt."[24]

Against the doubters, the tenacious Frenchman waged constant warfare in the columns of *The Sunspot* and the California press. Any article or address by a scientist opposing the sunspot theory, one journalist wrote, called forth a special reply from the Santa Clara observatory, and because Ricard's pronouncements were always tinged with humor and sarcasm, they quickly found their way onto the front pages of the newspapers.[25] When the chief of the U.S. Weather Bureau revealed his disdain for long-range forcasting by disputing both the sunspot theory and Ricard's belief that volcanic dust over Hawaii could affect Pacific weather, the Jesuit issued one of his "sizzling" replies. The chief and his experts "are 200 years behind the times." "America may be a paradise of fools, but the long-range forecaster is not contained within the embrace of that category." When the director of the Amherst Observatory miscalculated, according to Ricard's figures, the relationship between a particular group of sunspots and the aurora borealis, the lively Frenchman called him "a stubborn horse in an old pasture, refusing to be moved to brand new fields."[26]

Ricard's colorful controversies with the professional scoffers sent his popularity soaring. During the 1920's, his every opinion was newsworthy. Ricard
was quoted equally on sunspots and rain, science and religion, earthquakes
and Prohibition. When the findings of a University of California professor linking temblors and storms seemed to support the relationship that
Ricard had noted between earthquakes and sunspots, it was Ricard who
was quoted. Newspapers from San Francisco to New York flashed the word:
"Quakes due to Sunspots, says Ricard."[27]

On the subject of Prohibition, he was outspoken. His verbal broadsides at
the "bolsheviks" and "blue sneaks" who had taken "advantage of unnatural
times to force their narrow, unconstitutional laws upon America" always
made good copy in local newspapers. "That fanatics should, in the name of
a phantom law, wantonly destroy that which the Lord of heaven and earth
has created for the good of man" was a crime, declared Ricard who assiduously cultivated the vines clustered around his observatory in order to keep
his wine glass filled. When his opposition to the Volstead Act erupted in
editorials in *The Sunspot*, an embarrassed President Zacheus Maher implored the Jesuit provincial to use his influence to assure that the aging Ricard confine his comments to the weather and not "drag in the wets and drys"
when writing for the pages of his meteorological magazine.[28]

The old man's theological observations were sometimes more astute than
those of his contemporaries. That science and theology were irreconcilable
was unthinkable to Ricard. At the same time that Maher was complaining
to the Jesuit provincial of the modernist tendencies of one of the faculty
theologians who had told students that the biblical story of Noah need not
be taken literally, Ricard informed a visiting journalist that the scriptural
account of creation and the theory of evolution were not necessarily incompatible. "What does it matter what bones are found or what new theories, Darwinian or otherwise?" he declared. "Of course, we cannot interpret
the book of Genesis to meet the demands of today" in the same way we
once did.[29] On another occasion, after having chastized Luther Burbank and
David Starr Jordan for their "know it all" pronouncements of the subject
of religion, Ricard asked a reporter: "Do you think the astronomer is
troubled in his religious faith because he finds somewhere in the Bible that
Joshua commanded the sun to stand still? Must we give up all poetry and
become prosaic materialists for the sake of our astronomy? Would you become a quibbler over a choice of words, with so much glory and grandeur
before your eyes?"[30]

The Ricard Observatory

For more than thirty years, Ricard carried on his work in the picturesque vine-covered shacks in the college vineyard that housed his telescopes and scientific apparatus. In 1924, at the height of his popularity, the Knights of Columbus spearheaded a campaign among their members to erect on campus a modern observatory for the "Padre of the Rains," in recognition of his reputation as a weather forecaster. Though largely a special undertaking directed by Ricard, the Knights, and the Jesuit provincial, the project produced headaches for two university presidents.

Ground was broken in 1925, during the presidency of Zacheus Maher. Three years later, when Cornelius McCoy occupied the office, the edifice was still incomplete. The Knights, who enthusiastically agreed during their 1925 convention to erect the observatory, had a year later not yet reached their goal of $50,000. Fund raising was made more difficult when it was discovered that an impostor was making the rounds in San Francisco, soliciting money for the project in Ricard's name. Then an architect, who at first had offered to design the building as a work of love for the "Padre of the Rains," changed his mind and demanded a superintendency fee. Another source of trouble was Ricard himself, who, having grown increasingly independent of the university administration, tried to impose a "hands off" policy upon the president and resented his meddling in details of the building's construction.[31]

The most tedious if comical aspect of the observatory's construction concerned its main telescope. Eager to have the biggest and the best for the building's central dome, Ricard set his sights on a giant five-foot reflector that would rival the telescope possessed by the Mount Wilson Observatory. President Maher, who feared such a large machine would obligate Santa Clara for all time to sustain research commensurate with the cost and size of the instrument, tried to persuade Ricard to settle for a more modest telescope. But the stubborn astronomer would not be moved. "It is like buying a Rolls Royce when a Studebaker would do the work," Maher complained resignedly.[32]

After scouring Europe and America for a lens maker, Ricard reported in 1925 that he had found the right man in Canada. "A Vancouver gentleman, ranking high among authoritative scientists," was contracted to produce a sixty-inch mirror that would place Santa Clara in the foremost rank of the world's observatories. The five-foot reflector would be ready for operation

Jerome S. Ricard, popularly known as the "Padre of the Rains," sits by his telescope at the edge of the college vineyards, near the site of today's Ricard Observatory. *Courtesy: Archives, Univ. of Santa Clara.*

within a reasonable time and then would be joined to the mount and spec-troheliograph being manufactured separately in San Francisco.[33]

Three years later, after an expenditure of thousands of dollars on the glass and on three university-paid trips to California by the manufacturer to con-fer with Ricard, the observatory's fifty-foot central dome remained empty. When all three domes of the observatory were completed, the great tele-scope still had not materialized. Anxious inquiries from the university con-cerning the cause of the delay were always met with assurances of satisfac-tory progress from Vancouver and with requests for additional time to grind and polish the precious mirror. Although disappointed at the many delays in the completion of this glass, Ricard steadfastly refused to admit the possibility of fraud.

In 1928 word finally came that the long-awaited and much-publicized mirror had arrived in Oakland. A participant recalled that when the large packing crate was opened and when a thick coating of pitch that covered the contents was scraped off, it was discovered that instead of a polished glass sixty inches in diameter, the shipment contained a sixty-inch slab of concrete.[34]

A flurry of correspondence among an increasingly wearied President Mc-Coy, the Knights of Columbus, and the Vancouver police elicited a variety of explanations—including a suggestion from the lens maker that the block of concrete was really a composition which if subjected to treatment could be turned into glass. But no lens was forthcoming. Exasperated by five years' delay, McCoy offered to call it a draw. He would "close all negotiations" with the "Vancouver gentleman" and forego criminal proceedings if the lat-ter would return the funds forwarded to him over the years by the ingen-uous Ricard.[35]

"I am always humiliated when I see or think of the Observatory," McCoy observed many years later. "We built a barn and had no steed." When in 1941 the university purchased a sixteen-inch refractor in place of Ricard's chimerical five-foot mirror, McCoy from his home in Hollywood applauded the conclusion of the long episode with the comment, "We might at least have a colt in the barn."[36]

Although Ricard died at the age of eighty in 1930, soon after the comple-tion of the observatory, advocacy of the sunspot theory did not terminate im-mediately. His assistant for many years, Albert Newlin, inherited adminis-tration of the university weather station and continued to defend Ricard's views for many years after the old priest's death. He also expanded upon his mentor's system. During the depression, Newlin linked the eleven-year cycle of solar activity with drought, agricultural fertility, and, by extension, business conditions, thus prompting in 1934 headlines in San Francisco and New York that were reminiscent of Ricard in his heyday, "New Sunspots Forecast Better Times, End of Depression."[37] Newlin also interpreted another system of long-term weather forecasting based upon cycles of solar radiation, one fully developed in the 1930's by Dr. Charles Abbot of the Smithsonian Institution, as new confirmation of Ricard's theory. During his lifetime, however, Ricard himself had frequently distinguished between his own system of solar meteorology and the ideas Abbot had announced up to that time. Moreover, the latter's theory of long-range forecasting received no more acceptance by meteorologists than did Ricard's.[38]

With the passing of time, the "Padre of the Rains" and his theory of weather prediction were largely forgotten, his memory surviving chiefly in the recollections of generations of Santa Clarans. In the 1960's the development of America's space program and the attendant need to protect men and vehicles traveling outside the earth's atmosphere from destructive radiation resurrected curiosity about Ricard's view of the origin of sunspots. His belief that their appearance could be predicted piqued special scientific interest. But nothing came of the renewed inquiry, and the padre's papers were once again consigned to the archives.

The final verdict on Ricard's contribution to the science of solar observation and meteorology is yet to be written. One of his successors at the university observatory, citing a twelve-year study of the sunspot hypothesis, declared in 1956 that the theory could not be proved. "There seems to be some sort of complex relationship between the weather and sunspots, but Father Ricard's theory does not account for it." This critic thought that despite a few remarkable coincidences between the appearance of sunspots and terrestrial storms, Ricard's success in forecasting probably owed more to his shrewdness and salesmanship than to his theory.[39] Another analysis of his method and forecasts, one made by a student a few years later, suggested that Ricard was able to predict weather a month in advance with about 82 percent accuracy—a remarkable figure indeed. But the validity of the theory upon which he based his forecasts remained open to question.[40]

Contemporary meteorological research supports the more skeptical verdict. The relationship between weather and sunspots is not a simple one—if it were, it would long since have been uncovered. That there exists a correlation between fluctuations in solar activity and terrestrial weather, few experts deny. But the other factors affecting weather—including temperature, pressure, humidity, and wind speed—are complexly interrelated. Thus Ricard's theory is both narrow and difficult to assess.

Even if the sunspot theory of Jerome Sixtus Ricard has not won scientific acceptance, the exuberant Jesuit brought an avalanche of publicity to the mysterious sunspots and much controversy and discussion to the question of long-range weather forecasting. He also generated a great amount of public attention for Santa Clara, and he left the university the legacy of the Ricard Observatory, a monument to one of the most popular and colorful characters who ever walked the mission campus.

16
The Depression Years
1932–1940

In 1929 the balloon burst, and the prosperity of the 1920's shrank to the penury of the 1930's. The panic precipitated on Wall Street in October by the collapse of the stock market moved across the nation. As the grim reality of the Great Depression spread from New York to San Francisco, California became a refuge for the unemployed. Los Angeles, the city that had once invited settlers and tourists to its "everyman's Eden" with enticing advertisements, in 1936 rushed police guards to the border in a vain attempt to turn back the tide of jobless migrants pushing west. Only with the outbreak of World War II would the corner be turned and the depression ended. In the meantime, every institution in America was in shock.

How did the financial crisis affect higher education? As a group, universities fared surprisingly well, although the effects of the depression varied from place to place. Public universities suffered from reduced appropriations and lowered income from fees. Private institutions like Santa Clara lost income from endowments, private benefactions, and student tuition. Although enrollments fell at many colleges, the decline was usually not precipitous. In fact, during the 1931–32 school year, nationwide enrollment actually increased, only to fall again the following year. According to David D. Henry, "The most serious impact of the Depression upon higher education was psychological." Cutbacks in faculty positions and salaries increased tension between faculty and administration. Depression stringencies were a disillusioning experience for most students. "Not only were they thrown into the discomfiture of 'making ends meet' and sharing in the general worries of their parents' generation, but they felt that their future was uncertain and their aspirations were destroyed." As a consequence, the 1930's—like the 1960's—was a time of student unrest and a time in which many students involved themselves in social problems.[1]

Santa Clara's experience of the depression was in many ways typical. The impact of the crash was not felt immediately by the university. Enrollment did not suddenly plummet in 1929; in fact, it inched slightly upward, reaching an all-time high in 1931. Nor did the national economic crisis herald a sudden financial collapse for Santa Clara. The host of new buildings that were erected on the campus before the depression had not required deficit spending and did not burden Santa Clara with mortgaged classrooms. Proceeding cautiously on the pay-as-you-go basis of his predecessor, Zacheus Maher, President Cornelius McCoy continued construction in the years immediately following the crash.

But the depression's impact was cumulative. Within five years California was in severe economic trouble. Mortgage foreclosures terminated thousands of businesses, bankruptcies became endemic, and mass unemployment swept through the state until, by 1934, one fifth of the population was on public relief.[2] The university meanwhile had begun to feel the deepening crisis. In June, 1933, a year after he succeeded McCoy, President James Lyons reported that enrollment figures had fallen entirely below what they should be and that the decline in attendance had now reached a serious point. From a highwater mark of 491 reached in 1931, Santa Clara's total enrollment had dropped to fewer than four hundred students, a decline of nearly 20 percent.[3]

The situation worsened. Because "concessions of all kinds" had been made to those in need, President Lyons reported in 1935 that the resources of the university had been "subjected to a greater strain than at any previous time." As "an experiment and a good-will policy," the president had reduced rates and allowed delays in tuition payments during his first year in office. However, after confronting both a loss of $15,000 in deferred payments during the fall semester of 1932 and the opposition of the board of trustees, Lyons admitted that his experiment had proved rather disastrous and could not be continued. "We are forced to drop thirty or forty boys owing to their want and our financial crises."[4] In one bizarre case, the father of a senior student to whom the president had refused a diploma until his bills were paid angrily took his complaint to Rome in the vain hope of suing the beleaguered priest in an ecclesiastical tribunal.

When possible, concessions continued to be made to enable students to remain in school. There were occasional laments in the school newspaper about New Deal encroachments upon private enterprise, but no complaints when the Emergency Relief Agency came to the aid of forty undergraduates in 1934 by granting them fifteen dollars a month. Needy and deserving students received additional help the following year, when the university established six four-year scholarships.

In the face of falling tuition income, Lyons, like many other college administrators, was forced to economize. On October 1, 1932, all faculty salaries of more than $200 a month were reportedly reduced 15 percent. Intercollegiate baseball was dropped in the spring of 1933, and the next year publication of the college yearbook was suspended. Such cutbacks provoked resentment, but Lyons remained convinced that because of the depression they had to be made.[5]

Jousting Jesuits

Restive students and teachers were not the only adversaries Lyons faced in his battle to balance the university's budget. Unknown to the student body and to most of the faculty, he was clashing swords with Zacheus Maher, former Santa Clara president and since 1932 head of the California Province. Maher directed frequent and fervent appeals to the university for financial assistance, which from his point of view seemed neither unreasonable nor immoderate.

Despite the enrollment fluctuations of which Lyons complained, Santa Clara's economic condition was enviable. When the university's accounts were placed beside those of other Jesuit houses in 1933, they stood as "probably the best in the province." The following year, Santa Clara's condition was "very satisfactory," and in 1935 a Jesuit glowingly described the school to Father Louis Rudolph, incoming president, as "the plum" of the California Province.[6] Kept afloat by tuition, reallocated funds, and gate receipts from intercollegiate football games, Santa Clara passed through the worst years of the Great Depression free from debt, occasionally even ending the year (as in 1934) with a budgetary surplus.

By contrast, the California Province to which the university was intimately bound was hard pressed to pay its food bills. The separation of Oregon and California into two Jesuit provinces in 1932 had left the latter heavily indebted to the new province to the north. In addition the burden of sustaining several Jesuit schools in California weighed heavily upon Maher's shoulders. Whether some of these institutions would survive seemed uncertain during the darkest days of the depression. Forced into the strictest frugality and always in need of cash, Zacheus Maher looked frantically to Santa Clara for help.

In 1932 he approached President Lyons with a proposal: Would the university stand as security for a $50,000 loan the province was then negotiating on behalf of its needy institutions? Lyons was not insensitive to the provincial's plight. But he was also aware of his obligation as president to protect the financial health and the rights of the university. That Santa Clara should be saddled with the debts of other Jesuit schools or of the province itself seemed unjust. For this reason he resisted the request. Though warned by Maher that opposition would "not sit well with Father General," Lyons and his advisers knew that the rules of the order placed well-defined limits upon a provincial's power to interfere in the financial autonomy of an individual Jesuit house. They called Maher's bluff by referring the matter to Rome themselves. Lyons's position was sustained, and Santa Clara did not supply the collateral for the loan.[7]

The following year a new financial request appeared on the president's desk. In 1933 the university had agreed to receive on campus for a year a group of California Jesuit scholastics engaged in philosophy studies. Normally, the seminarians would have attended the Jesuit philosophate at Mount St. Michael's in Spokane, Washington, but to control the outflow of the province's resources Maher took the extraordinary step of enrolling the scholastics temporarily at Santa Clara. After the twenty-two philosophers were settled, Maher revealed that not only was he unable to pay their bills, but he asked as a gift to the province that the university accommodate forty more scholastics the following year. The provincial offered two alternatives: either Lyons could waive all recompense or he could establish a nominal rate for the scholastics' housing and education. In the latter case the university was asked to "waive payment until such time as the province may be in a position to pay."

Lyons was not pleased with the option. "Why should Santa Clara" alone "be asked to take the whole burden" of educating the province's young men? Annoyed by Maher's persistence, he bluntly informed the provincial that the proposal seemed "just another way of imposing upon Santa Clara" the discredited request of the previous year. He agreed to support the philosophers for one year, and once again he petitioned Father Ledochowski's intervention. In reply the father general ordered the philosophers to return the following autumn to Mount St. Michael's in Spokane.[8]

In the months that followed, the jousting between the two Jesuits continued, as each fought to protect the interests and responsibilities of his office in those perilous times. According to one source, Maher again requested security for a large loan from the university on behalf of the province in 1935, and once again he met a wall of opposition at Santa Clara.[9] Soon afterward, James Lyons was removed from the presidency of the university.

Because Lyons's term still had a year to run, some concluded that his repeated rejection of the provincial's financial requests had prompted his downfall. Separation of fact from conjecture is not possible because much of the pertinent documentation has yet to be opened to historical examination. It is true that Lyons's unwillingness to divide Santa Clara's spoils angered the provincial as well as the heads of the debt-ridden Jesuit schools in the province. But there was a history of disagreement between Maher and Lyons on a variety of subjects. This general incompatibility may have gradually eroded Maher's confidence in the young president's style of governance.[10]

Whatever the reason, on July 4, 1935, Lyons was ordered to the provincial office in San Jose for a conference. Father Louis Rudolph, Dean of Arts at Loyola University, had received a summons in Los Angeles the day before to travel to the same meeting. Upon their arrival both men were informed by the provincial that Rome had approved Rudolph's replacement of Lyons at Santa Clara. Neither seems to have had any foreknowledge of the purpose of the meeting, evidence of the secretive manner in which the mandates of Jesuit obedience were then executed. The transfer of authority occurred ten days later. Lyons was sent south to Loyola University in Los Angeles. Rudolph became president of Santa Clara on July 14, 1935.[11]

Combating Communism

The story of the Great Depression is not recorded exclusively on the pages of financial ledgers, nor are dollars and cents the sole measure of its impact. The 1930's were also a time of unprecedented social and political turmoil. Labor disputes provoked violence from the waterfront docks of San Francisco to the fruit-packing sheds of the Imperial Valley. And the frustration that drove thousands of dust-bowl migrants into the Golden State was a poignant element in the social impact of those years. Panaceas as well as scapegoats abounded. Messiahs offered cure-alls such as the Technocracy Movement, the Townsend Plan, and the International Church of the Foursquare Gospel as led by Aimee Semple McPherson.

From most of this unrest Santa Clara remained aloof and protected, a quiet backwater in an agitated sea. Produce from the college farm kept food on the dormitory tables during the worst years of the depression, sparing students the suffering experienced by the army of migrants laboring in the orchards and fields of the Santa Clara Valley. To an extent, political and social issues of the day were not neglected by Santa Clara's undergraduates. There were debates and controversies in the pages of the university newspaper. The future of capitalism, the defects of Technocracy, and the pros and cons of the New Deal all found a place alongside the latest sports scores. But sports dominated the journal out of proportion to all other topics during the 1930's. The turbulence outside rarely disturbed the tranquility of the little campus community.

But there were exceptions. One was the contemporary obsession with

The university as it appeared in 1940, before the postwar transformation of the Santa Clara Valley. The Alameda, a two-lane road connecting San Jose and the small town of Santa Clara, runs in front of the college grounds. In the distance, beyond the town, open fields can still be seen. *Courtesy: U.S. Army Air Corps photo, Archives, Univ. of Santa Clara.*

Communist subversion. Another was the vigilante lynching that occurred in San Jose in 1933.

Communism, the *Stanford Daily* declared in 1934, is "the twentieth century's No. 1 scare-word."[12] Bolshevism had frequently been blamed for the unwelcome outbursts of social criticism of the previous decade. The turmoil of the Great Depression was similarly ascribed to those who, as one Santa Clara alumnus put it, "wave red flags and sing songs of rebellion."[13] The efforts of the Communist Party to organize migrant laborers and cannery workers in the early 1930's had convinced many Californians that the entire labor movement was Communist inspired and that every strike was the work of Marxist agitators. As the depression worsened and as society grew more restive, so too did the tendency to paint all forms of social criticism with the red brush of radicalism. The primacy of the red menace in the eyes of many worried citizens was illustrated by a series of events that unfolded at several California colleges in 1934.

That autumn, while Californians nervously awaited the outcome of a gubernatorial election between an incumbent Republican, Frank Merriam, and a former Socialist, Upton Sinclair, a tide of protest surged through the California campuses. The first disturbance erupted in October at the University of California, Los Angeles, where a group of students pressured the administration for permission to hold an open forum to discuss election issues. The provost of UCLA responded by suspending five of the student leaders for reported Communist activities.[14] A series of student strikes and protests followed, although the majority of the student body supported the administration. When the worried provost summoned all universities and fraternities to join in a campaign against radicalism on November 1, some one hundred fifty athletes formed a vigilante patrol pledged to purge the UCLA campus of radicals.[15]

The spirit of confrontation spread quickly to other campuses. When inflammatory leaflets were circulated at San Jose State College that same week by an alleged Communist agitator, President Thomas MacQuarrie called upon "every true citizen on this campus" to eradicate the "festering sore." "If you know members of the group," he counseled students, "please feel quite free to take them to the edge of the campus and drop them off." "No more fooling," the president concluded, "No more mollycoddling."[16] A few days later a mass meeting held at Berkeley's Sather Gate by campus radicals to protest the suspensions at UCLA was met with a shower of eggs and tomatoes. Nonetheless, the meeting convinced an already jittery public that the University of California was a hotbed of subversives.[17]

On November 1, Santa Clara had its own politically charged event. While UCLA's vigilantes were mustering to purge the college of Communism and while the president of nearby San Jose State was issuing his call to arms, Santa Clara expelled the editor of its student newspaper, reportedly for radical activities. The *San Francisco Chronicle* broke the news: "Santa Clara ousts school editor as red."[18]

Two editorials published in the campus newspaper, *The Santa Clara*, preceded the expulsion. Disturbed by the ease with which a local congressman found reds under every university bed, editor Edward Horton, a junior from Richmond, California, posed a question: "Are we being drugged with Communism?" In his answer he criticized the congressman's tendency to "drag down everybody" who opposed him with the "general term—'Red,'" and Horton ridiculed the congressman's "century-late" laissez-faire economic philosophy.

A second editorial appearing in the same issue voiced a conviction in agreement with a pacifist movement that had been launched at Oxford University: "Students have nothing to gain by war." When antiwar students in England had the year before pledged never to fight for king and country, they had attracted a sympathetic response from students around the world. On many American campuses compulsory ROTC became the target of pacifist opposition. Because Santa Clara then had no military training program, Horton appealed for a different form of opposition. When the "war lords" ask the colleges to contribute men for the world's next armed conflict, the editor of *The Santa Clara* urged his fellows, "be intelligent." "Know what war has in store for you, know that you can gain nothing by it. Then serve notice to the people that would have you fight, that you will have nothing to do with their proposals."[19]

Such counsel—common enough in the 1960's—was a red flag in 1934. Horton, who two months earlier had lamented the "apparent" influence of the "red plague" in the nation's social unrest and labor uprisings, was himself painted in bright pink.[20]

University authorities were more annoyed by the fact that the two editorials had escaped the censorship of the faculty adviser than by their content. But some observers criticized the message. A few of the faculty, convinced that all forms of pacifism were "Moscow bred," were alarmed to see "open advocacy" of "Marxist philosophy" on the pages of *The Santa Clara*.[21] And some off-campus readers reacted similarly. Rapping the knuckles of the administration for its "woeful lack of censorship," one alumnus concluded angrily that the "irresponsible editorials" could have "emanated verbatim from Moscow."[22] The campus newspaper, a source of pride in recent years because of the awards it had won for outstanding journalism, was now an embarrassment. The controversy grew more heated two weeks later when authorities, without specifying the reason publicly, expelled the errant editor. The sacking, which *Time* magazine and the press in general ascribed to Horton's radical sympathies, stimulated a rash of national publicity for the university, as well as angry letters of protest from pacifist and radical student groups across the country.[23]

The episode also helped to earn Santa Clara a reputation for no-nonsense anti-Communism. In 1936, when the War Department approved the university's request for a campus ROTC unit, some university authorities attributed the decision to the school's strong stand against Communism and to its strict actions during the red scares of the thirties.[24] The headlines generated by the dismissal of its crusading student editor were not the only foundation for Santa Clara's anti-Communist reputation. When alumnus Lewis F. Byington, president of the Public Utilities Commission of San Francisco, delivered a radio address in 1934 that linked the nation's social unrest to "1,500,000 radicals in this country who are clamoring for a change in the nature of our government from its present form to a Communistic state," a university publication declared that the speech reiterated that which was fundamental in the teachings of Santa Clara. The administration also concurred when Byington declared that "The schools of America should no more consider graduating a student who lacks faith in our Government than a school of theology should consider graduating a minister who lacks faith in God."[25]

Steps to avoid the danger of graduating such a student were taken as early as 1934, when Provincial Zacheus Maher ordered that courses, lectures, and seminars on Communism be instituted by all Jesuit colleges in California. Compliance at Santa Clara followed the wave of anxiety regarding radical influences that swept over the state's campuses that autumn. In January, 1935, the university chaplain, Father Hugh Donavon, announced the inauguration of a series of compulsory chapel talks in which, it was promised, "the whole field of Communism and Atheism" would be explained, and "the inherent impossibility of their truth" demonstrated.[26] Donavon did not stint in his coverage. "The infiltration of the Soviet," a campus chronicler summarized, "into religion, the nation, industry, the press, labor, the theatre, schools and local civil life was exemplified freely" by the chaplain's lectures.[27] The study of Marxism was also incorporated into the university's political science and philosophy courses. Thus, the campus newspaper reported, every student "will be forearmed and prepared for the open defense of his country, his religion and his home" against "the revolutionary aliens" bent on destroying America.[28]

A Lynching in San Jose

Traditional values seemed threatened on many fronts during the thirties. The anti-red hysteria that swept through the state was merely one symptom of the profound disquiet that characterized the era. Lawlessness, too, was growing more fearful, as was brought home to Santa Clara in 1933. That autumn, shortly after school began, Brooke Hart, a former university student, was kidnapped and brutally murdered. Two weeks later an enraged mob in San Jose demonstrated its lack of confidence in the ability of traditional institutions to deal with the crime by perpetrating another: it lynched the two alleged abductors in the city park.

Neither act of violence, the kidnap-murder or the lynching, was unprecedented in the turbulence of the thirties. Kidnapping for ransom claimed its most famous victim in 1932 with the abduction and murder of the Lindbergh baby. Nor was vigilante violence—even lynching—uncommon. Bands of student vigilantes stalked the hills of Westwood, the site of UCLA, and of Berkeley in 1934, sometimes using force to purge the campus of radicals. Attacks on union sympathizers by mobs of masked strikebreakers characterized California's labor strife during the depression, and the lynching of blacks was a frequent event in the Southern states. California had a long tradition of vigilante action. From the 1840's, more lynchings occurred in the Golden State than anywhere outside the South, and more lynchings of white men than in any other state in the Union.[29]

The circumstances leading to the hangings of 1933 began on November 9 with the disappearance of Brooke Hart, the twenty-two-year-old son of a wealthy San Jose businessman. Having a few months earlier completed his studies at Santa Clara, Hart had assumed the vice-presidency of the family department store in San Jose. Despite a massive manhunt by police, no clues could be found to his whereabouts. A week after the disappearance a caller attempted to communicate details regarding the payment of ransom to Hart's parents' home on the Alameda, and a telephone tap led police to two suspects. According to newspaper accounts, Thomas Thurmond and Jack Holmes, men in their late twenties, soon confessed Hart's abduction and murder.

According to their statement, which police immediately released to the press, the two men had seized their victim at gunpoint in the parking lot behind the family store and had taken him to the San Mateo Bridge. There, under cover of darkness, they had bound his arms with baling wire, bashed in his head with a stone, and tossed him half-conscious and weighted down with cement blocks into the waters of San Francisco Bay.[30] Another ten days passed before his body could be found. Its recovery sent waves of anger and revulsion through the community.

Faint rumblings of possible vigilante action against the two suspects began several days before the recovery of the body, after police transferred the pair under heavy guard from San Francisco to the San Jose jail. At that time, Sheriff William Emig publicly warned his fellow citizens against mob violence.[31] At the university, where young Hart's disappearance had special significance, the news of his murder cast a deadening pall.[32] Reports published in a San Francisco newspaper that Santa Clara students were organizing a party to lynch the jailed suspects were branded by the university newspaper as entirely false. "We have heard some dark and ominous mutterings during the past week," an editorial penned anonymously by a campus Jesuit admitted, but "we fervently hope [they] will never flare into riotous anger." "It would be a gross miscarriage of justice to permit or participate in a mob retribution."[33]

From the governor's office in Sacramento, counsel of a markedly different tone emerged. As tension mounted quickly following the finding of Hart's remains, Governor James Rolph, Jr., publicly promised not to call out the National Guard "to protect those two fellows" in the San Jose jail.[34] No clearer summons to vigilante action could have been issued.

The recovery of Hart's body from the waters of San Francisco Bay on the morning of November 26 was the spark that set off an explosion of community violence. It was Sunday. All day long, an ever-increasing crowd converged on the San Jose jail. When darkness fell, rioting began. By nine o'clock the situation was out of hand. While hundreds of curious men and women stood looking on, drawn to the scene by the blow-by-blow reports of a local radio broadcaster, a mob of shouting, brick-throwing vigilantes began to assault the prison. Police resisted the rioters with tear gas until it ran out and then, around eleven o'clock, they stepped aside. From a discreet distance, the officers watched as the drama moved to its bloody denouement.[35]

After breaking down the door by using a pipe as a battering ram, a score of volunteer hangmen rushed into the jail and pulled their prey from the cells. Stripped of clothing and beaten, the two men were dragged across the street to the spreading acacia trees of St. James Park. The first victim offered

A mob of more than one thousand persons cheered as these men battered down the door of the San Jose jail to reach the alleged kidnap-slayers of Santa Clara student Brooke Hart in November, 1933. The two victims were dragged from their cells, beaten, and hanged in St. James Park across the street. *Courtesy: Wide World Photos.*

no resistance. While flashlights illuminated his nakedness and the crowd roared its approval, half a dozen men jerked the doomed man aloft. Disregarding the second victim's protests, a red-haired youth slipped a noose around his neck and he too was dispatched by half a dozen executioners. In a few minutes the deadly drama was over. "Bathed in the white light of a half moon," an eyewitness wrote, St. James Park now offered "a ghastly spectacle." As the bodies continued to dangle from the trees, "a sepulchral silence settled over the place."[36]

Public reaction to the lynching was as swift as it was short-lived. Governor Rolph lauded those responsible for the atrocity, whereas the press generally censured the mob murders. Numerous editorials inveighing against the contemporary penchant for vigilante justice appeared, some in newspapers that had kept a conspicuous silence, unlike the campus journal at Santa Clara, before the foreseeable tragedy.

The identity of the vigilantes and the question of their legal liability was the object of only momentary curiosity. Few papers were as bold as the *Stanford Daily* which, the day following the lynching, laid full responsibility on "a handful of Santa Clara students, roommates [and] buddies of murdered Brooke Hart."[37] No disclaimers issued from the mission campus, where the morality of lynching was now a much-discussed question. That some students had ignored a curfew and slipped out of the dormitories that night to join the swelling crowd in St. James Park no one could deny. After viewing their morning newspaper the next day, some Santa Clarans also claimed that a few familiar faces could be spotted in photographs of the mob gathered before the door of the besieged jail. The *San Francisco Examiner*, however, took pains to absolve the students of complicity, although it admitted that the ringleaders were mostly men in their early twenties. "The various versions of the attack on the jail," the *Examiner* concluded, "although conflicting as to detail, definitely eliminated rumors that the lynching had been organized and carried through by students of Santa Clara University, the alma mater of young Hart."[38]

In fact, in the flush of excitement that immediately followed the lynching, a few of the vigilantes openly admitted their identity and boasted of their role in the double execution. The public praise heaped upon them by no less a personage than the governor and the tacit approval bestowed by the local community encouraged such braggadocio. Later, as more thoughtful spokesmen voiced their shocked disapproval and as the gravity of the deed began to dawn on piqued consciences, a pall of protective silence gradually descended around the entire episode. Authorities in San Jose initiated no legal action. In the sobering aftermath, the consensus was that the ugly events in St. James Park should be forgotten as soon as possible.

Governor Rolph's role in the affair was less readily ignored or less quickly forgiven. He acted in what has been described as a desperate and deluded attempt to regain his popularity, which had been shaken by the depression.[39] For whatever reasons, "Sunny Jim" Rolph had not only encouraged the lynching but had openly and vividly congratulated those responsible. "That was a fine lesson for the whole nation," the governor announced from Sacramento the day after the hangings. "They made a good job of it." If any are arrested for the crime, he promised, "I'll pardon them all." Rolph wished he could hand over all convicted kidnappers to "those fine, patriotic citizens of San Jose who know how to handle such a situation."[40] Rolph's defense of lynching did nothing to aid his political career, which ended abruptly six months later when he collapsed and died during a reelection campaign. A wave of denunciation and angry editorials crossed the nation, protesting the irresponsibility of California's "Governor Lynch."[41]

Depression Distractions

College life during the 1930's had its grim intervals, but they did not dominate the campus atmosphere nor the consciousness of the average student. The typical Santa Clara undergraduate spent more time at football games and in traditional collegiate activities than he did at fretting about the red menace, vigilante violence, and other depression worries.

Authorities were forced by hard times to tighten purse strings but not to abolish fun, particularly athletics, which received unprecedented support and encouragement from the Santa Clara administration. President Lyons also compensated for the deprivations of the depression by sponsoring frequent entertainments and extravaganzas. They raised the eyebrows of some cost-conscious Jesuit superiors, who considered Lyons more suited to public-relations work than to the duties of the university presidency. But his productions did brighten college life during the early thirties.

Lyons had a penchant for fanfare, bunting-wrapped buildings, and grand opera, of which he was an avid devotee. He was at his best when staging special ceremonies and pageants. During his five years as president, a long list of celebrities and distinguished visitors responded to his invitations to visit the campus. After leaving the White House, Herbert Hoover made his first public appearance at the university on April 23, 1933. The former president, described by reporters as looking "pale, his face lined and drawn," came to Santa Clara to attend a memorial military mass for the crew of the *U.S.S. Akron*, a dirigible that had recently gone down in the Pacific.[42] That same year Guglielmo Marconi, father of wireless telegraphy, toured the campus and met with the aging Father Richard Bell, Santa Clara's radio pioneer. It was reported that, in anticipation of the early repeal of the Eighteenth Amendment, the famous inventor was banqueted in Nobili Hall and served fitting beverages from the college vineyard at Villa Maria.[43] A few months later the visit amid much fanfare of Augusto Rosso, Italy's ambassador to the United States, was climaxed by the granting of an honorary degree and by enthusiastic encomiums from the president regarding the Lateran Treaty of 1929, which established the sovereignty of the State of Vatican City. Lyons praised Benito Mussolini as "a man whom God has raised up."[44] James A. Farley, Roosevelt's campaign manager and postmaster general, paid the university a visit the following year.[45]

Lyons promoted other morale-building projects. In 1935 he announced the formation of the Faculty Club for the purpose of bringing about a mutual understanding of common problems pertaining to the University.[46] The Catala Club, a women's society he had helped organize in 1930, continued to sponsor special lectures and to raise scholarship funds for needy students. Lyons revived President's Day, an annual celebration he remembered from his own undergraduate years at Santa Clara, in 1935. For the celebration that year students and faculty staged an elaborate production of *Nazareth*, the Santa Clara Passion play. A special role was created for former child star Jackie Coogan, then a Santa Clara freshman. The resurgence of the university's Alumni Association testified to Lyon's interest in graduates and in Santa Clara's rising football fortunes. Homecoming, a practice abandoned for a decade, was resurrected, and a revitalized newsletter for alumni began to roll off the press.

Student publications also experienced new vitality. Since its founding in 1922 the campus newspaper, *The Santa Clara*, had gradually grown in size until by 1930 it was reputed to carry more news than any other Catholic student newspaper in the United States.[47] Directed by several talented student editors in quick succession, the campus weekly won national awards in collegiate journalism, including an All-American Pacemaker prize two years in a row.

In 1931 the Santa Clara *Owl*, the West's oldest college magazine when it had ceased publication in 1875, was revived as the literary supplement to the newspaper. Its reappearance after a lapse of more than fifty years was the

work of a gifted sophomore from Hollywood, James Pike, later the colorful
Episcopal bishop of California. Also responsible in large part for the success
of *The Santa Clara*, Pike was appointed editor of the paper in 1932. Dissatisfied with the courses offered at Santa Clara, which he found insufficiently
challenging (he was once booed in the student dining room when his classmates learned of his criticisms), Pike transferred to the University of California at Los Angeles during the summer of 1932. Hence his editorship of *The
Santa Clara* was short-lived.[48] Pike's keen interest in the campus journal survived the separation, however, inasmuch as he continued to guide its publication long-distance by supplying his co-workers with ideas and layouts
through the mail.[49]

The Glacier Priest

Among the famous persons who spoke to the campus community in the
thirties, no one was more familiar than Santa Clara's own Bernard R. Hubbard, popularly known as the "Glacier Priest." Though listed in the university bulletin as a member of the geology department, the peripatetic Hubbard
spent most of his time exploring Alaska and lecturing about his travels to
audiences across the country.

Hubbard's career as an explorer began when he was a youth climbing the
Santa Cruz mountains with camera, gun and dog.[50] Later he was dubbed
"Fossil" by his classmates at St. Ignatius College and at Santa Clara because
of his interest in geology. Hubbard entered the Jesuit order in 1908, when he
was twenty years old. Even as a religious he showed great resourcefulness in
finding opportunities for mountain climbing and exploration. Sent to Inns-
bruck, Austria, in the 1920's to complete his theological studies, Hubbard
devoted more than his spare time to probing and photographing the alpine
peaks and glaciers of the Austrian Tyrol. It is here that he earned the nickname *Gletscher Pfarrer*—"Glacier Priest"—which he carried all his life.[51]

In 1926 Hubbard returned to Santa Clara to teach Greek, German, and
geology, but it was not long before he again pulled on his hiking boots.
During summer vacation in 1927 he made his first major expedition to
Alaska to explore the Mendenhall and Taku glaciers. That trip, over country
never before traversed by man, brought the thirty-nine-year-old priest extended publicity.[52] So great was the interest generated by nationwide newspaper coverage of the expedition—beautifully illustrated by Hubbard's own
photographs of the glacial wonderland—that another trip was organized
the following year.

When Hubbard returned from the Alaskan wilderness in 1928, he announced that he was "the first human being ever to reach the rugged and almost inaccessible interior of Kodiak Island," where he found mountains six thousand feet high of which "no one had previously known the existence."[53] His knowledge of the Taku River region led the U.S. Coast and Geodetic Survey to seek his services the following summer as guide for a party erecting triangulation stations there. The summer of 1929 also found Hubbard trekking through the rarely visited and spectacular Valley of Ten Thousand Smokes toward the summit of the towering volcano Mount Katmai.

Frequently accompanied by strapping athletes from the Santa Clara football team ("chosen to stand hardship," a New York paper explained) and occasionally traveling alone (as in 1931, when he mushed a thirteen-dog-team one thousand six hundred miles from the interior of Alaska to the Bering Sea), Hubbard pursued his interests in both geology and the great outdoors. They had long since overshadowed his devotion to the classroom. In 1930 he was released from teaching at the university for full-time lecturing, writing, and further exploration of the Alaskan wilderness.[54]

Financing his trips with proceeds from his public lectures (any surplus was destined for the Jesuit missions in Alaska), Hubbard turned his attention in the early thirties to the volcano-torn Alaskan Peninsula. He had visited Aniakchak, "the largest active volcano in the world," for the first time in 1930. The next year Aniakchak erupted in a spectacular display of fire and molten rock. Hubbard returned to explore and photograph the volcano's still smoking crater. For two weeks he and his party of university athletes trekked around and through its smoldering dangers. The results of that expedition were described in *National Geographic*.[55] Hubbard returned frequently to the giant craters of Aniakchak, Veniaminof, and Katmai in succeeding years, as in 1934, when the National Geographic Society participated in his expedition to explore and map both the Alaskan Peninsula and the adjacent Aleutian Islands, whose topography had been greatly altered by the recent volcanic upheavals.[56]

When the adventures of this unusual Jesuit were serialized in *The Saturday Evening Post* in 1932, the name "Glacier Priest" became a household word. Sponsorship of his lecture tour and radio broadcasts by the National Broadcasting Company that same year enhanced Hubbard's finances as well as his fame.[57] Accompanied by a couple of his Alaskan sled dogs, Hubbard thrilled audiences across the country with stories of how he had traveled with Eskimos on a two-thousand-mile trip to the Arctic Circle, celebrated Mass on ice floes, narrowly escaped death while flying an airplane into the crater of a still active volcano, and hiked for weeks through the vast center of the mighty

"The Glacier Priest," explorer-photographer Bernard R. Hubbard, nurses a baby seal on King Island, Alaska, in 1938. *Courtesy: Archives, Univ. of Santa Clara.*

Aniakchak. "Half the year the highest paid lecturer in the world, the other half a wanderer among treacherous craters and glaciers": thus *The Literary Digest* described him in 1937. When he stepped down from the lecture platform at New York's Town Hall in May of that year, after eight months on the road, he had delivered more than 275 talks, "probably a world record," the *Digest* surmised.[58] Hubbard also wrote popular accounts of his travels. *Mush You Malemutes*, his first book, appeared in 1932; three years later he wrote *Cradle of the Storms*.

Although scientists occasionally accompanied him (Hubbard himself was largely self-trained), the overall scientific value of his thirty-odd expeditions to Alaska was not great. Indeed, his pretensions to expertise on a variety of highly technical subjects, as well as his proclivity for the spectacular and for what appeared to be self-serving publicity, earned him criticism from fellow Jesuits trained in geology and other scientific fields. Hubbard was effective in other ways, however, for his adventures repeated a harvest of publicity not only for himself but also for Santa Clara and especially Alaska. While university football teams were capturing headlines for Santa Clara in newspapers across America, the "Glacier Priest" was making the name of the university known in lecture halls from Los Angeles to New York.

Alaska loved him as its volunteer ambassador because of the worldwide attention he drew to the territory's natural wonders.[59] His lecture tours and radio broadcasts, as well as the coverage he received in magazines and newspapers, led a Juneau daily to conclude in 1932 that Bernard Hubbard had generated the most extensive and effective advertising that Alaska had yet received.[60]

But the most important result of his explorations was the thousands of feet of motion-picture and still film with which he illustrated his lectures. Those materials, which today are kept in the university archives, constitute one of the largest collections of images of Alaska in the 1930's. Hubbard's photographs provide a valuable visual record of many aspects of Alaskan geography and of the life of its native peoples that have long since disappeared.

"Fight for Santa Clara"

Nothing—neither the adventures of Hubbard nor the plays and pageants of President Lyons—publicized Santa Clara during the 1930's as much as intercollegiate athletics. Baseball, once the mission campus's favorite sport, had been virtually buried and forgotten during the depression decade.[61] Basketball and football, on the other hand, attained extraordinary popularity and, in the case of football, extraordinary financial success as fans by the tens of thousands flocked to Kezar Stadium to cheer on the Broncos to "fight for Santa Clara."

Obliged to compete with football for funds, fans, and players, basketball's acceptance had been slow in previous decades. Once considered a women's game, the sport was described as "dead or dying" at Santa Clara in 1918.[62] However, as a result of rule changes that introduced the fast break and more excitement into the game (rules were standardized nationwide for the first time in 1934), basketball emerged in the thirties as a major sport, second only to football in popularity. When a former campus basketball star, George Barsi, returned to the university as coach in 1935, the Broncos moved into the national spotlight. Within a few years, Santa Clara teams were competing in Madison Square Garden in New York City and in other places in the East as well as the Midwest. Before World War II brought the curtain down on intercollegiate competition, Barsi had developed such players as Ralph Giannini (Santa Clara's first basketball all-American), Bruce Hale, Stan Patrick, Marty Passaglia, Jim Rickert, and Robert Feerick.

In 1938, the Santa Clara team ventured over the Rockies for the first time in search of top-flight competition. That season the Bronco quintet—hailed by sportswriters as the university's best team ever—proved its worth by winning the Northern California Intercollegiate Conference championship, an honor that had eluded the team by narrow margins in the two previous seasons.

The 1939 squad was even more successful. Despite early losses to the University of San Francisco and Berkeley, Santa Clara rallied, and by the end of its regular season it had won seventeen out of the twenty games on its coast-to-coast schedule. In addition to a one-point forfeit to DePaul, the team had lost by a single basket to the USF Dons and by twelve points to California. The Broncos beat both USF and Berkeley in return matches. As the season drew to a close, hopes were high that Santa Clara would be invited to meet the winner of the Pacific Coast Conference for the right to represent the West Coast in that year's National Collegiate Athletic Association tournament in Kansas City. But before the Pacific Coast Conference committee could extend an invitation, Santa Clara authorities announced that no exception would be made to the four-day traveling restriction enforced at all Jesuit institutions, which required that student athletes miss no more than four days of school. Thus the Kansas City tournament slipped

from the grasp of the Broncos. That season's team, which *Newsweek* magazine rated fourth nationally, was clearly Santa Clara's most successful basketball squad until the postwar years.

King Football

If little Santa Clara, with its student body of fewer than five hundred,
attained surprising success in basketball, its football triumphs were nothing
less than spectacular. Often pitted against universities that had more men in
the freshman class than Santa Clara had in its entire enrollment, Bronco
teams in the 1930's toppled the biggest and the best opposition. Before the
outbreak of the war temporarily ended intercollegiate competition, Santa
Clara had not only developed many outstanding football players—including
all-Americans Nello Falaschi, Al Wolff, John Schiechl, and Ken Casanega
—it had also capped its best seasons with two consecutive Sugar Bowl victories.

In 1932 one sportswriter recalled that a few years earlier "Santa Clara was
just a warm-up for California, just a chance to give the Bears a chance to
work out the kinks and get ready for bigger game." But when the 1932 mission eleven upset the University of California for the first time in a decade,
twelve to zero (Santa Clara had not beaten Berkeley since rugby was abandoned), the writer concluded that those days were gone forever. Santa Clara
football was finally attaining a place in the sun.[63]

Football was financially profitable. As the 1933 season drew to a close and
the team sailed off to Honolulu for a Christmas Day game, it was estimated
that close to two hundred fifty thousand fans had watched the Broncos play
that year.[64] According to a survey made the following season, the percentage
gain in attendance at Santa Clara games had topped all colleges in the country. The absolute gain of more than one hundred thousand spectators made
Santa Clara the Pacific Coast's leader in increased attendance.[65]

The annual game against arch rival St. Mary's College was always a great
attraction, as in 1933 when an estimated sixty thousand fans paid to see the
Broncos and the Gaels play in San Francisco's Kezar Stadium. It was a hard-
fought contest, and as usual several players were sidelined with injuries.
For the first time in a decade, Santa Clara was not defeated, having held
the Gaels to a six to six tie. But the game (which, coincidentally, occurred
one week before the lynchings in St. James Park) ended in a riot quelled
only after club-wielding police reserves rushed onto the field to subdue the
battling players and thousands of roaring rooters. It was not the first time
nor the last that a Bronco-Gael match erupted in mayhem. Nor were such

outbursts characteristic of that rivalry alone. Violence and vandalism also attended the annual Big Game between California and Stanford. Violence had become such a perduring feature of Bronco–Gael competition, however, that one writer called the Little Big Game "too big to handle." "It has gotten out of the control of players and officials alike" and "out of control of the peace officers."[66]

The restoration of peace in Kezar Stadium did not end the squabbling. In the weeks that followed, rumors of a possible break circulated in the press as coaches and staff, drawing upon their arsenal of longstanding grievances, cross-fired accusations. On December 1 President Lyons, apparently hoping to beat St. Mary's to the punch, announced that in the best interests of Santa Clara he was reluctantly ending all athletic competition with the Gaels of Moraga. For the second time in a generation the bellicose Bronco–St. Mary's rivalry was severed.[67]

Although the "riots and unpleasantries" convinced a few sportswriters that perhaps a break was for the best, most observers disputed Lyons's decree.[68] "What good will be accomplished by all this?" complained USF's former president, Father Edward Whelan. That Santa Clara would abandon the one game that brought it any measure of financial prosperity in the football world, he informed the Jesuit provincial, did not make sense. Whelan asserted that some people had acted too hastily.[69] One disappointed journalist summed up the sentiment of many football fans when he declared simply that Lyons's decision meant "one great game shot to pieces."[70]

No one was more distraught at the termination of the rivalry than Edward J. Hanna, archbishop of San Francisco. Annoyed by the wave of adverse publicity the breach created for the church, Hanna instructed the two schools to mend their broken fences immediately. "As Archbishop," he told Father Maher, the Jesuit provincial, "I cannot permit public charges of unclean and unsportsmanlike actions affecting students of two Catholic institutions to go unnoticed." Putting the full weight of his episcopal authority behind the restoration of the Little Big Game, Hanna ordered each college to submit its grievances to him for arbitration. He also demanded that motion pictures of the contest whose roughness had helped precipitate the break be delivered to the chancery office for a private screening in order that accusations of foul play might be definitively resolved.[71]

President Lyons resisted Hanna's efforts to revive the football classic. Denying Hanna's assumption that the violence-ridden rivalry was worth saving, he wondered facetiously if the archbishop would pay for the hospital bills. And as for scandal, Lyons argued, the game itself and its unruly crowds

were just as scandalous as severed relations.[72] But if Lyons thought his arguments would change the mind of either Zacheus Maher or the archbishop,
he was wrong. After a blunt order from Maher declaring that he wanted
"the whole thing settled, and shortly," Lyons surrendered and sent to the
San Francisco chancery Santa Clara's list of grievances against St. Mary's,
which the arbitrating archbishop had long since demanded.[73] After nearly a
year of negotiation—much of it carried out by the Jesuit and Christian
Brother provincials—peace was restored in 1934, and the Little Big Game once
again returned to the gridiron.

  That Santa Clara played St. Mary's made a major difference two years
later. At the end of the 1935 season the Pacific Coast Conference gave notice
that its members would play a "closed shop" schedule the following year,
which would all but freeze California's nonconference teams out of competition with the major schools. The news was a stunning setback to institutions such as Santa Clara, USF, and the College of the Pacific. With the opportunity to distinguish themselves against good teams suddenly reduced
or eliminated, the independent schools, some observers predicted, would
soon "go to seed in their own little garden." Deprived of its profitable and
popular series with California, which had drawn crowds of nearly 60,000
annually in recent years, Santa Clara faced a situation that was described
as desperate.[74] Some state legislators, sympathetic to the plight of the independents, threatened cutbacks in state funds to the University of California
unless the new conference ruling was relaxed. Despite this and similar protests (including petitions from Santa Clara requesting Governor Merriam's
intervention), the "freeze-out" continued.

  One obvious solution was for Santa Clara to schedule more intersectional
games. As late as 1934, the Broncos still had not traveled to the East. That
possibility was precluded by the four-day restriction on travel enforced at all
Jesuit institutions. It was based on a policy of allowing no unreasonable interruption of studies for the sake of athletics.[75] Translated into practical terms,
it meant that a team could leave the campus for a weekend game no earlier
than a Wednesday evening and that it had to be back at the school the following Tuesday evening.[76] Whatever the faculty thought of it, the four-day
rule was viewed as an unnecessary handicap by the coaching staff. "You cannot get east, play a big-timer there, then return home in only four days," one
Santa Claran explained resignedly. (Airplane travel was prohibited at that
time.) "So we settle for the best schedule we can get."[77]

  Outside observers predicted a relaxation of the four-day rule in the aftermath of the Pacific Coast Conference exclusion, and in fact more exceptions

were conceded after 1936. But these were granted reluctantly and rarely by Jesuit superiors. Like Cinderella, the Santa Clara athlete was expected to return home before midnight on Tuesday in order to take his place alongside his fellows in class the following morning.

Thus Santa Clara's schedule was limited by both the Pacific Coast Conference policy and the four-day travel rule. All conference schools except Stanford had dropped the Broncos from their schedule, and Bronco head coach Maurice "Clipper" Smith resigned, reportedly in frustration. Santa Clara's football prospects appeared dim. Yet to the surprise of many observers, the team, now under the direction of popular Lawrence "Buck" Shaw, went on to its most successful season ever.

Sugar Is Sweet

On the eve of their last regular game of the 1936 season, Santa Clara stood as the only major undefeated and untied team in the nation. The Broncos had scored 118 points to their opponents' 7, and they were hailed as the best squad on the Pacific Coast by some sportswriters. Even New York's Damon Runyan sang the praises of the mission eleven and castigated the Pacific Coast schools for freezing the nonconference Broncos out of that year's Rose Bowl.[78] Although the team lost its final game of the season, to Texas Christian, the bowl bid that many sportswriters wanted for Santa Clara was already in the mail.

In December the news broke that Shaw's Broncos had been invited to play in the Sugar Bowl, founded three years before by Governor Huey Long of Louisiana as competition to the Rose Bowl in Pasadena. Arranged through the influence of alumnus George H. Casey, a member of Santa Clara's Board of Athletic Control and the president of the Pacific Fruit Exchange, the offer was accepted immediately, and a few weeks later the Broncos traveled to New Orleans for their encounter with Louisiana State University. In addition to the players and hundreds of rooters, the train that pulled out of the San Jose depot carried a unique cargo of two hundred thousand prunes. A gift from the San Jose Chamber of Commerce, they were to be distributed at station stops en route to New Orleans "to give as many non-California residents as possible a taste of Santa Clara Valley sunshine." Wrappers on the fruit advertised the valley's two most famous products, the Bronco football team and the prune. On New Year's Day, California's "prune pickers" scored an upset victory over heavily favored LSU, twenty-one to fourteen.[79]

Santa Clara's 1937 team played an even better season against better competition, including Stanford, USF, Marquette, and St. Mary's. Having ended

The Broncos celebrated many football victories in the 1930's. Though its student body then never surpassed 700, Santa Clara's teams played top-flight competition and they achieved two consecutive Sugar Bowl victories. *Courtesy: Henry F. Schmidt.*

the regular season with a perfect record, Santa Clara was invited to play in the Sugar Bowl against Louisiana State for a second time. Once more, the "Bronco Special" rolled out of the San Jose depot toward New Orleans, again leaving a trail of Santa Clara Valley prunes at whistle stops across five states. This year's larder also contained 150 gallons of prune juice for distribution to prominent citizens and public officials. On New Year's Day, Santa Clara defeated Louisiana State, six to zero, and thus the Broncos emerged as the only major college team in the country to finish the season undefeated and untied.[80]

With two Sugar Bowl victories and a national reputation to its credit, Santa Clara now found it easier to schedule games. In 1938, after vanquishing Stanford, Texas A & M, Arkansas, and Michigan State, Santa Clara saw its reign as king of the nonconference football powers come to an end when

St. Mary's toppled the mission eleven, seven to zero. That game also broke the Broncos' sixteen-game winning streak. Despite a second defeat later that year, to Detroit, Santa Clara had lost only three of its twenty-six games during three seasons. Offered a Cotton Bowl bid at the end of the 1938 season, the team turned the invitation down, preferring to stay home rather than spend a third Christmas in a row on the road.

In the few years that remained before World War II, Santa Clara teams were pitted against progressively tougher opposition. In 1940, an Associated Press poll rated the Broncos the eleventh best team in the nation. The following year, Santa Clara played and beat California for the first time since the conference "freeze-out." But with the entry of America into the war and the exodus of students into the armed forces, athletic competition gradually ground to a halt.

Football and "Worldly Wisdom"

Despite the general fanfare given the Broncos' gridiron triumphs, football did not enjoy universal and unqualified approval at Santa Clara. Athletics had always been encouraged at the university, especially the minor sports, because these did not interfere with study. But in the minds of some administrators and faculty members, football was another matter.[81] That an institution could carry out a commitment to "big time" football without compromising its academic purpose seemed dubious to them. Yet they did not question "at least the *worldly* wisdom," as President McCoy put it, of the policy of a prudent development of athletics.[82] "It's hard for us academic souls to take," Loyola's Jesuit president once confided to President Lyons, "but what can you do about it?"[83] As long as the bottom line in the university's ledgers showed an excess of profits over losses in athletics, football would retain a berth at the mission university.

Professing a commitment to both scholarship and solvency, Santa Clara bravely set its course between the Scylla of poverty and the Charybdis of compromised standards. Prosperity was assured and penury avoided by producing winning teams, an accomplishment that the board of athletic control performed with unquestioned skill. The board consisted of Charles Graham, owner of the San Francisco Seals; Harry McKenzie, prominent defense attorney; Emile Maloney, vice-president of Pacific Telephone; lawyer Norbert Korte; Brian Gagan, attorney for Wells Fargo; James A. Bacigalupi, president of Transamerica Corporation; attorney C. M. Castruccio; and George H. Casey, president of the Pacific Fruit Exchange. To this group of alumni, Santa Clara's athletic program owed much of its success.

The task of enforcing academic requirements and of keeping athletics in check fell to the university administration, a responsibility for which it was held accountable by authorities outside the institution. The four-day rule limiting athletic travel, for example, testified to the intention of Jesuit superiors to keep football and other sports subservient to academics. The California provincial subjected the university's athletic program—especially the account books—to continual scrutiny, and the head of the Jesuit Educational Association monitored academic performance by periodic visitations.

The fact that Santa Clara athletics was kept strictly in the hands of the faculty was singled out for praise by the director of the Jesuit Educational Association, Edward Rooney.[84] All measures proposed by the university's board of athletic control were subject to presidential veto, and the board itself was for years dominated by the dean of faculties, Father William Gianera, who prided himself on the stern demands, both academic and disciplinary, that he exacted of university athletes. The laxity that had stigmatized Santa Clara football in the early twenties, Gianera resolved, would never be repeated while he was in command.[85] Even Homer nodded on occasion, however, as in 1941, when Rooney discovered that close to 25 percent of Santa Clara's small student body were receiving athletic scholarships of one sort or another. At his command, a cutback was made in the school's devotion to sport.[86]

Whatever academicians thought of intercollegiate football, no one questioned its profitability. Income from football games was vital to Santa Clara during the depression years. After analyzing accounts in 1934, former president Cornelius McCoy stated flatly that Santa Clara "cannot go on without athletics."[87] Whereas other universities relied upon endowments, as President Lyons once observed to a fellow Jesuit, Santa Clara depended upon football revenues.[88] This view was confirmed by the California provincial, Father Francis Seeliger, in a report he delivered to the Jesuit faculty in 1939:

[Athletics] are not getting out of hand and at the same time, for the past few years, they have very fortunately proved profitable and a source of substantial support to the University. It will be impossible to reduce them in any material way and still continue the University on a paying basis.[89]

Football revenues were allotted to nonathletic budgets. The money from football was needed, President Lyons admitted, "to keep other [departments] afloat" and "to support our numerous charity-concession students."[90] Football also helped sustain nonpaying departments such as the College of Law, which was a recipient of athletic largesse in 1938, when President

Louis Rudolph directed that the gate receipts from Sugar Bowl games help pay for its new building, Bergin Hall.[91]

Public-relations value was another benefit frequently cited in football's defense. Intercollegiate athletics was one of the few means whereby a small college could gain national recognition. Santa Clara has received more publicity than ever before, President Lyons noted in 1934, because of the marked improvement of the football team.[92] After two successful bowl games in a row, one happy faculty member exulted that Santa Clara is "known from one end of the country to the other."[93] Athletics not only drew alumni back to their alma mater in droves, it supplied the one common bond that reliably united town and gown. Thousands of citizens from San Jose and Santa Clara turned out to cheer on the home team during games and to salute the returning heroes with banquets and with parades down the Alameda after the Sugar Bowl victories.

National football prominence also caused enrollment to climb. In 1937 applications for admission arrived at the office of the registrar in record numbers, and that autumn the student body boasted representatives from eight states that had never before sent students. For the first time in the school's history, autumn enrollment passed the 500-mark, necessitating the opening of the fourth floor of the Nobili Hall dormitory, unoccupied since it was constructed a decade earlier.[94]

The Drums of War

With the outbreak of World War II, the golden age of athletics at Santa Clara came to an end. Intercollegiate sports would survive the war, of course, and there would even be another bowl game in the mission school's future. But never again would Santa Clara athletes score as many triumphs as in the thirties, nor would football dominate the campus with the same all-absorbing intensity that it had during the depression years.

In some respects the decade of college life before the war was an idyllic time. Although cries of social protest did occasionally disturb the ordered tranquility within the college walls, most Santa Clara students dwelled in a world apart, distracted by football games and dances and protected from the worries that troubled the sleep of their elders. World War II would shatter that isolation and break into a thousand pieces a pattern of campus life that could never be put back together again.

The idyllic quality of campus life was in part the result of size. Santa Clara was by any standards a small university. The entire student body could be gathered together for one group photograph, and if he made the effort a professor could know the name of every student. Pupil and professor lived in a close daily contact, a circumstance that made possible a family spirit as well as the tight discipline that had been Santa Clara's hallmark for nearly a century. This circumstance would begin to change in the aftermath of World War II.

In the 1930's the university was still a country campus. Nearby San Jose boasted a population of sixty thousand, and although the little town of Santa Clara (population six thousand) had begun paving its streets in 1928, the march of material progress had not yet destroyed the rural quality of the Santa Clara Valley. From the tower of Nobili Hall, students could still gaze out upon green fields and orchards, country roads and clear vistas; and every spring a cloud of fruit blossoms carpeted the "Valley of Heart's Delight" as far as the eye could see. Thus the setting too was idyllic, but like the produce of its orchards, perishable. The postwar industrial boom, with its freeways, factories, and smog, would transform the face of the valley dramatically and irrevocably. College life, faculty-student relations, the curriculum, and the physical environment would never be the same after the war. As a new decade began, the halcyon days at bucolic Santa Clara were dwindling.

17
Years of War
and Years of Calm
1941–1958

During the 1930's the vast majority of Americans opposed the entry of the United States into another war. Their desire to remain aloof from the problems of the rest of the world, best symbolized perhaps by the staunch isolationism of California's senior senator, Hiram Johnson, received strong student support at Santa Clara. When pollsters visited the campus shortly after Hitler launched his blitzkrieg attack on Poland in September, 1939, they learned that 95 percent of the students they interviewed were against American entry into the war erupting in Europe.[1]

Nonetheless, the battles that flared in distant Poland, Denmark, and Norway soon began to affect America. Military orders pouring into its factories from France and Britain caused California's depressed economy to surge with new life. When France collapsed before Hitler's panzer divisions, leaving a defiant Britain to fight on alone, the United States began to prepare its own defenses with all possible speed.

Bowing to pressure from President Roosevelt, Congress passed the Selective Service Act in September, 1940. A few weeks later, on October 16, seventeen million men between the ages of twenty-one and thirty-five signed up for the draft. Included were eighty from Santa Clara, both students and professors, who filed into Seifert Gymnasium and enlisted with the university registrar.[2] That autumn, more upperclassmen than ever before volunteered for ROTC instruction, a sign that the grave situation in Europe and America's vast preparedness program were touching the lives of most students.[3]

While Santa Clara debaters argued the question of military aid to Britain in the spring of 1941, American neutrality yielded to Lend-Lease. The nation contemplated with growing concern the grim possibility of a complete German victory in Europe. "The world is tumbling into the abyss of war and destruction," a graduating senior wrote. "The future for our class is not inspiring."[4] Six months later, disaster in the Pacific confirmed those fears. Japan's surprise attack at Pearl Harbor on December 7, 1941, plunged the United States into world war for the second time in a generation.

The Wartime Campus

The declaration of hostilities against the Axis powers had an immediate impact upon the university. Two months later enrollment had dropped 9 percent. When the spring semester ended in May, a third of the senior class received commissions in the United States Army, along with their graduation diplomas.[5]

The sudden disappearance of many familiar faces was disquieting. Even if he remained in college, it was "difficult for a student to keep his mind entirely on his work," wrote campus historian Father Henry Walsh.[6] Signs of war, guideposts to an uncertain future, abounded.

In the immediate aftermath of Pearl Harbor, invasion of mainland America did not seem impossible. "Should, which God forbid, our coast be bombed," the California provincial instructed the Jesuit faculty in December, 1941, "let all be ready to give all-out aid to the sick and wounded, and help by word and example to keep up the morale of the people."[7] At night, fear of Japanese attack kept lights dimmed along the California coast, and blackouts, often ordered when least expected, plunged the campus into total darkness.

News from the Far East was grim in those early months. The Philippine Islands, Guam, Singapore, and Burma collapsed before an advancing enemy. The United States had yet to win a battle. Only the movement of men and matériel was auspicious for eventual victory. Troops en route to the Pacific front camped in and around the town of Santa Clara and, because departing students had left many rooms in Nobili Hall empty, the upper floor of that dormitory was opened up as quarters for officers.[8]

How did students feel about the war? Believing that they were living on borrowed time, they first reacted with despondency, according to campus journalists. Many students asked themselves, "What's the use of studying now?"[9]

The war touched certain lives in different ways. The day before he was scheduled to graduate, Wayne M. Kanemoto, a third-year law student, was evacuated from San Jose with other Nisei and Japanese aliens and transferred by train to Southern California. On May 30, 1942, while his classmates at Santa Clara were marching up the aisle to receive their diplomas, Kanemoto was marched by military police into the Santa Anita race-track reception center in Los Angeles. Soon afterward he was transferred to a detention camp in distant Arizona.[10]

War brought inevitable changes in academic routine. In 1942 Father Charles Walsh, who had been named president two years earlier, announced the inauguration of an accelerated program of study. It would remain in effect for the duration of the war. Created to let students complete as much of their schooling as possible before being drafted, the innovation lengthened the academic year to two semesters of sixteen weeks each and added a twelve-week summer session. Students could now finish college in three years rather than the normal four.[11]

The university, in cooperation with the Federal government, introduced the Engineering Science Management War Training Program to the curriculum. In this program nonstudent civilians were given specialized training in aircraft design, material inspection and testing, engineering mathematics, radio communication, and industrial office management. Instructors from private industry augmented the faculty. The program's courses were open to all high-school graduates so that they might replace in wartime industries men who had been called to military service. Thus for the first time women entered the classrooms of Santa Clara as teachers and as students.[12]

Spring, 1942, was a time of "constant uncertainty."[13] Although several hundred local citizens had taken advantage of the war training program, the university's regular daytime student body shrank daily as men between the ages of eighteen and forty-five became subject to the draft. Extracurricular activities ceased, and intercollegiate athletic competition was abandoned. Seven priests from the Jesuit community entered the armed forces as military chaplains. Because its students and all but two of its faculty had departed for the war, the law school closed its doors. "It is hard to take," President Walsh sighed, "to see everything crash about one's head."[14]

"Whether or not we should try to maintain any civilian students at all next term" was the dilemma facing the trustees in March, 1943.[15] "We may have some civilians," but "we simply do not know as yet."[16] After weighing the pros and cons, authorities elected to keep the school open. They hoped thereby to "maintain our reputation as a Liberal Arts College," to retain the lay staff "as far as possible, even at a sacrifice," and to preserve continuity in campus traditions by keeping "a skeleton student body" of all four classes.[17] The trustees then waited to see how many students would appear the next fall.

One hundred three young men registered in September, 1943. They were chiefly premedical or engineering students, undraftable seventeen-year-olds, or men physically ineligible for military service. That year's junior class boasted seven members.[18] In January enrollment fell even lower: the student body numbered just ninety-one.[19] Its customary faculty and students scattered to the battlefields of the South Pacific and North Africa, the campus now seemed abandoned.

A reporter from the *San Jose News* who visited the university one April morning in 1943 marveled at the silence that pervaded the place. The palm trees that lined the campus walks stood motionless. "No breath of air moved their fronds, and a high fog deadened the few sounds which echoed from the big dormitories." The reporter looked for people.

> On the tennis courts a few students slapped tennis balls across the nets, but no one stood watching them. In a lone dormitory window a boy in a bright red sweater gazed absently at a textbook propped on one knee. But the familiar shouting across the broad green lawns was gone. Down a long corridor walked two other students, talking in a low, quiet voice that hesitated to break the stillness which seemed to hang over the buildings.[20]

The arrival of Army convoys broke the silence in May, 1943. Santa Clara had been approved for a unit of the Army Specialized Training Program. Created to train officers in technical subjects, this program was introduced into more than one hundred colleges and universities during the war, bringing new life to empty classrooms. In California's larger universities, crash programs in engineering, dentistry, medicine, and foreign languages were instituted. Santa Clara was asked to provide training in basic and advanced engineering.[21]

The advent of the first group of 375 soldiers gave the university new purpose. Once again the place bustled with activity as administrators hurriedly converted the institution into a military training school. The faculty was augmented; the business office was introduced to the cost-accounting system of bookkeeping; aluminum trays borrowed from local canning companies were used to help convert the campus cafeteria into a mess hall. By July the Army had occupied more than 75 percent of the campus facilities.[22]

But to President Walsh's dismay the program ceased a year later as quickly as it had started. Almost without warning Santa Clara's soldier-students were called to active duty.[23] Scores of other colleges and universities across the country whose financial solvency depended upon military enrollments also lost great numbers of students. Stanford University, for example, bade goodbye to more than one thousand soldiers. When the program ended both Stanford and Santa Clara were confronted with the specter of crippling financial losses and drastic cuts in enrollment.[24]

Rumors that Santa Clara would close for the duration of the war were denied, but when the last convoy of trucks departed from the front gate in

March, 1944, registration plunged to an all-time low. The university now had sixty students, Walsh reported, most of them being 4-F's and seventeen-year-olds. With a large plant to maintain and very little revenue with which to maintain it, the university was facing "a crisis in our history." By September, current income had dropped more than 80 percent. "When this war is over, things will brighten up again," the president predicted, but in the meantime, Santa Clara's survival depended upon our "beating the highways and byways for discharged veterans, aliens, 4-F's, and youngsters of pre-induction age."[25] At the 1945 commencement—held in the Adobe Lodge because of diminished numbers—seven graduates stepped forward to receive diplomas.

To cope with the emergency created by the withdrawal of the soldiers, Walsh launched a hurried drive for funds. His aim was to raise $150,000, enough, he estimated, to "carry us through until the conclusion of the war permitted a return to normal enrollment."[26] Operational deficits incurred during 1944–45 were met with gifts and with cash obtained from the sale of properties. For $10,500 the university parted with its last 23 acres of land at Loyola Corners.[27] In 1945 Walsh sold Villa Maria, the college's old winery and vineyard on Steven's Creek. The sale of those 322 acres brought $40,759.[28]

Despite the relief provided by these emergency measures, the school's financial condition remained critical as long as the draft kept enrollment down. Symbolic of the degree to which the war dominated all aspects of the university's existence, a victory ship named *S.S. Santa Clara* in honor of the mission school was launched in Wilmington harbor, California, that spring.

Then in August, 1945, the scourge of war dramatically ended. While the few remaining students were preparing to return to school that August, Japan was forced to surrender by atomic holocaust. The war was over.

The Veterans Return

Another six months would pass before demobilization flooded the college campuses of America with veterans entitled to the benefits of the GI Bill. But the outlook for the future was bright. A few weeks after the war ended, harbingers of recovery were already in evidence. Santa Clara's first registration after World War II attracted 169 students. The Law School reopened, and the campus braced itself for the wave of veterans expected in the months ahead.

The man who guided the university through the wartime crisis did not preside over its return to normal times. Charles Walsh had inherited the presidential chair in 1940. At that time his sole administrative experience was

During World War II, when the university's enrollment once sank to 60 students, the Army's Specialized Training Program helped keep Santa Clara's doors open. Soldier-students line up in front of St. Joseph's Hall in June, 1943, for morning drill preceding classroom instruction in engineering. *Courtesy: Archives, Univ. of Santa Clara.*

his ten years as dean of studies at the Jesuits' secluded Los Gatos Novitiate. He had learned university administration in a trial by fire, and his health broke in the process. In October, 1945, Walsh resigned in favor of the man who had long since shouldered many of his presidential duties, William C. Gianera.

Few persons knew Santa Clara better than Father Gianera, whose association with the school began when he was an entering student in 1903. Even as a Jesuit, he spent most of his long life on the mission campus. Owing to his exceptional ability to deal with many details, young Gianera had been named dean of faculties in 1928, an all-embracing position that combined the functions of registrar, dean of admissions, academic vice-president, and dean of arts and sciences.[29] After a seventeen-year reign as dean, Gianera, now affectionately known to several generations of alumni and faculty as "Mr. Santa Clara," was named president. To his administration fell the responsibility of receiving the onrush of veterans who applied for admission after the war.

In September, 1946, the university registered a record 879 students. (Santa Clara's highest previous enrollment had been 556, on the eve of Pearl Harbor.) Two thirds of the student body were veterans. Nearly as many applicants as were accepted were turned away owing to lack of facilities.[30] Because the campus had been planned for a resident student population of approximately five hundred, the postwar deluge required many adaptations and innovations.

Housing was critically short. From the Navy the university purchased bunk beds for students who were crowded into the dormitories, usually three to a room. Off-campus accommodations were generally unavailable, and hence inconveniences were taken in stride. The campus newspaper reminded discomforted students that crowding was not as bad at Santa Clara as in a midwestern university where a student had been living in a closet.[31] Had it not been for the building programs of presidents Maher and McCoy, the situation would have been worse, and Santa Clara could not have met its responsibility of educating its share of veterans.

Married students with families posed a special problem. Barracks originally intended for the use of troops were obtained from military surplus to provide emergency housing. During the summer, vacationing veterans helped convert the steel structures into one- and two-bedroom apartments for themselves and their families. Laid out in neat rows near Ryan Field, the 112-unit housing tract was dubbed Veterans' Village.[32]

In 1947, for the first time in Santa Clara's history, enrollment broke the one thousand mark. As the shortage of classrooms and housing grew more critical, additional barracks were transformed into classrooms and laboratories. One, planted on the lawn in front of Nobili Hall, became a student store, replete with pool hall and soda fountain. It was dubbed the Bronco Corral. Mushrooming enrollments also necessitated academic innovations. The faculty was enlarged, the number of afternoon classes was increased, and a summer session was added to help veterans speed up their studies. In October, 1947, Charles J. Dirksen, dean of the College of Business, announced that for the first time women would be admitted to the school's evening program, which opened that autumn.[33]

Enrollments swollen by large numbers of veterans were, however, a passing phenomenon. Following the commencement of 1950, the largest in San-

ta Clara's history, the number of students attending under the GI Bill began
to wane. Former soldiers constituted 80 percent of the graduating class in
1950, but the following fall most entering freshmen had no military experience. Although the number of veterans declined by September, 1950, the loss
did not signal a return to small prewar enrollments.[34] An even greater flood
of students was expected in the 1950's. Their advent reflected California's dramatic postwar growth.

Planning for the Second Wave

Santa Clara was on "the threshold of a new era," as President Gianera reported in 1947. Although the surge of veterans would spend itself in several
more years, a second and bigger wave of students was expected. "The increase that I envision is more permanent," Gianera explained, "and will be a
result of the growth of population in the state of California and particularly
in our own locality."

From a prewar total of 6.9 million, it was estimated that California's
population would grow to 12.5 million by 1954 and to at least 15 million by
1960. The San Francisco Peninsula–San Jose region, from which Santa Clara
drew 60 percent of its students, would double its population by 1950. Industrial development would continue to skyrocket after the war, and the area
would shift rapidly from a rural to a suburban economy. "The factors shaping
our new development must be recognized early and cared for assiduously,"
Gianera declared, "if we are to take our proper place in the educational and
social scheme in which we will be involved."[35]

The challenge to accomplish major growth and the opportunities to
achieve it were at hand. If Santa Clara planned to move ahead securely in
postwar America, it must initiate fund-raising programs to insure endowments, campus development, higher salaries for an improved faculty, and
concomitant administrative reorganization. All universities and colleges were
faced with this challenge, but at the mission campus the steps to meet it were
at the beginning hesitant and sluggish.

Why was its evolution into the new academic world not more sudden
and spectacular? In the first place, no one anticipated the institution's potential for growth. The extent of its participation in the postwar boom exceeded
all estimates. Moreover, few decision makers appreciated the extent to which
the exploitation of new opportunities required adaptations in the university's governance. Tradition reigned strong at Santa Clara and also in the religious order that guided almost every aspect of its development. That Santa
Clara's needs and opportunities were beyond the capacity of time-honored

solutions was not yet conceded. Besides, money was scarce. The main concern of the university's postwar directors was to cope with the immediate crises created by mushrooming enrollments—and to solve them by recourse to traditional methods. To future administrators was left the burden of innovative long-term planning and of breaking the mold of past practice.

No one foresaw the scope of the change in enrollment. That the university would twenty years hence number its students in the thousands seemed inconceivable in 1947 and, indeed, undesirable. Of course the school was expected to grow after the war. "Santa Clara will have to expand to meet the demand which will inevitably be made on her," Father Gianera stated in 1947. "Never again will we be able to limit our enrollment [to 600 men] as in the past." But despite the expected transformation of what was virtually a country boarding school into an urban university, the president was determined that Santa Clara remain a small university.[36] "We feel that Santa Clara can point to a normal peacetime enrollment of approximately 1,500 students," the president predicted with assurance in 1948. "It is doubtful if Santa Clara will, within the reasonable future, ever accept" more than that number.[37] *The Monthly Santa Claran* described the same conservative estimate of students as very probable within the next quarter-century, in view of the population of the region.[38]

The fact that the university's enrollment doubled in less than ten years made some administrative reorganization imperative. The most significant innovation was a decision by Jesuit superiors to create the office of academic vice-president. In 1950 John Hynes became Santa Clara's first holder of that office, and James A. King, former dean of faculties, was named dean of the college of arts and sciences. The following year an academic council, composed of administrative officials and the deans of the various colleges, was organized to deal with problems stemming from postwar expansion. Apart from publication of a bulletin created to achieve closer faculty relations, the council did little and was rarely convened. Committees that might have served as channels of communication between the administration and the faculty remained virtually nonexistent.[39] Santa Clara continued as always to be a one-man institution, in which the president personally directed the details of administration.[40]

Development was another area demanding action. If Santa Clara was to improve the quality of its education while at the same time boosting enrollment, the consequent budgets for classroom expansion, faculty improvement, and higher salaries required an energetic commitment to fund raising. Endowment was inadequate to the university's needs and was woefully below that of many California colleges. In 1947, Stanford and the University of California reported funds of $36 million and $35 million, respectively. Even institutions comparable to Santa Clara in size, such as Pomona College, the University of Redlands, and Mills College, possessed investment reserves of several million dollars. In 1947 Santa Clara's endowment totalled $190,000.[41]

In the past, the university had relied upon the living endowment of its Jesuit faculty. But the decision to expand after the war meant that tuition income and the contributed services of these nonsalaried religious were no longer sufficient to sustain the institution financially. Once the majority, by 1949 the Jesuits constituted less than one half of the faculty. The number of lay professors had to be increased, and they had to be offered competitive salaries. A drive for endowment was begun.

A campaign had in fact been launched in 1944, in anticipation of the university's postwar requirements. Its foundation was $35,000 remaining from the alumni endowment insurance plan initiated by President Maher in the 1920's.[42] The campaign had been suspended a year later, however, when falling enrollments caused by the withdrawal of the Army Specialized Training Program forced the Walsh administration to search for emergency funds to balance its operating budget. But the crisis had underscored the importance of providing for future emergencies. "If the endowment fund had been established years ago," observed alumni president Harold McKinnon in 1945, that crisis "would not have been so acute."[43]

The strain that postwar expansion placed on Santa Clara's resources led President Gianera to renew the endowment push in 1947. His aim was to provide for future construction and especially to assure development of a comprehensive lay faculty.[44] Of far-reaching significance was the creation of an office of university development to guide the campaign. Starting with the reserve of $190,000, Gianera hoped to reach a sum of $1 million by the time the university celebrated its centennial in 1951.[45]

As in the case of Santa Clara's previous quests for funds, the results were disappointing. The university still had much to learn about raising money. Because an office of development was not created until the last twelve months of the drive, for several years the tasks of solicitation fell to devoted alumni volunteers rather than to professional fund-raisers. Alumni bore the brunt of the appeal itself. Fearing that an intensive public campaign would be a mistake because such efforts were generally not successful, the university preferred a quiet drive, without pressure or fanfare, limited solely to alumni.[46] This, despite the fact that in 1951 the total membership of the

Alumni Association was 4,191, of whom only about 25 percent were dues-paying members.[47] There were no efforts to cultivate large donors, whether individuals or corporations, and publicity was kept to a minimum. Despite complaints regarding the "vagueness of the facts and figures which have so far been made available," no detailed statement of university finances was ever released, not even to the faculty and staff. Public progress reports were forbidden until such time as the $1-million goal was attained.[48]

The endowment drive ended in March, 1951, the one-hundredth anniversary of the university's founding. When the final tally was computed, 60 percent, or $600,000, of the goal of $1 million was still unpledged.[49] The office of development, created the previous year, was then disbanded.

The Price of Impecunity

Without funds and without an effective development program, Santa Clara had no alternative but to continue to meet its requirements piecemeal as they arose. Despite a genuine concern to look ahead and to plan for the university's growth, its administrators focused their attention primarily on immediate, short-term projects. Because of the school's continued dependence upon tuition, flexibility was compromised and long-range planning remained a dream.

Strict economizing was necessarily the hallmark of Santa Clara's postwar development. Balancing the annual $1-million budget received the highest priority, earning for President Gianera a reputation for shrewd, tightfisted financing. "Plans for development of the University of Santa Clara are based primarily on good business management," he reported, "which means operating within the limits of existing income no matter what sacrifice that requires."[50]

And sacrifices there were. Budgetary restrictions were distributed through all of the institution's operations. Such construction as occurred was possible chiefly through the reception of legacies.

In 1948 the will of Delia L. Walsh, widow of alumnus James E. Walsh, investment banker and associate of James L. Flood, left $250,000 to Santa Clara. This gift, one of many that the couple had made to the school over the years, was the largest single bequest Santa Clara had ever received.[51] The following year work began on the James E. Walsh Dormitory and the Delia L. Walsh Administration Building, the first major construction projects at the university in ten years. With a view to expanded enrollments, President Gianera wisely made the administrative building large, though it greatly exceeded the size needed by his own small staff.

William C. Gianera spent most of his Jesuit life on the Santa Clara campus. After serving as dean of faculties from 1928 to 1945, he was president of the university during the post-World War II years 1945 to 1951. *Courtesy: Archives, Univ. of Santa Clara.*

In 1950 the estate of San Jose pioneer Isabel de Saisset provided funds for the erection of an art gallery and museum in memory of her brother, artist Ernest de Saissett, who had attended Santa Clara in the 1870's. That structure was completed in 1955. Authorities discussed construction of a new engineering building and a new student union, both urgently needed. They also pondered the purchase of property adjoining the campus to assure future expansion. The limitations imposed by lack of money left all these projects on the drawing boards.

Budgetary limitations also restricted faculty salaries. Wages were linked to tuition, which the trustees were determined to keep low so that attendance might remain within the financial reach of a wide spectrum of the Catholic population. When the board increased tuition from $320 to $350 a year in 1949, it did so reluctantly, fearing lest educational costs be raised "so high as to force Catholic students to State schools."[52] As a consequence, wages were not competitive. In 1950, when the following salary scale was reported, 75 percent of the faculty fell within the lowest paid categories of assistant professor and instructor.[53]

FACULTY SALARIES BY RANK, 1950–1951
(Law College not included)

Rank	Low	High	Median
Professor	$3,600	$6,000	$4,782
Associate Professor	3,400	5,450	4,066
Assistant Professor	3,000	4,550	3,318
Instructor	1,850	3,650	3,160

Low salaries helped to explain the low percentage of Ph.D.'s on the faculty, although some observers also ascribed their absence to poor recruitment. Since the 1930's there had been a few teachers with European doctorates on the faculty, including Jesuits Cornelius Deeney and Eugene M. Bacigalupi, both of whom had received ecclesiastical degrees from the Gregorian University. A layman, Umberto Olivieri, who had studied at the University of Rome, came to Santa Clara to teach Italian in 1932. The first professor with a Ph.D. from an American university who remained on the staff for more than a year was Lloyd L. Bolton, who joined the biology department in 1932. Other persons with advanced degrees soon followed, especially in the sciences, including Joseph F. Deck in chemistry in 1936.

In the postwar period several veteran faculty members returned to graduate school to complete their degrees, including Edwin A. Beilharz in history and Francis R. Flaim in biology. But as late as 1950 there were many departments without a single holder of the doctorate on the staff. No department except chemistry boasted more than one. "The undergraduate faculty at Santa Clara is badly in need of bolstering," warned Edward B. Rooney, head of the Jesuit Educational Association, when he visited the university in 1950. Out of a full-time faculty of sixty-one professors, only eight held the doctorate. "It is difficult to understand," Rooney observed, "why there has not been much more effort along this line in the past."[54]

A Place Apart

If low salaries made it impossible to compete with the best universities for professors, restrictions placed upon the faculty further diminished Santa Clara's attractiveness. In 1948 the university issued a manual, *Rules and Regulations*, that explained in no uncertain terms that there were definite limits beyond which academic inquiry should not range. "Members of the faculty are expected to maintain a conservative viewpoint," the manual warned, "not only within the University but also in social, political, civic and religious fields."[55]

The foundation of this conservative policy had been outlined in an address to the faculty a few years earlier by President Charles Walsh. "The University of Santa Clara refuses to profess such so-called 'academic freedom' as implies that there are no fixed truths, no fixed principles of thought and of action." Walsh went on to state that the university did not profess academic liberty without regard for the logical implications of Catholic theology and scholastic philosophy, the two fields he deemed to be at the very heart of educational philosophy and to which all other fields are necessarily subordinated. After enumerating some of the religious and philosophical certitudes to which professors were expected to adhere regarding the natural law, the indissolubility of marriage, the family, political philosophy, the relationship between capital and labor, the realm of economics, and the arts, Walsh singled out biological evolution for special mention. The university "holds that the theory of evolution is but a theory, . . . so certainly false that it would be extremely rash to maintain it."[56] Professors were expected to teach as fact only that which has been established beyond question and to distinguish facts from hypotheses and opinion. "Startling viewpoints" were out of place.[57] Thus Santa Clara placed the burden of proof on anyone advocating innovation, and it identified Catholicism with the status quo in social, political, and religious fields.

Nothing required that all members of the faculty practice the Catholic religion. But the university tolerated no expression of attitude in any form or forum that was "opposed to Catholic beliefs, or practices, or to the known attitudes of Catholic authorities."[58] Santa Clara's integrated educational philosophy required that everyone be "completely mastered by the same principles and the same aims, working together in perfect 'mesh.' " As the faculty expanded and diversified, that ideal became increasingly hard to maintain. The main difficulty, President Walsh conceded in 1940, "comes in trying to explain our system to non-Catholics who have never known the theological and philosophical bases upon which we stand."[59]

Student discipline also followed traditional lines. Although the requirement of daily Mass was fast disappearing, attendance at Sunday morning services was still obligatory. Catholics and non-Catholics alike were expected to make an annual three-day religious retreat, and all students filed into the college auditorium to hear an exhortation by the campus chaplain twice a month. Santa Clara was a place to which young Catholics came to be schooled in their faith as well as in secular learning. Courses in religious studies were required every semester. Scholastic philosophy—firmly considered "a powerful mental discipline"—remained "the integrating factor of the educational system of Santa Clara."[60] The curriculum was for the most part still prescribed.

With the passing of time, off-campus social functions had become an essential part of college life, but they were closely supervised. It took an earthquake in 1941 to persuade President Walsh that the practice of locking the doors of the dormitories at night should end for the sake of safety. After the war, the exits were once again sealed to prevent nighttime escapes. Unexplained absences after lights-out invited disciplinary action from the prefects who patrolled the hallways.[61] As a reminder of the nightly curfew, a local theater used to flash the hour on its movie screen as a warning to students to return to the campus before ten o'clock bed check. "Beer busts notwithstanding," summarized alumnus Stan Terra, Santa Clara was virtually "a secular seminary."[62]

Campus life was not without compensations. "The Santa Clara of my day was cozy and secure," recalled Paul Laxalt, a graduate of 1944 and later governor of Nevada and United States senator from that state. It was "at once our Linus blanket and our sheltered fortress." Though quick to concede the school's obvious limitations, alumni of Laxalt's day often agreed that its smallness, its informality, its all-male camaraderie, and its fierce school spirit made the Santa Clara of their recollections a "wonderful time and place." What they learned there—including the discipline—stood them in good stead in later life.[63] Many also conceded that trying to get around the protective

measures taken by the university was one of their greatest sources of entertainment.

Beginning the Second Century

When the university celebrated its one-hundredth anniversary in March,
1951, the celebration underscored the role that tradition still played on the
campus. Santa Clara's Passion play, *Nazareth*, which had not been performed
since 1939, was revived for the occasion. The spiritual climax of the centennial was a special "ecclesiastical triduum," or three-day retreat, held in the
spring. Led by cassock-clad altar boys, the entire student body proceeded
in solemn, silent pilgrimage to the campus shrine of St. Joseph, as it did every
year, to begin the retreat and to honor the patron saint who had guided the
college for the past one hundred years.

The academic highlight of the centennial year was a conference in March
on "Philosophy and the Social Sciences." The program featured Roscoe
Pound, former dean of Harvard Law School, philosopher Yves Simon, and
James B. Carey of the CIO as speakers. The main discussions were on "Labor
and Management," "Constitutional and Natural Rights," "The Family,"
and "The Social Sciences and our Human Destiny."[64]

In 1951 Santa Clara was still unique among mainstream educational institutions in the West. Even its size testified to its individuality. "In California,
where everything grows fast," observed *Time* magazine on the occasion of
the university's centennial, "even colleges and universities can become giants
within a few years. But California's oldest college has never gone in for big-
ness." On the mission campus the ideal of the small university still reigned
supreme. The advantages of smallness were obvious, but they were also
costly, and Santa Clara was finding it increasingly difficult to pay the price.
More important, in many essential areas the university seemed untouched
by the great changes occurring in the world of higher education. The period
after the World War II had been one of solid achievement and growth for
the school, but with its small, all-male student body, its seminary-like regimen, its prescribed curriculum, and its singular resistance to change, Santa
Clara seemed to *Time* magazine in 1951 "a place apart from the rest of the
brash and bustling state."[65]

Nineteen fifty-one marked the closing of an era. At the end of the
centennial year, President Gianera retired after more than twenty-five years
of dedicated administrative service. He was replaced by a man twenty years
his junior, thirty-nine-year-old Herman J. Hauck. Fresh from graduate
studies in English at Yale, Santa Clara's new president had only four years of

college teaching behind him and no administrative experience. He was the first of the university's chief executives to have studied at a secular institution.

Although the unreadiness of the Society of Jesus to implement wide-ranging reforms precluded the possibility of dramatic innovation, the 1950's were nonetheless a period of quiet transition. By the time Hauck's term drew to a close in 1958, several of the traditions that had for more than a century kept Santa Clara a small, undergraduate institution had been abandoned. Prodded on by accrediting agencies, the university took important steps in upgrading itself academically. A popular public speaker, Hauck made friends for the university and gained for it respect and greater recognition in educational and professional circles. Elected president of the Western College Association in 1955, he was that same year also appointed by Governor Goodwin J. Knight to be one of the nine commissioners heading the state's recently founded scholarship program, which brought many benefits both to higher education in California and to Santa Clara.

Other changes reflected shifts in society. In the late 1950's, Catholic colleges across the country were caught up in the debate over the question, "Where are the Catholic intellectuals?" It was the beginning of a period of critical self-examination. In sum, the events of the 1950's brought the university a step closer to the mainstream of contemporary higher education. Although not dramatic, they set the stage for the far-reaching innovations of the 1960's.

Fourth Down for Football

The Hauck administration soon faced events that were neither quiet nor academic. It was shaken by a crisis in its public relations a year after the new president came to office. The cause was the university's sudden abandonment of intercollegiate football.

Rebuilding a team after the war had not been easy, but by 1949 Santa Clara had regained its national reputation. That year it had received an invitation to travel to Miami to play in the Orange Bowl. It was the first such bid received by a California team. Santa Clara was not expected to win. In fact, oddsmaker Jimmy "the Greek" Snyder was so confident of the opposition's strength that he bet $250,000 in favor of Paul "Bear" Bryant's University of Kentucky team. Jimmy lost his wager. Santa Clara scored a twenty-one to thirteen upset over Kentucky, and coach Leonard Casanova's team returned home to fifteen thousand cheering fans and a victory parade down the Alameda led by California Governor Earl Warren.[66]

But the Orange Bowl was Santa Clara's last football "spectacular." Subsequent years were problem-plagued for the team. After three poor seasons in a row, attendance and income fell off alarmingly. The Little Big Game against St. Mary's, which used to fill San Francisco's Kezar Stadium to capacity, now drew more sea gulls than spectators. The number of independent teams against whom Santa Clara could compete also dwindled. By 1951 financial losses had forced the University of San Francisco, Saint Mary's, Portland, and Nevada to withdraw from competition in football, leaving Santa Clara no alternative but to play many of its games far from home.[67] The shrinking pool of local competitors repeatedly prompted the question: How much longer would football survive on the mission campus? In the three years since its Orange Bowl victory, it had won eight games, lost thirteen, and tied two.

Although the sport lost money in the fall of 1951, university spokesmen repeatedly said that there would be no change in Santa Clara's policy regarding football.[68] President Hauck himself enthusiastically defended the game. When the young president told a Touchdown Club luncheon in San Francisco in 1951 that football shared some of the dignity of the fine arts, grateful sportswriters headlined his unusual approach to the rugged gridiron sport. Describing football as an organized symphony of motion not unlike ballet, Hauck went on to explain that "in the Jesuit system of education we consider the academic side and athletics in much the same way. We try to develop a man's intelligence, his search for knowledge and truth right along with bringing his athletic ability to his fellow man." Thus the good things of the game should be salvaged and not jettisoned with the bad, and, Hauck concluded, "Sports shall survive."[69] Speaking to a group of alumni five months later, the president agreed to support football on the mission campus for two more seasons, that is, through 1953. The benefits that the game had showered on the college in the past and the chance that better seasons lay ahead seemed to demand as much.

Hauck's repeated guarantees were suddenly overturned nine months later by the Jesuit provincial, Joseph D. O'Brien. Santa Clara's 1952 season had been disastrous.[70] Football had caused deficits for two years running, and it was expected to lose more money in the following year. When the departure of coach Richard Gallagher was announced at the end of the season, it seemed to the provincial an opportune moment to reassess the future of Bronco football.

A special meeting was called in San Francisco to analyze accounts. After O'Brien and his advisers learned that nonathletic funds would have to be diverted to sustain the game in 1953, they agreed to apply the coup de grace to a dying enterprise. Despite the predicament in which the decision placed Santa Clara and especially its president, the provincial ordered that football be dropped immediately.

Father Hauck was dismayed. He requested a year's grace in order to keep the promise he had made to support the sport through 1953, but he was turned down. Appeals to Rome also failed, and the chagrined but obedient Jesuit had no choice but to implement his religious superior's mandate. Lest the impression be given to the public that the provincial was meddling in the university affairs, it was agreed that the president would present the decision as his own.[71]

On December 29, 1952, President Hauck made the bombshell announcement. He specified that exorbitant costs, rising competition from professional football games and from television, the platoon system, the increasing pressure to waive academic standards, and the lack of local opponents made it imperative that Santa Clara withdraw immediately from intercollegiate football. The decision, he said, was unavoidable and irrevocable.[72]

"Shocking in its suddenness": that was the common reaction to the news. If applauded by the faculty, Hauck's announcement left many alumni who had relied on the university's guarantees shaking their heads in disbelief. "Speechless," "greatly disappointed," and "outraged" were the words and feelings of many unhappy fans.[73]

There was no turning back. Protests notwithstanding, the final curtain had fallen on big-time football. But the price proved to be high. An embarrassment to many university personnel, the episode was a personal trial for its young president, who suffered through it in obedient silence. The episode also created a crisis of confidence in the university's word. The "dissatisfaction and discord" that the sudden slaying of the sport provoked among the alumni body would linger for years.[74] A striking example of the historic lack of communication that existed between the university's directors and their lay supporters, the decision and the manner in which it had been reached left scars that were visible long after football itself ceased to be an issue.

Football was not the only sport whose accounts were reexamined. Though they had generated greater deficits, baseball and basketball survived cutbacks and continued to be played. Santa Clara baseball teams won no conference pennants in the years immediately after the war, but they produced several athletes who played professional ball after graduation. Basketball, too, had its ups and downs. A record of twenty-one wins and four losses made the Broncos one of the outstanding teams in the West in 1946, but two years later they suffered what was described as their "worst basketball season in twenty years."[75] Later, coached by alumnus Robert Feerick, the Broncos scored some of their greatest triumphs. Beginning in 1952, Santa Clara competed three years running in the playoffs of the National Collegiate Athletic Association. With the demise of football, basketball emerged as the favorite campus sport.

Academic Progress

The painful football fiasco behind it, the university gladly turned its attention to other tasks. One of the first projects undertaken by the new administration was the accreditation of the university, which had long been urged by the Jesuit Educational Association and which President Hauck himself was eager to complete.

Under Edwin J. Owens—its first full-time dean, who served from 1933 to 1953—the Law College had been approved by the American Bar Association since 1937. That same year the Engineering Council for Professional Development had accredited the College of Engineering, making Santa Clara for twenty-four years the only Catholic college west of St. Louis with an approved engineering curriculum.[76] Abandoning its membership in the Northwestern Association, which had not reexamined the school since its original approval in 1932, the university asked in 1952 to be visited by the newly formed Western College Association. The College of Arts and Sciences received accreditation the next year. Also in 1953 the School of Business was approved by the American Association of Collegiate Schools of Business. In 1959 the chemistry department received accreditation from the American Chemical Society.

These new affiliations testified to past achievement by declaring that the university had met the requirements of basic academic respectability. No less important, they served as a stimulus to further progress. Accreditation committed the university to a continuing pursuit of academic proficiency and encouraged scholarly research by the faculty. It also established lines of communication between the university and the world of higher education at large, thus furnishing a yardstick by which future growth could be measured.

Accreditation also laid the groundwork for the reestablishment of graduate studies, which had been terminated in 1936. The chief obstacle to their resumption had been a dearth of faculty holding a doctoral degree. When this deficiency was corrected in 1957, the Jesuit Educational Association, overseer of the order's educational work in the United States, permitted the creation of programs leading to the master's degree in chemistry, English,

One of the features of Santa Clara's postwar growth was the increased laicization and professionalization of its faculty and administration. By 1949, Jesuits, once the majority, constituted less than one-half of the faculty. Pictured from left to right: O. Robert Anderson, professor of business administration; Charles J. Dirksen, dean of the Business College beginning in 1941; John B. Drahmann, named dean of the College of Sciences in 1968; Edwin J. Brown, professor of education; Robert J. Parden, named dean of the College of Engineering in 1955. *Courtesy: News Bureau, Univ. of Santa Clara.*

and history. Plans were also drawn up for beginning graduate instruction and for teacher-training courses in the department of education, which had been opened in 1951.

The programs that generated the widest response were initiated a few years later by the School of Business Administration and by the School of Engineering. Meeting the booming demand for professional training and technical expertise, programs leading to the master's degree in business administration and in engineering contributed significantly to the university's enrollment explosion of the 1960's. In 1957 Alma College, the theologate of the California Province of the Society of Jesus, located in the Santa Cruz Mountains, became affiliated with Santa Clara as its graduate school of theology.

Apart from ongoing efforts to upgrade the faculty, undergraduate studies changed little until 1958. In accord with the educational policy of the Society of Jesus, heavy requirements in theology and philosophy continued to dominate the core curriculum. As it had for decades, Santa Clara refused to grant the Bachelor of Arts degree to students untrained in Latin or Greek. As a result, in 1957, for example, all but one of the 193 graduating seniors received the Bachelor of Science diploma.[77] The following year, the classical requirement was abandoned, and equality was conceded among the humanistic disciplines.

That more far-reaching transformations did not take place was in part the result of the impoverished state of university finances, a condition made worse by postwar inflation. With a view toward boosting faculty salaries and covering recurring budgetary losses, the board of trustees subjected tuition charges to long-overdue reexaminations. Pointing out that nearby Stanford University charged $660, whereas Santa Clara's tuition remained at $380 as late as 1951, the board approved frequent raises, so that by 1958 the charge had advanced to $700 a year. But these increases were not sufficient, President Hauck observed, to relieve the "pinched salaries that squeeze our faculty into other colleges," even when supplemented one year by a Ford Foundation endowment grant of $340,000.[78] Fluctuating enrollments worsened the problem. For several years during the Korean War, the undergraduate student body dropped below the one-thousand mark. If the university had not had an ROTC program, the effect of the war on enrollment would probably have been even more severe.

But the war alone was not to blame for Santa Clara's enrollment worries. "We must become more development-minded," urged Academic Vice-President John Hynes, who compared the university's "present plan of operation" to that of a corner grocery in competition with a chain store.[79] Father James King, trustee and dean of the College of Arts and Sciences, agreed. "We have not, for a number of years, registered our quota of day students." King was also concerned by the low numbers of boarding students. Believing that its failure to provide adequate housing had in recent years caused the university to lose many such students to other institutions, King, an ardent advocate of expanded enrollments, urged immediate construction of new dormitories. "It is my persevering conviction," he concluded, "that any development of the University during the next ten years is very closely tied in with the amount of housing we are able to provide for our students." "If we wish to keep a quality faculty," he warned, enrollment will have to climb.[80]

Plans were laid for expansion. A Federal housing loan, the first ever obtained by Santa Clara, helped finance a new residence hall, named in honor of San Jose pioneer Edward McLaughlin. The addition of this fifth dormitory was, however, a mere stopgap. The campus was still incapable of housing more than seven hundred boarders, the remainder being forced to find off-campus housing.

Though unable to finance additional construction, the board of trustees did scrape together sufficient funds to begin purchasing properties on the periphery of the campus, upon which future administrations might build for expanded enrollments. The largest acquisition was six acres across the Alameda. Most of the land belonged to the ancient Eberhard Tanning Company, which had fronted the campus area since 1849, and whose pungent odors had for generations wafted through the campus. After first threatening condemnation proceedings, the university purchased the property in an out-of-court settlement in 1953.[81] This acreage and parcels added to it later served as the site for Bannan Hall, the Sullivan Engineering Center, the Orradre Library, and several dormitories.

Problems Resolved and Unresolved

By the time President Hauck left office in 1958, several important steps had been taken toward developing and modernizing the university. The purchase of new properties signalled a desire to grow. By seeking accreditation, the administration had formally committed the university to updating its standards and to bringing them more into conformity with those of other institutions of higher learning. The status of the faculty had improved through the establishment of inchoative tenure procedures and through salary increases in some categories. Faculty quality was better too, as evidenced by a 30 percent jump in the number of teachers holding the doctorate.[82]

Capping years of negotiation, permission had been obtained for the revival of graduate studies. The desire for a Catholic education continued to attract talented students to the university, including California's future governor, Jerry Brown. In 1955 a Santa Clara senior, Arthur Hull Hayes, Jr., was awarded a Rhodes Scholarship. Hayes was the first student from the mission campus to receive that distinction.

In some respects the university was more involved in the off-campus world, especially in the local community, than ever before. President Hauck was well known and respected for his educational work. Conferences on the economic future of the Santa Clara Valley and its industrial growth sponsored by the College of Business frequently brought Dean Charles Dirksen and his faculty into contact with local business leaders. In 1950 Anthony P. Hamman, alumnus and former assistant to the president, became city manager of San Jose, one of the fastest growing urban centers in the country. Through Father Walter Schmidt, campus chaplain and founder of the Santa Clara Valley Youth Center, the university participated in the postwar battle against juvenile delinquency in San Jose and Santa Clara.

In many critical areas, however, the university was at a standstill. The rest of the world seemed to be passing it by. The Santa Clara Valley was undergoing a radical transformation. Its population was expanding at an unprecedented rate, and fortunes were being made overnight as bulldozers swept its once fabled orchards into oblivion to make way for factories, freeways, and suburban housing. The "Valley of the Heart's Delight" was rapidly becoming "Silicon Valley," the center of California's flourishing semiconductor industry. But in the face of much of this activity, this university seemed a disinterested bystander.

Santa Clara had yet to capitalize on the challenge of the postwar era. Progress on all fronts was still linked to tuition income, which fluctuated in response to changes in enrollment. In 1958 undergraduate enrollment still was less than one thousand students. Faculty compensation, though much improved in the lower ranks of instructor and assistant professor, failed to keep pace with inflation and with the salaries offered by industry and by other educational institutions. Whether as teachers or as students, women were still conspicuous by their absence at Santa Clara. Of the one hundred fifty faculty members listed in the 1957–1958 university bulletin, only one was a woman. New construction proceeded at a snail's pace. Permission had been received to build an urgently needed engineering center to replace the antiquated Montgomery Laboratories, but six years would pass before funds could be raised to complete the project. Emergency appropriations had boosted the holdings of the main library from 65,000 to 91,500 bound volumes in six years, but the collections were still deficient.[83] Evaluating committees found it difficult to understand why such a venerable institution possessed so few books. Library facilities in the Varsi Library and in the library of the Law College remained grossly inadequate and overcrowded. And yet there were no concrete plans for a remedy.

Without productive endowment and without an aggressive fund-raising program, the university was in the doldrums. While the rest of the educational world underwent startling transformation, Santa Clara seemed becalmed in a sea of inactivity. A few months before he retired, President Hauck announced plans to construct new buildings and to expand the university's enrollment. But unless new means could be found to implement those plans, they would suffer the same fate as the unfulfilled dreams that had preceded them. If Santa Clara hoped to grow in size and scope and to share in California's extraordinary postwar progress, a breakthrough was needed.

18

Traditions Shattered
1958-1977

One of the priorities facing Patrick A. Donohoe when he became Santa Clara's president in 1958 was to push enrollment upward. The ratio of faculty to students in some departments was in "crisis condition."[1] The College of Arts and Sciences, for example, which had initiated a wide variety of new programs, lacked the numbers of students to make those programs financially feasible. A ratio of one professor to fewer than seven students could no longer be sustained.[2] "While size is in itself not an objective," Donohoe concluded, "a certain size is absolutely necessary to guarantee even the minimal standards of budget-practice."[3] If Santa Clara hoped to "stay alive financially" while maintaining a good academic program, it had to grow.[4]

The university's first president with a doctoral degree, Donohoe had completed his graduate studies in 1950 at St. Louis University. Having taught political science at the mission campus for seven years, he was familiar with Santa Clara's problems and eager to do something about them. Young and flexible, the new president began by questioning some of the university's long-held assumptions. In the name of progress, Donohoe soon cast aside many of the conventional ways of doing things. Later, urged on by reforms within the Jesuit order and the Catholic Church resulting from the *aggiornamento* of Pope John XXIII, Donohoe was able to introduce changes undreamed of by his predecessors. Indeed, the innovations that occurred in the wake of the Second Vatican Council were the most dramatic that the university had experienced in a hundred years. What Burchard Villiger had done for Santa Clara of the 1860's, Donohoe and his successor, Thomas D. Terry, did for the university of the 1960's.

Coeducation

Few changes were as significant as the decision to admit women students. That action not only brought economic and academic benefits to the university, but it also symbolized the institution's new willingness to move toward the mainstream of contemporary higher education. During the 1960's the notion of separate colleges for the sexes came under increasing criticism in the

United States. The reassessment was prompted by rising costs, shrinking application pools, increased competition for students, and shifts in youthful life styles. According to statistics compiled by Brubacher and Rudy, of the 300 separate colleges for women in the United States in 1960, only 146 still retained their distinctive identity by 1973. During that period, 160 of the nation's 261 men's colleges also opted for coeducation.[5] Santa Clara was among those colleges that abandoned their all-male tradition. The "only sane solution" to the university's quest for financial stability and academic proficiency, President Donohoe decided, was the admission of women. Thus Santa Clara, in order to increase its enrollment, joined the national trend.[6]

The question of limited coeducation had, in fact, come before the board of trustees several times before the 1960's. Women had already been enrolled in the graduate school, in the evening division, and in a nurses' training program offered in cooperation with nearby O'Connor Hospital. But the admission of women to the undergraduate student body had never before received serious consideration.

The chief obstacle to coeducation at Santa Clara was the possible opposition of local colleges operated by nuns. To avoid such a conflict the superior general of the Society of Jesus, John B. Janssens, had ordered that before coeducation could be extended to any Jesuit college or university in the United States, approval would first have to be obtained from the bishop in whose diocese the school was located. Thus the decision to accept women as undergraduates did not rest with the board of trustees alone.

The prospect of Santa Clara's receiving diocesan permission appeared unlikely in view of the larger number of Catholic women's colleges in the San Francisco Bay area. Nonetheless, President Donohoe, persuaded that he had nothing to lose and having obtained provincial permission, presented a request to the diocesan chancery in San Francisco. No response was immediately forthcoming. But he continued to press his case, each time arguing that a change in admission policy at Santa Clara would not undermine enrollments at the women's colleges. After several months' negotiation, in which the president's brother, Auxiliary Bishop Hugh A. Donohoe, assisted the university, Archbishop John J. Mitty of San Francisco approved coeducation at Santa Clara.[7]

On the night of March 21, 1961, a few days after the university celebrated its 110th anniversary, Donohoe startled the campus community with one of the surprise announcements that would become characteristic of his presidency. Beginning the following autumn, women would be admitted to all departments of the university. The next morning a special edition of the campus newspaper carried a banner headline that broke the news to the all-male student body: "TRADITION SHATTERED." Santa Clara had become the first Catholic coeducational institution of higher learning in California.

Reaction to the news was mixed. The campus newspaper staff expressed "regrets that the administration has been forced to make this decision." Although student body president Jerry Kerr conceded that coeducation was "a necessary step" because "Progress has to be served," other student leaders were unhappy with the decision. "I don't think anyone will quit," declared one of them, "But I feel sorry for the freshmen and sophomores. They're going to have to go through this long period of co-education [during] their years here and they won't like it." "I am proud to say that I attended the Santa Clara that was," grumbled another young man, "the Santa Clara that was part of the famous tradition." The reaction of Alumni Association president Richard Lautze typified that of many recent graduates. "I am very happy. I have four daughters."[8]

The explosion in the number of admissions that followed the decision was greater than anyone had anticipated. Coeducation, accompanied by a greater selectivity in admissions, marked a turning point in the university's history. During Donohoe's nearly ten years in office, Santa Clara grew from a 1,500-student, all-male university to a coeducational institution with a total enrollment of more than 5,000. The size of the faculty tripled.[9] The sudden increase in the size and caliber of the student body was accompanied by improvements in faculty salaries and classroom facilities, thus enabling the university to serve its new clientele proficiently. Although the admission of women was not the sole cause of Santa Clara's unprecedented growth in the 1960's, that action—in concert with improved funding, academic advances, and an ambitious building program—played a leading part.

Financing Private Education

When a university was expanding as was Santa Clara, new sources of income had to be found. When Patrick Donohoe took command in 1958, the need to find new ways to finance the institution was critical. If rising faculty salaries were to be maintained, if scholarship funds were to expand, and if the university hoped to compensate for its lack of endowment, a wider spectrum of financial support was indispensable. Moreover, if campus facilities were to keep pace with student increases, new goals had to be attained in fund raising for capital improvements. The university could not survive on tuition and fees alone. The old expedient, common in many colleges, of forcing the faculty to finance institutional growth through the instrumentality of low salaries was no longer feasible.

When the university announced its inauguration of coeducation, Martha Patricia O'Malley of Phoenix, Arizona, became its first woman applicant. In 1961 Santa Clara became the first Catholic coeducational institution of higher learning in California. *Courtesy: Mr. & Mrs. Paul Conley.*

Annual increases in tuition provided only a partial answer. By 1968 that charge had jumped to $1,620 a year, double what it had been a decade earlier—though still in line with tuitions at comparable private institutions in California. Despite record increases, tuition income did not pay the full cost of education.

Administrative reorganization with a view toward greater efficiency provided another part of the solution. As the university expanded, greater specialization of functions affected all areas of its governance, academic as well as financial. Offices were reorganized and expanded with new or reassigned personnel. Outside experts were brought in to draw up long-range projections. The development office, headed after 1967 by the university's first lay vice-president, Lee Case, expanded its constituency beyond the alumni body and began to seek grants, federal loans, and corporate gifts with a new vigor and on a new scale.

Few innovations were as far-reaching as the creation of a board of regents in 1959. It marked the beginning of significant lay participation in university affairs and paved the way for the subsequent increase of lay influence within the university's highest governing board, the board of trustees. Organized to guide the development program, the regents constituted a group of prominent men and women who opened new avenues of financing to the institution. Either through their own gifts or through the funds they raised, the regents were largely responsible for the building program that transformed the face of the campus in the 1960's. In 1965 a subsidiary group was formed, the board of fellows, whose long-range goal was the increase of the university's permanent endowment.

The most effective fund raiser in Santa Clara's history was San Francisco hotelier Benjamin H. Swig. Elected to the board of regents in 1960 and its chairman from 1962 until 1966, Swig was personally responsible for raising millions of dollars for libraries, theaters, classrooms, and laboratories. "You take care of the educational process," he was once said to have told Jesuit administrators, "and I'll take care of the business end."[10] Swig not only persuaded others to contribute, he also gave generously from his own wealth. No less important was the élan and vigorous leadership that Swig gave as regent and later as chairman of the board of trustees at a critical time in the university's history. Much of the success as well as the enhanced reputation that Santa Clara began to enjoy in the 1960's was attributable to this well-known benefactor.

"I must confess my greatest love is Santa Clara," Swig often stated, a surprising admission for a man of such broad and numerous philanthropies.[11]

What motivated this Jewish philanthropist to such devotion to a Catholic institution? The question was frequently posed. No doubt his close personal friendship with President Donohoe was a factor, but also, Swig said, he had discovered "something special" at Santa Clara. "No one pressured me into this relationship. I did not inherit it by reason of my religious tradition or cultural heritage or old schoolboy loyalty. I discovered some pretty wonderful people working here for a fine institution—deeply rooted in the history of our State. It challenged me, and I saw an opportunity to help."[12]

The campaign to develop the university, masterminded by Swig, Donohoe, and others, produced quick, tangible results. New buildings arose across the campus in the 1960's at the rate of more than one a year. The annual budget jumped from $2 million to nearly $10 million in the space of twelve years. In 1964 President Donohoe reported that more than $14 million had been raised for new programs in the past five years, $6.3 million from private sources and $7.7 in the form of government loans.[13] Between 1958 and 1968 gifts totaled $18.4 million, the greatest amount ever raised by the university in a like period.[14]

The Building Boom

The decision to expand enrollment was accompanied by the biggest building program in the university's history. To accommodate a mushrooming student population, most of the existing classroom buildings were remodeled, and a host of new structures were erected.

First priority was given to the construction of dormitories. By 1966 eight new halls, many of them financed by loans from the Federal government, boosted the resident student population from 700 to nearly 2,000. The Graham Residence Center, the university's first new housing for women, was dedicated in 1963. The first four halls to be built in the center honored Mae Swig, late wife of the chairman of the board of regents, and three women regents, Paloma O'Neill, Vera Strub, and Marian Hancock. With the addition of two more residence halls, named for regents Philip Sanfilippo and Dr. Salvatore V. Campisi, the center was completed. Housing for men also grew by leaps and bounds. James Dunne Hall was opened in 1962. Four years later, Benjamin H. Swig Hall, a $2-million, eleven-story structure, the tallest in the city of Santa Clara, began to provide housing for an additional 450 men.

Other structures arose at the university. A student union, planned since before World War II, became a reality in 1963 with the completion of the $2.5-million Benson Center. For the university's varsity football program, resumed on a small scale in 1959 under the direction of alumnus George P. Malley, Buck Shaw Athletic Stadium was built. It was financed by the Bronco Bench, a nonprofit organization created to support Santa Clara athletics.

A growing student body and the creation of new academic programs required additional classrooms. The postwar growth of the School of Engineering at a time when the demand for engineers was described as "little short of hysterical" made better laboratories as well as a larger faculty mandatory.[15] When he came to office, President Donohoe inherited blueprints for a three-unit, $1.5-million engineering center, for which funds were subsequently raised.

Financed with contributions from alumni and from industry, the new engineering complex was dedicated in 1961 in ceremonies attended by California Governor Edmund G. Brown; by alumnus James K. Carr, undersecretary of the interior in the Kennedy administration; and by alumnus Thomas J. Bannan, president of Western Gear Corporation. It was named in honor of the school's recently retired dean, George L. Sullivan, a member of the faculty since 1912 and the holder of California's first license in mechanical engineering. Two of the three buildings of Sullivan Center were dedicated to alumni from the 1890's, George L. Turel and Dr. James D. Murphy, and the third acknowledged contributions from the family of Philip L. Bannan, Sr. Five Bannan sons had attended Santa Clara, three of whom were graduates of the engineering school. Ten years after moving into its new quarters, the School of Engineering, under the direction of Dean Robert J. Parden since 1955, reported an enrollment of more than 300 undergraduates and nearly 700 graduate students.

Other buildings rose in rapid succession. The School of Law had partially outgrown its home in Bergin Hall. In 1963 a new law library, the gift of attorney Edwin A. Heafey, university alumnus and regent, enabled the school to anticipate the growth in enrollment it would experience in the 1970's.

In 1966 the superior general of the Society of Jesus, Pedro Arrupe, visited Santa Clara to dedicate Daly Science Center. This sprawling complex of classrooms and laboratories, built at a cost of $1.4 million, recognized the contributions of Edward J. Daly, president of World Airways and then chairman of the university's board of regents.

In 1967 the remodeling of Kenna Hall provided new facilities for the burgeoning School of Business. Unique among business schools for the emphasis that its curriculum gave to the liberal arts, the school had profited greatly from the postwar demand for professional business training. Led by Dean Charles J. Dirksen since 1941, it had launched into graduate studies in

1959, first with a successful master's degree program and later with a small doctoral program. When the American Assembly of Collegiate Schools of Business issued its first list of approved master's degree programs in the United States in 1963, Santa Clara was among the thirty-one institutions thus accredited. Boasting a total enrollment of about one thousand five hundred students when it moved into its new quarters in Kenna Hall in 1967, the School of Business had tripled its numbers of students in six years.

Of all the new buildings erected in the 1960's, the Orradre Library was perhaps the most painfully needed. Replacing the outdated Varsi Library, whose every feature had for years been criticized by accreditation committees, the new, $1.8-million edifice had a capacity of nearly seven hundred thousand volumes. The sixth new building to arise in three years, it was opened in 1964 and named for its chief benefactor, California rancher and university regent Michel Orradre.

Physical expansion was accompanied by innovations in the academic sphere. In the College of Arts and Sciences, administered since 1961 by Thomas D. Terry, a substantial increase in courses in the social sciences and the fine arts occurred. Evidencing a new-found willingness to experiment, the university adopted a controversial plan of instruction in 1964. Dubbed the Santa Clara Plan, the new program divided the academic year into three eleven-week terms. The number of courses a student could take was limited to four (or three in the upper division), and class days were restricted to four days a week. The purpose of the Santa Clara Plan was to encourage students to develop habits of independent study and to permit them to concentrate in depth on a few subjects at a time.

More significant for the upgrading of the university's academic life were changes affecting the faculty. Not only did the number of faculty members increase greatly during the decade of Donohoe's presidency, but compensation rose as much as 50 percent in some categories. By 1968 salaries in the College of Arts and Sciences ranged from $7,200 for beginning instructors to $16,500 for full professors—a significant improvement in relation to the $4,500–$8,000 range offered a decade earlier.[16] Salaries for nonacademic personnel were also upgraded. While faculty salaries and fringe benefits grew, rank and tenure procedures became standardized. Improvements in the manner of granting sabbatical leaves encouraged scholarly research. Newly created administrative councils and committees gave the faculty more consultative voice in the administration of the university. Academic progress, evidenced especially by improvements in the quality of faculty and students, received recognition in 1976, when a Phi Beta Kappa chapter was approved for the university, making Santa Clara the only Catholic university west of St. Louis to be thus honored.

The Spirit of Vatican II

Campus traditions were shattered on many fronts in the 1960's. Coeducation, spiraling enrollments, greater lay control, systematic fund raising—all represented a break with concepts that had for generations guided Santa Clara's development. With the exception of a brief protest against the admission of women on the part of some disgruntled males, these changes were recognized as progress and generally applauded. No less innovative if more controversial was the about-face in policy which occurred as the university opened its doors ever more widely to the secular world.

Long considered a "safe and quiet" bastion of "protective Catholicism," Santa Clara's self-understanding as well as its public image was profoundly transformed by the events of the 1960's and early 1970's.[17] The university's old paternalism and authoritarianism gave way to an atmosphere of few restraints, an atmosphere in which self-government and self-discipline played the leading roles. In the classroom and in the dormitory a new spirit of freedom and open inquiry gained the ascendancy. Much of this change stemmed from the profound shift in attitudes within American society in that decade, a shift that created a host of new problems for contemporary higher education. For Catholic institutions, a second set of challenges was generated by the wave of reform that swept through the Catholic Church in the aftermath of the Second Vatican Council. Together, these stimuli forced the Catholic university to study its commitment in a vastly changing world. After 1967, at Santa Clara as elsewhere, controversy became a fact of everyday life.

No single event more dramatically illustrated the revolution in attitudes than a Christian-Marxist conference sponsored by the university's Center for the Study of Contemporary Values. Convoked in 1967 in the spirit of Vatican II's call for dialogue "with the world and with men of all shades of opinion" and its invitation to "believers and unbelievers, alike" to work for "the rightful betterment of the world in which we live," the conference brought together scholars of national reputation to discuss "past problems between the churches and Marxism, as well as new openings for possible accord in both theory and practice."[18]

The first meeting of its kind in the Far West, the conference attracted wide press coverage. Its topic and the appearance on campus of Herbert Aptheker, a leading American communist, and Bishop James A. Pike, Santa Clara's controversial former student, also prompted demonstrations of angry protests. Letters and telephone calls from irate parents and alumni poured into the president's office, condemning the conference: What was happening at Santa Clara? Had the university abandoned its Catholic heritage?

President Donohoe answered the criticism with a sharply worded defense of academic freedom. The policy that his declarations represented was a far cry from that of a similar address made by President Walsh some twenty-seven years earlier. The difference in viewpoints helps explain why the *aggiornamento* of the 1960's left many alumni of that earlier time nonplussed. The change in attitudes that had taken place at Santa Clara in those years was nothing less than dramatic.

Drawing from the writings of John Henry Newman and the decrees of Vatican II, Donohoe insisted on the university's right and obligation to encourage free and open exchange of ideas. That it had failed to do so in the past, he readily conceded. "If ever we sought dramatic evidence to validate George Bernard Shaw's cynical assertion that a Catholic University is an impossibility," he declared, "we would have to look no further than the ranks of those who once attended Santa Clara." To the "vocal minority" of alumni and friends who raise "an elephantine hue" every time the university sponsors a controversial program, to those who "think and demand that the university be a controlled experiment utterly divorced from the world of reality," to those who "cannot distinguish between dialogue and espousal," Donohoe replied that "paternalism is blessedly dead." "The essence of today's academic scene . . . is the fact that neither administration nor trustees stand *in loco parentis.*"

The Catholic university has to grow up. So do Catholic alumni and friends of the university. The formal work of the institution is not to prepare monks and nuns, but citizens of the world—and the world is made up of a vast spectrum of ideas ranging from Mao to Robert Welch.

We sincerely think, therefore, that in bringing to campus speakers of various backgrounds and allegiances, we are being true to ourselves as a university. We are opposed to no men and we are afraid of no ideas. We are confident that our faculty and our students are of such a caliber that neither one nor the other will be exposed to undue peril.

We need the support of alumni and friends. We will, however, never buy it by "knuckling under" nor compromise the integrity proper to the life of the intellect.[19]

The lowering of the barriers that had long separated mission campus academe from the world at large affected all aspects of campus life. The classroom, student government, faculty rights, and dormitory life—all began to be reexamined.

It was inevitable that Santa Clara's tightly structured curriculum, an object of student complaint even in the 1950's, would eventually be subject to reappraisal. For generations, every undergraduate with the exception of engineers had been required to take 24 semester units of scholastic philosophy before graduating. In addition, Catholics had to complete 16 units of theology. Although one of the university's stated aims was to give a student a liberal education and "knowledge of the society in which he lives," students were rarely exposed to alternative philosophical systems.[20] Moreover, training in economics, sociology, anthropology, and the creative arts was neglected in favor of the established curriculum. In 1958, out of a total of 128 units required for graduation, only 21 were elective.

Long considered excessive by accrediting committees, this curricular imbalance came under increasing on-campus fire, too, during the sixties. "We had to change," said Jesuit philosopher Austin Fagothey. "Students were beginning to feel spoon-fed and indoctrinated."[21] Professors complained of the deadening effect of lecturing to captive, hostile audiences, and chairmen of theology and philosophy, eager to upgrade the professional performance and morale of their faculties by putting them on equal footing with other departments of the university, began to press for reduced requirements.

Demands for greater freedom and flexibility, coupled with the necessity of adjusting the curriculum to a quarter plan, prompted gradual cutbacks. By 1968 the requirement in philosophy had been reduced to three courses. Two years later this requirement, once the hallmark of Santa Clara training, was dropped entirely. After 1970, the only university-wide graduation requirement was three courses in religious studies, with a broad selection of courses from which to choose.

These sharp breaks with the past were not effected without strong protest and sometimes heated in-house debate. Austin Fagothey, veteran of thirty years' teaching, along with many other faculty members, regretted that the study of philosophy had become wholly voluntary under the new system. But Fagothey probably gave the view of the majority of the faculty of the 1960's when he conceded that "the broader, less confined look" had made Santa Clara a "far, far better school educationally than before."[22]

The spirit of change permeated all aspects of university life. Even the administrative structure of the university was transformed, beginning at its highest level with the board of trustees. In 1959 Donohoe had created the board of regents, an organization separate from the trustees, whose primary purpose was fund raising and development. In view of their active role in the newly created regents' organization, lay persons as trustees seemed to Donohoe redundant. Consequently, three years after the creation of the board of regents, lay membership on the trustees was allowed to lapse. From 1962 until 1967 all trustees were Jesuits. The only exception was the university attorney, Victor Chargin, who was succeeded in 1964 by Edward A. Panelli.

In 1966 new reasons appeared for reconstituting a mixed board. The Vatican Council had called for increased lay participation in the church. Giving lay persons financial responsibility for the university as regents without an attendant voice in its ultimate decision-making body, the board of trustees, now seemed inappropriate. Moreover, the legal separation of the Jesuit community from the university corporation was already under study. Donohoe and other Catholic university presidents were convinced that laicization of the trustees would place their institutions in a better legal position to receive Federal aid. Consequently, Santa Clara joined the trend in Catholic higher education toward secularization. In 1967 Donohoe announced a return of lay persons to the Santa Clara board.

During Donohoe's term Jesuits still constituted the majority of board members, but under his successor the secularization of control increased. During the campus turmoil of the late 1960's President Thomas D. Terry requested a change in the bylaws that would allow a larger and more varied board incorporating more lay counsel. For the first time in its history Santa Clara was governed by a board whose lay members constituted the majority.

The university's relationship with the Jesuit order was altered by another innovation. On February 16, 1968, as his final act as rector-president, Father Donohoe legally separated the Jesuit community and its function from the university and its functions. Though highly controversial, Donohoe's action followed the example set by other colleges run by the Society of Jesus. The Jesuits of Boston College, Georgetown, Creighton, Holy Cross, and Fordham had also recently legally separated their religious communities from their educational institutions.

What did this action mean? It reflected the altered composition of the board of trustees, and it removed any ambiguities regarding the powers of the board. Santa Clara was no longer a family business, administered and controlled exclusively by the religious order. By forming the Jesuit community into a religious, nonprofit corporation, separate and distinct from the university, Donohoe assured that control over Santa Clara's character and its future rested solely in the hands of its board of trustees.

Other considerations also influenced the decision. As mentioned, it was hoped that legal separation would remove any potential legal obstacles to the university's continuing to receive Federal funds. It also relieved the Society of Jesus of heavy financial responsibility for the institution. The separation of

Patrick A. Donohoe, president of the university from 1958 to 1968, and Benjamin H. Swig, chairman of the university's board of trustees since 1970. *Courtesy: News Bureau, Univ. of Santa Clara.*

the office of president from that of rector of the religious community gave the university greater immunity from ecclesiastical interference, a source of the authoritarianism and paternalism that had characterized and sometimes caricatured its education in the past. Finally, the change gave the Jesuit community greater flexibility at a time when the order was beginning to reevaluate, in light of a recent general congregation, its educational ministry.

Legal separation did not mean that the Jesuits were suddenly separating themselves from Santa Clara. The bylaws of the university still required that the president be a member of the Society of Jesus and that he serve, along with an established number of other Jesuits, on the board of trustees. The stated purpose of the institution continued to be education in the Catholic and Jesuit tradition. The California Province, insofar as it was able in view of its several institutional commitments, continued to supply Santa Clara with teachers and administrative officers. The Jesuit community remained a major financial contributor to the university.

Separate incorporation was meant to benefit both the Jesuits and the university. Under the new arrangement, Jesuits were hired on the basis of their professional qualifications, as were lay persons. They were also to be paid on the same scale as their lay colleagues. The Jesuit community's living and operating costs were to be covered by income from salaries, from the operation of its cemetery, and from gifts and stipends received. The surplus was then given to the university as an unrestricted donation. Thus legal separation not only made it clear that the Jesuit community was self-supporting, it also clarified its position as a major benefactor and fund-raiser of the university. Separation, its defenders said, did not sound the death knell of the order's historic commitment to the mission campus. Rather, concluded Father Leo P. Rock, rector of the religious community, it was "a much better, healthier way to assure the Jesuit presence at Santa Clara."[23]

Is Santa Clara Still Catholic?

The task of working out the details of separate incorporation and of explaining it to the public fell to Patrick Donohoe's successor. In 1968 Donohoe was called from Santa Clara to become provincial of the California Jesuit province. The man selected to follow him, Father Thomas D. Terry, had served for five years as dean of the College of Arts and Sciences during Donohoe's administration. Trained in agricultural chemistry at the University of California at Davis, where he received his doctorate, Terry was academic vice-president at Loyola University when tapped to become Santa Clara's new president. During his tenure the professionalization of the university made its greatest strides.

Probably no president had to deal with as many controversies as did Terry. Separate incorporation was merely one of the many changes that had to be explained and justified. The uproar created by the Christian-Marxist encounter of 1967 proved a portent of problems to come as the university opened its doors even wider to the secular world. The following year a much-publicized campus address by Eldridge Cleaver strained relations with many of the university's alumni and friends to the breaking point. Antiabortion groups were offended a few years later by the appointment of Congressman Don Edwards as a member of the board of regents. Student sit-ins, antiwar demonstrations, and the introduction of unchaperoned visiting hours in the men's and women's dormitories also had to be interpreted to a questioning public. Time and time again, Terry was called upon to answer the question, Is Santa Clara still a Catholic university?[24]

No topic required more repeated explication than the policy on guest speakers. That the bewilderment experienced by many older alumni was partly the university's fault, Terry readily admitted. "We changed our policy and have not sufficiently informed our alumni and friends of that change."[25]

The question of who should speak on a Catholic campus had a troubled history, which was confused by the assumption that the university approved and taught whatever any guest said.[26] For many years, the message of any speaker enjoyed the university's endorsement—otherwise, the person was not allowed to speak. "Alumni of that era," Terry said, "understandably find it difficult to comprehend how Santa Clara could give a platform to such persons as Herbert Aptheker and Cleaver." "The real world is made up of many speakers and ideas which the University does not endorse." But "the University recognizes a responsibility to present the main questions of the day to its students in an effective way. To the student today, this means hearing both sides of the question from speakers representing opposite views." The university must and will, he concluded, live up to this responsibility in spite of any pressure.[27]

Terry explained, as had Donohoe before him, that the purpose of the university's speaker's policy was to open the campus to the world. "This indicates no weakening of our commitment to fundamental Christian values, but rather a confidence that this commitment will be strengthened by facing the important problems of our times."[28] Even if some people use an open forum "not to study or to investigate, but to offend or irritate certain groups on campus or to sensationalize or trivialize certain questions," the president said, "putting up with this sort of nonsense may sometimes be part of the price of having a truly open forum." "Catholic universities, like other universities, stand for the discussion of ideas, not the suppression of ideas." The board of trustees concurred with the president's views. Santa Clara is "opposed to narrow indoctrination or proselytizing of any kind," they declared. It is a community wherein "freedom of inquiry and freedom of expression enjoy the highest priority."[29]

This shift in policy regarding speakers did not mean that the university had abandoned its religious tradition. Terry frequently said that dedication to value-oriented education "informed by Catholic principles" remained Santa Clara's goal. One formal statement of the university's aims and objectives issued by the board of trustees in 1968 and another in 1975 sought to make that commitment manifest.[30]

No one could claim, however, that Catholic Santa Clara was still cast in the mold of the 1940's or even of the 1950's. There were few, if any, schools that were the same as they once were. Much had changed after 1960, including the Catholic Church. "At Santa Clara, we are trying to keep pace with the Church," Terry said in defense of his breaks with tradition. "That is what helps make Santa Clara distinctive." We are still a Catholic university, he stated, "but we are very different today than we were 15 years ago." To remain the same would be tragic, he concluded. "It would rob the University of all its academic improvement and gains in that period."[31]

Years of Protest

Interpreting the present campus scene to alumni of past generations was one challenge; justifying the past to the student generation was another. Terry had frequent occasion to do both. During his presidency universities throughout the country faced the challenge of student unrest and campus disruption. Santa Clara was not immune to that ferment, although student protest never reached the level of intensity that it did elsewhere.

United States military intervention in Cambodia in spring, 1970, triggered the greatest outburst of student protest. Demonstrations at Santa Clara took the form of class boycotts, teach-ins, and antiwar rallies. When Governor Ronald Reagan ordered the closure of the colleges and universities of the state for two days to ease tensions, that action indirectly caused Santa Clara to shut its doors, too. When learning that students from nearby state campuses planned to rally at Santa Clara to force its closure, the administration sought to avoid a confrontation by shutting down the university.

When classes resumed, tension mounted again. This time the focus of student and faculty protest was the president's annual review and award ceremony for the ROTC. Carrying placards declaring, "Off ROTC," "Stop the War Machine," and "Get Out of Southeast Asia," a group of twenty demonstrators walked onto Stanton Field and lay down in the path of the parading cadets.[32] A few weeks later, academic vice president James Albertson announced that the spring term would end almost a week early to "minimize tensions for students and faculty."[33]

Other issues sparked sit-ins. The first occurred in 1969, when seventy students occupied the office of the dean of students to protest the firing of two student prefects for having violated dormitory visiting-hour regulations. A second sit-in occurred three years later, occasioned by a controversial reorganization of personnel on the student services staff. Before calm was finally restored several students who had occupied the administration building were arrested for trespassing and less than a month later the dean of students resigned.[34]

The enrollment of racial minorities also became a focus of controversy. In the past Santa Clara's student body had been composed almost exclusively of white students, predominantly of upper-middle-class background and of Irish and Italian ancestry. Blacks were conspicuous by their absence. Apparently it was not until 1949 that a Negro student was admitted to the mission campus.[35] Mexican-Americans, too, were few, notwithstanding their large percentage among the local population and the fact that Santa Clara had in the past exercised a special attraction for students of Hispanic background, beginning with native Californios and Latin Americans in the nineteenth century.

In 1968 only about 3 percent of the university's undergraduate population could be described as belonging to a racial minority.[36] Responding to strongly expressed community need, the university launched a major effort to recruit students from the black and Mexican-American communities. The major obstacle in the way of the effort was that most minority students could not afford to come to Santa Clara.[37] Thus the challenge was to raise a larger amount of financial aid. By 1976, when minority students constituted 16 percent of the total student body, the university was contributing $1.1 million in scholarships and grants. About a third of that amount went to minority students.[38]

Not only disadvantaged minorities, but also median-income families were finding private schooling prohibitive. It was becoming increasingly difficult for private colleges to compete with the nearly free education offered by state-supported institutions. As educational costs mounted, administrators predicted that the number of persons who could afford to pay Santa Clara's annual $2,718 tuition (as of 1976) would inevitably shrink. Compe-

Antiwar protestors try to halt the annual review parade of the campus ROTC on May 13, 1970. *Courtesy: News Bureau, Univ. of Santa Clara, C. Paige Abbot Photo.*

tition for qualified students who could afford to come to the university was therefore expected to become extremely keen in the late 1970's.

Santa Clara fared remarkably well in the struggle for students. It had clearly become one of the nation's most attractive Catholic undergraduate universities. Its ability to draw students was helped by increasing funds for student aid, an essential trend for private colleges that hoped to avoid restricting their clientele solely to the rich and to the very poor who were on scholarships. In 1976 more than 60 percent of the university's full-time students received some form of financial assistance. That figure contrasted dramatically with the two full-time scholarships offered in 1926.[39]

No scholarship program had a more beneficial impact than the one created in 1957 by the State of California. Fourteen years after it was launched, about a fourth of Santa Clara's student body from California and approximately a third of the freshman class were enrolled with state assistance. By 1976 that number had grown to 1,100, a third of all undergraduates. Santa Clara ranked third among private colleges selected by California State Scholarship winners, following the University of Southern California and Loyola Marymount.[40]

More Buildings

At Santa Clara as elsewhere, the day-to-day business of education continued through the 1970's, though confrontations between students and administrators temporarily captured the headlines. During President Terry's tenure, enrollment climbed to new heights every year, reaching 7,010 students in 1976. Undergraduate enrollment was limited by policy at 3,150 in 1969, although it crept slightly higher in the 1970's. At the same time the academic administration of the university was systematized and made increasingly more professional by James Albertson, academic vice-president. Responsibility for administering the four undergraduate colleges and their greatly expanded programs fell to their respective deans, Father John H. Gray of humanities, John B. Drahmann of sciences, Charles J. Dirksen of business, and Robert J. Parden of engineering. To meet faculty and student requests for greater participation in decision making, the university's entire committee structure was reorganized and expanded. The faculty senate, too, was reorganized and given greater responsibility. The board of trustees, now partly religious and partly lay, played a greater role in the university's governance than ever before.

Buildings, too, were a measure of institutional growth. In 1970 trustee chairman Benjamin H. Swig launched a major campaign to raise $10.5 million for endowment and new construction. Not meant to expand enrollment, this campaign aimed rather at enhancing the university's academic programs and at consolidating growth attained in the last decade. Before President Terry retired in 1976, four major new buildings had been erected and four others renovated.

The successful drive concluded with the dedication of a $2-million classroom building in 1973. Named for the late trustee and alumnus Berchman A. Bannan, this hall provided classrooms and offices both for the undergraduate college and for the law school. Long considered a financial drain, the College of Law had in the 1970's come into its own. Reorganized and riding the wave of popularity of careers in law, the college's enrollment had shot up from fewer than three hundred students in 1969 to more than eight hundred by 1973.[41] Its dramatic growth in numbers under Dean George J. Alexander, especially in the categories of women and minorities, required expanded facilities. Bannan Hall helped relieve the pinch, as did a two-story addition to the law library erected that same year, a gift of Benjamin Swig and alumnus Edwin A. Heafey.

The most spectacular architectural form to rise across the campus skyline was the $4.6-million Leavey Activities Center. When erected in 1975 this controversial structure was the largest permanent air-supported structure in the world. Named for alumnus Thomas A. Leavey, one of the founders of Farmers Insurance Group, who donated $500,000 toward its completion and additional funds for later improvements, the innovative pavilion occupied nearly two acres. Under its translucent domes were facilities for the university's large intramural program, including a swimming pool and a 5,000-seat basketball arena honoring benefactor Harold J. Toso, founder of Mission Equities Corporation and outstanding athlete of the class of 1925.

A grant from the S. H. Cowell Foundation paved the way for the erection of Cowell Health Center in 1975. This facility, supported also by gifts from Mr. and Mrs. Frank Hagan and from Dr. James B. Ludwig, university medical director, replaced the fifty-year-old Donohoe Infirmary, which was remodeled as the Alumni House.

The following year the university dedicated a new $3-million theater named for the late motion-picture producer, Louis B. Mayer, whose Mayer Foundation had contributed $750,000 toward its completion. The edifice was also supported by a $750,000 gift from Benjamin Swig and by the university's Board of Fellows, which contributed proceeds from its annual Golden Circle Theatre Party to the building fund. Mayer Theatre and the Fess Parker Studio Theatre replaced the so-called Lifeboat, temporary quarters for campus dramatics since the demolition of the historic Ship in 1962.

The Bicentennial

In 1976, while the United States celebrated the 200th anniversary of national independence, Santa Clara prepared a celebration of its own. The academic year 1976–1977, a year of special celebration on the mission campus, served as a reminder that the roots of American history stretch to the West as well as to the East. That year marked the bicentennial of Mission Santa Clara's founding and the conclusion of the university's 125th year.

It also witnessed the inauguration of a new administration. Disabled by persistent health problems, President Terry announced his resignation, effective June 30, 1976. After a nationwide search, the trustees chose as his successor William J. Rewak, rector of the campus Jesuit community. The forty-three-year-old priest had joined the Santa Clara faculty in 1970 as assistant professor in English, after completing his doctoral studies at the University of Minnesota. On January 12, 1977, the bicentennial of the founding of Mission Santa Clara, he became president of California's oldest institution of higher learning. The inauguration took place in the mission before the assembled students, faculty, and friends of the University.

Seated in the mission sanctuary with the incoming president were three men who had in recent years done more than any other individuals to shape and mold the institution. Present were Patrick A. Donohoe and Thomas D. Terry, who had successively presided over Santa Clara during the period of greatest change in its history. Beside them was Benjamin H. Swig, chairman of the board of trustees. While the two former presidents looked on, Swig read the appointment investing the new president with his rights and duties of office.

The institution whose administration Rewak received was remarkably different from that inherited by Donohoe some twenty years earlier. In 1958 Santa Clara's all-male student body numbered 1,100. In 1977 more than 7,000 students were enrolled, a third of them women. In the intervening years, academic programs had multiplied, full-time faculty had increased fourfold, and the face of the campus had been transformed by the biggest building campaign in the school's history. In 1958 Santa Clara had been governed exclusively by Jesuits, with only token lay participation. Twenty years later its highest governing body was a board of trustees whose majority were lay persons. Testimony to the progress of the past two decades, the university's popularity and academic reputation were at an all-time high.

Perhaps the greatest contrast between past and present lay in the liberalization of campus attitudes. Ten years had passed since the Christian-Marxist symposium of 1967. The winds of reform that had swept through the campus since then had been almost unrelenting. They had brought storms of controversy as the institution struggled to retain its distinctive Catholic character while at the same time making its education relevant to the needs of a rapidly changing world.

The gales of the sixties and the seventies left behind them a revitalized institution. Santa Clara emerged dedicated to open intellectual inquiry on a scale hitherto deemed impossible and, indeed, unacceptable. Stripped of the narrow sectarianism of the past, the university still professed a dedication to Catholic education. The modes of implementing religious principles had, of course, changed with the times, and their further integration would continue to challenge the custodians of the university's future. But President Rewak's inaugural address suggested that the commitment to value-oriented education, as well as academic excellence, had survived intact. The promotion of both would be the goal of his administration.

A university's diamond purpose, he said, is to foster intelligence. to emphasize the importance of value judgments, and to inspire creative action. If a Catholic institution hoped to achieve its Christian purpose, it must be a place where freedom of inquiry is paramount. Repeating a counsel often voiced by his two predecessors, Rewak observed that "We cannot change the world if we do not see it as it is."

As a Jesuit Catholic university, we look both at the revelation of Sinai and the dark search of atheism; we look at totalitarianism and measure it against freedom; we study Karl Marx to enlighten our study of democracy; we hear the words of the drug culture and measure them against the Word that gives Life. All of man's striving and all of man's hope are grist for the mill of contemplation. For if we do not investigate we cannot know; and if we do not know, we can never make a moral choice.[42]

A university exists not merely to impart facts, the president concluded, but also to help a student make responsible ethical decisions. "The making of a moral judgment is a unique, rational, human activity," and right and wrong "are matters of indispensible importance within the educational enterprise." Finally, he concluded, the spirit of Jesuit education demands that work and study "result in action—in charity."

Unless our university, by its dynamism and commitment fires students to make an impress upon their world, it has failed its most distinctive purpose: helping to create a social, economic, and political environment where man can forge his intellectual and spiritual freedom.

For if we do not make the large plans, if we do not seek for truth, if we do not honor moral choice, and if we do not creatively forge a society free of oppression and prejudice, then we may as well be blown away with the dust of time.[43]

19
Conclusion

In 1969 sociologist Andrew M. Greeley authored a study of the evolution of Catholic higher education in the United States. He entitled his volume *From Backwater to Mainstream.* With only slight exaggeration that title might be reversed to describe the course of Santa Clara's first century. The college entered the mainstream of nineteenth-century education soon after its founding. But by the end of the century, driven by forces from within and without, it had drifted into an educational backwater. There it remained for decades, more or less disdainful of the course followed by most American colleges. Santa Clara's academic isolation was not definitively ended until the late 1960's, when the university rejoined the mainstream by conforming its standards to those of secular higher education.

Santa Clara's journey was not unique, although few Catholic institutions enjoyed the prominence of the school during its earliest decades. As Greeley's title suggests, the majority of the Catholic colleges and universities that survived into the twentieth century traveled the same final course. Indeed, one of the conclusions to be drawn from Santa Clara's later history is that it exemplifies most of the generalizations usually made about American Catholic higher education.

Santa Clara's developmental journey was also paradigmatic in its movement toward secularism. According to Richard Hofstadter, the drift toward secularism is the oldest and longest theme in the history of American higher education.[1] By shifting the purpose of education away from intellectual and spiritual formation, that movement threatened to leave all denominational colleges in an academic backwater. Every traditional college, Protestant as well as Catholic, then faced the challenge of coming to terms with the new learning and with the host of problems it brought in its wake. Some institutions adjusted quickly and in the process abandoned their denominational character. Others could not cope with the new directions and closed their doors. Still others, like Santa Clara, survived through compromise. They surrendered to some of secularism's demands, but they did so with reluctance and only after delaying for as long as possible. Thus the history of the University of Santa Clara is a case study of the dilemma that secularization posed for denominational education. Because of the influence that Jesuit educational practice exerted on American Catholic higher education, the story of how Santa Clara met the challenge of that dilemma is of more than local significance.

Mainstream

When Santa Clara opened its doors in 1851, American higher education was still the almost-exclusive preserve of religious denominations. Although Santa Clara's initial popularity was partly owing to the circumstances of its founding in gold rush California, its success was also explained by the fact that it was a representative college. In the mid-nineteenth century, when the paradigm of American higher education was the small church-related institution, Santa Clara stood securely in the mainstream.

The moral relevance of education was generally accepted at the time. Thus Santa Clara's philosophy of education was in line with contemporary American ideals. Its dedication to religious and intellectual formation was typical of the age. To be sure, its Italian Jesuit origin gave Santa Clara a distinct cast. This was seen, for example, in its seminary-like regimen. The college's controls on student behavior, if somewhat more rigorous than most, nonetheless represented a contemporary pedagogical ideal shared by religious and secular educators alike.

Santa Clara also shared contemporary academe's belief in the efficacy of the classical curriculum. What made the college unique was that it continued to cling to that ideal long after other institutions had abandoned it for more diversified courses of study. After the Civil War, when industrialization began to make new demands of schools, training in practical subjects eroded the position of Latin and Greek in American higher education. Santa Clara—like many Jesuit colleges—bowed to public demand by inaugurating a department of commercial instruction, but it did not grant collegiate status to its business curriculum. At Santa Clara the classics still reigned supreme.

The college also recognized the value that nineteenth-century society gave to science. Training in scientific subjects received almost as much emphasis at Santa Clara as did Latin and Greek. This fact was explained not only by student demands for practical training, but also by Santa Clara's setting in a mining region and by the fact that its Italian faculty was trained in scientific subjects. For years the college bulletin proudly drew attention to the school's scientific instruments and its mineral collection, which, it was claimed, testified to Santa Clara's desire to "keep pace with the progress of science" and stay in the educational mainstream.[2]

Planted in an educational vacuum and sustained by a well-trained European faculty, the college flourished. In 1857, six years after its founding, the newly chartered institution began conferring degrees, including the first college diploma bestowed in the State of California. During its first sixty years approximately 5,500 students passed through its classrooms. Only 370 of these, however, received the Bachelor's degree.[3] The number of students enrolled in collegiate studies in any given year probably never surpassed 100. And of these only a handful stayed long enough to graduate. Their lack of interest in college diplomas was characteristic of the age. Until late in the nineteenth century, college training was a luxury, not a necessity. Nor was the presence of younger students atypical. Until the last quarter of the century, most American colleges retained preparatory departments.[4]

Santa Clara's success could also be measured by the careers of its graduates. Several first-generation alumni attained positions of prominence in law and politics. The names of Murphy, McClatchy, Breen, Burnett, Vallejo and Estudillo made the student roster read like a roll call of early California history. The college's chief competitor being merely "the little denominational school" in Oakland known as the College of California, Santa Clara's early directors were convinced that their young college was "easily first" in California.[5]

Backwater

With the passing of time the college slowly lost its position of self-confident superiority. By the end of the century its situation was admittedly critical. The secularization of American higher education posed an enduring dilemma for Santa Clara's directors and for Jesuit educators everywhere. They wanted to run classical schools, but they also wanted to keep their classrooms filled. How can we preserve our liberal arts tradition, they asked themselves, and at the same time keep our colleges relevant to the needs of modern society? That question was not easily answered. Because changes in the direction of relevancy seemed to require a surrender of cherished educational ideals, such changes were resisted. As a consequence, Santa Clara found itself in an educational backwater. Plagued by many of the difficulties that forced scores of other denominational colleges, Protestant and Catholic alike, to close their doors, Santa Clara came close to joining the casualty list.[6]

By the end of the century its problems were many. As a result of the spectacular rise of rival institutions, the mission campus faced stiff competition for the first time in its history. Its buildings looked inferior, its academic standards suffered by comparison, and its time-honored course of classical studies was seriously challenged by the principle of electivism. By 1910 the faculty complained that they could no longer "reasonably hope for more than a fraction of the desirable class of students."[7]

In addition to its other woes, the college was charged with boarding facilities that had become a distraction to faculty energies. The tasks of supervision seemed to devour personnel at the very time when academic tasks were making increased demands on the faculty. Traditional discipline had become onerous to enforce. By the end of the nineteenth century the fortunes of "poor little Santa Clara," as one Jesuit described it, had so deteriorated that plans were laid for closing the school or moving it elsewhere in hopes of giving it new life.[8]

That the school did not close was owing to reforms implemented during the presidency of James P. Morrissey. The decision to remain at Santa Clara meant that the institution would have to continue to cope with many of the problems that had impeded its growth. Nonetheless, Morrissey's reorganization of the school signaled the beginning of a new phase of development. In 1912 Santa Clara ended its college period and inaugurated the era of the modern university.

Santa Clara's flowering as a full-fledged university was, however, a slow and sometimes painful evolutionary process. The school's educational philosophy remained static and, for the most part, conservative. Academic policy continued to be dictated by Jesuit tradition rather than by contemporary professional norms. Despite the creation of professional schools, authentic graduate programs in the arts and sciences were left undeveloped. Library facilities remained inadequate, student scholarships were meager, and the faculty generally lacked professional academic training. Morrissey had nudged the university closer to the mainstream, but decades passed before the entry was complete.

The period after World War II brought the most rapid modernization. The enrollment explosion of the postwar years, a new-found appreciation of secular values, increased dependence upon lay faculties, and a quest for professional accreditation made a sheer necessity of change. The final steps toward standardization and professionalism were begun in the 1950's and swiftly carried to completion in the 1960's and 1970's. The university, emboldened by reforms that transformed both the Catholic Church and the Jesuit order after the Second Vatican Council, brought its education into line with the prevailing pattern of American higher education.

Problem Areas

What kept Santa Clara in the backwater so long? Several factors must be taken into account. For the most part, they were the same factors that impeded the full development of Catholic higher education in general. Obviously, external events such as the appearance of rival institutions and the rapid development of secular education served to diminish Santa Clara's growth. Just as obviously, the university's evolution was at times hindered internally by excessive devotion to tradition. A Procrustean attachment to custom blinded its directors to the opportunities hidden in accepting educational innovations; it also hid the disadvantages of clinging to outdated practices. The spirit of adaptation that had guided the frontier school's missionary founders yielded to conservatism as the century grew on and as the founders grew older. The continuation of this conservatism showed that resistance to change was not limited to clerics of European origin. Perhaps the most dramatic illustration of Jesuit conservatism was the hostile reception given President James Morrissey and his reforms. Nor did the situation improve radically after his departure. The battle against electivism and vocationalism, the slowness with which Latin and Greek were abandoned, and the perduring patterns of nineteenth-century student discipline all revealed a great reluctance to leave the well-trod path of tradition.

What was the source of the inflexibility that characterized not only Santa Clara but Catholic higher education itself? Some authorities ascribe it to the static world view that underlay the Catholic philosophy of education. Jesuit educators at Santa Clara, as Catholics elsewhere, believed that the Church had "an organic 'integrity of vision' about the meaning of the world and of life," and that the purpose of a Catholic college was to pass on to its students this unchanging vision of reality. Catholic colleges "were not so much concerned with the pushing back of the frontier of truth," therefore, "as with passing on a given tradition of truth in which little in the way of addition or alteration was necessary."[9] Indeed, changes in that system were often fiercely resisted. It was the Jesuit colleges that embodied the classical pedagogical ideal most satisfactorily, writes historian Philip Gleason, and it was they who were among the severest critics of modern trends.

To an age whose education was secular, scientific, and technical in spirit, particularized in vision, flexible in approach, vocational in aim, and democratic in social orientation, the Jesuits thus opposed a system that was religious, literary, and humanistic in spirit, synthetic in vision, rigid in approach, liberal in aim, and elitist in social orientation. There was no place in it for interchangeable parts, electivism, or

vocationalism. These were simply the educational heresies that sprang from the
radical defect, the loss of a unified view of reality.[10]

It was not pedagogical theory alone that kept Santa Clara from a more
flexible response to educational change. Local circumstances were also important. The multiple commitments of the California Jesuit province ad-
versely affected the university's development. "We are scattered about like
water," complained a priest who opposed the extension of the Society's educational ministry into Los Angeles in 1910 because he foresaw the sacrifices
that the new undertaking would demand of Santa Clara.[11] James Morrissey
agreed. "With very little strength, we try to tackle the biggest tasks," he
complained to Father General Wernz in 1913. Morrissey pointed out that
the California Jesuits had begun a new school in Los Angeles although "there
are not sufficient men for the already existing colleges." "The situation cries
out for remedy." Five years later his successor, Walter Thornton, declared
flatly, "We don't have enough [Jesuits] to sustain a University"; nor, he
might have added, were there sufficient resources to hire qualified laymen in
their stead.[12] Possessing only limited amounts of money and men, the province nonetheless multiplied its communities, which obviously made Santa
Clara's educational task more difficult. The multiplication of commitments
drained the institution of desperately needed personnel and increased the
strain on those left behind.

The Jesuits were not the only persons who attempted more than they
could accomplish in the field of education. The temptation to fill the land
with colleges was one that every church and religious denomination found
difficult to resist. A hallmark of the college-founding movement of the nineteenth century was unrestrained expansion. Spurred on by denominational
rivalry as well as by religious zeal, the churches multiplied institutions with
scant regard for their ability to sustain them. One of the reasons for the high
mortality rate among American colleges in the late nineteenth century was
precisely the churches' inability to resist this proliferation and the attendant
squandering of their resources. According to statistics compiled by Edward
J. Power, less than 30 percent of the Catholic colleges founded between
1850 and 1899 endured. The most obvious reason for their failure is that the
many colleges "overburdened a thin, impoverished Catholic population."[13]

Santa Clara survived, but the Jesuits' tendency to multiply institutions
without anticipating the consequences had serious repercussions. These were
academic as well as financial. When joined to their bias against secular schooling, proliferation seriously hindered the Jesuits' ability to provide the uni-

versity with professionally trained teachers. By 1900 the culture of professionalism had come to dominate all aspects of American life, including higher
education. According to historian Burton Bledstein, the modern American university itself had come into existence to serve and to promote professional authority in society. It had not yet dawned on the Jesuit leadership,
however, that teaching in a college or university was a special profession
requiring appropriate training. "For the past thirty years our scholastics have
been trained irrespective of the fact that we have colleges to run," one unhappy member of the Santa Clara faculty complained in 1910. "The ordinary
Jesuit is trained to be a secular priest, not a college man."[14]

Even Morrissey's dedication of the university to a broadened curriculum,
designed to meet the needs of career-minded students, did not correct this
deficiency. In one of his last letters to the superior general of the order,
Morrissey strongly urged that young Jesuits be allowed to attend good American graduate schools in preparation for careers in college teaching. "This
matter has to be urged," he said, "since we are already too late."[15]

All things considered, Morrissey was a visionary who was nearly a generation ahead of his time. Despite the urgent need for men specifically prepared
for university work, twenty years slipped by before Jesuits were permitted
to enroll in secular American universities. In the 1930's the California Jesuit province, then headed by Father Zacheus Maher, allowed a few of its
young men to pursue advanced degrees at the University of California and
at Stanford. When Peter M. Dunne completed his course in 1934, he became
the first California Jesuit with a doctorate from an American university.
Another eleven years passed before a Jesuit with a Ph.D., Charles Casassa,
joined the handful of lay faculty already so qualified at Santa Clara.[16]

The Financial Formula

Perhaps no single factor explains so fully the tortuous course that Santa
Clara navigated during the first half of the twentieth century as the absence
of solid financing. Because of the tendency toward excessive proliferation,
this was a problem that confronted many church-related colleges. Even from
the beginning, insolvency placed strict limitations on what Santa Clara's
directors could accomplish. It was perhaps symbolic that its very site was
chosen not on account of its exceptional advantages, but because Nobili,
having no means at his disposal, was not free to select a better one.[17]

Lack of funds discouraged long-range planning, postponed separating the
high school from the college, frustrated attempts to relocate the institution,
and severely handicapped the ability to respond to the great changes affecting

American education at the turn of the century. Though necessity finally forced the acceptance of a broader selection of courses, the ardor with which Santa Clara embraced the curricular expansion was cooled by its inability to hire many lay professors or to train Jesuits in secular academic specialties.

Financial stringencies had numerous effects. Dependent chiefly on tuition income, the university found it hard to maintain customary standards for admission in times of low enrollment. In order to sustain Santa Clara, we "have been compelled to become licensed Wholesale Liquor Dealers," a priest grumbled in 1911 in disapproving reference to Jesuit wine production, "and to supply what was further wanting by almost uninterrupted begging."[18] One of the reasons why intercollegiate football was supported so enthusiastically on the mission campus was that it helped to balance the annual budget, thus making some academic improvements possible.

As they struggled to pay Santa Clara's debts, successive presidents complained of the lack of financial support they received from the public. "Santa Clara has always been self-supporting," someone wrote in 1907, "and for over fifty years has been giving more than she has received." "Apart from a few donations she has had no benefactions. Alone and unaided she has built her own structures, paid and fed her own professors, all out of her earnings and the sacrifices of her generous sons, who, content with frugal living as pay, enabled her treasurer to pay all expenses."[19] The hope that someday a great benefactor would appear and endow the university has been "a dream," another Jesuit complained in 1926.[20]

Who was at fault in the failure of Santa Clara's appeals for assistance? Why, after nearly a century, was the university destitute of any endowment? In 1901, when Kenna's fund drive collapsed, the Jesuits claimed that "illiberality" on the part of the Catholic public was to blame. The laity, it was said, habitually "gave little or nothing to Catholic education."[21] A decade later President Morrissey voiced the same complaint. After expressing gratitude for the $50,000 in gifts that Santa Clara had received in 1911-1912, the president observed that during the same period the University of California had accepted "donations from private individuals amounting to more than $800,000" and that a desire to provide "religious help" to Catholic students at that university had "forced" Archbishop Riordan to devote $100,000 to building a Newman Center in Berkeley. "If the Catholic people of this community would but contribute as liberally to the endowment and upbuilding of the University of Santa Clara as private individuals contribute to the State-aided University of California," Morrissey speculated, "the plans and hopes of the University of Santa Clara would be realized tomorrow."[22]

Several factors explain the insufficient response of the public to the needs of Catholic institutions. The Catholic church in America was primarily a church of impoverished immigrants. Catholic students are "generally speaking, poor," a California Jesuit observed in 1884, and consequently "our resources . . . will increase, and with them our means of doing good" only "as our Catholics rise in the social scale."[23] Moreover, many Catholics, working class immigrants and "hard-pressed to secure money for their daily needs," no doubt preferred public schools over tuition-charging institutions like Santa Clara.[24]

Catholics were found among the wealthier classes too, and although many preferred more distinguished institutions, especially after the turn of the century, some enrolled their sons at Santa Clara. Even so, the number of potential patrons among Santa Clara parents was never large, and the number of alumni whom the college could claim was even smaller. Besides, wealthy Catholics were subject to appeals for assistance from a host of Catholic institutions. Both Santa Clara and St. Ignatius College, for example, frequently looked to the same wealthy families for funds, a fact attested to by the "rather warm feeling" that their rivalry generated and by the enthusiasm with which many Jesuits from both schools welcomed the opportunity to move Santa Clara to distant Los Angeles.[25]

On the other hand, the Jesuits were perhaps guilty of "poor business capacity," as some laymen alleged in explanation of Santa Clara's economic problems.[26] The tendency of the California Province to assume more institutional commitments than it could adequately sustain was certainly a factor; proliferation and the overstretching of resources did not make Santa Clara's task any easier. In the nineteenth century, when its account books occasionally showed black, excess revenue was drained off and distributed to other, more needy Jesuit communities. Thus encumbered with the reputation of a worthy provider, Santa Clara was denied funds needed for its own development.[27]

The problem did not disappear in the twentieth century. The university's fortunes remained intimately bound to those of the Jesuit province. The clash between President Lyons and Father Zacheus Maher over the provincial's access to Santa Clara revenues highlighted the problem during the crisis of the Great Depression. Another example of the problem occurred during World War II, when the province's desire to sustain its institutions led President Walsh to permit a $50,000 private loan from the university to the Jesuits' hard-pressed Loyola High School in Los Angeles. At the same time, in 1944, the university was engaged in a $150,000 emergency fund drive and was

selling properties left and right to cover its operational deficits.[28] Such solic-
itude was advantageous to the high school, but it caused serious problems
in the management of a modern university.

Because the distinction between the university and the religious community was not drawn until 1968, the Jesuit superior general (always a European) and especially the California provincial were intimately involved in
all aspects of the university's governance. That relationship often benefited
the university. The great innovations of the 1960's, for example, were implemented by the Jesuit leadership. At other times, however, interference by
religious superiors who knew little about university management stifled
growth and reduced the president to a mere puppet.

No detail was too small for some provincial's scrutiny. Whether liquor
should be served at the 1952 homecoming (it should not); whether pictures
of women in evening gowns or swimsuits should be excluded from the college yearbook (they should); and which persons should receive honorary degrees from the university—all were grist for the mill of provincial decision-
making. As late as the 1950's, Santa Clara's rector-presidents were obliged to
keep the provincial abreast of activities by submitting detailed biweekly
reports.

The regulations of the Society of Jesus placed particularly precise controls
on expenditures. In 1933 Provincial Zacheus Maher reminded Father James
Lyons that the maximum amount that the rector-president could spend on
his own authority was $250! Amounts beyond that were subject to pro-
vincial approval; if the sum was more than $2,500, "then we must get Father
General's permission."[29] Postwar inflation bent that rule only slightly. As late
as 1954 President Hauck had to ask the provincial's leave to purchase a new
vegetable chopper for $500 and a new hamburger-patty machine for $625
for the university kitchens.[30] President Donohoe's success as a builder was
sometimes the result of his ability at skirting such regulations. When plans
were being made for the new $1.8 million Orradre Library, the limits that
the order placed on presidential spending were bypassed by forming a nonprofit foundation, independent of the university, to underwrite the project.[31]

Fund raising did not have a bright history at Santa Clara, another factor
that kept it in the backwater. Jesuits frequently complained that Santa Clara's
efforts to obtain aid were harmed by the impression of wealth that the institution sometimes communicated to the public.[32] "I was slightly astonished,"
President Hauck remarked in 1953, "to hear from one alumnus recently, that,
in the minds of many alumni, Santa Clara was rich."[33] In fact that myth had
a long history, having been a source of complaint as early as 1901.[34]

Though it had no basis in fact, Santa Clara's image of wealth could in part be blamed on school administrators. Not until the late 1950's was a financial statement released to reveal the troubled nature of university accounts. In previous years potential patrons remained unconvinced of the real urgency of Santa Clara's polite requests for financial assistance.

All of the early fund drives lacked the organization and flair for promotion that have come to be associated with an efficient modern appeal. Maher's campaign of 1922, for all its fanfare, was a dismal failure. The emergency drive for operating expenses during the years of World War II and the centennial endowment drive of 1946 sponsored by the alumni fell far short of their objectives. The record of fund raising at Santa Clara, an outside consultant reported in 1957, shows that contributions never exceeded 25 percent of a fund goal. Even at that late date it was said that, except for the alumni association, the Catala Club was "the most organized group of friends of the University, followed by faculty wives."[35]

In an institution that is simultaneously trying to stay alive financially and to improve itself academically, the role of the president is of crucial importance. Santa Clara's chief executives varied in their ability to raise money. Kenna, the first of the twentieth-century presidents, surpassed all his predecessors in this important area; but even he suffered serious setbacks, as evidenced by the poor response to his call for help in keeping the college at Santa Clara in 1901. Morrissey, assisted by the men he gathered around him, was more successful than many. Paradoxically, it was his frequent absences from the university on fund-raising tours that contributed to his removal from office. Several of the legacies that came to Santa Clara after his departure were the fruit of contacts he had made during his brief administration. By contrast, President Gleeson, upon whose money-making talents the transfer to Mountain View chiefly hinged for five years, was described by a coworker as having "no knowledge" in money matters.[36] The same could be said of some of his successors who had little experience—financial, academic, or administrative—for the burden placed upon them. No doubt it was the priests' inexperience in such matters that led a lay consultant to suggest in 1911 that Santa Clara needed a department of publicity and finance, staffed by an experienced lay executive, to organize the institution's campaigns for funds.[37] Nearly a half-century passed, however, before a permanent office of development was established. The Jesuit leadership was loathe to share with nonclerics anything more than token participation in the university's governance.

It would be incorrect to place only blame on the shoulders of some of the university's clerical administrators. Much of the school's success and indeed its survival was directly attributable to its Jesuit staff. Though dependent upon instructional income and bereft of any money endowment, Santa Clara, like many Catholic institutions, possessed an endowment in men that few other colleges could match. The dramatic growth the college experienced after World War II would diminish the impact of that boon, but undoubtedly the school's greatest asset during its first one hundred years were the Jesuits who filled its classrooms and administrative offices without benefit of salary.

That the religious order had accomplished impressive results with modest resources cannot be denied. "It is said that the fathers are not business men," a Jesuit apologist observed in 1901, but "let us ask any business man to attempt and achieve with the same means at Santa Clara's disposal what Santa Clara has done." "Let a business man build up so much with so little," the writer concluded, "and the objection will have some weight."[38] Despite their personal and collective shortcomings and despite the setbacks that their work sometimes suffered, the university's overseers had indeed accomplished much at Santa Clara of which they might rightly boast.

Return to the Mainstream

By the 1970's most of the deficiencies that held back the university's modernization had been overcome. To the financial crisis of the postwar era, largely brought on by faculty salary increases, a number of responses had been made, including coeducation and an increase in enrollment and in tuition. Greatly expanded lay participation at all levels of university life, including the board of trustees, was another response. To be sure, some problem remained unresolved. As a consequence of imbalanced hiring in the past, women continued to be underrepresented in the ranks of the tenured faculty. Spiraling inflation and mounting educational costs raised the specter of continuing rises in tuition. Santa Clara's endowment remained behind that of many institutions of comparable size. After 125 years the university had failed to establish even one fully endowed teaching chair. The persistence of these problems could not, however, detract from the positive actions that the institution had made in a short span of time.

Implicit in all these reforms was an ideological adjustment. The suspicion with which Santa Clara had long regarded its secular counterparts disappeared in the 1960's as the university rushed to bring its academic standards and practices into full conformity with those of American higher education. Considered a place apart in 1951, the mission campus clearly stood in the mainstream two decades later.

Behind this transformation profound forces were at work. Santa Clara's

On January 12, 1777, six months after the signing of the Declaration of Independence, Mission Santa Clara was founded. The reconstructed mission church marks the historic heart of the University of Santa Clara campus. *Courtesy: News Bureau, Univ. of Santa Clara.*

aggiornamento did not occur in a vacuum. Nor was Santa Clara the only Catholic institution to experience dramatic change in the 1960's. The trend toward secularization pervaded Catholic higher education during that decade. Historians continue to weigh the causes of the transition. Some, like Philip Gleason, have traced it to the assimilation of Catholics as they entered the mainstream of contemporary American life.[39] Delayed for generations by their immigrant status, Catholics had by the mid-twentieth century moved from ghettos into upper-middle-class suburbs. The election of John F. Kennedy to the presidency is frequently cited as a symbol of the shift. As the Catholic population rose in status and power, so too did its colleges and universities cast aside "the posture of an immigrant religious group" and took on "the posture of a typically American educational institution."[40]

The new stance of Catholic schools also reflected the ideological shift that occurred in the church at mid-century. As Catholicism moved from the era of counter-reformation to the age of ecumenism, a change both symbolized and accelerated by the Second Vatican Council, the old relationship between secular knowledge and religious truth underwent reexamination. In almost all Catholic institutions, including the American colleges, the postconciliar age was characterized by "a growing acceptance of the notion that 'the secular' is an autonomous sphere which is in itself good."[41] Norms, values, and methods once viewed as inimical to the Catholic educational ideal were perceived as worthy of study and in some instances, of emulation.

The embrace of the secular world was not an unmixed blessing. Catholic institutions like Santa Clara, after having corrected their historic defects, were next faced with the challenge of justifying their existence as Catholic institutions regardless of their educational value.[42] In the rush to conform to the standards of academic excellence that prevailed in secular education—"or at least those kinds of excellence which [were] thought to prevail there"— Catholic institutions ran the danger of losing their distinctive features.[43] As their former function of facilitating ethnic acculturation disappeared, they groped for new purpose; as the fear that attendance at secular institutions would destroy faith passed, Catholic schools faced the specter of a crisis in student recruitment. What was the raison d'être of the Catholic colleges in the secular age, and how would they survive? What were Santa Clara's prospects as a Catholic institution?

In reply, it should first be noted that there were many paths to secularization. The degree to which Catholic institutions severed their ties with the religious orders that had previously owned and operated them varied considerably. In some instances, the break was complete, resulting in the total laicization of the board of trustees, the abandonment by the religious group of positions of institutional control, and adoption of new goals that, for all intents and purposes, left the Catholic institutions indistinguishable from their secular counterparts.

Santa Clara's experience was less drastic if more typical. It exhibited a continuity of values and outlook. The university retained a "mosaic of characteristics," as President Rewak described it in 1977, "the elements of which are not necessarily unique, but when seen together exhibit an emphasis, a form, a characteristic, a spirit which would be difficult to reproduce without the Jesuit tradition."[44] The architects of the university's modernization had, for example, opted for a mixed board of trustees, integrating elements of both lay and clerical influence. Moreover, the Jesuit commitment to the institution, a factor of key importance in sustaining its Catholic character, continued. Not that lay persons were less capable than clerics of guiding Catholic institutions; but, as Philip Gleason notes, religious orders are self-perpetuating bodies "of their nature disinclined to organizational hara-kiri," and hence the presence of significant numbers of religious remained the principal means by which most Catholic institutions preserved their distinctive religious character.[45] To assure the retention of its Jesuit ambiance, Santa Clara remained committed to recruiting competent Jesuits for service in all areas of university life, social, administrative, and academic. Moreover, members of the order continued to hold many key administrative posts.

Even allowing for rhetorical excesses, an institution's statement of purposes provides clues to its character. One hundred twenty-five years after its founding, Santa Clara continued to specify religious as well as academic priorities, with adaptations having been made in light of changed circumstances. In an ecumenical and secular age the university was officially committed to creating a community enriched by men and women of diverse religious and philosophical backgrounds, a community in which freedom of inquiry received the highest priority. At the same time, the university remained dedicated to the development of an academic community informed by Catholic principles. In conformity with its long tradition, Santa Clara aimed at providing its undergraduates with a value-oriented education as a framework for living.

It was an announced goal of the university to encourage scholarly investigation of all aspects of the religious dimension of human experience, with a view both to societal and personal enrichment. "The University, as a forum for intellectual and moral exploration," President Rewak said, "must constantly question and investigate the principles of our social, political, and economic structures." The educational purpose of the mission campus was "the development of moral as well as intellectual values, an education of the whole person, an education constantly seeking to answer not only 'what is' but 'what should be.' "[46]

The implementation of ideals is never an easy undertaking. The translation of the institutional priorities listed in college bulletins into concrete programs and effective policies is particularly challenging. The University of Santa Clara claims commitment both to education of high quality and to the preservation of its Catholic and Jesuit traditions. Achieving a religious commitment without falling into the narrowness of the past is a continuing challenge. To what extent the university will be able to escape the homogenization of American higher education as it conforms to mainstream norms poses a more serious challenge. Its stated purpose is to continue to accomplish both—to retain its religious distinctiveness while maintaining a heritage of academic excellence. Thus the mission university's task is to integrate its future promise with its unique past.

Reference Matter

Appendixes

A: Enrollments

Academic Year	Students	Academic Year	Students	Academic Year	Students	Academic Year	Students
1851	12	1884–85	259	1918–19	335	1952–53	1,256
1851–52	44	1885–86	244	1919–20	359	1953–54	1,245
1852–53	50	1886–87	235	1920–21	372	1954–55	1,362
1853–54	85	1887–88	256	1921–22	382	1955–56	1,385
1854–55	111	1888–89	263	1922–23	399	1956–57	1,498
1855–56	130	1889–90	244	1923–24	236	1957–58	1,595
1856–57	137	1890–91	234	1924–25	359	1958–59	1,635
1857–58	151	1891–92	223	1925–26	328	1959–60	1,892
1858–59	125	1892–93	200	1926–27	344	1960–61	2,325
1859–60	140	1893–94	185	1927–28	436	1961–62	2,849
1860–61	130	1894–95	172	1828–29	475	1962–63	3,544
1861–62	134	1895–96	236	1929–30	513	1963–64	3,517
1862–63	146	1896–97	239	1930–31	461	1964–65	3,895
1863–64	211	1897–98	252	1931–32	553	1965–66	4,334
1864–65	184	1898–99	201	1932–33	476	1966–67	4,434
1865–66	183	1899–00	223	1933–34	316	1967–68	5,000
1866–67	216	1900–01	228	1934–35	506	1968–69	5,248
1867–68	191	1901–02	257	1935–36	561	1969–70	5,613
1868–69	202	1902–03	272	1936–37	584	1970–71	5,902
1869–70	218	1903–04	311	1937–38	667	1971–72	6,049
1870–71	225	1904–05	353	1938–39	683	1972–73	6,041
1871–72	210	1905–06	359	1939–40	694	1973–74	6,185
1872–73	186	1906–07	330	1940–41	699	1974–75	6,794
1873–74	224	1907–08	326	1941–42	754	1975–76	7,010
1874–75	227	1908–09	349	1942–43	580	1976–77	7,020
1875–76	246	1909–10	353	1943–44	714[a]	1977–78	7,295
1876–77	231	1910–11	292	1944–45	196		
1877–78	208	1911–12	288	1945–46	431		
1878–79	209	1912–13	349	1946–47	1,000		
1879–80	204	1913–14	358	1947–48	1,279		
1880–81	198	1914–15	358	1948–49	1,441		
1881–82	190	1915–16	341	1949–50	1,450		
1882–83	242	1916–17	336	1950–51	1,397		
1883–84	259	1917–18	309	1951–52	1,322		

NOTE: In most instances figures are taken from the roster of students in the annual bulletin. They include divinity students enrolled at the Los Gatos Jesuit Novitiate and at the Alma College campus. Summer-school enrollments are not included. The figures for 1851-54 are approximate and are drawn from sometimes conflicting contemporary sources. All figures represent total annual enrollments, not autumn registration figures.

[a] Includes 529 ROTC and ASTP soldier-students.

B: Degrees Conferred

Year	B.A.	B.Phil.	B.S. Sci- ences	B.S. Engin- eering	B.S. Com- merce	M.A.	M.S.	M.B.A.	J.D.	Ph.D.	Bach. Sacred Theol.	Master Sacred Theol.	M.A. Theol.	Other[a]
1857	1													
1858	1													
1859	1		1			1								
1860	1		—			1								
1861	1		—			—								
1862	1		3			—								
1863	—		—			1								
1864	2		1			—								
1865	—		1			1								
1866	1		1			1								
1867	—		2			—								
1868	—		3			—								
1869	1		—			—								
1870	1		1			—								
1871	2		2			1								
1872	1		7			2								
1873	—		4			1								
1874	1		5			—								
1875	2		2			—								
1876	2		4			—								
1877	—		11			—								
1878	3		6			2								
1879	1		5			—	3							
1880	2		8			1	2							
1881	—		5			—	—							
1882	2		5			—	1							
1883	1		2			1	—							
1884	—		10			—	—							
1885	—		5			—	1							
1886	—		6			—	—							
1887	1		11			—	—							
1888	7		12			—	—							
1889	2		11			3	—							
1890	2		12			1	—							
1891	3		15			—	1							
1892	8		—			—	—							
1893	1		—			4	—							
1894	2		—			—	—							
1895	2		—			1	—							
1896	3		—			—	—							
1897	6		—			—	—							
1898	10		—			—	—							
1899	5		—			—	—							
1900	8		—			—	—							

NOTE: Statistics through 1970 are drawn from data in university bulletins and in annual commencement programs; those after 1970 are from the office of the university registrar.

[a]"Other" includes other bachelor degrees, certificates, and credentials.

Year	B.A.	B.Phil.	B.S. Sciences	B.S. Engineering	B.S. Commerce	M.A.	M.S.	M.B.A.	J.D.	Ph.D.	Bach. Sacred Theol.	Master Sacred Theol.	M.A. Theol.	Other[a]
1901	11		—			1	—							
1902	3		—			—	—							
1903	7		—			—	—			1				
1904	5		—			—	1			—				
1905	6		—			—	1			—				
1906	7		—			1	—			—				
1907	11		—			3	1			—				
1908	15		3			—	—			1				
1909	8	1	—			1	—			2				1
1910	18	—	—			—	—			3				—
1911	12	—	1			3	—			1				—
1912	11	—	7			2	—		1	—				—
1913	14	—	3			3	—		—	—				—
1914	4	—	1			—	—		12	1				3
1915	5	—	1	5					6	—				1
1916	8	—	6	7					16	—				1
1917	2	—	6	7					14	1				3
1918	5	—	4	4					6	—				1
1919	1	—	2	2					—	—				1
1920	5	—	8	8					3	—				1
1921	2	—	3	7					2	—				1
1922	2	—	5	4					8	—				1
1923	2	—	5	10					8	2				2
1924	3	14	—	9					7	—				2
1925	3	17	—	14					15	—				1
1926	10	12	—	14					16	—				9
1927	5	1	6	12	9	—	—		—	—				2
1928	5	5	10	13	5	—	—		4	—				2
1929	4	13	1	13	11	—	—		3	—				1
1930	5	—	39	16	—		1		9	—				—
1931	2	26	12	24	18	—	—		9	2				—
1932	9	18	5	21	10	—	—		8	—				—
1933	11	15	13	17	11	1	—		8	1				—
1934	6	5	26	21	11	—	1		4	1				2
1935	5	1	30	12	10	—	—		5	1				1
1936	8	3	27	6	7	—	—		1	—				—
1937	5	1	30	11	9	—	—		5	—				—
1938	2	5	28	7	10	—	—		9	—				1
1939	9	9	33	14	15	—	—		6	—				—
1940	9	1	36	11	17	—	—		8	—				—
1941	7	3	49	9	17	—	—		5	—				—
1942	4	2	34	18	9	—	—		4	—				—
1943	—	1	43	13	14	—	—		—	—				—
1944	—	—	12	15	—	—	—		—	—				—
1945	2	—	3	—	2	—	—		—	—				—
1946	1	—	9	2	—	—	—		—	—				—
1947	3	—	24	18	20	—	—		4	—				1
1948	1	—	31	43	31	—	—		19	—				1
1949	3	—	51	43	62	—	—		29	—				1
1950	6	—	87	75	85	—	—		24	—				2

Appendixes

Year	B.A.	B.Phil.	B.S. Sciences	B.S. Engineering	B.S. Commerce	M.A.	M.S.	M.B.A.	J.D.	Ph.D.	Bach. Sacred Theol.	Master Sacred Theol.	M.A. Theol.	Other[d]
1951	5	—	64	57	76	—	—	25	—					1
1952	5	—	74	53	75	—	—	14	—					2
1953	2	—	83	44	67	—	—	7	—					—
1954	7	—	70	35	63	—	—	13	—					—
1955	8	—	53	44	51	—	—	9	—					1
1956	18	—	53	44	68	—	—	12	—					1
1957	2	—	58	60	43	—	—	18	—					—
1958	10	—	68	49	64	—	—	22	—		9	10		—
1959	4	—	54	52	54	—	—	35	—		16	12		—
1960	60	—	16	65	74	3	—	34	—		14	12		—
1961	66	—	23	53	91	2	—	8	26	—	9	10		1
1962	59	—	23	36	79	4	14	15	32	—	11	11		7
1963	70	—	24	46	73	4	18	82	35	—	7	19		10
1964	119	—	22	44	80	4	33	132	22	—	2	19	11	5
1965	171	—	38	58	89	8	51	130	14	—		11	11	
1966	252	—	43	55	107	22	76	186	30	—	8	18	—	—
1967	277	—	59	57	126	31	64	152	26	2	1	13	3	16
1968	368	—	47	63	137	28	98	130	46	2	1	15	7	2
1969	365	—	62	72	144	48	96	179	58	1	—	1	1	—
1970	362	—	65	65	148	53	142	216	56	4	—	10	5	—
1971	241	—	146	81	164	89	128	246	62	9	—	16	5	—
1972	237	—	283[b]	60	125	91	108	254	104	3	—	—	—	1
1973	447	—	100	47	158	124	95	275	187	4	—	—	—	1
1974	223	—	263	51	171	106	101	294	206	3	—	—	—	1
1975	256	—	265	58	215	169	122	259	219	4	—	—	—	1
1976	225	—	262	58	236	170	95	216	272	4	—	—	—	2
1977	212	—	213	50	216	149	108	317	263	6	—	—	—	3
1978	233	—	265	48	275	173	100	392	222	5	—	—	—	1
Total	4684	153	3651	2030	3652	1316	1461	2007	2347	64	78	177	43	98

[b]Includes some B.A. degrees granted through the college of sciences.

C: *Members of the Board of Trustees Since 1855*

Joseph S. Alemany, O.P., 1855–57
Joseph Bixio, S.J., 1855–56
Peter H. Burnett, 1855–56
Joseph Caredda, S.J., 1855–62, 1877–1903
Nicholas Congiato, S.J., 1855–58
Peter DeVos, S.J., 1855–58
James A. Forbes, 1855–56
William M. Lent, 1855–?
Aloysius Masnata, S.J., 1855–62, 1877–87
Charles Messea, S.J., 1855–62
John Nobili, S.J., 1855–56[a]
George O'Doherty, 1855–56
Decius Salari, S.J., 1855–56
Francis Veyret, S.J., 1855–62, 1877–78
C. Walsh, 1855–?
Richard J. Whyte, S.J., 1855–59
Anthony Maraschi, S.J., 1855–57
Archibald A. Ritchie, 1855–?
Michael Accolti, S.J., 1856–62
Gregory Mengarini, S.J., 1856–75[a]
Anthony Goetz, S.J., 1856–62
Emmanuel Nattini, S.J., 1856–62, 1877–80
Felix Cicaterri, S.J., 1857–61[a]
Anthony Ravalli, S.J., 1859–62
Aloysius Bosco, S.J., 1859–70[a]
Florence J. Sullivan, S.J., 1859–62
William Moylan, S.J., 1860–61
Santo Traverso, S.J., 1860–70[a]
Burchard Villiger, S.J., 1861–62
Edmund Young, S.J., 1870–?, 1877–92
Henry Imoda, S.J., 1870–?, 1877–86
Patrick J. Kelly, S.J., 1871–?, 1877–87
Charles Pollano, S.J., 1871–75,[a] 1880
Paul Raffo, S.J., 1875–?
Angelo Affranchino, S.J., 1875–?
John Pinasco, S.J., 1875–?, 1880–83, 1887–93
Aloysius Brunengo, S.J., ?–1870,[a] 1877–80
Vincent Testa, S.J., 1877–92, 1897
Joseph Isolabella, S.J., 1878–79, 1886–88
Anthony Cichi, S.J., 1880–1906
Robert E. Kenna, S.J., 1883–88, 1892–97, 1899–1912
Aloysius Raggio, S.J., 1888–92, 1900–1931
T. Demasini, S.J., 1889–93
Aloysius Jacquet, S.J., 1892

Jeremiah Collins, S.J., 1892–1900
William H. Culligan, S.J., 1893–1900, 1907–10, 1911–18
Michael Shallo, S.J., 1893–98
Joseph W. Riordan, S.J., 1892–99, 1916–19
Laurence Gallagher, S.J., 1899–1907
Richard A. Gleeson, S.J., 1900–1910
Jerome S. Ricard, S.J., 1900–1930
Patrick Foote, S.J., 1903–7
John D. Walshe, S.J., 1906–8
Charles M. Lorigan, 1907–20
Henry D. Whittle, S.J., 1908–11
William McMillan, S.J., 1910
John J. Laherty, S.J., 1910–13
James P. Morrissey, S.J., 1910–13
Walter F. Thornton, S.J., 1913–18
Richard H. Brainard, S.J., 1913–16
Richard H. Bell, S.J., 1913–24
Nathaniel S. Purcell, S.J., 1916
Timothy L. Murphy, S.J., 1918–21
Cornelius A. Buckley, S.J., 1918–22
Eugene S. Oliver, S.J., 1919–21
Clarence C. Coolidge, 1920–46
Zacheus J. Maher, S.J., 1921–26
John J. Hayes, S.J., 1921–38
William I. Lonergan, S.J., 1922–25
Joseph Georgan, S.J., 1924–31
John A. Lennon, S.J., 1925–28
Cornelius J. McCoy, S.J., 1926–32
William C. Gianera, S.J., 1928–51
Joseph R. Crowley, S.J., 1930–51
Eugene M. Bacigalupi, S.J., 1931–53
Paul F. Galtes, S.J., 1931–34
James J. Lyons, S.J., 1932–35
James H. Strehl, S.J., 1934–50
Louis C. Rudolph, S.J., 1935–40
Edward J. Zeman, S.J., 1938–42, 1953–60
Charles J. Walsh, S.J., 1940–45
Ernest P. Watson, S.J., 1942–53
James A. Bacigalupi, 1943–50
George H. Casey, 1943–53
Constantine M. Castruccio, 1943–52
Austin J. Fagothey, S.J., 1943–73
John P. O'Connell, S.J., 1943–54
Victor A. Chargin, 1946–64

[a]Because Trustee records prior to 1877 are incomplete, only those pre-1877 dates marked with an *a* are certain.

Charles H. Graham, 1946–48
Vincent H. O'Donnell, 1948–62
Charles F. Guenther, S.J., 1950–69
Herman J. Hauck, S.J., 1951–58
Arthur H. Kenny, 1951–62
Carroll M. O'Sullivan, S.J., 1951–54
Berchman A. Bannan, 1953–62
James A. King, S.J., 1953–58
Edward R. A. Boland, S.J., 1954–69
Wilfred H. Crowley, S.J., 1954–64
Harold J. Toso, 1955–62
Patrick A. Donohoe, S.J., 1958–68
Alexis I. Mei, S.J., 1958–73
Wilson Aldridge, S.J., 1960–61
Raymond F. Copeland, S.J., 1961–73
Joseph S. Brusher, S.J., 1962–66
Anthony F. Frugoli, S.J., 1962–66
Walter E. Schmidt, S.J., 1962–77
Thomas D. Terry, S.J., 1962–66, 1968–76
Joseph J. Pociask, S.J., 1964–67
Edward A. Panelli, 1964–
John F. Dullea, S.J., 1966–67
Joseph T. Keane, S.J., 1966–69
William J. Perkins, S.J., 1966–77
Edward J. Daly, 1967–77
Edwin A. Heafey, 1967–
Thomas E. Leavey, 1967–71
Theodore J. Mackin, S.J., 1967–71
Michel P. Orradre, 1967–
Benjamin H. Swig, 1967–
James S. Albertson, S.J., 1969–74

Louis I. Bannan, S.J., 1969–
John M. Ottoboni, 1969–75
Leo P. Rock, S.J., 1969–75
Philip S. Sanfilippo, 1969–
Laurence L. Spitters, 1969–
Francis X. Duggan, 1970–75
Witold Krassowski, 1970–73
Mary Woods Bennett, 1971–
John F. O'Hara, 1971–77
Cornelius M. Buckley, S.J., 1973–
William F. Donnelly, S.J., 1973–78
Paul J. Goda, S.J., 1973–
Timothy J. Healy, 1973–
Patrick C. Heffernan, 1974–
Joseph B. Ridder, 1974–
Robert L. St. Clair, S.J., 1974–
William J. Rewak, S.J., 1974–
Timothy J. O'Keefe, 1975–
Stephen A. Privett, S.J., 1975–
Kathleen D. Sidenblad, 1975–
Lyndon J. Farwell, S.J., 1977–
Robert M. Senkewicz, S.J., 1977–
Francis R. Smith, S.J., 1977–
James S. Torrens, S.J., 1977–
Jerome W. Komes, 1977–
Nathan Shapell, 1977–
William Joseph Naumes, 1977–
Norman J. Martin, S.J., 1978–
Donna Duhe, 1978–
John B. M. Place, 1979–
Harold J. Toso, 1979–

Appendixes

D: Presidents and Other Officers

Presidents

John Nobili, S.J., 1851–56
Nicholas Congiato, S.J., 1856–57
Felix Cicaterri, S.J., 1857–61
Burchard Villiger, S.J., 1861–65
Aloysius Masnata, S.J., 1865–68
Aloysius Varsi, S.J., 1868–76
Aloysius Brunengo, S.J., 1876–80
John Pinasco, S.J., 1880–83
Robert E. Kenna, S.J., 1883–88
John Pinasco, S.J., 1888–93
Joseph W. Riordan, S.J., 1893–99
Robert E. Kenna, S.J., 1899–1905
Richard A. Gleeson, S.J., 1905–10
James P. Morrissey, S.J., 1910–13
Walter F. Thornton, S.J., 1913–18
Timothy L. Murphy, S.J., 1918–21
Zacheus J. Maher, S.J., 1921–26
Cornelius J. McCoy, S.J., 1926–32
James J. Lyons, S.J., 1932–35
Louis C. Rudolph, S.J., 1935–40
Charles J. Walsh, S.J., 1940–45
William C. Gianera, S.J., 1945–51
Herman J. Hauck, S.J., 1951–58
Patrick A. Donohoe, S.J., 1958–68
Thomas D. Terry, S.J., 1968–76
William J. Rewak, S.J., 1976–

Prefects of Studies

Gregory Mengarini, S.J., 1855
Michael Accolti, S.J., 1856–61
Alphonso Biglione, S.J., 1861–62
Aloysius Masnata, S.J., 1862–68
Aloysius Varsi, S.J., 1868–76
Aloysius Brunengo, S.J., 1876–80
John Pinasco, S.J., 1880–83
Robert Kenna, S.J., 1883–88
John Pinasco, S.J., 1888–93
Joseph Riordan, S.J., 1893–99
John Ford, S.J., 1899–1901
Walter Thornton, S.J., 1901–2
James P. Morrissey, S.J., 1902–4
John Ford, S.J., 1904–6
Joseph Lydon, S.J., 1906–10
James P. Morrissey, S.J., 1910–11
William Boland, S.J., 1911–12

Deans of the Faculties

Cornelius A. Buckley, S.J., 1912–22
William I. Lonergan, S.J., 1922–25
John A. Lennon, S.J., 1925–28
William C. Gianera, S.J., 1928–45
James A. King, S.J., 1945–50

Academic Vice-Presidents

John M. Hynes, S.J., 1950–53
Joseph C. Diebels, S.J., 1953–56
Alexis I. Mei, S.J., 1956–68
James Albertson, S.J., 1968–73
William F. Donnelly, S.J., 1973–78
Paul L. Locatelli, S.J., 1978–

Deans of the College of Arts and Sciences

James A. King, S.J., 1946–48
Charles S. Casassa, S.J., 1948–49
James A. King, S.J., 1949–58
Hugh M. Duce, S.J., 1958–60
Alexis I. Mei, S.J., 1960–61
Thomas D. Terry, S.J., 1961–66

Deans of the College of Humanities

John M. Hynes, S.J., 1966–68
John H. Gray, S.J., 1968–

Deans of the College of Sciences

Elmer H. Luthman, S.J., 1966–68
John B. Drahmann, 1968–

Deans of the School of Law

James H. Campbell, 1911–18
Lawrence E. O'Keefe, 1918–19
Clarence C. Coolidge, 1920–33
Edwin J. Owens, 1933–53
Byron J. Snow, 1953–55 (Acting)
Warren P. McKenney, 1955–59
Leo A. Huard, 1959–70
George A. Strong, 1970 (Acting)
George J. Alexander, 1970–

*Deans of the
School of Engineering*
George L. Sullivan, 1919–55
Robert J. Parden, 1955–

*Deans of the
School of Business*
William H. Pabst, 1922–29
Edward J. Kelly, 1929–41
Charles J. Dirksen, 1941–

Prefects of Discipline
Joseph Caredda, S.J., 1855–89
H. J. Gallagher, S.J., 1889–92
Joseph W. Riordan, S.J., 1892–93
Robert E. Kenna, S.J., 1893–97
Joseph A. Mulligan, S.J., 1897–1900
Walter F. Thornton, S.J., 1900–1902
James P. Morrissey, S.J., 1902–4
Patrick J. Foote, S.J., 1904–7
Joseph P. Lydon, S.J., 1907–9
Francis J. Burke, S.J., 1909–13
Joseph T. Morton, S.J., 1913–15
Joseph A. Sullivan, S.J., 1915–18
Silverius Eline, S.J., 1918–19
Joseph A. Sullivan, S.J., 1919–21
Joseph R. Crowley, S.J., 1921–24
Cornelius J. McCoy, S.J., 1924–26
William C. Gianera, S.J., 1926–28
Joseph M. Georgen, S.J., 1928–29
Harold E. Ring, S.J., 1929–30
Joseph R. Crowley, S.J., 1930–35
Thomas Saunders, S.J., 1935–36
John P. O'Connell, S.J., 1936–46
Edward M. Stretch, S.J., 1946–51

Vice-Presidents for Student Services
Edward M. Stretch, S.J., 1951–52
Raymond J. Kelley, S.J., 1952–58
James E. Sweeters, S.J., 1958–1961
Wilfred H. Crowley, S.J., 1961–64
William J. Perkins, S.J., 1964–67
Mark F. Ferber, S.J., 1970–72

Dean of Men
Jerald G. McGrath, 1963–68

Deans of Women
Helen K. Reedy, 1962 (Acting)
Viola F. Kamena, 1962–69

Deans of Students
Joseph T. Keane, S.J., 1967–68
Jerald G. McGrath, 1968–70
Richard J. Scheurer, 1970–71 (Acting)
Stephen G. Olivo, S.J., 1971–72
George F. Giacomini, Jr., 1972–78

Vice-President for Student Services
George F. Giacomini, Jr., 1978–

Vice-Presidents for Finance
Edward J. Zeman, S.J., 1958–60
Charles F. Guenther, S.J., 1960–68
Marc Callan, 1968–73
Patrick A. Donohoe, S.J., 1973–75 (Acting)
José A. Debasa, 1975–78

*Vice-President for
Business and Finance*
José A. Debasa, 1978–

*Vice-Presidents for
Development/Public Relations*
Charles F. Guenther, S.J., 1958–60
Walter E. Schmidt, S.J., 1960–67
Lee Case, 1967–69
Anthony P. Hamann, 1969–71
Herbert G. Carhart, 1971–74
Norbert J. Stein, 1974–76
Eugene F. Gerwe, 1977–

E: Student Body Presidents

1912–13	Chauncey Tramutolo	1946–47	William H. McInerney
1913–14	Rodney A. Yoell	1947–48	William V. Mulkenbuhr, Jr.
1914–15	Louis T. Milburn	1948–49	John Diepenbrock
1915–16	Thomas Boone	1949–50	Patrick H. Walsh, Jr.
1916–17	Nicholas Martin	1950–51	Joseph D. Farrell
1917–18	Albert Aloysius Quill	1951–52	Reid Cerney
1918–19	Norbert Korte	1952–53	John W. McMahon
1919–20	H. C. Veit	1953–54	John B. Vasconcellos
1920–21	Roy W. Fowler	1954–55	Robert J. Williams
1921–22	J. Thomas Crowe	1955–56	Jerald G. McGrath
1922–23	Porter T. Kerckhoff	1956–57	Gerald T. Kirrene
1923–24	Henry J. Miller	1957–58	Kenneth J. Murphy, Jr.
1924–25	Ernest Bedolla	1958–59	Donald J. Eaton
1925–26	Saied N. Karam	1959–60	Louis M. Castruccio
1926–27	Charles F. Scherf	1960–61	Jerrold E. Kerr
1927–28	Earle J. Reynolds	1961–62	Samuel J. Sebastiani
1928–29	Berchman A. Bannan	1962–63	Richard J. Bell
1929–30	Timothy Connolly	1963–64	Patrick M. Callan
1930–31	Albert J. Ruffo	1964–65	William L. Jaeger
1931–32	Anthony P. Hamann	1965–66	Michael Ranahan
1932–33	Richard E. Doyle	1966–67	Harold W. Mack, Jr.
1933–34	James F. Green	1967–68	Craig Needham
1934–35	William Harp	1968–69	John M. Ottoboni
1935–36	James A. Bacigalupi, Jr.	1969–70	Gary M. Horgan
1936–37	John Filippini	1970–71	Daniel Walker, Jr.
1937–38	Patrick C. Heffernan	1971–72	Edgar A. Suter
1938–39	John F. O'Hara	1972–73	Richard C. Hagan
1939–40	Paul V. Claudon	1973–74	William Everhart
1940–41	Patrick J. McGarry, Jr.	1974–75	Robert Dawson
1941–42	Edmund C. Hurlbutt	1975–76	Christopher Nance
1942–43	Francis J. Murphy	1976–77	Michael Ray
1943–44	Norman E. McGurk	1977–78	Paul Wagstaffe
1944–45	Samuel Conti	1978–79	Wayne Higgins
1945–46	Joseph Radigan		

F: Presidents of the Alumni Council

(from its founding on April 27, 1881)

1881–82	Bernard D. Murphy
1882–85	Hon. James T. Breen
1885–87	Charles F. Wilcox
1887–88	William C. Kennedy
1888–90	James H. Campbell
1890–91	Hon. John M. Burnett
1891–93	Daniel C. Nealon
1893–94	Thomas J. Dillon
1894–95	Joseph R. Ryland
1895–96	Lewis F. Byington
1896–97	James F. McCone, M.D.
1898–99	Clarence C. Coolidge
1899–1900	William F. Humphrey
1900–1901	John H. Barrett
1901–03	John J. O'Gara
1903–04	James A. Emery
1904–07	John J. O'Toole
1907–08	Joseph F. Cavagnaro
1908–09	Hon. Bradley J. Sargent
1909–10	Rev. Thomas J. O'Connell
1910–11	Charles M. Cassin
1911–12	Hon. Thomas I. Bergin
1912–13	Victor A. Scheller
1913–14	Alexander Keenan, M.D.
1914–16	John J. Barrett
1916–18	Joseph T. McDevitt
1918–19	John R. Riordan
1919–20	John J. O'Toole
1920–21	James P. Sex
1921–23	Chauncey Tramutolo
1923–25	Joseph T. McDevitt
1925–27	Frank M. Heffernan
1927–28	William J. Kieferdorf
1928–29	Roy A. Bronson
1929–30	Adolph B. Canelo
1930–31	Charles H. Graham
1931–32	Louis O. Normandin
1932–33	William Knightly
1933–34	Thomas J. Riordan
1934–35	Harold J. Toso
1935–36	Victor A. Chargin
1936–37	George H. Casey
1937–38	Francis X. Farry
1938–39	Rodney A. Yoell, M.D.
1939–40	Brian E. Gagan
1940–41	Norbert J. Korte
1941–42	Joseph A. Schenone
1942–43	Marshall E. Leahy
1943–44	Vincent H. O'Donnell
1944–45	Edward M. Fellows
1945–46	Harold R. McKinnon
1946–47	Warren L. Morey
1947–48	Baldo A. Ivancovich
1948–49	Robert E. Grady
1949–50	John M. Burnett
1950–51	Arthur H. Kenny
1951–52	John A. Cronin
1952–53	Paul J. Dias
1953–54	Paul F. Kelly
1954–55	William V. Regan, Jr.
1955–56	Arthur P. Calou
1956–57	James A. Arnerich
1957–58	Francis J. Murphy
1958–59	Kenneth J. Friedenbach
1959–60	John F. O'Hara
1960–61	Richard J. Lautze
1961–62	Ralph M. Grady
1962–63	William H. McInerney
1963–64	Frank Fiscalini
1964	Joseph C. Tobin
1964–66	Joseph T. Nally
1966–68	Patrick C. Heffernan
1968–70	Leo W. Ruth, Jr.
1970–71	William J. Adams, Jr.
1971–72	Robert F. Lautze
1972–73	Robert F. McCullough
1973–74	Gerald T. Kirrene
1974–75	R. Donald McNeil
1975–76	Bart C. Lally, M.D.
1976–77	Edward S. Gallagher, M.D.
1977–78	Kenneth Murphy
1978–79	Kathleen Bui

G: Nobili and St. Clare
Outstanding Student Medal Winners

Nobili Medal Winners

1876	James Franklin	1921	Harold J. Cashin
1877	James W. Enright	1922	John F. O'Shea
1878	Joseph Cavagnaro	1923	John T. Lewis
1879	Anselmo Volio	1924	Charles Harrington
1880	L. Olcese	1925	Raymond A. Ferrario
1881	Ignatius Schmitt	1926	Raymond J. Hulsman
1882	Frank Meyer	1927	George L. Andre
1883	D. R. Prince	1928	Alvin J. Wolf
1884	John G. Leibert	1929	George G. Gabel
1885	Joseph G. Hooper	1930	Timothy P. Connolly
1886	John A. Cull	1931	Albert J. Ruffo
1887	O. D. Stoesser	1932	George J. Schelcher, Jr.
1888	Joseph M. Pierson	1933	Vincent Cullinan
1889	Raphael Ruiz	1934	James F. Green
1890	Charles Walsh	1935	Frank C. Sobrero
1891	John O'Gara	1936	James A. Bacigalupi, Jr.
1892	Walter DeMartini	1937	William J. Adams, Jr.
1893	Francis Sargent	1938	Louis M. Farasyn
1894	Charles J. Welch	1939	John F. O'Hara
1895	William Fleming	1940	Carlin A. Treat
1896	James A. Emery	1941	Alan J. Williams
1897	Manuel Alvarado	1942	Roger M. Garety
1898	Henry Guglielmetti	1943	James O. Beaumont
1899	William Johnson	1944	(not awarded)
1900	William Kieferdorf	1945	(not awarded)
1901	John A. Clark	1946	(not awarded)
1902	Robert F. Keefe	1947	Robert H. Passalacqua
1903	John M. Regan	1948	William V. Molkenbuhr, Jr.
1904	Joseph T. Curley	1949	Frank L. Keegan
1905	John O. McElroy	1950	John F. Gallagher, Jr.
1906	Robert H. Shepherd	1951	Harry E. Williams
1907	George J. Fisher	1952	Reid C. Cerney
1908	Ernest P. Watson	1953	John W. McMahon
1909	Reginald L. Archbold	1954	John B. Vasconcellos
1910	Daniel J. Tadich	1955	Arthur H. Hayes, Jr.
1911	William I. O'Shaughnessy	1956	Jerald G. McGrath
1912	Paul R. Leake	1957	Roderick D. McNeil
1913	Louis T. Milburn	1958	Kenneth J. Murphy, Jr.
1914	William T. Shipsey	1959	Donald J. Eaton
1915	Thomas C. Boone	1960	Wells J. Longshore
1916	James D. Coyle	1961	William V. Regan, III
1917	Albert A. Quill	1962	Francis J. Muller
1918	Rudolph J. Scholz	1963	Jerold A. Hawn
1919	James B. O'Connor	1964	Patrick M. Callan
1920	Alfred J. Abrahamsen	1965	William L. Jaeger

1966	Thomas H. Bender
1967	Michael M. McHale
1968	Craig E. Needham
1969	John M. Ottoboni
1970	Kevin D. Eagleson
1971	Dean Joseph Miller
1972	Bruce A. Labadie
1973	Richard C. Hagan
1974	Edmund C. Hurlbutt, Jr.
1975	Vernon H. Granneman
1976	Michael A. Hindery
1977	Timothy P. Meissner
1978	Pierce Murphy

St. Clare Medal Winners

1967	Laura E. Arnold
1968	Lynda S. Lange
1969	Mary K. Maloney
1970	Kathleen A. Simas
1971	Judith A. Little
1972	Jeanne G. Huber
1973	Maureen A. Gilbert
1974	Rita C. Beamish
1975	Theresa Merdes
1976	Susan J. Lindner
1977	Jana L. Garland
1978	Canice Evans

H: Recipients of Honorary Degrees

1876 George Davidson

1901 James V. Coffey
Clay M. Greene
Rev. William D. McKinnon
John J. Montgomery
Bernard J. Reid
Irving M. Scott
Charles W. Stoddard
Dr. George Chismore
Charles K. McClatchy
Dr. Aloysius P. O'Brien
Charles D. South
Dr. Walter S. Thorne
John A. Waddell

1903 Gen. James F. Smith
John M. Burnett
James H. Campbell
Delphin M. Delmas
James D. Phelan
William C. Lorigan
Charles F. Lummis
Franklin Hichborn
Bernard D. Murphy

1905 Charles Dillon Perrine
Bryan J. Clinch

1906 Martin V. Merle

1907 James V. Coleman
Henry A. Dance
Frank J. Murasky
Miles P. O'Connor
Joseph Scott
George Wharton James
Frank J. Sullivan
Godfrey C. Buehrer
Dr. Alexander T. Leonard
George A. Stanley
Edward White
Matthew J. Walsh

1909 Rev. John J. Prendergast
Alexander G. McAdie

1912 Curtis Holbrook Lindley
William G. Lorigan

1913 Samuel Couten

1924 John Joseph Tynan

1925 Richard H. Bell, S.J.

1926 Zephyrin Engelhardt, O.F.M.
George A. O'Meara, O.S.A.
Brother Leo, F.S.C.
James A. Bacigalupi
Dr. John Gallwey
L. Hudner
Dr. Alexander S. Keenan
Frank Hamilton Spearman

1928 Dr. Frederick C. Gerlach
John Steven McGroarty
Joseph J. Trabucco
Michael Williams

1930 Col. Charles Egbert Stanton
Maurice Timothy Dooling, Jr.
Joseph George Hooper
David M. Burnett
Dr. Thomas Edward Bailly
Hunter Sherman Armstrong

1933 Dr. Oliver D. Hamlin

1934 Agusto Rosso
Capt. Joseph Sigall

1935 Monroe E. Deutsch

1938 Dr. John Casson Geiger
William J. Kieferdorf
Victor A. Scheller

1939 George H. Casey

1940 Gen. Albert J. Bowley
Sen. Hiram W. Johnson

1942 Col. Ernest T. Barco

1947 Gov. Earl Warren

1948 Warren H. McBryde
Bro. Albertus Alfred, F.S.C.

1951 Edward G. Jacklin, S.J.
Victor A. Chargin
Harold R. McKinnon

1952 Edwin J. Owens

1954 James F. Twohy

1955 Robert F. Benson
Most Rev. Jose Maria Cuenco

1959 G. Allan Hancock

1960 Sidney L. Schwartz
      Edwin W. Pauley

1961 John E. O'Neill
      Gov. Edmund G. Brown

1962 Sen. Barry Goldwater
      Most Rev. Joseph T. McGucken
      Eunice Kennedy Shriver
      Berchman A. Bannan
      Benjamin H. Swig

1963 Bro. Timothy Michael, F.S.C.
      Edwin A. Heafey, Sr.
      George W. Artz
      J. E. Wallace Sterling
      Alfred J. Hitchcock

1964 Rabbi Alvin I. Fine
      Sen. Thomas H. Kuchel
      Thomas E. Leavey
      Michel Orradre

1965 Charles J. Dirksen
      Vice-President Hubert H. Humphrey
      Arthur Hull Hayes

1966 Paul L. Davies
      Arthur G. Coons
      William P. Fay

1967 Edward J. Daly
      Charles E. Rothwell
      Gov. Paul D. Laxalt

1968 James Kennedy Carr
      Morris L West
      Robert D. Clark
      Joseph L. Alioto
      Patrick A. Donohoe, S.J.
      Sen. Edward M. Kennedy

1969 Henri de Lubac, S.J.
      Sen. Mark O. Hatfield

1970 Dr. Walter Rapaport
      Fess Parker

1971 Dorothy Kirsten
      Bob Hope
      Bernard J. Lonergan, S.J.
      Carl Rogers

1972 Harold J. Toso
      Edwin A. Beilharz

1973 Charles Casassa, S.J.
      Albert J. Ruffo
      Thomas J. Bannan
      Paul N. McCloskey, Jr.

1974 John T. Noonan, Jr.
      Patrick C. Heffernan
      Austin J. Fagothey, S.J.

1975 Robert Wise
      Matthew Oscar Tobriner
      Helen Hayes

1976 George Cleve
      Norman Kaplan
      John H. Bunzel
      Stanley Mosk

1977 Joseph Naumes
      Jill Uris
      Leon Uris
      Roy Wilkins
      Alfonso J. Zirpoli

1978 Ramsey Clark
      Frederick Copleston, S.J.
      Martin A. Pasetta

Notes

The following abbreviations are used in the Notes:

AALA   Archives of the Archdiocese of Los Angeles, Los Angeles, California
AASF   Archives of the Archdiocese of San Francisco, San Francisco, California
ACPSJ Archives of the California Province of the Society of Jesus (Santa Clara materials), Los Gatos, California
ADS   Archives of the Diocese of Seattle, Seattle, Washington
AHSI   Archivum Historicum Societatis Iesu (California Collection), Rome
AMPSJ Archives of the Missouri Province of the Society of Jesus, the Pius XII Memorial Library, St. Louis University, St. Louis, Missouri
AOPSJ Archives of the Oregon Province of the Society of Jesus, Crosby Library, Gonzaga University, Spokane, Washington
AUSC   Archives of the University of Santa Clara, Santa Clara, California
BL   Bancroft Library, University of California, Berkeley, California
CSL   California State Library, Sacramento, California

1. Introduction

1. Alexis de Tocqueville, *Democracy in America* (New York, 1899), vol. 1, pp. 313, 308–10.

2. Donald G. Tewksbury, *The Founding of American Colleges and Universities Before the Civil War* (New York, 1969), pp. 31, 211. Tewksbury's list of permanent colleges and universities in California includes only those institutions that were chartered.

3. John S. Brubacher and Willis Rudy, *Higher Education in Transition: A History of American Colleges and Universities, 1636–1976* (New York, 1976), pp. 59–60, 70.

4. Tewksbury, p. 8.

5. Brubacher and Rudy, pp. 70–71; Tewksbury, pp. 16–17, 68–69.

6. E. N. Kirk, *Discourse Before the S.P.C.T.E.W.* (pamphlet, 1856), quoted in Tewksbury, pp. 74–75.

7. *Daily Evening Picayune* (San Francisco), 18 February 1852.

8. Richard Hofstadter and C. DeWitt Hardy, *The Development and Scope of Higher Education in the United States* (New York, 1952), pp. 10–14.

9. *Ibid.*, p. 31.

10. Burton J. Bledstein, *The Culture of Professionalism: The Middle Class and the Development of Higher Education in America* (New York, 1976), p. 127.

11. Brubacher and Rudy, p. 100.

12. *Ibid.*, p. 329.

13. Tewksbury, p. 72.

14. *Ibid.*, pp. 57–58.

15. John Swett, *Public Education in California* (New York, 1969), p. 264.

16. William J. Rewak, S.J., "Statement of Purpose and Planning Priorities," Presidential Papers, AUSC.

17. Hofstadter and Hardy, p. 56.

2. The Setting: Gold Rush California

1. Michael Accolti, "Osservazioni sopra una lettera dall' Arcivo. di San Francisco, Cal., al Rdo. P. Felice Sopranis, S.J. Visitatore in data del 23 Dicembre 1863," MS[1863], ACPSJ. The Italian text of Accolti's description reads, " . . . il di seguente potemmo meter piedi sulle desiate sponde di quel non so come chiamare, se Palazzina, Bordello o Babilonia, che va sotto il nome di San Francisco."

Because Accolti, Nobili, and the other European Jesuits who emigrated to California usually employed the English version of their first name, especially when corresponding in English, the anglicized forms they adopted will be used in this study. Hence, Michele, Giovanni, and Guiseppe become Michael, John, and Joseph.

2. Maynard J. Geiger, O.F.M., ed. and trans., *Palou's Life of Fray Junipero Serra* (Washington, D.C., 1955), p. 97.

3. Maynard Geiger, O.F.M., *Franciscan Missionaries in Hispanic California, 1769–1848, a Bibliographical Dictionary* (San Marino, Calif., 1969), p. 44.

4. Quoted in Arthur Dunning Spearman, S.J., *The Five Franciscan Churches of Mission Santa Clara, 1777 to 1823* (Palo Alto, Calif., 1963), p. 36.

5. Dorothea Louise Schmitt, "History of the Santa Clara Valley: The American Period, 1846–1865," unpublished M.A. thesis, 1928 (Univ. of Calif., Berkeley), pp. 133–34. See also R. F. Peckham, "An Eventful Life" (scrapbook, 1877), BL, p. 29.

6. *San Jose Daily News*, 15 May 1892.

7. Geiger, *Franciscan Missionaries*, p. 251.

8. Zephyrin Engelhardt, O.F.M., *The Missions and Missionaries of California* (San Francisco, 1916), vol. 4, pp. 587–88. González Rubio informed Bishop Alemany in 1852 that no ecclesiastical superior "had ever authorized Father Real to alienate any part of this building [Franciscan residence] or any other ecclesiastical property" at Mission Santa Clara. See José María de Jesús González to Joseph S. Alemany, 30 March 1852, AUSC.

9. [John Nobili], "History of Santa Clara Mission, Doc[ument] No. 16th," n.d., Presidential Papers, AUSC.

10. William Kelly, *An Excursion to California, Over the Prairie, Rocky Mountains, and Great Sierra Nevada, with a Stroll Through the Diggings and Ranches of That Country* (London, 1851), vol. 2, p. 329.

11. Leonard Pitt, *The Decline of the Californios: A Social History of the Spanish-Speaking Californians, 1846–1890* (Berkeley, Calif., 1966), p. 214.

12. John B. McGloin, S.J., "The California Catholic Church in Transition, 1846–1850," *California Historical Society Quarterly*, vol. 42 (March, 1963), p. 39.

13. *Ibid.*, p. 46.

14. Charles Toto, Jr., "A History of Education in California, 1800–1850," unpublished Ph.D. dissertation, 1967 (Univ. of Calif., Berkeley), pp. 109–11.

15. McGloin, p. 43.

16. *Ibid.*; Joseph W. Riordan, S.J., *The First Half Century of St. Ignatius Church and College* (San Francisco, 1905), pp. 13–17.

17. Lauro de Rojas, "California in 1844 as Hartnell Saw It," *California Historical Society Quarterly*, vol. 17 (March, 1938), p. 24.

18. John McLoughlin to Pierre De Smet, 14 October 1844, De Smetiana, AMPSJ.

19. Biagio Accolti-Gil fu Egidio, *Padre Michele Accolti* (Bari, Italy, 1915). Further biographical information is contained in John B. McGloin, S.J., "Michael Accolti, Gold Rush Padre and Founder of the California Jesuits," *Archivum Historicum Societatis Iesu*, vol. 20 (1951), pp. 306–15.

20. Michael Accolti to John Roothaan, 24 May 1849, AHSI.

21. Accolti to J. B. A. Brouillet, 14 April 1849, ADS.

22. Quoted in Accolti to Roothaan, 24 May 1849, AHSI.

23. Brouillet to Louis Elet, 25 July 1849, quoted in Gilbert J. Garraghan, S.J., *The Jesuits in the Middle United States* (New York, 1938), vol. 2, pp. 401-2. Garraghan records that Brouillet's letter (which quotes a letter he had received from González Rubio) was addressed to Roothaan, but an examination of the original in the Jesuit Archives in Rome indicates that it was, in fact, sent to Father Elet in St. Louis and then relayed to Roothaan.

24. Accolti to Roothaan, 24 May 1849, AHSI.

25. "Du projet d'une station en Californie" [1849], AHSI.

26. Roothaan to Elet, 17 February 1849, in Garraghan, vol. 2, p. 395.

27. Accolti to Roothaan, 24 May 1849, in Garraghan, vol. 2, pp. 396-97.

28. Michael Accolti, "Osservazioni," 1863, ACPSJ.

29. Accolti to William S. Murphy, 8 November 1852, AMPSJ; Joseph Joset to [Charles] Jenkins, 1 September 1849, AOPSJ.

30. Garraghan, vol. 2, p. 329. See also John Bernard McGloin, S.J., "John Nobili, S.J., Founder of California's Santa Clara College: the New Caledonia Years, 1845-1848," *British Columbia Historical Quarterly*, vol. 17, p. 221.

31. Accolti, "Osservazioni," ACPSJ.

32. Accolti to Roothaan, 29 February 1850, in Garraghan, vol. 2, pp. 404-5.

33. Accolti, "Osservazioni," ACPSJ.

34. Garraghan, vol. 2, p. 404.

35. José M. González Rubio to John Nobili, 1 February 1850, AMPSJ.

36. Accolti to Roothaan, 28 March 1850, in Garraghan, vol. 2, p. 407.

37. Accolti, "Osservazioni," ACPSJ.

38. Kelly, vol. 2, p. 328.

39. Accolti to Murphy, 8 November 1852, AMPSJ. An entirely different picture of the priest José María Pinyero is recorded by Pedro Isodoro Combet, a Chilean gold miner who greatly admired his character and praised his ministry in San Jose. See Edwin A. Beilharz and Carlos U. López, *We Were 49ers!, Chilean Accounts of the California Gold Rush* (Pasadena, 1976), p. 165.

40. Accolti to Brouillet, 28 March 1850, ADS.

41. Accolti to Roothaan, 12 June 1850, in Garraghan, vol. 2, p. 410.

42. Accolti to Roothaan, 28 March 1850, in Garraghan, vol. 2, p. 407.

43. *Ibid.*

44. *Ibid.*

45. Accolti to Roothaan, 29 February 1850, in Garraghan, vol. 2, p. 405.

46. Accolti to De Smet, 17 June 1850, AMPSJ.

47. Nobili to De Smet, 28 March 1850, AMPSJ.

48. Kelly, vol. 2, pp. 294-95.

49. Accolti, "Osservazioni," ACPSJ.

50. Accolti to Murphy, 8 November 1852, AMPSJ.

51. John Bernard McGloin, S.J., *California's First Archbishop: the Life of Joseph Sadoc Alemany, O.P., 1814-1888* (New York, 1966), p. 125.

52. Francis J. Weber, "The Long Lost Ecclesiastical Diary of Archbishop Alemany," *California Historical Society Quarterly*, vol. 44 (December 1965), pp. 323, 325.

53. Garraghan, vol. 2, p. 412.

54. Accolti, "Osservazioni," ACPSJ; Geiger, *Franciscan Missionaries*, p. 251.

55. *Alta California* (San Francisco), 11 February 1851.

56. Accolti, "Osservazioni," ACPSJ.

57. Garraghan, vol. 2, p. 413.

58. Joseph Alemany to Nobili, 4 March 1851, Presidential Papers, AUSC.

59. According to a long-standing tradition, it was on March 19, 1851, that Nobili took possession of Santa Clara. An entry in the summary of Jesuit correspondence concerning California (AHSI) supports that tradition: "Possessionem init. 19 martio 1851." That Bishop Alemany was in the area on this date is established by the entry in his diary for March 19th: "Preach at San Jose or Pueblo and remain for three days. Try to obtain funds for a school." See Weber, p. 325.

3. From Franciscan Mission to Jesuit College

1. *Daily Evening Picayune* (San Francisco), 18 February 1852.

2. Joseph S. Alemany [memorandum to Pope Piux IX regarding property grants to Jesuits, Dominicans, and Sisters of St. Dominic in California], 1854, AASF.

3. Michael Accolti to William S. Murphy, 8 November 1852, De Smetiana, AMPSJ.

4. John Nobili to Murphy, 13 March 1852, Presidential Papers, AUSC.

5. "Inventorio General," 21 March 1851 (photocopy), AUSC.

6. "Veduta della chiesa e casa di Santa Clara come si trovava nel 1851," AHSI, and "Delineatio aedium et fundi Sta. Clara, tavola prima," n.d., AHSI.

7. Nobili to Murphy, 13 March 1852, Presidential Papers, AUSC.

8. [Accolti], "Financial Report: 'Estratto dello Stato Economico del Collegio di Santa Clara dalla morte del P. Nobili, Marzo 1856 fino al Maggio 1863' " [9 May 1863], ACPSJ.

9. James Alexander Forbes to Accolti, 16 May 1852, "Letter Book of James Alexander Forbes," vol. 1, CSL.

10. *Alta California* (San Francisco), 16 May 1851.

11. John Paul Harney, S.J., "A History of Jesuit Education in American California," unpublished Ph.D. dissertation, 1944 (Univ. of Calif., Berkeley), p. 38. There are no records indicating on precisely what day Santa Clara's first session began, but in a letter to Father Roothaan, Nobili states that he initiated classes "in the beginning of May," 1851. See Nobili to John Roothaan, 20 July 1851, AHSI. An unclear reference in a diary of Bishop Alemany suggests that the date was May 8, 1851. See Joseph S. Alemany, "Diary," 1850–1853, AALA. That Nobili viewed the former mission as a school by May 1 is indicated by inscriptions in his hand in two of the college's early books. For example, inscribed on the title page of a copy of Baudrand's *L'Ame Elevée à Dieu*, AUSC, is: "Santa Clara College S. Iesu, May 1st, A.D. 1851."

12. *Daily Evening Picayune* (San Francisco), 18 February 1852.

13. Rockwell D. Hunt, *History of the College of the Pacific, 1851–1951* (Stockton, Calif., 1951), pp. 4–10; Mary Dominica McNamee, S. N.D., *Light in the Valley, the Story of California's College of Notre Dame* (Berkeley, Calif., 1967), pp. 16–32.

14. *Daily Evening Picayune* (San Francisco), 18 February 1852.

15. Nobili to Murphy, 12 March 1852, De Smetiana, AMPSJ.

16. Nobili to John Roothaan, 20 July 1851, AHSI; Nobili to Murphy, 12 March 1852, De Smetiana, AMPSJ.

17. Nobili to [William Hart], 22 February 1853, Presidential Papers, AUSC; William R. Bulkley to the Common School Marshal of the Township of Santa Clara, 12 December 1853, Presidential Papers, AUSC; Harney, p. 43; *Alta California* (San Francisco), 11 July 1854.

18. Edward J. Power, *A History of Catholic Higher Education in the United States* (Milwaukee, 1958), pp. 112–13.

19. Roothaan to Accolti, 14 January 1851, "Epist. Praep. Gen.," ACPSJ.

20. Accolti to Lordo, 2 July 1851, AHSI.

21. Forbes to Accolti, 16 May 1852, "Letter Book," vol. 1, CSL.

22. Forbes to Accolti, 17 September 1852, "Letter Book," vol. 1, CSL.

23. Forbes to William Heath Davis, 30 December 1853, "Letter Book," vol. 2, CSL; Forbes to Nobili, 10 January 1854, Presidential Papers, AUSC.

24. James F. Reed, "Statement," 15 February 1854, AUSC; John M. Murphy, "Statement," 18 February 1854, AUSC; District Court of the United States, Northern District of California, *Opinions Delivered by his Honor, Ogden Hoffman, District Judge, in the Cases of J. W. Redman and Others, and Thomas O. Larkin, Claiming the "Orchard of Santa Clara,"* (San Francisco, 1858).

25. Hubert H. Bancroft, *The History of California, 1848–1859* (San Francisco, 1888), vol. 6, pp. 564–65.

26. Santa Clara College, "Journal [of Finance], 1852–1856," AUSC.

27. Forbes to Nobili (deed), 1 July 1854, Presidential Papers, AUSC.

28. Andrés Pico to A. C. Campbell, 14 May 1852, Presidential Papers, AUSC; Campbell to Nobili, 20 March 1852, Presidential Papers, AUSC.

29. [Accolti], "Financial Report," ACPSJ. See also Joseph W. Riordan, S.J., *The First Half Century of St. Ignatius Church and College* (San Francisco, 1905), pp. 45–67, which offers the most complete published account of the ill-fated Mission Dolores School.

30. Nobili to W. Hart, 28 June 1854, quoted in Riordan, *First Half Century*, p. 62.

31. Forbes to James L. Folsom, 2 September 1852, "Letter Book," vol. 1, CSL.

32. Pierre De Smet to George Carrell, 14 May 1850, De Smetiana, AMPSJ; De Smet to Charles Lancaster, 19 May 1850, De Smetiana, AMPSJ.

33. Joseph W. Riordan, S.J., "Notes for the History of Santa Clara College," n.d., AUSC.

4. The Nobili Years, 1851–1856

1. *A Statement in Behalf of the College of California* (1860), p. 13, BL.

2. John Swett, *History of the Public School System of California* (San Francisco, 1876), pp. 1–16.

3. William Warren Ferrier, *Origin and Development of the University of California* (Berkeley, Calif., 1930), pp. 50–51.

4. *Ibid.*, p. 50.

5. Hero Eugene Rensch, "Educational Activities of Protestant Churches in California, 1849–1860," unpublished M.A. thesis 1929 (Stanford Univ.), quoted in William Hanchett, "The Question of Religion in the Taming of California, 1849–1854," *California Historical Society Quarterly*, vol. 32 (June, 1953), p. 127.

6. *A Statement*, p. 3; John Swett, *Public Education in California* (New York, 1969), p. 264.

7. Antonio R. Soto, "Chicanos and the Church in San José, California, 1848–1908," unpublished draft of chapter for a dissertation in sociology to be completed (Univ. of Calif, Berkeley), p. 18.

8. Leonard Pitt, *The Decline of the Californios: A Social History of the Spanish-Speaking Californians, 1846–1890* (Berkeley, 1966), p. 228.

9. José Estudillo to [William Heath Davis], 8 May 1859, William Heath Davis Collection, CSL.

10. Joseph W. Riordan, S.J., "General Rules for Prefects and Teachers," Presidential Papers, AUSC.

11. Jesús María Estudillo, "Diary," entries for 29 April 1861 and 27 April 1861, BL.

12. James Alexander Forbes to José Antonio Aguirre, 3 December 1852, "Letter Book of James Alexander Forbes," vol. 1, CSL.

13. W. R. McQuoid to H. H. Bancroft, "Biographical Sketch," 13 September 1888, BL; Bernard D. Murphy, "Dictation" [1888?], BL.

14. *Pittsburgh Catholic*, 21 August 1852, which contains a letter from B. J. Reid, who taught at Santa Clara during its founding years.

15. *The Pacific* (September, 1852), quoted in William Warren Ferrier, *Ninety Years of Education in California, 1846–1936* (Berkeley, Calif., 1937), p. 206; the reporter referred both to Santa Clara College and to the Notre Dame Academy in San Jose.

16. Donald G. Tewksbury, *The Founding of American Colleges and Universities Before the Civil War* (New York, 1969), p. 25.

17. Ferrier, *Ninety Years of Education*, p. 206; Ferrier, *Origin and Development of the University of California*, p. 149; *A Statement*, p. 2, BL.

18. Michael Accolti to William S. Murphy, 8 November 1852, De Smetiana, AMPSJ. See also Louis B. Wright, *Culture on the Moving Frontier* (New York, 1961), p. 144.

19.* John Nobili to School Commissioners, 13 December 1853, Presidential Papers, AUSC; Swett, *Public School System of California*, pp. 22–23; Swett, *Public Education in California*, p. 116. See also Paul Goda, S.J., "The Historical Background of California's Constitutional Provisions Prohibiting Aid to Sectarian Schools," *California Historical Society Quarterly*, vol. 46 (June, 1967), pp. 149–71.

20. *California Christian Advocate*, 16 January 1854, quoted in *Alta California* (San Francisco), 2 March 1854. The author of the article in the *California Christian Advocate* was Charles Maclay.

21. *Daily Evening Picayune* (San Francisco), 18 February 1852; *Alta California* (San Francisco), 8 April 1854.

22. *Alta California* (San Francisco), 8 April 1854.

23. John Nobili to Hiram Grimes, 13 April 1852, Presidential Papers, AUSC.

24. Bernard J. Reid to Nobili, 31 August 1852, Presidential Papers, AUSC.

25. Forbes to Accolti, 14 September 1852, "Letter Book," vol. 1, CSL.

26. *Alta California* (San Francisco), 2 March 1854.

27. *Alta California* (San Francisco), 18 July 1854.

28. Nobili to [anonymous], n.d., Presidential Papers, AUSC; *Prospectus of Santa Clara College, 1854–1855*.

29. *The Redwood* (student publication), vol. 9 (October, 1909), p. 25.

30. William I. Lonergan, S.J., "Another California Jubilee, Santa Clara University, 1851–1926," *America*, vol. 34 (27 March 1926), p. 563.

31. Bryan J. Clinch, "The Jesuits in American California," *Records of the American Catholic Historical Society*, vol. 17 (June, 1906), pp. 136–37.

32. *Ibid.*, p. 139. To some Jesuits recently arrived from Europe and unaccustomed to frontier conditions, the early school seemed "a heap of irregularity," Accolti once conceded. But with typical optimism, he advised complainers that in America one kept one eye "on the way things are at present" and the other on how "they probably will be in the future." Michael Accolti, "Osservazioni" [1863], ACPSJ.

33. *Daily Evening Picayune* (San Francisco), 18 February 1852.

34. *Ibid.*

35. *Ibid.*

36. Nobili to Hiram Grimes, 13 April 1852, Presidential Papers, AUSC.

37. Eliza M. Roland to Nobili, 31 December 1852, Presidential Papers, AUSC.

38. J. F. Hutton to Nobili, 8 July 1852, AUSC; J. F. Hutton to Frank Hutton, 3 February 1853, AUSC.

39. Edward S. Hereford to Margaret S. Hereford Wilson, 29 March 1858, Benjamin Davis Wilson Papers, Huntington Library, San Marino, Calif.

40. [Author Unknown] to [Father], [*ca.* 1853], Presidential Papers, AUSC.

41. John Nobili, "Prospectus of Santa Clara College" [*ca.* 1855], Presidential Papers, AUSC.

42. Accolti to Pierre De Smet, 15 April 1853, De Smetiana, AMPSJ; Accolti, "Osservazioni," ACPSJ.

43. Accolti to Rev. P. Richard, O.M.I., 18 May 1853, Archives Deschatelets, Scholasticat St. Joseph, Ottawa, Canada; Accolti, "Osservazioni," ACPSJ.

44. Clinch, vol. 17, p. 139.

45. *Prospectus of Santa Clara College, 1854–1855*. See also Edward G. Holley, "Academic Libraries in 1867," *College and Research Libraries*, vol. 37 (January, 1976), p. 20.

46. J. M. O'Sullivan, S.J., "The Old California Hotel," AUSC, "Deed of Francisco Arce and Gertrudis Bernal to Martin Murphy," 6 September 1854, AUSC; "Deed of Martin Murphy to the President and Board of Trustees of Santa Clara College," 3 April 1855, AUSC; "College Account Book, 1852–56," p. 68, AUSC.

47. Nicholas Congiato to Peter Beckx, 19 March 1856, typescript translation from "Précis Historique" (1856), AUSC; *Daily Herald* (San Francisco), 6 March 1856.

48. Congiato to Beckx, 19 March 1856, Presidential Papers, AUSC.

49. *Daily Evening Picayune* (San Francisco), 18 February 1852.

50. John Bernard McGloin, S.J., *California's First Archbishop: the Life of Joseph Sadoc Alemany, O.P., 1814–1888* (New York, 1966), p. 125.

51. Nobili, "Prospectus."

52. Congiato to B. A. Maguire, 18 February 1856, De Smetiana, AMPSJ.

53. *Alta California* (San Francisco), 17 July 1855.

5. Italy Comes to California, 1854–1861

1. Charles W. Eliot, quoted in Laurence R. Veysey, *The Emergence of the American University* (Chicago, 1965), pp. 6–7.

2. Edward J. Power, *A History of Catholic Higher Education in the United States* (Milwaukee, 1958), p. 90. Power reports that after the Civil War, Europeans constituted only 10 percent of the total teaching staff. By the turn of the century that figure had dropped even more.

3. The only first presidents of Jesuit colleges founded before 1900 who were not foreign-born were Patrick Mulledy of Holy Cross and Joseph Rigge of Marquette. See William V. Bangert, S.J., *A History of the Society of Jesus* (St. Louis, 1972), pp. 491–95. Bangert mistakenly includes Rockhurst College (founded in 1910 in Kansas City, Missouri) among the Jesuit colleges established before 1900.

4. Estimates are based on data drawn from *Catalogus Provinciae Taurinensis Societatis Iesu*, 1051 to 1909, AUSC. Turinese jurisdiction over Jesuit activities in both California and Oregon commenced in 1854 and ended in 1909, when the California Province was formed by uniting the former California and Oregon missions.

5. John P. Frieden, S.J., "The Society of Jesus in California," *Echoes of the Golden Jubilee* (Santa Clara, Calif., 1901), p. 66. In the eyes of an admiring former student, Accolti was "one of the most polished gentlemen on this coast." See Jesús María Estudillo, "Diary," entry for 10 May 1867, BL. See also O. P. Fitzgerald, *California Sketches* (Nashville, 1880), p. 145.

6. John Bernard McGloin, "John Nobili," *British Columbia Historical Quarterly*, vol. 17 (1953), p. 216.

7. Autobiographical material contained in *Woodstock Letters* (a Jesuit newsletter published in vols. 1–80, 1872–1951, at Woodstock College, Md.), AUSC.

8. Bryan J. Clinch, "The Jesuits in American California," *Records of the American Catholic Historical Society*, vol. 17 (June, 1906), p. 447; Mel Gorman, "Stereochemical Concepts in the Molecular System of Joseph Bayma," *Proceedings of the Tenth International Congress of the History of Science* (1962), pp. 899–901; *Dictionary of American Biography* (New York, 1929), vol. 2, pp. 79–80.

9. Robert Ignatius Burns, S.J., *The Jesuits and the Indian Wars of the Northwest* (New Haven, 1966), p. 55.

10. Michael O'Ferrall, S.J., "Five Years at the Golden Gate," *San Francisco Monitor*, 29 March 1872.

11. *Thistleton's Illustrated Jolly Giant* (San Francisco), 1 December 1873, quoted in John Bernard McGloin, S.J., *Eloquent Indian: The Life of James Bouchard, California Jesuit* (Stanford, Calif., 1950), p. 145.

12. Peter Beckx to Joseph Bayma, 12 July 1869, ACPSJ.

13. John A. Waddell, "Some Memories of Earlier College Days in Santa Clara, 1866–1926" (dictation), AUSC; O'Ferrall.

14. Michael Accolti to John Roothaan, June, 1850, in Gilbert J. Garraghan, S.J., *The Jesuits in the Middle United States* (New York, 1938), vol. 2, p. 411; Beckx to Matteo Ciravegna, 18 April 1870, Prov. Taur. 1010, AHSI.

15. Waddell, AUSC.

16. Alexander Cody, S.J., *A Memoir, Richard A. Gleeson, S.J., 1861–1945* (San Francisco, 1950), p. 13.

17. *Santa Clara College Catalog, 1910–1911*. See also William J. McGucken, S.J., *The Jesuits and Education: The Society's Teaching Principles and Practices, Especially in Secondary Education in the United States* (New York, 1932).

18. John J. Barrett, "Address," *Echoes of the Golden Jubilee* (Santa Clara, Calif., 1901), p. 46.

19. *Santa Clara College Catalog, 1910–1911*.

20. *Ibid.*; Joseph A. Walsh, S.J., "Jesuit College Education after the War," *Jesuit Educational Quarterly*, vol. 6 (1944), p. 168.

21. Barrett, p. 46.

22. Dennis J. Kavanagh, S.J., "The Jesuits in California," ACPSJ.

23. Garraghan, vol. 3, p. 120.

24. Kavanagh, ACPSJ.

25. William Warren Ferrier, *Origin and Development of the University of California* (Berkeley, 1930), p. 34.

26. William B. Faherty, S.J., *Better the Dream, Saint Louis: University and Community, 1818–1968* (St. Louis, 1968), p. 169. See also Power, *Catholic Higher Education*, pp. 57, 85.

27. *San Jose Daily Mercury*, 17 March 1901.

28. "Programme of the Exercises of the Tenth Annual Commencement of the Students of Santa Clara College" 1861, AUSC.

29. "Meetings of the Teachers and Prefects of Santa Clara College," entry for 15 August 1864, AUSC. See also Rockwell D. Hunt, *History of the College of the Pacific, 1851–1951* (Stockton, Calif., 1951), p. 43.

30. *Prospectus of Santa Clara College, 1854–1855*.

31. John W. Padberg, S.J., *Colleges in Controversy, the Jesuit Schools in France from Revival to Suppression, 1815–1880* (Cambridge, 1969), p, 233.

32. Jesús María Estudillo, "Diary," entries for 15 January 1861 and 7 March 1864, BL.

33. Richard J. Purcell, "Gregory Mengarini," *Dictionary of American Biography*, vol. 12, pp. 535–36. See also Gloria Ricci Lothrop, ed. and trans., *Recollections of the Flathead Mission, Containing Brief Observations both Ancient and Contemporary Concerning this Particular Nation, by Fr. Gregory Mengarini, S.J.* (Glendale, Calif., 1977).

34. John Paul Harney, S.J., "A History of Jesuit Education in American California," unpublished Ph.D. dissertation, 1944 (Univ. of Calif., Berkeley), p. 55.

35. *Ibid.*, pp. 54–55.

36. "House Consultations of Santa Clara College," entry for 2 [Accolti], "Financial Report" [9 May 1863], ACPSJ.

37. B. J. Reid (diary, 25 August 1851–11 October 1852), entry Reid Papers, AUSC.

38. [Accolti], "Financial Report" [9 May 1863], ACPSJ.

39. *Souvenir of Santa Clara College, 1851–1901* (Santa Clara, Calif.

40. *Ibid.*, p. 44. See also "Monthly Report of Accounts, 1857–187(

6. The End of the Era of Adobe, 1861–1865

1. John Bernard McGloin, S.J., *Eloquent Indian: The Life of Jame* ___ornia *Jesuit* (Stanford, Calif., 1950), p. 101.

2. *Alta California* (San Francisco), 27 May 1861.

3. Kevin Starr, *Americans and the California Dream, 1850–1915* (New York, 1973), p. 123.

4. Burchard Villiger to [Maryland provincial], 8 June 1861, Archives of the Maryland Province of the Society of Jesus, Baltimore. See also John J. Ryan, S.J., *Memoir of the Life of Rev. Burchard Villiger of the Society of Jesus* (Philadelphia, 1906).

5. Villiger to John P. Frieden, 14 December 1900, ACPSJ.

6. Villiger to Joseph S. Alemany [August, 1861], AMPSJ; Villiger, "Autobiography," *Woodstock Letters*, vol. 32 (1903), p. 78, AUSC; "Monthly Report of Accounts, 1857–1870," AUSC.

7. Villiger to Frieden, 14 December 1900, ACPSJ.

8. *Souvenir of Santa Clara College, 1851–1901* (Santa Clara, Calif., 1901), p. 44.

9. Henry L. Walsh, S.J., "The Annals of Santa Clara College and University, 1851–1951," typed manuscript, vol. 1, part 1, p. 71, AUSC.

10. Jesús María Estudillo, "Diary," entry for 15 November 1862, BL.

11. Villiger to Frieden, 14 December 1900, ACPSJ.

12. Villiger, "Autobiography," p. 78.

13. *Prospectus of Santa Clara College, 1879–1880.*

14. Estudillo, entry for 26 October 1864, BL. For a summary of Neri's career, see Mel Gorman, "Chemistry at the University of San Francisco, 1863–1906," *Journal of Chemical Education*, vol. 41 (November, 1964), p. 628.

15. *Prospectus of Santa Clara College*, 1855–1856, 1857–1858, and 1879–1880; "Father Messea's Life Work Ended," *San Jose Mercury* (?), 12 August 1897, Messea File, AUSC.

16. *Alta California* (San Francisco), 20 August 1866. The account of a visit by Mr. Anderson from Scotland, published in the Philadelphia *Argus* (ca. December, 1860) is quoted in Bryan J. Clinch, "The Jesuits in American California," *Records of the American Catholic Historical Society*, vol. 17 (September, 1906), pp. 316–17.

17. Gorman, p. 628. See also *The Redwood* (student publication), vol. 11 (April, 1912), p. 236.

18. *Souvenir*, p. 46.

19. Estudillo, entry for 16 January 1864, BL.

20. Villiger to Frieden, 14 December 1900, ACPSJ.

21. Villiger to [Maryland provincial], 8 June 1861 and 3 September 1861, Archives of the Maryland Province of the Society of Jesus, Baltimore.

22. *San Francisco Weekly American Flag*, 10 July 1864, and *Thistleton's Illustrated Jolly Giant* (San Francisco), 1 November 1873, both quoted in John Bernard McGloin, S.J., *Eloquent Indian: The Life of James Bouchard, California Jesuit* (Stanford, Calif., 1950), pp. 144–45.

23. *Woodstock Letters*, vol. 18 (1889), pp. 246–47, AUSC.

24. "Bond [of] President of Santa Clara College for Forty Stand of Arms, etc.," 9 May 1862, Military Records, California State Archives, Sacramento.

. *The Redwood*, vol. 9 (October, 1909), p. 26.

26. Estudillo, entries for 5 April 1861, 26 April 1861, 19 February 1862, and 15 May 1862, BL.

27. Villiger to Frieden, 14 December 1900, ACPSJ.

28. Alemany to Felix Sopranis, 23 December 1862, quoted in John Bernard McGloin, S.J., *California's First Archbishop, the Life of Joseph Sadoc Alemany, O.P., 1814–1888* (New York, 1966), p. 203.

29. All Jesuit schools in the United States charged tuition, with the single exception of Regis High School in New York City, which was endowed by benefactors at its founding. See John W. Donohue, S.J., *Jesuit Education: An Essay on the Foundations of its Idea* (New York, 1963), p. 195.

30. See Joseph W. Riordan, S.J., *The First Half Century of St. Ignatius Church and College* (San Francisco, 1905), pp. 109–214 *passim*, for a description of the financial crisis at St. Ignatius College.

31. "Monthly Report of Accounts, 1857–1870," AUSC.

32. Alemany to Cardinal Alessandro Barnabo, 18 August 1867, quoted in McGloin, *Alemany*, pp. 234–35.

33. Villiger to Frieden, 14 December 1900, ACPSJ. Accolti was less sanguine at the appearance of Saint Mary's. "The purpose of this new institution is ostensibly to put down Santa Clara," he complained privately. Because of its lower tuition, "a great number will rush there," he predicted, and "for two or three years" Santa Clara will suffer. However, even the loquacious Accolti agreed with Villiger that "it suits us best to wait" in patient silence. [Accolti], "Financial Report" [May, 1863], ACPSJ. Saint Mary's tuition and room and board fee is listed in that college's 1864 Commencement program.

34. Riordan, p. 145.

35. *San Francisco Weekly American Flag*, 10 July 1864, quoted in McGloin, *Eloquent Indian*, p. 144.

36. Roy W. Cloud, *Education in California* (Stanford, 1952), p. 47. Accolti placed the value of the buildings, lands, and equipment of Santa Clara at not less than $250,000. See California Department of Education, *Report, 1864–1865*, p. 408.

37. Riordan, pp. 145–46.

7. Early Student Life

1. Laurence R. Veysey, *The Emergence of the American University* (Chicago, 1965), pp. 28, 32–35; Edward J. Power, *A History of Catholic Higher Education in the United States* (Milwaukee, 1958), p. 126.

2. Michael Accolti, "Financial Report," 8 May 1863, ACPSJ; Accolti to Col. J. L. L. Warren, 25 September 1864, J. L. L. Warren Papers, BL.

3. Accolti to Warren, 25 September 1864, Warren Papers, BL.

4. *Ibid.*

5. *Ibid.*; "Regulations for the Students of Santa Clara College," Broadside [*ca.* 1880], AUSC.

6. *Catalogue of Santa Clara College, 1875–1876*.

7. John Nobili to Hiram Grimes, 13 April 1852, Presidential Papers, AUSC.

8. Accolti to Warren, 25 September 1864, Warren Papers, BL.

9. J. Campbell Shorb, "Priests No Alarmists" (pamphlet, Santa Clara, Calif., 1873), AUSC.

10. Zachariah Montgomery, "Address of Hon. Z. Montgomery before the Graduating Class of 1872 at Santa Clara College" (pamphlet, Santa Clara, Calif., 1872), AUSC.

11. "Regulations" (broadside), AUSC.

12. Nobili, "Regulations for the Day Scholars of S.C.C., S.J.," Presidential Papers, AUSC.

13. "Regulations" (broadside), AUSC; *Catalogue of Santa Clara College, 1865–1866*; see also "Meetings of the Teachers and Prefects of Santa Clara College, 1856–1899," AUSC.

14. Jesús María Estudillo, "Diary," entry for 15 May 1862, BL.

15. "Meetings of Teachers and Prefects," entry for 29 December 1864, AUSC.

16. "Regulations" (broadside), AUSC.

17. Henry L. Walsh, S.J., "The Annals of Santa Clara College and University, 1851–1951," typed manuscript, vol. 1, part 1, p. 197, AUSC.

18. [Joseph W. Riordan, S.J.], "General Rules for Prefects and Teachers," n.d., Presidential Papers, AUSC; "Meetings of Teachers and Prefects," entries for 2 March 1869 and 2 January 1869, AUSC.

19. "Meetings of Teachers and Prefects," entry for 4 August 1874, AUSC.

20. "Meetings of Teachers and Prefects," entry for 20 July 1865, AUSC.

21. Walsh, vol. 1, part 1, p. 55.

22. Veysey, p. 35.

23. United States Government, Department of the Interior, Bureau of Education, *The Discipline of the School* (Washington, D.C., 1881).

24. Estudillo, entry for 29 August 1864, BL.

25. Walsh, vol. 1, part 1, p. 143, AUSC.

26. Estudillo, entry for 21 April 1862, BL.

27. "Meetings of Teachers and Prefects," entry for 14 November 1865, AUSC.

28. *Ibid.*, entry for 19 August 1866.

29. Estudillo, entries for 17 January 1861 and 24 January 1861, BL.

30. *Ibid.*, entry for 2 June 1864.

31. *The Monthly Santa Claran*, vol. 5 (April, 1937).

32. Walsh, vol. 1, part 1, p. 148, AUSC; T. J. O'Connell, S.J. [reminiscences], AUSC.

33. D. J. Kavanagh, S.J., "The Jesuits in California," ACPSJ.

34. Walsh, vol. 1, part 2, p. 50, AUSC.

35. [Fragment from diary of student in a "Secret Society," Santa Clara College], AUSC.

36. [Riordan], "General Rules," Presidential Papers, AUSC.

37. Kavanagh, ACPSJ.

38. *California Farmer and Journal of Useful Sciences* (San Francisco), 30 March 1876; "Head Prefect's Log: 1869–1886," entries for September–October 1875, AUSC.

39. Kavanagh, ACPSJ.

40. *Woodstock Letters*, vol. 37 (1908), pp. 108–11, AUSC.

41. Joseph W. Riordan, S.J., *The First Half Century of St. Ignatius Church and College* (San Francisco, 1905), p. 61, regarding Veyret.

42. *Woodstock Letters*, vol. 37 (1908), pp. 108–11, AUSC.

43. *California Farmer and Journal of Useful Sciences* (San Francisco), 30 March 1876.

44. "Meetings of Teachers and Prefects," entry for 20 July 1865, AUSC.

45. "Regulations" (broadside), AUSC.

46. John A. Waddell, "Some Memories of Earlier College Days in Santa Clara, 1866–1926" (dictation), AUSC.

47. "Meetings of Teachers and Prefects," entry for 2 January 1869, AUSC.

48. *The Monthly Santa Claran*, vol. 2 (March, 1934).

49. "Meetings of Teachers and Prefects," entry for 5 January 1874, AUSC.

50. *Ibid.*, entries for 18 April 1870 and 13 November 1865.

51. *Ibid.*, entry for 2 January 1875.

52. Waddell, AUSC.

53. [Riordan], "General Rules," Presidential Papers, AUSC.

54. "Meetings of Teachers and Prefects," entry for 20 July 1865, AUSC.

55. *Ibid.*, entry for 27 October 1868.

56. *Ibid.*, entries for 4 December 1868 and 2 January 1869.

57. *The Redwood*, vol. 1 (April, 1903), p. 246.

58. "Meetings of Teachers and Prefects," entry for 20 May 1869, AUSC.

59. For example, see Estudillo, entry for 23 January 1864, BL.

60. Joseph W. Riordan, S.J. [notes for history of Santa Clara College], n.d., AUSC.

61. "Catalogus Alumnorum Collegu Stae Clarae, Soc. Iesu, Cal., 1868–1890," AUSC.

62. "Regulations" (broadside), AUSC.

63. "Head Prefect's Log: 1891–1896," entry for 25 May, 1891, AUSC.

64. *The Redwood*, vol. 1 (April, 1903), p. 246.

65. *Woodstock Letters*, vol. 39 (1910), pp. 111–12, vol. 14 (1885), p. 371, AUSC. See also Estudillo, entries for 28 and 30 March 1867, BL.

66. *Catalogue of Santa Clara College, 1866–1867; Catalogue of Santa Clara College, 1887–1888.*

67. "Meetings of Teachers and Prefects," entries for 20 July 1865, 2 January 1869, and 2 March 1869, AUSC.

8. Progress Amid Poverty, 1865–1880

1. *The Owl*, vol. 2 (April, 1871).

2. Rockwell D. Hunt, *History of the College of the Pacific, 1851–1951* (Stockton, Calif., 1951), pp. 33–45; John Swett, *Public Education in California* (New York, 1969), p. 265; William Warren Ferrier, *Origin and Development of the University of California* (Berkeley, Calif., 1930), pp. 344, 374.

3. *Souvenir of Santa Clara College, 1851–1901* (Santa Clara, Calif., 1901), p. 46; "Monthly Report of Accounts, 1857–1870," AUSC.

4. Joseph W. Riordan, S.J., *The First Half Century of St. Ignatius Church and College* (San Francisco, 1905), pp. 337–38; Richard A. Gleeson, S.J., "My Golden Jubilee Thoughts," pp. 11–12, AUSC.

5. Henry Woods, S.J., "The California Mission of the Society of Jesus," *Woodstock Letters*, vol. 13 (1884), p. 163, AUSC. See also Bryan J. Clinch, "Jesuits in American California," *Records of the American Catholic Historical Society*, vol. 17 (June, 1906), pp. 318–19.

6. Over the years, the nickname of this local landmark was attributed to many causes. For various versions, see *The Santa Clara*, 12 March 1926 and 31 March 1938, and an undated clipping from the *San Jose Mercury Herald* [*ca.* 19 January 1941] in "SCU Clipping Scrapbook, 1939–1942," AUSC. Modern fire and safety codes led to the razing of the Ship in 1962.

7. *Alta California* (San Francisco), 11 August 1870, and *Prospectus of Santa Clara College*, 1879–1880.

8. B. J. Reid [diary, 25 August 1851–11 October 1852], entry for 20 June 1852, B. J. Reid Papers, AUSC.

9. Jesús María Estudillo, "Diary," entry for 26 February 1864, BL.

10. *Alta California* (San Francisco), 11 August 1870.

11. "Address Delivered by John T. Doyle, Esq. at the Inauguration of the New Hall of Santa Clara College on Tuesday, August 9th 1870" (pamphlet, San Francisco, 1870), AUSC.

12. Because no class listings according to divisions have survived, the estimates above were drawn from the record of the distribution of prizes contained in the 1875 commencement program.

13. *Souvenir*, pp. 46–47.

14. Aloysius Varsi to [Peter Beckx], 4 August 1869, AHSI; "Monthly Report of Accounts, 1870–1886," AUSC.

15. "Monthly Report of Accounts, 1870–1886," AUSC.

16. *Thistleton's Illustrated Jolly Giant* (San Francisco), 18 July 1874, quoted in John Bernard McGloin, S.J., *Eloquent Indian: The Life of James Bouchard, California Jesuit* (Stanford, Calif., 1950), p. 147.

17. "Annual Financial Reports, 1886–1907," AUSC. Vineyard income appears to have fluctuated widely, from $500 to $10,000 annually.

18. *Souvenir*, p. 60. See also Thomas D. Terry, S.J., "California Grapes and California Missions," *Agricultural History*, vol. 49 (January, 1975), pp. 292–93.

19. Richard B. Spohn, "The Sacred Heart Novitiate, 1888–1963," *Western Jesuit*, vol. 38 (September, 1963), pp. 4–14.

20. *Alta California* (San Francisco), 11 August 1870.

21. *Woodstock Letters*, vol. 21 (1892), pp. 428–30, AUSC.

22. "Monthly Report of Accounts, 1870–1886," AUSC. See also "Liber Consultationum Domesticarum" [1855–1894], entry for 30 December 1876, AUSC.

23. "Philalethic Society Records, 1856–1874," AUSC.

24. John J. O'Toole, "The House of Philhistorians and Public Life," *The Redwood* (student publication) vol. 8 (June, 1909), p. 413.

25. *Woodstock Letters*, vol. 30 (1901), p. 138, AUSC.

26. "100 Years of Debating at the University of Santa Clara, 1857–1957, NSHSSA State Qualifying Tournament, April 27, 1957," AUSC. See also William J. McGucken, S.J., *The Jesuits and Education* (New York, 1932), p. 195, and *America*, vol. 34 (27 March 1926), p. 564.

27. *The Redwood*, vol. 8 (June, 1909), p. 413.

28. *Prospectus of Santa Clara College, 1865–1866.*

29. Edward J. Power, *A History of Catholic Higher Education in the United States* (Milwaukee, 1958), pp. 138–39.

30. Celia Einarsson, "The Santa Clara College Press and Its Imprints, 1866 to 1900," unpublished M.A. thesis, 1969 (San Jose State College, San Jose, Calif.).

31. Henry L. Walsh, S.J., "The Annals of Santa Clara College and University, 1851–1951," typed manuscript, vol. 1, part 1, pp. 93, 116, AUSC.

32. Einarsson, pp. 40–41.

33. *The Owl*, vol. 2 (March, 1870), p. 85.

34. Samuel H. Winklebleck, "History of 'The Owl,'" *The Owl*, vol. 38 (June, 1951), p. 8. Regarding the question of which school, Santa Clara or Berkeley, published first, see *The Owl*, vol. 8 (September, 1873), p. 34.

35. *The Owl*, vol. 10 (October, 1875), p. 68.

36. "Liber Consultationum Domsticarum" [1855–1894], entry for 12 September 1875, AUSC.

37. *Souvenir*, p. 48, and George O'Connell, S.J., "The Jesuit Mission of California," *Woodstock Letters*, vol. 20 (1891), pp. 361–62, AUSC.

38. McGloin, *Eloquent Indian*, p. 147.

39. *Thistleton's Illustrated Jolly Giant*, 1 November 1873, quoted in McGloin, *Eloquent Indian*, p. 145.

40. *The Advocate* (San Francisco), 24 June 1869.

41. Robert D. Cross, *The Emergence of Liberal Catholicism in America* (Chicago, 1958), p. 89. See also John Higham, *Strangers in the Land: Patterns of American Nativism 1860–1925* (New Brunswick, N.J., 1955).

42. Michael Accolti to Pierre De Smet, 15 April 1853, De Smetiana, AMPSJ.

43. Paul Goda, S.J., "Historical Background of California's Constitutional Provisions Pro-

hibiting Aid to Sectarian Schools," *California Historical Society Quarterly*, vol. 46 (1967), p. 167, and Joseph Bayma, S.J., "The Liberalistic View of the Public School Question," *The American Catholic Quarterly Review*, vol. 2 (1877), p. 11.

44. Cross, p. 96.

45. Goda, p. 165.

46. Oscar Lewis, *George Davidson, Pioneer West Coast Scientist* (Berkeley, 1954).

47. "Address by Doyle," AUSC.

48. *Souvenir*, p. 47.

49. "California Historical Society, 1852–1922," *California Historical Society Quarterly*, vol. 1 (July, 1922), pp. 9–15. Another society of the same name had been formed as early as 1852, but no record exists of its having survived beyond the year of its formation.

50. Power, pp. 85–86; Gilbert J. Garraghan, S.J., *The Jesuits in the Middle United States* (New York, 1938), vol. 3, p. 122.

51. *Prospectus of Santa Clara College, 1858–1859*. See also Power, p. 242.

52. "Historia Domus, 1877," ACPSJ.

53. Peter Beckx to Aloysius Varsi, 4 December 1877, "Epist. Praep. Gen.," ACPSJ. Beckx responded to Varsi's complaints by advising him "not to insist too much on the abolition of the Commercial Course" because it appeared *post factum* "to be working out well and useful."

54. *Prospectus of Santa Clara College, 1877–1878*; *San Jose Daily Mercury*, 15 May 1892.

55. *Prospectus of Santa Clara College, 1877–1878*.

56. John Roothaan to Michael Accolti, 14 January 1851, "Epist. Praep. Gen.," ACPSJ. The papers of B. J. Reid, pioneer member of Santa Clara's first lay faculty, were donated to the university in 1978 by his great grandson, Alfred D. Reid, Jr., a graduate of the class of 1955.

9. A College in Conflict, 1880–1893

1. "Monthly Statements, 1870–1886," AUSC.

2. *Dictionary of American Biography* (New York, 1929), vol. 2, pp. 79–80; *Woodstock Letters*, vol. 21 (1891), pp. 317–25, AUSC.

3. Mel Gorman, "Stereochemical Concepts in the Molecular System of Joseph Bayma," *Proceedings of the Tenth International Congress of the History of Science* (1962), p. 901.

4. *Ibid.*, pp. 889–901; Mel Gorman, "Chemistry at the University of San Francisco, 1863–1906," *Journal of Chemical Education*, vol. 41 (November, 1964), p. 628.

5. Francis A. Tondorf, "Joseph Bayma," *Dictionary of American Biography*, vol. 2, p. 79; Pietro Paulo Gonella to Peter Beckx, 20 February 1869, Prov. Taur. 1010, AHSI.

6. Gorman, "Chemistry at San Francisco," p. 628; *Report of the Eleventh Industrial Exhibition of the Mechanics Institute of the City of San Francisco* (San Francisco, 1876), p. 204.

7. Antonio Piolanti, "Giuseppe Bayma," *Enciclopedia Cattolica* (Florence, Italy, 1949), vol. 2, pp. 1086–87. The series of seventeen articles that occasioned the condemnation of Bayma's theories by the Holy Office is found in *The Catholic World*, vols. 18–21 (1873–1875), under the titles "The Principles of Real Being," "Matter," "Substantial Generations," and "Space." A summary of the decree by the Holy Office is published in *Enchiridion Symbolorum, Definitionum et Declarationum de Rebus Fidei et Morum* (Rome, 1967), pp. 607–8.

8. William C. McGuire, "Joseph Bayma, 1816–1892," *The Owl*, vol. 31 (May, 1941), p. 9. See also *Dictionary of American Biography*, vol. 2, pp. 79–80; *Woodstock Letters*, vol. 21 (1891), p. 3, AUSC.

9. Joseph W. Riordan, S.J., *The First Half Century of St. Ignatius Church and College* (San Francisco, 1905), p. 247. Both California schools may, in fact, have borrowed the idea from Georgetown University, where an association of alumni was planned in 1880 and organized in June of the following year. See John Gilmary Shea, *History of Georgetown University* (Washington, D.C., 1891), pp. 274–75.

10. *San Jose Herald*, 28 April 1881; *Souvenir of Santa Clara College, 1851–1901* (Santa Clara, Calif., 1901), p. 48; "Historia Domus, 1881," ACPSJ.

11. *University of Santa Clara Diamond Jubilee Volume, 1851–1926* (Santa Clara, Calif., 1926), pp. 77–79; *San Jose Mercury*, 27 May 1912.

12. "Monthly Statements, 1886–1902," AUSC.

13. *Souvenir*, p. 60.

14. "Liber Consultationum Domesticarum" [1885–1894], entry for 4 October 1884, AUSC.

15. *Souvenir*, p. 49.

16. *The Monthly Santa Claran*, vol. 5 (May–June, 1937); "Liber Consultationum Domesticarum" [1855–1894], entry for 15 October 1894, AUSC.

17. John S. Brubacher and Willis Rudy, *Higher Education in Transition: A History of American Colleges and Universities, 1636–1976* (New York, 1976), p. 243. See also William Warren Ferrier, *Origin and Development of the University of California* (Berkeley, Calif., 1930), p. 381.

18. *Woodstock Letters*, vol. 14 (1885), p. 374, AUSC.

19. "Historia Domus, 1885," ACPSJ.

20. *Souvenir*, p. 56.

21. Joseph W. Riordan to Father Superior, 21 January 1909, ACPSJ.

22. John Frieden to [Rudolph Meyer], 29 August 1897, AHSI; Frieden to [Meyer], 18 March 1898, AHSI; Frieden to [Meyer], 29 April 1897, AHSI.

23. Riordan to Meyer, 16 April 1895, AHSI.

24. Frieden to Meyer, 20 August 1897, AHSI; Fortunato Guidice to Luis Martín, 18 September 1893, Prov. Taur. 1011, AHSI; Dominic Giacobbi to Joseph Sasia, 11 November 1894, Prov. Taur. 1011, AHSI.

25. Riordan, p. 280.

26. "Liber Consultationum Domesticarum" [1855–1894], entry for 1 August 1883, AUSC. A Jesuit source of a later generation, claiming information "faithfully narrated" to him "by one who heard the details from Father Kenna," relates that under Congiato "an effort was made to establish if possible the old *Ratio Studiorum*, not only in the matter of studies, but in the distribution of time." Classes were allegedly scheduled so that "little or no time was allowed for athletics"; even baseball was terminated on orders from Congiato. Only by appealing the controversy to Rome, so the story goes, did Kenna succeed in restoring a more realistic regimen of study and recreation to Santa Clara. See D. J. Kavanagh, S.J., "Jesuits," ACPSJ.

27. "Liber Consultationum Domesticarum" [1885–1894], entry for 1 August 1883, AUSC.

28. "Permission Slip" [1880's], AUSC; *The Monthly Santa Claran*, vol. 5 (May–June, 1937).

29. Nicholas Congiato to Anton Anderledy, 8 September 1887, AHSI.

30. Peter Beckx to Congiato, 7 March 1884, ACPSJ.

31. Anderledy to Congiato, 17 October 1884, ACPSJ; Congiato to Anderledy, 8 September 1887, AHSI.

32. Laurence R. Veysey, *The Emergence of the American University* (Chicago, 1965), p. 60. Statistics regarding Jesuit schools are in *Woodstock Letters*, vol. 13 (1884), p. 425, AUSC.

33. *Woodstock Letters*, vol. 13 (1884), pp. 162–63, AUSC.

34. Beckx to Congiato, 7 March 1884, ACPSJ. The conflict over the classics occurred simultaneously with Congiato's effort to prevent students at the college from leaving the campus unchaperoned.

35. Anderledy to Congiato, 17 October 1884, ACPSJ.

36. Anderledy to Congiato, 17 October 1884, ACPSJ; "Liber Consultationum Domesticarum" [1855–1894], entry for April 1885, AUSC.

37. Riordan, p. 276.

38. *Ibid.*, p. 283.

39. *Catalogue of Santa Clara College, 1892.*

40. Riordan, p. 283.

41. William B. Faherty, S.J., *Better the Dream, Saint Louis: University and Community, 1818–1968* (St. Louis, 1968), pp. 207, 257; Anderledy to Sasia, 1 March 1889, ACPSJ; Rudolph Meyer, "Memoriale de Vista California Missione, Anno 1889," ACPSJ.

42.ʹ Meyer, ACPSJ.

43. Anderledy to Sasia, 14 April 1890 and 27 February 1891, ACPSJ.

44. Meyer, ACPSJ; "Liber Consultationum Domesticarum" [1855–1894], entry for 3 December 1889, AUSC.

45. Meyer, ACPSJ.

46. *Woodstock Letters*, vol. 20 (1891), p. 367, AUSC.

47. Riordan, p. 266.

48. *Woodstock Letters*, vol. 13 (1884), p. 162, AUSC.

49. Meyer, ACPSJ; Anderledy to Congiato, 30 March 1885, ACPSJ.

50. *Catalogus Provinciae Taurinensis Societatis Iesu, 1885*, AUSC.

51. *Woodstock Letters*, vol. 13 (1884), p. 425, AUSC.

52. *Ibid.*, p. 162.

53. *Ibid.*, p. 162.

54. *Ibid.*, p. 163.

55. *Woodstock Letters*, vol. 26 (1897), pp. 487–88, AUSC.

56. *Woodstock Letters*, vol. 21 (1892), p. 439, AUSC.

57. John W. Padberg, S.J., *Colleges in Controversy, the Jesuit Schools in France from Revival to Suppression, 1815–1880* (Cambridge, 1969), p. 140.

58. *Woodstock Letters*, vol. 13 (1884), p. 162. Regarding the University of California's change in admission policy, see John Swett, *Public Education in California* (New York, 1969), p. 266.

59. John W. Caughey, *California: A Remarkable State's Life History* (Englewood Cliffs, N.J., 1970), pp. 393–94.

60. Franklin Hichborn, "California Politics, 1891–1939" (typed manuscript, Univ. of Santa Clara, Orradre Library), vol. 1, pp. 80–84.

61. William Warren Ferrier, *Ninety Years of Education in California: 1846–1936* (Berkeley, Calif., 1937), p. 193.

10. The Search for "A Broader Place," 1892–1905

1. Donald G. Tewksbury, *The Founding of American Colleges and Universities Before the Civil War* (New York, 1969), pp. 15, 23–24, 28.

2. Clifford M. Drury, "Church-Sponsored Schools in Early California," *The Pacific Historian*, vol. 20 (summer, 1976), pp. 158–66.

3. *Souvenir of Santa Clara College, 1851–1901* (Santa Clara, Calif., 1901), p. 50.

4. *San Jose Daily Mercury*, 15 May 1892; "Liber Consultationum Domesticarum" [1855–1894], AUSC; Joseph W. Riordan to Father Superior, 21 January 1909, ACPSJ.

5. Robert Kenna to Luis Martin, February 1900, AHSI.

6. *The Monthly Santa Claran*, vol. 3 (November 1934); Riordan to Fr. Superior, 21 January 1909, ACPSJ; [Meyer?], "Some Hints for the New Superior of the California Mission," AHSI.

7. "Liber Consultationum Missionis Californiae ab anno 1891 ad 1907," minutes for 9 November 1899, ACPSJ; Riordan to Fr. Superior, 21 January 1909, ACPSJ.

8. Riordan to Fr. Superior, 4 January 1911, ACPSJ; Riordan to Fr. Superior, 21 January 1909, ACPSJ.

9. "Liber Consultationum Domesticarum" [1855–1894], entry for 25 January 1893, AUSC; Riordan to Fr. Superior, 21 January 1909, ACPSJ.

10. "Historia Domus, 1894–1895," ACPSJ.

11. Riordan to Fr. Superior, 21 January 1909, ACPSJ.

12. "Liber Consultationum Missionis Californiae ab anno 1891 and 1907," minutes for 9 November 1899, ACPSJ; Souvenir, pp. 53–54.

13. Souvenir, pp. 3–6.

14. Riordan to Fr. Superior, 21 January 1909, ACPSJ.

15. Souvenir, p. 44.

16. Martín to John Frieden, 4 May 1901, ACPSJ.

17. Riordan to Fr. Superior, 21 January 1909, ACPSJ.

18. Woodstock Letters, vol. 31 (1902), p. 465, AUSC; The Redwood (student publication), vol. 1 (April, 1903), p. 252.

19. San Jose Mercury, 7 June 1904 and 22 August 1904; "Liber Consultationum Missionis Californiae ab anno 1891 ad 1907," minutes for 8 June 1904, ACPSJ; see also [anonymous], University of Santa Clara: A History (San Francisco, 1912), p. 19.

20. The Redwood, vol. 2 (October, 1904), pp. 30–31.

21. San Jose Mercury, 22 February 1903.

22. San Jose Mercury, 12 May 1903. See also The Redwood, vol. 1 (May, 1903), p. 315.

23. "Local Scientists Invent a New System of Wireless Telegraphy," San Francisco Call, 6 March 1904; unidentified clipping, 7 April 1904, "Santa Clara College Clipping Scrapbook, 1902–1906," AUSC.

24. The Redwood (1924), p. 27. Evidence is inconclusive and contradictory regarding voice communication by Bell. According to the recollections of a workman who assisted him, it was in 1907 that Bell sent his first voice-message by radio. See Frank G. Schmidt, "Memories of Father R. Bell, S.J.," 11 Nov. 1957, AUSC.

25. Jane Morgan, Electronics in the West, the First Fifty Years (Palo Alto, 1967), pp. 7–31.

26. Arthur Dunning Spearman, S.J., John Joseph Montgomery, Father of Basic Flying, 1858–1911 (Santa Clara, 1967), pp. 13–14.

27. Tom Day Crouch, "To Ride the Fractious Horse: the American Aeronautical Community and the Problem of Heavier-than-air Flight, 1875–1905," unpublished Ph.D. dissertation, 1976 (Ohio State Univ.), pp. 98–115.

28. Spearman, p. 60.

29. The Monthly Santa Claran, April, 1937.

30. San Francisco Examiner, 30 April 1905.

31. Quoted in Spearman, p. 90.

32. Victor Lougheed, Vehicles of the Air, a Popular Exposition of Modern Aeronautics with Working Drawings (Chicago, 1911), p. 138.

33. Carolyn Gallant de Vries, Andrew Putnam Hill: Biography of an Artist-Conservationist (privately published by the author, 1975). See also Herbert C. Jones, "History of the Acquisition of the Big Basin Park," BL, and Carolyn de Vries, "Andrew P. Hill and the Big Basin, California's First State Park," San José Studies, vol. 2 (November 1976), pp. 70–92.

34. San Jose Morning Times, 28 May 1912.

35. The Redwood, vol. 12 (April, 1913), p. 285.

36. The Irish Review, vol. 39 (April, 1911), p. 210. See also The Redwood, vol. 10 (October, 1910), pp. 2–10, 30–31.

37. Henry L. Walsh, S.J., "The Annals of Santa Clara College and University, 1851–1951," typed manuscript, vol. 1, part 2, pp. 108–110, AUSC.

38. "Head Prefect's Log, 1891–1896," entries for 25 and 28 October 1895, AUSC; *Pacific Calendar and Catholic Church Bulletin* (St. Joseph's Church, San Jose, Calif.), December, 1898, p. 27; *The Monthly Santa Claran*, vol. 2 (March, 1934).

39. *Pacific Calendar*, December 1898.

40. *The Redwood*, vol. 2 (September, 1903), pp. 39–40; *The Redwood*, vol. 2 (November, 1903), pp. 171–72.

41. Ray Allen Billington, *Frederick Jackson Turner: Historian, Scholar, Teacher* (New York, 1973), pp. 264–65.

42. "Historia Domus, 1900–1901," ACPSJ.

43. *San Jose Mercury*, 6 November 1905; *San Jose Mercury*, 14 December 1905.

44. Unidentified newspaper clipping [*ca.* 1909], baseball file, AUSC.

45. James A. Rockliff, S.J. [questionnaire regarding the transferral of Santa Clara College to Los Angeles, 1910], ACPSJ.

46. [Anonymous, S.J.], "The Necessity of Establishing Professional Schools in Connection with Our Schools in California," 1903, AHSI; "Memoriale of Rev. Father Provincial after the Annual Visitation of Santa Clara College, Santa Clara, California, June 11, 1911," ACPSJ.

47. Alexander J. Cody, S.J., *A Memoir, Richard A. Gleeson, S.J., 1861–1945* (San Francisco, 1950), pp. 51–52.

48. *Pacific Calendar*, August, 1898; July, 1899; and November, 1899; Joseph S. Brusher, S.J., *Consecrated Thunderbolt; Father Yorke of San Francisco* (Hawthorne, N.J., 1973), p. 38.

49. *San Jose Mercury*, 26 May 1905.

50. *Pacific Calendar*, September, 1897.

51. *Echoes of the Golden Jubilee* [of Santa Clara College], September, 1897.

52. Henry Woods, S.J., "Jesuit Colleges and the University of the United States" (San Francisco, 28 June 1900), AHSI; [Anonymous, S.J.], "The Necessity," AHSI; George de la Motte to Martín, 29 November 1908, AHSI; Frieden to Martín, 25 January 1903, AHSI.

53. Frieden to Martín, 26 January 1903, AHSI; [anonymous, S.J.], "The Necessity," AHSI.

54. John S. Brubacher and Willis Rudy, *Higher Education in Transition: A History of American Colleges and Universities, 1636–1976* (New York, 1976), p. 310; Woods, AHSI.

55. *Pacific Calendar*, October, 1902; *The Redwood*, vol. 3 (September, 1904), p. 272.

56. *Catalog of Santa Clara College, 1907–1908.*

57. *Catalog of Santa Clara College, 1906–1907.*

58. *Pacific Calendar*, October, 1902.

59. *Echoes of Golden Jubilee*, p. 46.

60. *The Redwood*, vol. 1 (April, 1903), p. 242.

61. Interview with Richard Twohy, Jr., S.J., Santa Clara, Calif., August 1971, and interview with Thomas Terry, S.J., Santa Clara, Calif., June 1971. James Twohy later claimed that the Harvard years "added virtually nothing to the formal pattern of my education. The *Ratio*, for better or worse, had done for me by then!" See James Twohy to Herman Hauck, 22 May 1954, Presidential Papers, AUSC.

11. Los Angeles Beckons, 1901–1911

1. *San Jose Mercury*, 24 October 1904.

2. Richard A. Gleeson to Rev. J. O'Connell, December 1909, AASF.

3. *Woodstock Letters*, vol. 39 (1910), pp. 251–52, and vol. 36 (1907), p. 378, AUSC.

4. "Head Prefect's Log, 1896–1907," entry for 18 April 1906, AUSC.

5. Patricia B. Curran, "The Earthquake of April 18, 1906, in the Santa Clara Valley," *Santa Clara County Pioneer Papers, 1973: A Collection of Three Award Winning Scholarship Papers and Other Articles* (Santa Clara, 1973), p. 12.

6. *The Monthly Santa Claran*, vol. 8 (April, 1937).

7. Donald G. Tewksbury, *The Founding of American Colleges and Universities Before the Civil War* (New York, 1969), p. 26.

8. *Woodstock Letters*, vol. 39 (1910), pp. 251–52, AUSC.

9. *Ibid.*, p. 252.

10. Robert Kenna to Thomas J. Conaty, 24 December 1909, AALA.

11. "Minister's Log, 1909–1912," entry for 10 January 1910, AUSC.

12. [Morrissey statement, 22 October 1910], ACPSJ.

13. *Ibid.*

14. In August, the California provincial received word from Rome that "Father Assistant says there is no difficulty about going ahead with that building at Santa Clara. May it realize all your hopes." Edward Mullan to James A. Rockliff, 8 August 1910, ACPSJ.

15. Kenna to Rockliff, January, 1911 (copy), ACPSJ. Kenna, deputed by Herman J. Goller to act on his behalf in negotiations with Conaty, summarized the history of the Jesuits' efforts to gain a house in Los Angeles. The California Province, established in 1909, embraced not only the former California Mission but most of the territory that had earlier constituted the Rocky Mountain Mission, i.e., the states of California, Washington, Oregon, Idaho, Montana, and the Dakotas, as well as lower Alaska. Goller served as provincial from 8 September 1909 until his death on 5 November 1910.

16. Francis J. Weber, "What Ever Happened to Saint Vincent's College?" *The Pacific Historian*, vol. 14 (winter, 1970), pp. 77–79.

17. Kenna to Rockliff, January, 1911, ACPSJ.

18. Because he was about to be named "socius," or assistant to the provincial, Rockliff had been summoned to the Oakland consultation. Though he arrived from New York after it had "practically been decided to accept the offer" of Saint Vincent's, Rockliff recorded a few months later that it was due "solely" to his advice that the provincial and his consultors agreed not to accept the college immediately, and instead elected to wait a year. "More could not be urged by one who was a stranger to the Province and its resources," Rockliff explained later in defense of his role at the Oakland meeting. See Rockliff's comments in Richard A. Gleeson [memorandum, *ca.* 25 July 1911], ACPSJ.

19. Rockliff [questionnaire regarding the removal of Santa Clara College to Los Angeles, December, 1910], ACPSJ.

20. Gleeson [memorandum], ACPSJ.

21. Rockliff [questionnaire], ACPSJ.

22. F. A. Ruppert to Rockliff, 25 December 1910, ACPSJ.

23. Rockliff [questionnaire], ACPSJ.

24. *Ibid.*

25. "Minister's Log, 1910–1913," entries for 6 and 11 December 1910, AUSC.

26. James A. Morrissey to Rockliff, 21 March 1911, ACPSJ.

27. Kenna to Rockliff, 27 December 1910, ACPSJ.

28. Joseph Riordan to Rockliff, 4 January 1911, ACPSJ.

29. William H. Culligan to Rockliff, *ca.* December 1910, ACPSJ.

30. Ruppert to Rockliff, 25 December 1910, ACPSJ.

31. Rockliff [questionnaire], ACPSJ.

32. Morrissey to Rockliff, 29 December 1910, ACPSJ.

33. George de la Motte to Rockliff, 28 December 1910, ACPSJ.

34. Richard Bell to Rockliff, 29 December 1910, ACPSJ.

35. Paul Arthuis to Rockliff, *ca.* December, 1910, ACPSJ.

36. J. D. Walshe to Rockliff, 29 December 1910, ACPSJ; John Laherty to Rockliff, 9 January 1911, ACPSJ.

37. Henry Woods to Rockliff, *ca.* December, 1910, ACPSJ; Laherty to Rockliff, 9 January 1911, ACPSJ; D. J. Kavanagh to Rockliff, 2 Janaury 1911, ACPSJ.

38. D. J. Mahony to Rockliff, *ca.* December, 1910, ACPSJ.

39. Arthuis to Rockliff, *ca.* December 1910, ACPSJ.

40. Woods to Rockliff, *ca.* December 1910, ACPSJ.

41. J. S. Ricard to Rockliff, 26 December 1910, ACPSJ.

42. Bell to Rockliff, 29 December 1910, ACPSJ.

43. Laherty to Rockliff, 9 January 1911, ACPSJ.

44. Morrissey to Rockliff, 21 March 1911, ACPSJ.

45. "Liber Consultationum in Missione Californiae et Montium Saxosorum habitarum, 1907–1931," ACPSJ; Gleeson [memorandum], ACPSJ.

46. According to the results of Rockliff's questionnaire, eight of the fourteen Santa Clara Jesuits polled opposed the transfer of the school.

47. Rockliff to Conaty, 18 May 1911, AALA.

48. "Liber Consultationum, 1907–1931," ACPSJ.

49. Laherty to Rockliff, 9 January 1911, ACPSJ.

50. Arthuis to Rockliff, *ca.* December, 1910, ACPSJ.

51. Herman J. Goller to Conaty, 8 May 1910, AALA.

52. Rockliff to Conaty, 13 April 1911, ACPSJ.

53. In an attempt to assuage the disappointment felt by Conaty and others at the collapse of collegiate studies at Saint Vincent's, the Jesuits offered two $200 scholarships to Santa Clara to Los Angeles students who wished to transfer there for their college education. Rockliff to Conaty, 18 May 1911, AALA.

54. Paul J. Harney, "A History of Jesuit Education in American California," unpublished Ph.D. dissertation, 1944 (Univ. of Calif., Berkeley), p. 240.

55. Morrissey to Rockliff, 21 March 1911, ACPSJ.

12. From College to University, 1910–1917

1. Dennis J. Kavanagh, "The Jesuits in California," ACPSJ; Kavanagh to James A. Rockliff, 2 January 1911, ACPSJ.

2. "Catalogus Secundus: Provincia Taurinensis," 1899, Archivo della Provincia Torinese della Compagnia di Gesu, Turin, Italy.

3. Kavanagh, "Jesuits," ACPSJ.

4. "Santa Clara University Scrapbook, 1904–1913," unidentified clipping, AUSC.

5. Robert Kenna to James D. Phelan, 12 May 1912, James Duval Phelan, Correspondence and Papers, BL. The Mountain View property was subsequently set to orchard; its sale in 1923 helped finance the construction of Kenna Hall.

6. Herman J. Hauck, S.J. [Building and Equipment of the Santa Clara Campus], Presidential Papers, AUSC.

7. "Liber Consultationum in Missionae Californiae et Montium Saxosorum habitarum, 1907–1931," entry for 15–17 November 1911, ACPSJ.

8. Hauck [Building and Equipment], AUSC. Morrissey states that the total cost of constructing and furnishing the two halls was $250,000. See *The Morning Times* (San Jose) 1 April 1912.

9. *University of Santa Clara, a History, 1777–1912* (Santa Clara, Calif., 1912), p. 50.

10. George de la Motte to Rockliff, 28 December 1910, ACPSJ.

11. Patrick Foote to Rockliff, 28 December 1910, ACPSJ; F. A. Ruppert to Rockliff, 25 December 1910, ACPSJ; Joseph Vaughan, S.J., [recollections], AUSC; William H. Culligan to Rockliff, *ca.* December, 1910, ACPSJ.

12. Culligan to Rockliff, *ca.* December, 1910, ACPSJ; Kavanagh to Rockliff, 2 January 1911, ACPSJ.

13. Ruppert to Rockliff, 25 December 1910, ACPSJ; Vaughan, [recollections], AUSC.

14. John Laherty to Rockliff, 9 January 1911, ACPSJ.

15. Vaughan, [recollections], ACPSJ.

16. *General Catalog of the University of Santa Clara, 1912–1913.*

17. Vaughan [recollections], AUSC; Kavanagh, "Jesuits," ACPSJ; *The Monthly Santa Claran*, vol. 2 (February, 1934).

18. Henry L. Walsh, S.J., "The Annals of Santa Clara College and University, 1851–1951," typed manuscript, vol. 1, part 2, p. 68, AUSC; *The Monthly Santa Claran*, vol. 3 (February, 1935); Kavanagh, "Jesuits," ACPSJ.

19. *San Jose Daily Mercury*, 12 June 1913.

20. *General Catalog of the University of Santa Clara, 1912–1913.*

21. *Santa Clara College Catalog, 1910–1911*; *General Catalog of the University of Santa Clara, 1912–1913.*

22. Henry Woods to Rockliff, *ca.* December, 1910, ACPSJ.

23. John S. Brubacher and Willis Rudy, *Higher Education in Transition: A History of American Colleges and Universities, 1636–1976* (New York, 1976), p. 252.

24. *Santa Clara University Bulletin, Institute of Law, 1912–1913.*

25. George Leonard Sullivan, "Engineering and the Sullivans come to Santa Clara, Memorial Edition" (Santa Clara, Calif., 1956), AUSC.

26. James Morrissey to Patrick W. Riordan, 9 November 1912, AASF.

27. *University of Santa Clara, a History, 1777–1912*, p. 32.

28. *The Morning Times* (San Jose), 1 April 1912.

29. *The Monthly Santa Claran*, vol. 4 (February, 1936); Addison C. Posey to Patrick A. Donohoe, 19 April 1960, Presidential Papers, AUSC.

30. Vaughan, [recollections], AUSC.

31. Richard Bell to Rockliff, *ca.* December, 1910, ACPSJ.

32. Kavanagh, "Jesuits," ACPSJ.

33. Franz X. Wernz to Rockliff, 13 May 1913, ACPSJ.

34. Wernz to Rockliff, 31 March 1913, ACPSJ.

35. Morrissey to Rockliff, 21 March 1911, ACPSJ.

36. Vaughan, [recollections], AUSC.

37. Morrissey to Wernz, 31 January 1913 and 25 April 1913, AHSI; Sullivan, "Engineering and the Sullivans," AUSC.

38. Wernz to Rockliff, 27 May 1913, ACPSJ.

39. Vaughan, [recollections], AUSC.

40. Morrissey to Bishop Charles J. O'Reilly, 6 July 1917, Archives of the Diocesan Chancery, Lincoln, Nebraska.

41. Morrissey to Rockliff, 29 December 1910, ACPSJ. Morrissey quotes Walter Thornton.

42. Robert F. Sesnon to Morrissey, 16 February 1912, Presidential Papers, AUSC.

43. Thornton to Wernz, 6 October 1913, AHSI.

44. Thornton to Wernz, 6 October 1913, AHSI.

45. *The San Francisco Evening Post*, 24 November 1913; *San Jose Times Star*, 24 November 1913.

46. *University of Santa Clara Diamond Jubilee Volume, 1851–1926* (Santa Clara, Calif., 1926), pp. 33–35.

47. Sullivan, "Engineering and the Sullivans," AUSC.

48. de la Motte to Wernz, 29 November 1908, AHSI.

49. Rejecting the arguments of "lost vocations, etc., etc.," Morrissey urged that Jesuit seminarians be prepared early for university careers in one of his last letters to the father general before leaving Santa Clara. See Morrissey to Wernz, 31 January (?) 1913, AHSI.

Morrissey is remembered at Santa Clara through a scholarship established in his honor in 1976 by Addison Posey, alumnus of the class of 1915.

50. "Plan of Union of Santa Clara and St. Ignatius Universities," 1915, AHSI. The author of this proposal was probably Santa Clara's Henry Woods, S.J.

13. Doughboys and Quarterbacks, 1917–1930

1. *The Redwood* (student publication), vol. 17 (February, 1918), p. 188.

2. *The Redwood*, vol. 16 (May, 1917), pp. 409–10.

3. *The Sacramento Bee*, 17 January 1931; Justin McGrath, "Lafayette, We are Here," *The Commonweal* (11 February 1931), pp. 409–10. In the 1930's, the university's ROTC drill field was named in Stanton's honor.

4. *The Redwood*, vol. 17 (February, 1918), pp. 162, 171.

5. *America*, vol. 19 (24 August, 1918), p. 488. See also *The Monthly Santa Claran*, vol. 5 (October, 1936).

6. *The Redwood*, vol. 17 (February, 1918), p. 162 and vol. 17 (April, 1918), p. 285.

7. *The Redwood*, vol. 17 (February, 1918), p. 198, and vol. 17 (April, 1918), p. 310.

8. *The Redwood*, vol. 17 (December, 1917), pp. 146–47.

9. *The Redwood*, vol. 17 (March, 1918), pp. 251–52, and vol. 17 (February, 1918), p. 199.

10. "Minister's Log: 1917–1921," entry for 21 October 1918, AUSC.

11. *Ibid.*, entry for 23 October 1918.

12. Gary Fleming, "The Last Great Pestilence," *San Jose Mercury*, 4 January 1976.

13. *Santa Clara Journal*, 6 March 1920; *San Jose Mercury*, 4 March 1920.

14. Unidentified clippings, April 1921, "Sullivan Clipping Scrapbook," AUSC.

15. Michael A. Kiely, Chairman, Football Field Committee, to [Alumni and Friends], 25 March 1914, AUSC.

16. Unidentified clippings, *ca.* 1920, "Sullivan Clipping Scrapbook," AUSC.

17. *The Daily Palo Alto*, quoted in *The Redwood*, vol. 16 (December, 1916), p. 184.

18. *San Francisco Call*, 2 March 1919.

19. Unidentified clipping, 23 October [1919], "Sullivan Clipping Scrapbook," AUSC.

20. Unidentified clipping, October, 1920, "Sullivan Clipping Scrapbook," AUSC; *Santa Clara Journal*, 12 October 1921.

21. Unidentified clipping, October, 1920, "Sullivan Clipping Scrapbook," AUSC.

22. Unidentified press accounts of Murphy statement of 6 April 1921, in "Sullivan Clipping Scrapbook," AUSC.

23. *Catholic Herald* (Sacramento), 23 April 1921; *Santa Cruz News*, 9 April 1921.

24. *Leader*, 16 April 1921; unidentified clipping, *ca.* 1921, "Sullivan Clipping Scrapbook," AUSC.

25. Zacheus Maher to Alumni, April 1922, Phelan Papers, BL; *San Francisco Examiner*, 22 July 1921; unidentified clipping, 23 August 1922, "Sullivan Clipping Scrapbook," AUSC.

26. "Head Prefect's Log, 1919–1925," entry for 23 August 1921, AUSC.

27. Henry L. Walsh, S.J., "The Annals of Santa Clara College and University, 1851–1951," typed manuscript, vol. 1, part 2, p. 118, AUSC.

28. *San Francisco Call*, 30 December 1921 and 6 January 1922; *San Francisco Examiner*, 20 December 1921.

29. *San Jose Mercury*, (?) August 1922, "SCU Clipping Scrapbook, 1920–26," AUSC. See also *San Francisco Call*, 22 August 1922.

30. Randy Andrada, *They Did it Every Time: The Saga of the Saint Mary's Gaels* (San Francisco, 1975), p. 37.

31. Andrada, pp. 46–47.

32. Clipping from *Thirty Five* (Oakland, Calif.), 22 November 1923, in "SCU Clipping Scrapbook, 1922–26," AUSC.

33. *The Evening News* (San Jose), *ca.* 28 November 1922, "SCU Clipping Scrapbook, 1922–26," AUSC.

34. E. V. Quill to James D. Phelan, 28 August 1923, Phelan Papers, BL.

35. Walsh, vol. 1, part 2, p. 134, AUSC.

36. Unidentified clippings, 15 November 1929, "SCU Clipping Scrapbook, 1926–30," AUSC.

37. *The Santa Clara*, 21 November 1929.

38. Edward J. Power, *Catholic Higher Education in America, a History* (New York, 1972), pp. 279–80.

14. The House That Zach Built, 1921–1926

1. Unidentified clippings in Zacheus Maher file, AUSC; "The Drive, or How We Failed to Raise $500,000 in 1922" (clipping scrapbook), Edward Zeman Papers, AUSC; *Santa Clara Journal*, 22 February 1922.

2. *University of Santa Clara Diamond Jubilee Volume, 1851–1926* (Santa Clara, Calif., 1926), p. 86.

3. *Santa Clara Journal*, 22 February 1922; "USC Campaign Bulletin," 1922, Phelan Papers, BL.

4. Maher to James T. Conaty, 15 October 1921, AALA; *Diamond Jubilee*, pp. 49–50.

5. *Ibid.*, p. 51.

6. Maher to James D. Phelan, 16 September 1924, Phelan Papers, BL.

7. Unidentified clipping, "SCU Clipping Scrapbook, 1922–26," AUSC.

8. "The Drive," AUSC; unidentified clipping, "Sullivan Clipping Scrapbook," AUSC.

9. "USC Campaign Bulletin," 1922, Phelan Papers, BL; "The Drive," AUSC.

10. "USC Campaign," BL; "The Drive," AUSC.

11. "The Drive," AUSC.

12. *San Jose Mercury*, 18 February 1922.

13. "USC Campaign," BL.

14. *San Jose Mercury*, 23 June 1921; *The Redwood*, vol. 21 (November, 1921), p. 27. The one-hundredth anniversary of the establishing of Mission Santa Clara on its present site was celebrated in 1922.

15. "The Drive," AUSC.

16. Maher to Alumni, April 1922, Phelan Papers, BL; Maher to Friends and Alumni, 22 April 1922, in "The Drive," AUSC.

17. Maher to Friends and Alumni, 22 April 1922, in "The Drive," AUSC.

18. Maher to Phelan, 27 January 1923, Phelan Papers, BL; unidentified clipping *ca.* 1926, "SCU Clipping Scrapbook, 1922–26," AUSC.

19. "The Drive," AUSC.

20. Maher to Phelan, 27 January 1923, Phelan Papers, BL.

21. *Diamond Jubilee*, pp. 48–49.

22. Phelan to Maher, 7 February 1923, Phelan Papers, BL.

23. Maher to Alumni, April, 1922; "USC Campaign," BL.

24. Henry L. Walsh, S.J., "The Annals of Santa Clara College and University, 1851–1951," typed manuscript, vol. 1, part 2, pp. 131–32, AUSC.

25. *Diamond Jubilee*, pp. 48, 37; F.M. Heffernan to Alumni, 20 February 1926, Phelan Papers, BL.

26. Phelan to Maher, 7 February 1923, Phelan Papers, BL; Maher to Phelan, 10 February 1923, Phelan Papers, BL; "Historia Domus, 1924–25," AUSC; *San Jose Mercury News*, 24 July 1923.

27. Phelan to Maher, 28 January 1926, Phelan Papers, BL.

28. C. J. McCoy to Edward Boland, 25 September 1952, AUSC.

29. "SCU Clipping Scrapbook, 1922–26," AUSC. For statistics regarding "prep" schools in 1915, see John S. Brubacher and Willis Rudy, *Higher Education in Transition: A History of American Colleges and Universities, 1636–1976* (New York, 1976), p. 243.

30. "Plan of Union of Santa Clara and St. Ignatius Universities, 1915," ACPSJ; *Diamond Jubilee,* p. 99.

31. Charles Budde, S.J., "History of Bellarmine College Preparatory," *ca.* 1934, AUSC; *Diamond Jubilee,* p. 94; *The Monthly Santa Claran,* January, 1947.

32. "Meeting of Jesuit Staff [Minutes]," *ca.* 1923, AUSC; *Diamond Jubilee,* p. 94.

33. Unidentified clipping, *ca.* September, 1925, "SCU Clipping Scrapbook, 1922–26," AUSC.

34. Unidentified clippings, September, 1925, "SCU Clipping Scrapbook, 1922–26," AUSC; Maher to Piet, 17 September 1925, ACPSJ.

35. Maher to Piet, 17 September 1925, ACPSJ; "Historia Domus, 1925–26," AUSC.

36. Maher to Piet, 17 September 1925, ACPSJ; Walsh, vol. 2, part 2, p. 20, AUSC.

37. Budde, AUSC.

38. Francis Dillon to Piet, 9 April 1926, ACPSJ.

39. Herman J. Hauck, "Rector's Notes [File]," AUSC; Maher to Piet, 16 July 1926, MS, AUSC.

40. Piet to Wlodimir Ledochowski, 12 March 1927, ACPSJ.

41. Dillon to Piet, 9 April 1926, ACPSJ.

42. *Ibid.*

43. Ledochowski to Piet, 8 April 1927, ACPSJ.

44. James Hayes to Piet, 13 September 1929, ACPSJ.

45. Hayes to Piet, June, 1930, ACPSJ; Hayes to Piet, 5 October 1929, ACPSJ; John Cosgrave to Piet, 9 June 1930, ACPSJ; Budde to Piet, 3 July 1930, ACPSJ.

46. Lewis McCann to Piet, 11 May 1934, ACPSJ.

47. *Bellarmine College Preparatory Catalogue, 1974–75.*

48. Walsh, vol. 2, part 2, pp. 9–10, AUSC.

49. Edward J. Power, *A History of Catholic Higher Education in the United States* (Milwaukee, 1958), pp. 242–43.

50. *The Call* (San Francisco), 26 December 1922; *Santa Clara Journal,* 24 February 1923; Maher to Phelan, 20 April 1923, Phelan Papers, BL.

51. Maher to Piet, 16 July 1926, ACPSJ; *Quinquennial Digest of Recommendations from the Annual Reports of the Interprovince Committee on Studies* (Jesuit Educational Association, 1926), ACPSJ.

52. Unidentified clippings, Maher File, AUSC.

53. *San Francisco Examiner,* 13 October 1921; *San Francisco Chronicle,* 14 October 1921; *San Francisco Bulletin,* 15 October 1921, all in "Sullivan Clipping Scrapbook," AUSC.

54. *San Francisco Examiner,* 5 December 1921, and unidentified clipping, *ca.* February, 1926, "SCU Clipping Scrapbook, 1922–26," AUSC.

55. *The Monitor* (San Francisco), 27 February 1926, "SCU Clipping Scrapbook, 1922–26," AUSC.

15. Fire and Sunspots, 1926–1932

1. Unidentified clippings, *ca.* September, 1926, "SCU Clipping Scrapbook, 1926–30," AUSC.

2. Unidentified clipping, "SCU Clipping Scrapbook, 1926–30," AUSC.

3. Unidentified clipping, 11 March 1930, "SCU Clipping Scrapbook, 1930–33," AUSC.

4. Unidentified clipping, *ca.* September, 1926, "SCU Clipping Scrapbook, 1926–30," AUSC.

5. Edward Shipsey, S.J., "Santa Clara, the Small University" (pamphlet, San Jose, Calif., *ca.* 1932), pp. 15–16.

6. C. J. McCoy, "Why Catholic Education," AUSC; unidentified clipping, *ca.* September, 1926, "SCU Clipping Scrapbook, 1926–30," AUSC.

7. In 1931, the University of California demanded an A or B in at least ten of the fifteen units in specified subjects it required for admission, and no grade lower than a C was allowed in any of the fifteen units. See Verne A. Stadtman, *The University of California, 1868–1968* (New York, 1970), p. 265.

8. Several professors listed "Ph.D." after their names in the university bulletin in 1926. But an examination of historical records reveals that they were recipients of degrees, usually honorary, bestowed by Santa Clara itself in recognition of years of service. In a few other instances, the degrees received by Jesuits for graduate studies at Rome's Gregorian University were translated in the bulletin as "Ph.D.," though they were not the exact equivalent of the American doctorate.

9. *The Monthly Santa Claran*, vol. 2 (April, 1935); unidentified clipping, *ca.* 13 March 1933, AUSC.

10. Unidentified clipping, *ca.* September, 1926, "SCU Clipping Scrapbook, 1926–30," AUSC.

11. Capping years of negotiation with the archbishop of San Francisco, the mission's status as a parish had been terminated in 1926. "For the sake of the University and the general fitness of things," as Zacheus Maher put it, a new site "removed from the campus" was selected for St. Clare's Church, which was erected nearby as successor to the old mission parish. See Maher to Joseph M. Piet, 16 February 1927, ACPSJ.

12. *The Santa Clara*, 28 October 1926; Henry L. Walsh, S.J., "The Annals of Santa Clara College and University, 1851–1951," typed manuscript, vol. 2, part 2, pp. 38ff, AUSC.

13. "Santa Clara Mission Restoration Brochure," AUSC; *The Santa Clara*, 28 October 1926.

14. See, for example, the account of Anderson's visit printed in Edith Buckland Webb, *Indian Life at the Old Missions* (Los Angeles, 1952), pp. 236–37.

15. *The California Missions, A Pictorial History* (Menlo Park, Calif., 1964), p. 165.

16. Webb, p. 236.

17. *San Jose Mercury Herald*, 9 February [1928], "SCU Clipping Scrapbook, 1926–30," AUSC; Arthur Dunning Spearman, S.J., *The Five Franciscan Churches of Mission Santa Clara, 1777 to 1823* (Palo Alto, Calif., 1963), p. 126.

18. Luis Rodés to McCoy, 17 December 1928, Presidential Papers, AUSC.

19. *Woodstock Letters*, vol. 29 (1900), p. 522, AUSC.

20. *The Sunspot*, vol. 1 (August 1915), p. 13.

21. Unidentified clipping, 3 May 1921, "Sullivan Clipping Scrapbook," AUSC; *Oakland Tribune*, 20 January 1922.

22. J.S. Ricard, "Long Range Weather Forecasting and its Methods," *Popular Astronomy* (April 1911), p. 226. See also *Oakland Tribune*, 14 September 1924.

23. Unidentified clippings, *ca.* March, 1926, "SCU Clipping Scrapbook, 1926–30," AUSC; *San Francisco Monitor*, 4 June 1921.

24. *San Francisco Monitor*, 4 June 1921; *San Francisco Examiner*, 12 January 1914.

25. Unidentified clipping, 9 March 1930, "SCU Clipping Scrapbook, 1930–34," AUSC.

26. Unidentified clipping, *ca.* April, 1926, "SCU Clipping Scrapbook, 1926–30," AUSC; *The Sunspot*, vol. 12 (May, 1926), p. 7; *San Jose Mercury*, 13 February 1922.

27. *San Francisco Examiner*, 26 October 1925, and other press clippings in "Newlin Clipping Scrapbook," AUSC. Because of Ricard's ongoing interest in seismology, the Observatory that bore his name was also equipped with instruments for recording the intensity

and duration of earthquakes. In 1929 two Galitzin seismographs from Estonia and two others of American make were installed in the underground vault beneath the Observatory to replace the instruments that Ricard had acquired after the earthquake of 1906.

28. *San Francisco Call*, 2 November 1921, and unidentified clipping, *ca.* May 1921, "Sullivan Clipping Scrapbook," AUSC; Maher to Piet, 8 October 1925, ACPSJ.

29. Maher to Piet, 22 October 1925, ACPSJ; "Sullivan Clipping Scrapbook," AUSC.

30. Unidentified clipping, *ca.* 1926, "SCU Clipping Scrapbook, 1922–26," AUSC.

31. C. J. McCoy to Piet, 23 August 1926, ACPSJ.

32. Zacheus Maher to Piet, 21 October 1925, ACPSJ.

33. Unidentified clipping, "SCU Clipping Scrapbook, 1922–26," AUSC.

34. T. S. Shearman to Ricard, 1 May 1929, Presidential Papers, AUSC; [John J. Jones] to L. H. Coquette, 19 November 1929, Presidential Papers, AUSC.

35. W. J. Bingham to W. J. Quinn, 14 February 1929, Presidential Papers, AUSC; McCoy to John J. Jones, 12 March 1930, Presidential Papers, AUSC.

36. McCoy to Francis Seeliger, 25 August 1941, Presidential Papers, AUSC. The refractor that Santa Clara purchased in 1941 had an interesting history. First used in 1882 in New York by Lewis Smith, a self-taught observer and discoverer of comets, it was at one time the third largest refractor in the country. See H. T. Kirby-Smith, *U.S. Observatories, a Directory and Guide* (New York, 1976), pp. 99–100.

37. *San Francisco Chronicle*, 21 December 1934; *New York Times*, 21 December 1934; *The Evening News* (San Jose, Calif.), 19 December 1934.

38. *San Jose Mercury*, 18 January 1935.

39. *San Jose Mercury News*, 11 March 1956.

40. Dave Goodreau, "An Evaluation of Ricard's Method of Weather Forecasting," senior thesis, 1964 (Univ. of Santa Clara), AUSC.

16. The Depression Years, 1932–1940

1. David D. Henry, *Challenges Past, Challenges Present: An Analysis of American Higher Education Since 1930* (San Francisco, 1975), pp. 13–14, 18, 27.

2. Walton Bean, *California: An Interpretive History* (New York, 1968), p. 409.

3. *The Monthly Santa Claran* (June, 1933). The president claimed that the university was "quite able to care for 250 or 300 more" students and "should have more in any case" than the fewer than 400 then enrolled. Because enrollment did not reach the quota Lyons desired until the tide of veterans on the G.I. Bill arrived in 1946, it appears that Santa Clara did not operate at full capacity until after World War II.

4. *The Monthly Santa Claran* (July, 1935); James Lyons to Anthony P. Hamman, 28 December 1932, AUSC.

5. Lyons to Zacheus Maher, 28 May 1934, ACPSJ.

6. C. J. McCoy, "Revisor's Report," 1933 and 1935, ACPSJ; Louis C. Rudolph, S.J., interview with author, 20 February 1971.

7. Lyons to Maher, 14 November 1933, ACPSJ; Joseph Crowley to Maher, 31 July 1932, ACPSJ.

8. Maher to Lyons, 24 October 1933 and 2 November 1933, ACPSJ; Lyons to Maher, 31 October 1933, 14 November 1933, and 29 November 1933, ACPSJ.

9. Louis C. Rudolph, S.J., interview with author, 20 February 1971.

10. In addition to their several disagreements over the question of Santa Clara's financial aid to the Province, Lyons and Maher had differed on other issues. Lyons's severance of athletic relations with Saint Mary's College in 1933, for example, had annoyed the archbishop of San Francisco, embarrassed Maher, and complicated relations between the provincial and the chancery office. That Lyons had allowed a disagreement between the university and a

senior student who was denied a diploma because of his debts to the school to mushroom into a dispute requiring Roman adjudication was also believed to have antagonized not only the provincial, but also the Jesuit father general. These and other differences, coupled with Lyons's alleged extravagance at Santa Clara during the Great Depression, may all have helped undermine his position.

11. Louis C. Rudolph, S.J., interview with author, 6 June 1976.

12. *The Stanford Daily*, 9 November 1934.

13. *The Monthly Santa Claran* (September, 1934).

14. *San Francisco Chronicle*, 2 November 1934.

15. Verne A. Stadtman, *The University of California, 1868–1968* (New York, 1970), pp. 298–99.

16. *San Francisco Chronicle*, 2 November 1934; *San Francisco Examiner*, 2 November 1934.

17. Stadtman, p. 299.

18. *San Francisco Chronicle*, 2 November 1934.

19. *The Santa Clara*, 18 October 1934; Edward J. Horton to author, 2 September 1976.

20. *The Santa Clara*, 6 September 1934.

21. Henry L. Walsh, S.J., "The Annals of Santa Clara College and University, 1851–1951," typed manuscript, vol. 2, part 2, p. 258, AUSC; annotated clipping from *The Santa Clara*, 18 October 1934, Presidential Papers, AUSC.

22. Cyril J. Smith to Lyons, 28 October [1934], Presidential Papers, AUSC.

23. *Time*, 19 November 1934. After graduating from the University of California at Berkeley, Edward J. Horton followed a career in public administration and teaching. The author is grateful to him for his cooperation in supplying information for this chapter.

24. Louis C. Rudolph, S.J., interview with author, 20 February 1971. The president of the Jesuits' Loyola University in New Orleans claimed similar advantages when seeking an ROTC unit for his institution. Army officials favored Catholic universities, he felt, because they "are sure of our attitude in regard to radicalism." Harold Gaudin to Rudolph, 3 December 1938, Presidential Papers, AUSC.

25. *The Monthly Santa Claran* (September, 1934).

26. Clippings from *Santa Clara Journal*, 18 January 1935, Presidential Papers, AUSC.

27. Walsh, vol. 2, part 2, p. 258, AUSC. At the University of San Francisco, a similar series of lectures given by Jesuit Raymond Feely later developed into a compulsory course on the "dynamics and tactics of communism," the first course of its kind required of all undergraduates by an American university. See John B. McGloin, S.J., *Jesuits by the Golden Gate* (San Francisco, 1972), p. 222.

28. *The Santa Clara*, 10 January 1935.

29. Bean, p. 410.

30. *San Jose Mercury*, 10, 17, and 26 November 1933.

31. *San Jose Mercury*, 23 and 25 November 1933.

32. Unidentified clipping, "SCU Clipping Scrapbook, 1930–35," AUSC; *The Monthly Santa Claran* (October, 1934).

33. *The Santa Clara*, 23 November 1933. The anti-lynching editorial, which was sometimes cited by the San Francisco press after the hangings, was written by the faculty moderator of the campus journal, Jesuit scholastic Wilfrid H. Crowley. Wilfrid H. Crowley, S.J., interview with author, 10 September 1976.

34. Bean, pp. 410–11.

35. *San Jose Mercury*, 27 November 1933; *The Stanford Daily*, 27 November 1933.

36. *San Jose Mercury*, 27 November 1933; *The Stanford Daily*, 27 November 1933.

37. *The Stanford Daily*, 27 November 1933.

38. *San Francisco Examiner*, 28 November 1933.

39. Bean, pp. 410–11.

40. *Call-Bulletin* (San Francisco), 27 November 1933; *San Francisco Chronicle*, 28 November 1933.

41. Bean, pp. 410–11.

42. Unidentified clipping, 24 April 1933, "SCU Clipping Scrapbook, 1933–35," AUSC; *San Jose Mercury Herald*, 24 April 1933.

43. Arthur Spearman, S.J., "The Marconis' Visit to Santa Clara," AUSC.

44. *The Monthly Santa Claran* (July, 1935).

45. Wishing to honor the university's distinguished guest, whom he understood to be a nonsmoker and a nondrinker, the president held a soft-drink reception for the postmaster general and presented him with an appropriate gift—a carton of chewing gum. Walter J. Kropp, S.J., interview with author, 27 April 1976; F. C. Mitchell to James A. Farley, 11 August 1965, James F. Twohy Papers, AUSC.

46. *The Monthly Santa Claran* (July, 1935).

47. Walsh, vol. 2, part 2, p. 154, AUSC.

48. Santa Clara's influence on James Pike's intellectual development and the reasons for his departure became a source of dispute and confusion in later years. Biographers, and sometimes even Pike himself, would suggest that his two years on the mission campus had been a time of religious crisis that occasioned his having "lost his faith" as a Catholic and his having transferred to UCLA. See *Time* (11 November 1966) and William Stringfellow and Anthony Towne, *The Death and Life of Bishop Pike* (New York, 1976). This claim surprised faculty acquaintances and classmates, who remembered Pike as a precocious and devout student, one who frequently attended daily Mass and even talked of becoming a priest. The recollections of those who knew him at the time lend weight to the contention that young Pike chose to pursue his education elsewhere for reasons other than a fundamental disaffiliation with Catholicism. Although in a letter to a campus Jesuit Pike cited his mother's illness, the family's "bad" financial situation, and a stepfather who "does not appreciate the value of a Catholic education" (Pike to J. F. Giambastiani, 14 June 1932, AUSC), information obtained from interviews with his contemporaries supports the conclusion that Pike left Santa Clara primarily because he was dissatisfied with its academic program. Author's interviews with J. F. Giambastiani, S.J., 15 October 1975; Walter Kropp, S.J., 9 January 1976; Brougham Morris, 6 December 1976; John Pagani, 9 September 1976; and Bernard Lawler, 29 January 1977.

49. Pike to Giambastiani [summer, 1932], AUSC, and Edward J. Horton to the author, 2 September 1976. See also Linda Larson, "Who is the Owl?" *The Owl* (spring, 1976), pp. 31–32.

50. *The Literary Digest*, vol. 123 (8 May 1937), pp. 25–28.

51. Arthur Spearman, S.J., "Father Bernard R. Hubbard (1888–1962)," *Woodstock Letters*, vol. 93 (fall, 1965), pp. 466–73, AUSC.

52. Clipping from *Chicago Sunday Tribune*, ca. January, 1928, in "SCU Clipping Scrapbook, 1926–30," AUSC; *New York Evening Post*, 28 January 1928.

53. "Rev. Bernard R. Hubbard, S.J., Biographical Notes," in "SCU Clipping Scrapbook, 1930–33," AUSC; "Back from Alaska," leaflet for talk in San Francisco Civil Auditorium [10 March 1933], AUSC. See also *The Redwood* (1929 and 1930).

54. *New York City Times*, 1 October 1930, and Bernard R. Hubbard, S.J., "A World Inside a Mountain: Aniakchak, the New Volcanic Wonderland of the Alaska Peninsula, is Explored," *National Geographic*, vol. 60 (September 1931), p. 319.

55. *National Geographic*, vol. 60 (September, 1931), pp. 319–45.

56. *National Geographic*, vol. 65 (May, 1934), pp. 625–26.

57. "SCU Clipping Scrapbook, 1930–33," AUSC.

58. *The Literary Digest*, vol. 123 (8 May 1937), p. 26.

59. *Daily Alaska Empire* (Juneau), 1930, in "SCU Clipping Scrapbook, 1930–33," AUSC.

60. *Daily Alaska Empire* (Juneau), *ca.* September, 1932, in "SCU Clipping Scrapbook, 1930–33," AUSC.

61. "SCU Clipping Scrapbook, 1939–40," AUSC.

62. *The Redwood* (student publication), vol. 17 (March, 1918).

63. Unidentified clipping, *ca.* September, 1932, "SCU Clipping Scrapbook, 1930–33," AUSC.

64. *The Monthly Santa Claran* (October, 1934).

65. *The Monthly Santa Claran* (October, 1935); unidentified clipping, 28 November 1934, "SCU Clipping Scrapbook, 1933–35," AUSC.

66. Unidentified clipping, November, 1933, "SCU Clipping Scrapbook, 1933–35," AUSC.

67. Unidentified clipping, December, 1933, "SCU Clipping Scrapbook, 1933–35," AUSC.

68. Unidentified clipping, December, 1933, "SCU Clipping Scrapbook, 1933–35," AUSC. *The Stanford Daily* (6 December 1933) extended "a big hand to little Santa Clara for their unlimited gumption in cutting St. Mary's off short," despite the loss of "a sure 60,000 gate." "If a few more of the colleges displayed such courage," the student editors felt, "the dirty football bugaboo would soon be eliminated."

69. Edward Whelan to Maher, 5 December 1933, ACPSJ.

70. Unidentified clipping, December, 1933, "SCU Clipping Scrapbook, 1933–35," AUSC.

71. Edward J. Hanna to Lyons, 11 December 1933, ACPSJ; Hanna to Lyons, 15 December 1933, ACPSJ.

72. Lyons to Maher, 7 December 1933, ACPSJ.

73. Maher to Lyons, 29 May 1934, ACPSJ.

74. Unidentified clipping, *ca.* December, 1935, "SCU Clipping Scrapbook, 1933–35," AUSC.

75. James Bacigalupi to William C. Gianera, 7 December 1936, ACPSJ. Bacigalupi, member of Santa Clara's Board of Athletic Control, quotes a conversation with Maher, whom he visited in Rome with a view to effecting a relaxation of the four-day rule.

76. Francis Seeliger to California Jesuit Rectors, 10 August 1937, ACPSJ.

77. Unidentified clipping, *ca.* November, 1938, "SCU Clipping Scrapbook, 1937–39," AUSC.

78. *New York American*, 18 November 1936.

79. Unidentified clipping, December, 1936, "SCU Clipping Scrapbook, 1936–37," AUSC.

80. Assorted clippings, "SCU Clipping Scrapbook, 1937–39," AUSC.

81. Walsh, vol. 2, part 2, p. 289, AUSC.

82. McCoy, "Revisor's Report," 1934, ACPSJ.

83. Hugh Duce to Lyons, 15 November 1934, Presidential Papers, AUSC.

84. Edward B. Rooney, "Report," 10 December 1938, ACPSJ.

85. *Los Angeles Times*, 15 May 1946.

86. Rooney, "Report," 1941, ACPSJ.

87. McCoy, "Revisor's Report," 1934, ACPSJ.

88. Lyons to Duce, 19 November 1934, ACPSJ.

89. Seeliger, "Memoriale," 18 April 1939, ACPSJ.

90. Lyons to Maher, 2 October 1934, ACPSJ.

91. Louis Rudolph, S.J., interview with author, 20 February 1971.

92. *The Monthly Santa Claran* (October, 1934).

93. "Historia Domus, 1937–1938," AUSC.

94. *Ibid.*; Walsh, vol. 2, part 3, pp. 338, 343, AUSC.

17. Years of War and Years of Calm, 1941–1958

1. Henry L. Walsh, S.J., "The Annals of Santa Clara College and University, 1851–1951," typed manuscript, vol. 2, part 3, pp. 394, AUSC.

2. *The Santa Clara*, 17 October 1940.

3. Unidentified clipping, "SCU Clipping Scrapbook, 1939–42," AUSC.

4. *The Santa Clara*, 15 May 1941.

5. Walsh, vol. 2, part 3, p. 346, AUSC.

6. *Ibid.*, p. 425.

7. Francis J. Seeliger, "Memoriale," (December, 1941), ACPSJ.

8. Walsh, vol. 2, part 3, pp. 425–27, AUSC.

9. *The Owl* (March, 1942, and October, 1942).

10. Wayne M. Kanemoto, [talk to young Japanese-Americans, 1973], AUSC. See also *San Jose Mercury*, 2 June 1943.

11. *University of Santa Clara Catalogue, 1941–1942.*

12. George Leonard Sullivan, "Engineering and the Sullivans Come to Santa Clara, Memorial Edition" (Santa Clara, Calif., 1956), AUSC.

13. "Historia Domus: August, 1936 to September, 1948," AUSC.

14. Walsh to Marshall E. Leahy, 17 February 1943, AUSC.

15. "House Consultations" [25 April 1939 to 9 May 1945], minutes for 29 March 1943, AUSC.

16. Walsh to Leahy, 17 February 1943, AUSC.

17. "House Consultations" [1939–1943], minutes for 29 March 1943, AUSC.

18. *The Santa Clara*, 9 September 1943.

19. Walsh, vol. 2, part 3, p. 461, AUSC.

20. *San Jose News*, 16 April 1943, in "SCU Clipping Scrapbook, 1942–48," AUSC.

21. *The Santa Clara*, 11 February 1943; Walsh, vol. 2, part 3, pp. 453–54, AUSC.

22. Walsh to Edward Whelan, 24 July 1943, Presidential Papers, AUSC; unidentified clipping, "SCU Clipping Scrapbook, 1942–1948," AUSC; Walsh, vol. 2, part 3, pp. 453–54, AUSC.

23. *The Santa Clara*, 11 May 1944.

24. *San Jose News*, 19 February 1944.

25. Walsh to Friends, 7 February 1945, Alexander Leonard Papers, AUSC; Walsh to Bertrand Gearhart, 24 March 1944, Presidential Papers, AUSC.

26. *The Santa Clara*, 7 September 1944; Walsh to Alumni and Friends, 30 June 1945, ACPSJ.

27. J. J. Tormey to Walsh, 24 February 1944, Properties File, AUSC. See also "University of Santa Clara Board of Trustees, Minutes of Meetings, 1926–1955," minutes for 25 February and 21 July 1944, AUSC.

28. *San Jose Mercury*, 21 August 1945; C. C. Coolidge to Walsh, 20 August 1945, AUSC.

29. C. J. McCoy to Joseph M. Piet, 30 May 1928, ACPSJ.

30. *The Santa Clara*, 7 November 1946.

31. *The Santa Clara*, 17 October 1946.

32. *The Santa Clara*, 14 November 1946.

33. Unidentified clipping, "SCU Clipping Scrapbook, 1942–1948," AUSC.

34. *The Owl*, vol. 37 (June, 1950); *The Santa Clara*, 13 September 1950.

35. *The Monthly Santa Claran* (January, 1947).

36. *Ibid.*, and *The Monthly Santa Claran* (May 1947).

37. William C. Gianera to [Joseph O'Brien] 16 September 1948, ACPSJ; unidentified clipping, "SCU Clipping Scrapbook 1942–48," AUSC.

38. *The Monthly Santa Claran* (October, 1950).

39. *The Monthly Santa Claran* (March, 1951).

40. John Hynes, S.J., "Report to Provincial," July, 1951, ACPSJ.

41. "The University of Santa Clara Builds for a Second Century," brochure, 1947, AUSC.

42. *The Santa Clara*, 23 March 1944.

43. Harold R. McKinnon to Alumni, 4 August 1945, Presidential Papers, AUSC.

44. *The Monthly Santa Claran* (February, 1951).

45. *The Monthly Santa Claran* (June–July, 1947).

46. Will Williams, Jr. to Gianera, 2 January 1950, AUSC; Williams to O'Donnell 14 Sept. 1950, AUSC; "Minutes of the Development Meeting, November 10, 1950," Presidential Papers, AUSC.

47. "Membership Report of Alumni Association of Santa Clara," September, 1951, AUSC.

48. Williams to Gianera, 2 January 1950, Presidential Papers, AUSC.

49. *The Monthly Santa Claran* (March, 1951).

50. "Report of the President 1950–1951," AUSC.

51. *The Monthly Santa Claran* (April, 1948).

52. "USC Board of Trustees, Minutes of Meetings, 1926–1955," minutes for 5 September 1948, AUSC. Nearby Stanford University charged $600 for three quarters in 1949. Tuition at the College of the Pacific was $275 a semester.

53. "Annual Survey for the Central Association of College and University Business Officers, Questionnaire re Fees, Enrollment, and Salaries, 1950–51," Presidential Papers, AUSC.

54. Edward B. Rooney, S.J., "Report on the University of Santa Clara, Santa Clara, California, March 7–11, 1950," ACPSJ. See also Rooney, "Report on University of Santa Clara," 1938, ACPSJ.

55. "Rules and Regulations, University of Santa Clara," 1 January 1948, p. 19, AUSC.

56. Walsh, "Presidential Address, September 12, 1940," *The Owl*, vol. 31 (October, 1940), pp. 10–13.

57. "Rules and Regulations," 1948, p. 19, AUSC.

58. "Rules and Regulations," 1948, p. 20, AUSC.

59. Walsh, "Presidential Address," pp. 10–13.

60. "The University of Santa Clara Builds for a Second Century," brochure, AUSC.

61. Walsh to James Kelly, 18 September 1941, Presidential Papers, AUSC.

62. Stan Terra, "Santa Clara Revisited," *The Best of Santa Clara Today, 1973–1974* (Univ. of Santa Clara Publicity Office, 1974).

63. Paul Laxalt, "Voices of Dissent—Constructive or Destructive," *The Santa Claran* (summer, 1967).

64. *The Redwood*, 1951.

65. *Time*, vol. 57 (19 March 1951), p. 79.

66. Jimmy Snyder, *Jimmy the Greek* (Chicago, 1976), p. 97.

67. Although the rule that forbade absences from class by athletes for more than four days was still in effect, in 1950 Father Gianera lifted the ban on airplane travel for the first time.

68. *San Francisco Chronicle*, 25 December 1952; *San Francisco Examiner*, 25 November 1952.

69. *San Francisco Chronicle*, 31 September 1951; *San Francisco Examiner*, 31 September 1951.

70. *Oakland Tribune*, 25 November 1952.

71. Herman J. Hauck to Joseph D. O'Brien, 27 November 1952, ACPSJ; "House Consultations [1945–1954], minutes for 1 December 1952, AUSC; Herman J. Hauck, S.J., interview with author, 7 June 1976, Los Angeles, California.

72. Hauck to Alumni and Parents, 4 January 1953, ACPSJ.

73. *San Francisco Chronicle*, 30 December 1952; *San Jose News*, 30 December 1952; *San Francisco News*, 31 December 1952; *San Francisco Examiner*, 6 January 1954.

74. Kelly to Santa Clara Alumni, 31 July 1953, Presidential Papers, AUSC.

75. *San Jose News*, 23 February 1949.

76. Sullivan, AUSC.

77. James A. King to Hugh Duce, 24 June 1957, Presidential Papers, AUSC.

78. *The Santa Claran* (May–June, 1953 and January–February, 1956).

79. Hynes, "Report to Father President," January, 1953, Presidential Papers, AUSC.

80. James A. King to Alexis Mei, 10 May 1957, Presidential Papers, AUSC; King to Hauck, 23 September 1957, Presidential Papers, AUSC.

81. "SCU Clipping Scrapbook, 1950–54," *passim*, AUSC; *The Santa Claran* (January–March, 1953).

82. Rooney, "Report on the University of Santa Clara," 1950, ACPSJ; "University of Santa Clara Board of Trustees, Minutes of Meetings, 1956–59," minutes for meeting of 16 September, 1956; AUSC.

83. University of Santa Clara, "Report to the Western College Association," 1952 and 1958, AUSC.

18. *Traditions Shattered, 1958–1977*

1. [Patrick A. Donohoe, S.J.], "The Possibility of Coeducation at the University of Santa Clara, the University of San Francisco, and Loyola University of Los Angeles [1959], typescript, ACPSJ.

2. [Donohoe], "Some Thoughts on Santa Clara's Future—the Next Decade" [1959], ACPSJ.

3. [Donohoe], "Santa Clara and Coeducation?," typescript memorandum, ACPSJ.

4. [Donohoe], "Possibility of Coeducation," ACPSJ.

5. John S. Brubacher and Willis Rudy, *Higher Education in Transition: A History of American Colleges and Universities, 1636–1976* (New York, 1976), p. 69.

6. [Donohoe], "Possibility of Coeducation," ACPSJ; Donohoe to John Baptist Janssens, 23 December 1960, ACPSJ. President Herman J. Hauck's view on coeducation is explained in *Newsweek*, 23 September 1957.

7. Donohoe to John J. Mitty, 18 March 1960, 2 June 1960, and 22 December 1960, ACPSJ. Patrick A. Donohoe, S.J., interview with author, 16 November 1976.

8. *The Santa Clara*, 22 March 1961.

9. *The Santa Claran* (Fall, 1965); *The Santa Clara Views* (February, 1968).

10. Donohoe, "A Tribute for a Friend," *The Santa Clara*, 17 November 1975. See also Walter Blum, *Benjamin H. Swig, The Measure of a Man* (San Francisco, 1968).

11. *Santa Clara Today* (December, 1972).

12. "Remarks by Mr. Swig given at the dedication dinner," Benjamin H. Swig Residence Hall for Men, 20 September 1966, program, AUSC.

13. "Report of the University of Santa Clara, Santa Clara, California, to Western College Association and Committee on Accreditation, California State Board of Education," 1969, Presidential Papers, AUSC. The tentative budget for fiscal 1957–1958 was set at $2.1 million, according to University of Santa Clara Board of Trustees, Minutes of the Meetings, 1956–59; minutes for 8 September 1957, AUSC.

14. "Annual Reports, 1958–68," Business Office, Univ. of Santa Clara.

15. *The Monthly Santa Claran* (February, 1952). See also "School of Engineering: a twenty-five year projection, first draft" [1961], AUSC.

16. "University of Santa Clara, Report to the Western College Association," 1958, Presidential Papers, AUSC; "Report of the University of Santa Clara," 1969, Presidential Papers, AUSC.

17. Eugene Bianchi, "Christian-Marxist Encounter at Santa Clara," *The Santa Claran*

(Winter, 1968). For a general description of campus attitudes on the eve of the period of change, see Julian Foster, "Some Effects of Jesuit Education: A Case Study," in Robert Hassenger, ed., *The Shape of Catholic Higher Education* (Chicago, 1967), pp. 163–90.

18. *The Santa Clara Views* (November, 1967).

19. *The Santa Claran* (Fall, 1967).

20. "University of Santa Clara, Report to the Western College Association" November, 1952, p. 55, Presidential Papers, AUSC.

21. Stan Terra, "Santa Clara Revisited," *The Best of Santa Clara Today, 1973–1974* (Univ. of Santa Clara Publicity Office, 1974).

22. *Ibid.*

23. *The Santa Claran* (Fall, 1970).

24. *Santa Clara Today* (February, 1973).

25. *Santa Clara Today* (June, 1976).

26. *Santa Clara Today* (March, 1976).

27. *Santa Clara Views* (December, 1970) and *Santa Clara Today* (June, 1976).

28. *The Santa Clara Views* (December, 1970).

29. *Santa Clara Today* (March, 1976).

30. Board of Trustees, "Our Concept of Education," 19 November 1968, *University of Santa Clara Bulletin*, 1969; board of trustees, "A Statement of Purpose," 22 January 1975, *University of Santa Clara Bulletin*, 1976.

31. *Santa Clara Today* (February, 1973).

32. *The Santa Clara Views* (May, 1970, and June, 1970). When a photograph of that episode snapped by a newsman from the *San Jose Mercury-News* was picked up by the wirephoto service, the clash between Santa Clara's side-stepping cadets and the supine protestors received nationwide publicity.

33. *Santa Clara Views* (May, 1970).

34. *Santa Clara Views* (May, 1969); *Santa Clara Today* (October, 1972, and December, 1972).

35. Melvin Lewis, a high-school athlete from Santa Monica, California, admitted in 1949, seems to have been the first black to enter the university. See *San Jose News*, 11 February 1949, in "SCU Clipping Scrapbook, 1948–50," AUSC. A brief entry in the Jesuit house consultation minutes for 3 December 1947 records the university's admission policy at that time. "Our position on the question of admitting colored students was discussed, and it was determined that there is no opposition—the same requirements for all students." "House Consultations [1945–1954]," AUSC.

36. "Minority Affairs: Other Institutions, Report, 1968," Presidential Papers, AUSC.

37. *San Jose Mercury-News*, 27 October 1968.

38. *Santa Clara Today* (June, 1976); statistical data supplied by David P. Arata, University Registrar, and financial data by Richard J. Toomey of the Financial Aid Office.

39. *Santa Clara Today* (November, 1976).

40. *The Santa Clara Views* (November, 1971); *Santa Clara Today* (April, 1977).

41. *Santa Clara Today* (November, 1973).

42. William J. Rewak, S.J., "Inaugural Address," 12 January 1977, AUSC.

43. *Ibid.*

19. Conclusion

1. Andrew M. Greeley, *From Backwater to Mainstream, A Profile of Catholic Higher Education* (New York, 1969); Richard Hofstadter and C. Dewitt Hardy, *The Development and Scope of Higher Education in the United States* (New York, 1952), p. 3.

2. *Prospectus of Santa Clara College*, 1872–1873.

3. Santa Clara graduates constituted a small percentage of the state's total. Of the estimated nine thousand Bachelor of Arts and Bachelor of Science diplomas granted by California colleges and universities between 1857 and 1912, only 370, or approximately 4 percent, were bestowed by Santa Clara. This estimate is drawn primarily from figures in various issues of the *Annual Report of the Commissioner of Education* (Washington, D.C.: Government Printing Office) and the Santa Clara College catalogues.

4. Philip Gleason, "American Catholic Higher Education: A Historical Perspective," in Robert Hassinger, ed., *The Shape of Catholic Higher Education* (Chicago, 1967), p. 36.

5. Henry Woods to James A. Rockliff, *ca.* December, 1910, ACPSJ. See also Nicholas Congiato to B. A. Maguire, 18 February 1856, de Smetiana, AMPSJ.

6. Greeley, p. 13. He describes the plight of many of these institutions in the early 1900's. They were "small, in constant financial difficulty, academically inferior, static in educational philosophy, traditional in curriculum and pedagogy, rigid in discipline and student life, clerical in faculty administration, and isolated almost completely from the mainstream of American higher education."

7. F. A. Ruppert to Rockliff, 25 December 1910, ACPSJ.

8. William H. Culligan to Rockliff, *ca.* December, 1910, ACPSJ.

9. Greeley, p. 11.

10. Gleason, p. 46.

11. J. S. Ricard to Rockliff, 26 December 1910, ACPSJ.

12. James Morrissey to Franz X. Wernz, 31 January 1913, AHSI; Walter Thornton to Wlodimir Ledochowski, 10 April 1918, RASJ.

13. Edward J. Power, *Catholic Higher Education, a History* (New York, 1972), pp. 61–62.

14. Burton J. Bledstein, *The Culture of Professionalism: The Middle Class and the Development of Higher Education in America* (New York, 1976); Ricard to Rockliff, 26 December 1919, ACPSJ.

15. Morrissey to Wernz, 31 January 1913, AHSI.

16. In 1946 Charles S. Casassa, S.J., having just completed a doctorate in philosophy at the University of Toronto, joined the Santa Clara faculty. Casassa later became president of Loyola University in Los Angeles. The first Jesuit in the California Province to earn a doctorate from an American institution was Peter Masten Dunne, who obtained his degree in history at the University of California, Berkeley, in 1934.

17. Joseph W. Riordan to Rockliff, 4 January 1911, ACPSJ.

18. Kavanagh to Rockliff, 2 January 1911, ACPSJ.

19. *Santa Clara College Catalog*, 1907–1908.

20. *University of Santa Clara Diamond Jubilee Volume, 1851–1926* (Santa Clara, Calif., 1926), p. 48.

21. *Souvenir of Santa Clara College, 1851–1901* (Santa Clara, Calif., 1901), p. 51.

22. *University of Santa Clara, A History, 1777–1912*, p. 37.

23. *Woodstock Letters*, vol. 12 (1884), pp. 162–63, AUSC.

24. Robert D. Cross, *The Emergence of Liberal Catholicism in America* (Chicago, 1958), p. 135.

25. Patrick Foote to Rockliff, 28 December 1910, ACPSJ.

26. *Souvenir*, p. 51.

27. Thomas W. McKey to Rockliff, 28 December 1910, ACPSJ.

28. Joseph King to Henry Walsh, 28 March 1944, and Walsh to King, 7 April 1944, in Herman J. Hauck, [Rector's Index], AUSC.

29. Zacheus Maher to James Lyons, 7 November 1933, ACPSJ.

30. Hauck to Carroll M. O'Sullivan, 5 September 1954, ACPSJ.

31. Patrick A. Donohoe, S.J., interview with author, 30 August 1977.

32. *Souvenir*, p. 51.

33. *The Santa Claran* (May–June, 1953).

34. See *Souvenir*, p. 51.

35. "The Survey, Analysis and Plan for the University of Santa Clara," prepared by G. A. Brakeley & Co., August, 1957, Presidential Papers, AUSC.

36. Joseph Tomkin to Rockliff, 19 May 1913, ACPSJ.

37. John E. Pope, "Report on Santa Clara University Site," February, 1911, ACPSJ.

38. *Souvenir*, p. 51.

39. See Gleason, pp. 27–30.

40. Greeley, p. 9.

41. Gleason, p. 51.

42. *Ibid.*, p. 52.

43. Greeley, p. 81.

44. William J. Rewak, S.J., "Statement of Purpose and Planning Priorities," 1977, Presidential Papers, AUSC.

45. Gleason, p. 31.

46. Rewak.

Index

Abbot, Charles, 228
Abortion: protests about, 298
Academia dei Nobili Ecclesiastici (Rome), 15, 53
Academic freedom: restrictions on, 224, 272–73; defended, 292–93, 298–99, 304–5, 320
Academic vice-president, of university, 264, 267, 302, 331
Accolti, Michael, 7f, 21 (illus.), 14–27 *passim*, 38–41 *passim*, 53, 62, 344; search for faculty, 29–31, 41, 46–49 *passim*; educational philosophy of, 80f, 106; mentioned, 35, 52, 68, 99, 107, 345, 348
Accounting: study of, 108, 110, 216
Accreditation of university, 210, 275–83 *passim*, 291, 309
Administrative organization, 65f, 266–67, 277, 279, 288, 294–97 *passim*, 302, 316f, 320, 331–32
Admissions to university: requests for, 37, 257, 286, 300; requirements, 43f, 146–47, 170, 215, 285f, 313, 371
Adobe Lodge, 69, 99, 100 (illus.), 211, 217, 263
Adobe Wall: photograph of, 121
Aeterni Patris: of Pope Leo XIII, 113
Agriculture, College of, 172
Aguirre, José Antonio, 40
Alameda, The: parades along, 75, 135, 257, 275; mentioned, 9, 27, 205 (illus.), 235 (illus.), 239, 281
Albertson, James, 300, 302
Alexander, George J., 302–3
Alemany, Joseph Sadoc, 13, 22–26 *passim*, 34f, 41, 66, 75–77, 114
Alfonso XIII, King of Spain, 200f
Algebra: study of, 108
Alma College (Calif.), 280
Alumni: athletics and, 145, 192f, 244, 255, 257, 276–77; business careers, 302f; careers in dramatics, 103, 143; in medicine, 150, 290; fund-raising and, 113, 117, 132f, 195–201 *passim*, 268–69, 316; gatherings of, 62, 84; governmental careers, 40, 102, 148, 152–53, 238, 282, 290; honorary degrees to, 135; journalists, 102, 273; legal careers, 48, 58, 102, 150, 172, 260; opinions of, 237f, 273–74, 277, 286, 292–93, 298–99; organized, 113, 175; photographs of, 48, 60; priests, 5, 147, 166; role in Spanish-American War, 147–48; teachers, 172
Alumni Association, 195, 201f, 244, 286, 316, 352
Alumni Council: presidents of, 334 (listed)
Alumni House, 303
Alumni Science Hall, 195, 201f
Alviso, Ignatius, 39
American Assembly of Collegiate Schools of Business, 291
American Association for the Recognition of the Irish Republic, 186

American Association of Collegiate Schools of Business, 278
American Bar Association, 278
American Chemical Society, 278
Americanism controversy: and California Jesuits, 55, 117–25, 353
American Protective Association, 147
Amherst College (Mass.): opposes teaching of evolution, 150
Amherst Observatory (Mass.), 223
Anderledy, Anton, 120, 122
Anderson, Mr. (visitor from Scotland), 71, 347, 363
Anderson, Robert O., 279 (illus.)
Anthropology: study of, 294
Anti-Catholicism, *see* Catholicism; Nativism
Anti-Communism, *see* Communism
Apothecary: at college, 99
Aptheker, Herbert, 292, 298
Aquinas, St. Thomas: study of, 112–13
Architecture: Victorian, 68ff, 100–101 (illus.), 217ff; study of, 151, 172; mentioned, 95–96, 115f, 167, 218–20, 303. *See also* Mission Church
Architecture, College of, 172
Archives, of university, 24, 248
Army Specialized Training Program (ASTP), 262, 264, 268
Arrupe, Pedro, 290
Art, *see* Fine Arts
Arts, College of, *see* Humanities, College of
Arts and Sciences, College of, 278, 284, 291, 297; deans of, 264, 267, 281, 331. *See also* Humanities, College of; Sciences, College of
Assaying: study of, 69, 71, 73 (illus.)
Astronomy, *see* Ricard, Jerome S.; Ricard Observatory
Atheism: study of, 305. *See also* Communism
Atherton, F., 75
Athletics: justification of, 61, 85, 144, 189, 276; criticized, 144–45, 162, 188, 255–56; regulations regarding, 145–46, 249–50, 252–53, 256, 367, 369; facilities, 61, 91, 192, 194, 290, 303; school colors, 192; mascot, 192; during Depression, 234; publicity value of, 248–49, 257; and Bronco Bench, 290. *See also names of specific sports*
Augustine and Evolution, 212
Aviation: Santa Clara and, 135, 137–40, 246, 252

Bacigalupi, Eugene M., 271
Bacigalupi, James A., 255, 367
Bancroft, A. L., 104
Bancroft, H. H., 107
Bandini, Alfred, 39
Bank of Italy, 197

Bannan, Berchman A., 302
Bannan, Philip L., 290
Bannan, Thomas J., 290
Bannan Hall, 281, 303
Barry, Kevin, 186
Barsi, George, 249
Baseball, 85, 86 (illus.), 100 (illus.), 145, 156 (illus.), 190, 231, 248–49, 277
Basketball, 248–49, 277–78, 303
Bayma, Joseph, 53, 54 (illus.), 111–13, 135, 211, 352; opposes public education, 106; designs mission gardens, 126 (illus.)
Beardsley, Aubrey, 143
Beaumont, George, 143
Beckx, Peter, 55, 352
Beilharz, Edwin O., 271
Bell, Alexander Graham, 138
Bell, Richard, 135–37, 159 (illus.), 162, 211, 244, 355
Bellarmine College Preparatory, see High School
Benson Center, 289
Bergin, Thomas I., 48 (illus.), 49, 58
Bergin Hall, 257, 290
Berryessa, F., 39
Big Basin Park (Calif.), 135, 140–42, 143, 149 (illus.)
Biology: study of, 71, 271f.
Bishops (Catholic), see names of specific persons and San Francisco, Archbishop of
Bixio, Joseph, 74
Blacks, 300, 371
Bledstein, Burton, quoted, 3, 312
Board of Athletic Control, 253, 255f, 367
Board of Fellows, 288, 303
Board of Trustees, see Trustees
Boggio, John Baptist, 99
Bolland, E. R. A., 203
Bolton, Lloyd L., 271
Boone, Daniel, 82
Bosco, Aloysius, 98, 103
Bosqui, Edward, 104, 107
Boston College (Mass.), 72, 295
Breen, Eugene, 83 (illus.)
Breen, James, 308
Bronco Bench, 290
Bronco Corral, 265
"Broncos," origin of, 192
Brouillet, J. B., 15–18 passim, 23
Brown, Edwin J., 279 (illus.)
Brown, Gov. Edmund G., Sr., 290
Brown, Gov. Jerry (Edmund G., Jr.), 282
Brubacher, John S.: quoted, 4, 285
Brunengo, Aloysius, 108–10
Bryant, Paul, 275
Buck Shaw Athletic Stadium, 290
Budgets and Budgeting: college supports other Jesuit works, 232–34, 313–15; in 1920's, 201–3, 206–10 passim, 358; during Depression, 230–34, 243, 255–56, 364–65; during World War II, 261–63, 314, 316; in postwar era, 269, 280, 284, 286–89, 317, 370; faculty and, 231, 271, 280ff, 286, 311–12; restrictions upon, 125, 243, 315; growth stifled, 176–79 passim, 312–17. See also Debts; Endowment; Financial Support; Fund Drives
Buildings: poor condition of, 26–27, 131, 194–95, 199, 308; major construction drives, 68–72 passim, 78,

167ff, 194–203, 288, 289–91, 302–3, 304; "mission" architectural style, 167; administrative offices, 68–69, 91 (illus.), 100 (illus.), 126 (illus.), 156–57, 159 (illus.), 167, 168 (illus.), 269; art gallery and museum, 271; chapels, 49, 61, 95, 115–17, 132–33, 167, 216–21; classrooms, 49, 69–72, 108–10, 290–91, 302; dormitories, 43f, 49, 61, 95f, 167ff, 216, 265, 269, 273, 281, 289, 300; gymnasiums, 61–62, 64, 167, 197, 202–3, 303; infirmaries, 69, 87, 202–3, 303; Jesuit residences, 26 (illus.), 27, 68–69, 91 (illus.), 100 (illus.), 156–57, 159 (illus.), 167, 168 (illus.); laboratories, 69f, 71–72, 73 (illus.), 203, 290, 307; libraries, 100 (illus.), 167, 211 (illus.), 216f, 290–91, 302–3; observatories, 167, 216, 221–29 passim; cafeteria, 262, 265; student refectory, 87; student union, 271, 289; theaters, 61–62, 91 (illus.), 95–96, 100 (illus.), 216 (illus.), 303; value of (1860's), 78, 348
Bulkley, William, 110
Bull-and-bear fights, 62
Burbank, Luther, 224
Burnett, Gov. Peter, 19, 40, 60, 110
Burnett, John M., 60 (illus.), 308
Business and Finance: vice-presidents for, 332
Business, School of, 210, 215–16, 278f, 279 (illus.), 282, 290f, 302, 332. See also Commercial Course
Byington, Lewis F., 238

California: aviation in, 137–40; Chinese in, 99, 105, 115; Civil War in, 67, 73–75; conservation in, 140, 142f, 149 (illus.); Democratic party in, 74; during Depression of 1930's, 230–45 passim; early mail service to, 20, 29; gold rush in, 7, 11–19 passim, 25, 33, 37, 43, 69, 71, 307; governors of, 19, 32f, 40, 60, 74f, 110, 197, 236, 240–43 passim, 275, 282, 290, 299; growth of Los Angeles, 158; influenza epidemic (1918), 184; labor unrest in, 115, 230, 234–39 passim; lynchings in, 236, 239–43, 365; Mexican War and, 11–14 passim, 49; mining industry, 69, 71, 99; mission preservation, 115–17, 218–20; missions secularized, 9–14 passim; nativism in, 40f, 53, 105–6, 147, 200; panic of 1873, 115; panic of 1893, 129; parks, 140, 142f, 149 (illus.); Progressivism in, 135; public school system of, 5, 13, 38, 42, 67, 106, 115; schools in Spanish-Mexican periods, 13, 30; and Spanish-American War, 147–148; prosperity of 1880's, 115; prosperity of 1920's, 197, 200; radio broadcasting in, 135–37, 355; state treasurer of, 40; and transcontinental railroad, 67, 95f; vigilante movements in, 236–37, 239–43; water needs, 222–23; and World War I, 181–84; and World War II, 230, 257–66 passim, 282f
California, Baja, 14
California, higher education in: anti-war protests, 237f, 299, 301 (illus.); degrees conferred, 48f, 93, 308, 372; developments in, 37ff, 128–29, 146–51 passim, 274; during World War II, 262; first Catholic coeducation, 286; early colleges, 1, 5, 27–28, 37, 92–93, 130, 308; in 1930's, 230, 236–42 passim; opposition to classics, 57; public-private competition, 128f, 300–301; state scholarship program, 210, 301–2. See also names of specific colleges
California Historical Society, 104, 107, 352
California Hotel, 31 (illus.), 44, 49, 61, 70 (illus.), 100 (illus.), 154, 167
California Mission (Jesuit): founding of, 52, 55, 61;

relation to college, 66, 98, 112, 117, 124–28 passim, 134f, 155; visitors to, 65, 124–25; clash with Italy, 117–25 passim. See also California Province; Jesuits

California Province (Jesuit): creation of, 52, 158, 166, 357; relationship with college, 158–65 passim, 175, 206–13 passim; 232–34, 238–39, 253–56 passim, 276–77, 285, 297, 311–15 passim, 364–65; over-extension of, 165, 180, 311–14 passim; and education of Jesuits, 179–80, 312, 372; theologate of, 209, 280; and World War II, 260. See also California Mission; Jesuits; Roman church authorities

California Redwood Park Commission, 142

California State Scholarship Program, 301–2

California, University of, see University of California

California Wesleyan College, see University of the Pacific

Californios: attend Santa Clara, 39f, 300

Campbell, James Havelock, 211

Campbell, W. W., 223

Canada, 18, 22, 225, 227

Candalaria's Fandango House, 62f

Canisius College (N.Y.), 51

Caredda, Joseph, 114, 120 (illus.)

Carleton College (Minn.), 79

Carr, James K., 290

Casanega, Ken, 250

Casanova, Leonard, 275

Casassa, Charles S., 312, 372

Case, Lee, 288

Casey, George H., 253, 255

Carey, James B., 274

Castro, José, 33

Castruccio, C. M., 255

Catalá, Magín, 9

Catala Club, 244, 316

Catholic University (Washington, D.C.), 158

Catholic World, The, 113, 352

Catholic-Protestant tensions, 1ff, 20, 22, 40–43, 106, 200. See also Nativism; Protestants

Catholicism, in California: mission system, 8–9, 32; early troubles of, 11–14, 18–23 passim; and Californios, 39; served by Santa Clara, 4–5, 14–24 passim, 271; opposition to, 2, 40ff, 53, 105–6, 150, 200; loyalty of, 147–48, 181f, 191, 196, 212–13; and secular education, 146–51 passim; contemporary change in, 275, 295, 319. See also Colleges, Catholic

Catholicism, in U.S., see Americanism controversy; Colleges, Catholic

Cecilian Society, 103

Center for the Study of Contemporary Values, 292

Chanute, Octave, 137f

Chaplain: of university, 238, 273

Chargin, Victor, 295

Charles IV, King of Spain, 218, 220

Charter of university, 27–28, 47

Chase, Hal, 145

Chemistry: study of, 53, 69, 71, 92, 124, 271, 278

Chicanos, see Mexican-Americans

Chile, 30, 341

China, 53, 93

Chinese: and college, 99, 105, 115

Chisholm, Roderick, 193

Christian Apologetics, 211

Christian Brothers, 77, 252

Christian-Marxist Symposium (1967), 298, 304

Church-State tensions, see Jesuits: oppose public education; Colleges, Catholic: oppose secular education

Cicaterri, Felix, 53, 63–64, 65

Cichi, Anthony, 72, 83 (illus.), 135

Civil engineering, 151–52

Civil War: and college, 67, 73–75; mentioned, 1ff, 92, 105, 108, 307

Classical studies: curriculum, 71, 142, 151–52; development of, 171–72, 177, 210, 280, 310; in denominational colleges, 3, 307–8; philosophy of, 55–58, 108; relevance debated, 57, 118–24, 150, 307–9 passim; mentioned, 47, 92. See also Greek; Latin

Coeducation: during World War II, 261; in evening school (1947), 265; undergraduate, 284–87 passim, 287 (illus.), 292, 317; mentioned, 214, 370. See also Women

College Echo (Berkeley), 105

College of California (Berkeley), 1, 38, 41, 130, 308. See also University of California, Berkeley

College of Notre Dame (California), 28, 38, 130

College of the Pacific, see University of the Pacific

Colleges, American: anti-war protests in, 237, 299; classics at, 307; coeducation at, 284–85; discipline in, 79, 307–8; high mortality rate of, 130, 308; proliferation of, 1, 311; retain prep schools, 204, 308; secularization of, 306ff

Colleges, Catholic: academic freedom at, 298–99; aims of, 3f, 212–13; commercial studies at, 108; compete with Protestant colleges, 2, 20, 41; elementary education at, 28–29; engineering studies at, 278; European faculties, 51, 345; fate of, 311; football at, 193; in California, 1, 38, 158–65 passim, 285; journalistic studies at, 103; law studies at, 172; oppose electivism, 3f, 170–71; oppose secular education, 146–51, 306–7; problems of, 275, 310–14 passim, 372; promote classics, 124; ROTC at, 365; secularization of, 4, 292–93, 295, 306–7, 319–20. See also specific institutions

Colleges, Protestant: in California, 1, 38; educational philosophy of, 2–5 passim; compete with Catholic colleges, 2, 20, 41; oppose secular education, 306–7; secularization of, 3f. See also specific institutions

Collegiate studies, at Santa Clara, 28, 47, 49, 92, 96, 133, 170–72, 205

Columbia University, 79

Coltelli, Angelo, 87

Commencement, 58–59, 172–73, 263, 265

Commercial Building, 100 (illus.), 108–10, 203

Commercial Course: study of, 47, 57, 103, 109–10, 122, 151, 307; opposition to, 57, 108, 124; expanded, 108–10, 352; director of, 173 (illus.). See also Business, School of

Communism, 196, 236–39, 292–93, 305, 365

Competition: among students, 59

Conaty, James T., 158–65 passim, 358

Congiato, Nicholas, 49, 53, 61, 63, 119–23 passim, 128, 353

Congregation of the Holy Cross, 51

Congregationalists, 1, 79

Conservation, 135, 140, 142, 149 (illus.)

Contemporary Values, Center for the Study of, 292

Contraception, 212

Coogan, Jackie, 244
Copeland, Charles T., 152–53
Cotton Bowl, 255
Cowell Foundation, 303
Cradle of the Storms, 248
Creighton University (Neb.), 222, 295
Cross, Robert D.: quoted, 106
Crowley, Wilfred D., 365
Curriculum: in early years, 27f, 92; classics emphasized, 55–58; disagreements over, 107–10, 120–24, 148, 150; electivism opposed, 151–53; reorganized, 170–72; described (1926), 215–16; postwar expansion of, 284; Santa Clara Plan, 291, 294; core requirements changed, 293–94. *See also specific subjects*

Daly, Edward J., 290
Daly Science Center, 290
Dancing, 92, 110
Dartmouth College (N.H.), 1
Darwinism: teaching of, 150–51, 224, 272
Davidson, George, 107
Dávila, Agustín, 217
Davis, William Heath, 40
Day students, 27, 82, 170, 281
Deans of colleges: listed, 331–32
Deans of faculties, 210, 264, 267, 270; listed, 331
Deans of men: listed, 332
Deans of students, 300; listed, 332
Deans of women: listed, 332
Debating: classroom, 31 (illus.); study of, 55, 59, 99, 102–3; organizations, 84, 86; teacher of, 86 (illus.); topics, 134, 259
Debts: in early years, 34ff, 63f, 68, 78, 93, 97, 111, 125; Kenna and, 114; Morrissey and, 176; during World War II, 263; avoided in 1920's, 202. *See also* Budgets and Budgeting; Endowment; Financial Support; Fund Drives
Deck, Joseph F., 271
Deeney, Cornelius, 143, 271
Degrees: requirements, 57–58, 123–24, 210, 215–16, 280, 293–94; conferred, 40, 48f, 58, 122–24, 133, 263, 308, 372; listed, 326–28; graduate, 123; master's, 60, 172, 278, 280, 290–91; doctoral, 291; honorary, 107, 135, 315, 337–38 (listed), 363
De la Motte, George, 158, 162
Delmas, Delphin, 58, 102, 133, 135, 182
De Paul University (Ill.), 249
Depression (1930's): and Bellarmine College Preparatory, 209; impact on American higher education, 230; and Santa Clara, 230–46 *passim*, 314; mentioned, 153, 202
De Saisset Art Gallery and Museum, 271
De Saisset, Ernest, 271
De Saisset, Isabel, 271
De Smet, Peter, 14f, 18, 35
De Studio Religiosae Perfectionis, 112
Development, office of: 266, 267–68, 288; urged in 1911, 316; vice-presidents for, listed, 332
Development, of university: plans for, 280–83, 286–92 *passim*
Devivier, W., 211
García Diego y Moreno, Francisco: death of, 13
Dillon, Francis, 208
Dirksen, Charles J., 265, 279 (illus.), 282, 290, 302

Discipline: controversies about, 43, 55, 86–88, 111, 118–20, 131, 161–62, 169–77 *passim*, 298; described, 79–91, 273–74; evolving concept of, 160ff, 164, 169–70, 174, 273–75, 292–93, 297–300 *passim*, 309f, 353; in American colleges, 79, 84; philosophy of, 80, 307f; punishments, 82, 88–89. *See also* Students: regimen of; Jesuits: philosophy of education
Disease: effect on mission, 9; at college, 49, 98, 134, 184, 203. *See also* Hygiene; Infirmaries
Donahue, Peter, 222
Donavon, Hugh, 238
Donohoe, Catherine, 203
Donohoe, Hugh A., 285
Donohoe Infirmary, 203, 303
Donohoe, Joseph, 105
Donohoe, Patrick A., 95, 284–98 *passim*, 296 (illus.), 304, 315
Donovan, Joseph, 181, 184
Downie, Harry, 219
Doyle, John T., 96, 107
Drahmann, John B., 279 (illus.), 302
Dramatics: study of, 58, 92, 99, 102–3, 142f; performances, 84, 133, 143, 186, 197, 216 (illus.), 244, 274. *See also* Buildings: theaters; *and names of specific plays*
Duce, Hugh, 255
Dueling, 59
Dunne (James H.) Hall, 289
Dunne, Peter M., 312, 372
Dye, Job F., 39

Earthquakes: effect of on Santa Clara, 9, 49, 95–96, 154–56, 167, 273; study of, 224, 363–64
Eberhard Tannery, 205 (illus.), 281
Economics: study of, 215, 294
Ecumenism, 3, 292, 319f
Education: study of, 215, 280; teacher of, 279 (illus.)
Edwards, Don, 298
Electivism, 3–4, 151–53, 171–72, 273f, 293–94, 309f
Elementary education: at the college, 28, 30, 58, 92, 96, 110, 170, 308
Elements of Molecular Mechanics, The, 112
Eliot, Charles W., 51, 152–53
"Eloquentia Perfecta," 99
Emergency Relief Agency, 231
Emig, William, 240
Endowment: of college, 129, 195–96, 199, 267–68, 280, 286, 288, 302, 313–17 *passim*
Engineering Council for Professional Development, 278
Engineering, College of: founding of, 171f, 175f, 179; degrees in, 216, 280, 290; during World War II, 261–62, 264; growth of, 278, 290; buildings of, 271, 290; deans of, 175, 279 (illus.), 302, 332 (listed); mentioned, 191–92, 203
Engineering Science Management War Training Program (ESMWT), 261
England, 55, 111f, 186, 259
English: study of, 40, 55, 108, 124, 214f, 304
Enrollment: figures, in 1800's, 27f, 50, 92, 96, 115; in 1900's, 193, 230–31, 304, 325 (listed, 1851–1978); fluctuations, 123, 129f, 280–83 *passim*, 364; small size of, 214, 250, 256ff, 267, 273f, 302, 308; during World War II, 260–63, 264; postwar, 265–67, 284–86, 292, 309, 317; mentioned, 205, 257, 283

Epidemics, *see* Disease
Estudillo, Jésus María, 39f, 308
Estudillo, José G., 40
Europe: and background of University, 7, 14–15,
    51–55, 307f, 310. *See also* Italy: Jesuits from
Evening Division, 265, 285
Evergreen, The (glider), 140
Evolution: teaching of, 150–51, 212, 224, 272
Examinations, 59

Faculty: anti-war protests, 299–300; and coeducation,
    284, *286; consultative role, 291, 302; growth of, 29,
    51–53, 92, 215, 284, 286, 304; Italians, 271; lay, 25,
    110, 268, 279, 309, 352; living accommodations of,
    45, 69; non-Catholic, 272–273; organizations of, 244,
    267, 291, 302, 316; prefecting duties, 82–84, 128, 131,
    160ff, 169, 273, 309; professionalism of, 179–80, 215,
    271–72, 278f, 297, 309, 311–12, 363, 372; publica-
    tions, 53, 61, 103–4, 111–13, 211–12, 248; quality of,
    47, 52–55, 71–72, 92, 111–13, 165, 280f, 291; rank of,
    291; recruitment of, 25, 29ff, 46f, 125–28, 311; re-
    search, 72, 111–13, 135–40, 211–12, 291; restrictions
    upon, 125, 272–73; salaries, 25, 176, 231, 266f, 271
    (listed), 280ff, 286, 291 (listed), 297; Spanish-
    speaking, 39; tenure, 281, 291; women, 317; work-
    load, 179; and World War II, 260–61; mentioned,
    99, 103, 143. *See also* Italy; Jesuits
Faculty Club, 69, 244. *See also* Adobe Lodge
Fagothey, Austin, 294
Falaschi, Nello, 250
Farley, James A., 244, 366
Farmers Insurance Group, 303
Feerick, Robert, 249, 278
Federal Aid, *see under* Financial Support
Fees, student, 39, 43, 75, 215. *See also* Tuition
Fence: surrounding college, 62, 67, 81, 87, 131, 145,
    168ff
Fencing: classes in, 62, 110
Fess Parker Studio Theater, 303
Finance: study of, 210, 216
Finances, *see* Budgets and Budgeting; Debts; Endow-
    ment; Financial Support; Fund Drives
Financial Support: college seeks self-sufficiency, 97–99,
    114–15, 234; Federal programs, 231, 261–66 *passim*,
    281, 288f, 295; football revenues, 250, 255ff; gifts, 64,
    177, 202–3, 269ff, 280, 288–91 *passim*, 302–3, 313–14;
    from Jesuit community, 297; State programs, 42,
    275, 301–2; wealthy image of college, 97, 133, 232ff,
    314–16 *passim*. *See also* Budgets and Budgeting; En-
    dowment; *names of individual benefactors*
Fine Arts: study of, 92, 99, 151, 271, 291, 294
Fires: on campus, 156–57, 159 (illus.), 217–18, 221
    (illus.)
First Book of Ethics, The, 212
Fitzgerald, Justin, 145
Flaim, Francis R., 271
Flood, James C., 75
Flood, James L., 269
Flynn, Hubert, 192
Football, 143–45, 186–93, 248–57, 258, 275–78; men-
    tioned, 232, 246, 289–90, 313, 367, 369. *See also*
    Athletics
Forbes, James Alexander, 26, 30–35 *passim*, 39f, 43

Ford Foundation, 280
Fordham University (N.Y.), 51, 193, 295
Foster, Julian, 371
France, 53, 71, 98, 181, 187, 221, 259
Franciscans, 8–12 *passim*, 24, 68. *See also names of specific
    persons*
Fribourg, College of (Switzerland), 53
Frémont, John C., 11
French: study of, 27, 92, 108
Freiden, John, 118
From Backwater to Mainstream, 306
Fund Drives: Kenna and, 113f, 132f; to relocate college,
    134, 154–57; competition with St. Ignatius College,
    160, 180; Morrissey and, 167; in 1922, 196–202; to
    restore mission, 218; for observatory, 225; during
    World War II, 263, 268, 314ff; postwar, 266–69
    passim, 316; contemporary, 288–89, 292, 302. *See also*
    Budgets and Budgeting; Debts; Financial Support

Gagan, Brian, 255
Gallagher, Desmond, 143
Gallagher, Richard, 276
Gallant Journey, 140
Galvin, James, 83 (illus.)
Gaudin, Harold, 365
Geology: study of, 124, 245
Geometry: study of, 108, 124
Georgetown University (Washington, D.C.), 29, 51,
    72, 93, 193, 295, 352
Gerlach, Fred, 144
German: study of, 27, 92, 245
G.I. Bill, 263–66, 364
Gianera, William C., 203, 256, 264–69 *passim*, 270
    (illus.), 274, 369
Giannini, Ralph, 249
"Glacier Priest," *see* Hubbard, Bernard R.
Gleason, Philip: quoted, 310, 319f
Gleeson, Richard, 55, 134, 154–157 *passim*, 166, 316
Golden Circle Theatre Party, 303
Goller, Herman J., 158ff, 163ff, 166
Gompers, Samuel, 143
Gonzaga University (Wash.), 51
González Rubio, José María de Jesús, 13f, 17, 341
Gorman, Mel: quoted, 72, 112
Grabhorn Press, 212
Graduate Studies, 172, 278, 280, 290–91, 309. *See also*
    Degrees
Graham, Charles, 83 (illus.), 145, 255
Graham Residence Center, 289
Grammar School: at the college, 28, 30, 58, 92, 96, 110,
    170, 308
Gray, John H., 302
Great Awakening, The, 1
Greek: study of, 3, 27, 55–58 *passim*, 245; declining
    importance, 122–24, 171–72, 177, 215, 280, 307. *See
    also* Classical studies
Greeley, Andrew M.: quoted, 306, 372
Greene, Clay M., 103, 133
Gregorian University, *see* Pontifical Gregorian Uni-
    versity
Griffith, Michael, 83 (illus.)
Grounds: described, 26, 44, 194, 262; expansion of, 26,
    50, 98, 132ff, 163, 167, 271, 281; illustrations of, 10,

26, 44, 63, 70, 91, 101, 235; worth of (1860's), 78, 348. *See also* Mission gardens; Properties
Guadalupe River, 8, 9, 85
Guglielmetti, Henry, 83 (illus.)

Hagan, Frank and Mrs., 303
Hale, Bruce, 249
Hamman, Anthony P., 282
Hancock, Marian, 289
Handball, 85
Hanna, Edward J., 66, 191, 206, 251f, 364
Hardin, Barry, 145
Harland, Henry, 143
Harmon, Robert, 187
Hart, Brooke, 239–243 *passim*
Hartnell, William, 14
Harvard University (Mass.), 1, 51, 79, 102, 144, 151f, 274, 356
Hastings School of Law (Calif.), 48
Hauck, Herman J., 274–83 *passim*, 315, 370
Hawaii (and Hawaiians), 27, 41, 192, 223, 250, 259
Hayes, Arthur Hull, Jr., 282
Hayes, James, 209
Heafey, Edwin A., 290
Health, *see* Hygiene
Hennessy, Francis, 83
Henry, David D.: quoted, 230
Henry Garnett, 143
Hereford, E., 75
Herrold, Charles D., 136
Hichborn, Franklin, 129, 135
High School: of the college, 28, 56ff, 92, 96, 115, 133, 170, 182, 201; curriculum, 58, 110, 171–72; separated from college, 204–10, 308, 312
Hill, Andrew P., 140–43 *passim*, 149 (illus.)
History: study of, 56, 215
Hofstader, Richard: quoted, 5–6
Holmes, Jack, 239
Holy Cross College (Mass.), 295
Honorary degrees, 107, 135, 244, 315, 337–38, 363
Hoover, President Herbert, 221, 243–44
Horton, Edward J., 238f, 365
Hubbard, Bernard R., 245–48
Humanities, College of, 215, 261; deans, 331. *See also* Arts and Sciences, College of
Huntington, Collis P., 102
Hyde, Douglas, 135
Hygiene, 9, 45, 82, 95, 169. *See also* Disease
Hynes, John, 267, 280–81

Immigration: Catholic, 2f, 51–55, 314, 319. *See also* Catholicism; Italy; Nativism
Imoda, Henry, 53
Imperial Valley, California, 234
In loco parentis: demise of, 4, 293
Indians, 8f, 14f, 61f, 218. *See also* Mission Santa Clara
IRA, 186
Ireland (and Irish), 3, 40, 53, 55, 114, 147, 185–86, 300
Isbell, Olive Mann, 37
Italian: study of, 92, 271
Italy (and Italians): Jesuits from, 30, 47–55 *passim*, 71f, 111–13, 118–21 *passim*, 169, 307f, 345, 353; mentioned, 3, 7, 14–15, 108, 244, 271, 300. *See*

also Turin, Italy (Jesuit province of); Jesuits
Ivancovich, John, 143

James, Henry, 143
Janssens, John B., 285
Japan (and Japanese), 160, 259f
Jesuit Educational Association, 210, 256, 272, 278
Jesuits: athletics and, 61f, 144, 187ff, 253–57, 276f, 353; business capacity of, 34ff, 80, 93, 97, 99, 114, 269, 314–17 *passim*; contemporary education and, 292–99 *passim*, 304–5, 317–20 *passim*; disagreements among, 55, 117–23, 174–75, 207–10, 232–34, 364f; education of, 125, 127–28, 179–80, 311–12, 359, 363, 372; educational philosophy of, 4, 55–59, 79–91 *passim*, 118–24, 272–73, 306–11 *passim*, 353; financial support from, 268, 297, 317; found college, 7, 24–31 *passim*, 59; manpower shortage, 25, 29ff, 46–49 *passim*, 125–28, 165, 180, 311–12; oppose secular education, 106, 146–53 *passim*, 179–80, 213–15 *passim*, 312; opposition to, 2, 19, 22, 53, 74, 98, 105–6; parish work of, 5, 22, 127, 158, 363; scholastics, 87, 98, 117, 122–28 *passim*, 166, 169, 175, 233. *See also* California Mission; California Province; Roman Church authorities
Jesuits, *see specific names*; Roman Catholic authorities
Jews, 90, 289
Jimmy "The Greek" Snyder, 275
John Carroll University (Ohio), 51
Johns Hopkins University, 222
Johnson, Sen. Hiram, 259
Jordan, David Starr, 142, 224
Joset, Joseph, 17f
Journalism: study of, 103, 151, 171
Junior Dramatic Society, 134

Kanemoto, Wayne K., 260
Kavanagh, D. J., 143
Keefe, Robert, 145
Keith, William M., 39
Kenna Hall, 201–8 *passim*, 290, 358
Kenna, Robert, 113–24 *passim*, 128f, 131–35 *passim*, 140–43 *passim*, 149 (illus.), 154–61 *passim*, 166; mentioned, 186, 212, 313, 316, 353
Kennedy, John F., 290, 319
Kerr, Jerry, 286
Kezar Stadium (San Francisco), 190, 249ff, 276
King, James, 267, 281
King, Thomas Starr, 75
Kino, Eusebio Francisco, 14
Knight, Gov. Goodwin J., 275
Knights of Columbus, 225, 227
Know-Nothing Movement, 40f
Korean War, 280
Korte, Norbert, 255
Ku Klux Klan, 143, 200

Labor movement, in California, *see under* Unionism
Lafayette College (Penn.), 150
Laity: at university, 320. *See also* Faculty, lay; Trustees, lay participation
Languages: study of, 27, 45, 56, 61, 151, 171, 215. *See also specific languages*
Larkin, Thomas O., 32–33

Lateran Treaty, 244
Latin: study of, 3, 27, 55–58, 215; declining importance of, 122–24, 171–72, 177, 280, 307. *See also* Classical Studies; Greek
Latin America: students from, 39, 115, 300
Lautze, Richard, 286
Law School: beginnings, 108, 110, 151, 171f, 179; buildings for, 48, 202, 283, 290, 302; aided by athletic income, 256–57; growth of, 210, 215, 261, 278, 290, 302–3; deans listed, 331
Leavey, Thomas A., 303
Leavey Activities Center, 303
Ledochowski, Wlodimir, 208, 213, 232–33
Leo XIII, Pope, 113
Leonard, Thomas P., 121 (illus.)
Lessons in Scholastic Philosophy, 212
"Letter A": punishment, 88–89
Lewis, Melvin, 371
Laxalt, Sen. Paul, 273
Libraries, 26, 47, 69, 90, 92, 212, 283, 309. *See also names of specific libraries*
Lick Observatory (Calif.), 223
Lifeboat (theater), 303
Light Eternal, The, 143
Lindsley (President, University of Nashville), 130
Liquor: forbidden, 82, 315. *See also* Wine
Literary Congress: of college, 102; founder of, 86 (illus.)
Literary Digest, The, 248
Literary Studies, 142
Literature: study of, 55f, 92, 123–24, 171
"Little Big Game," 190–92
Liturgy, 212. *See also* Religion
Lockheed Aircraft, 138
Long, Gov. Huey, 253
Los Angeles: proposed move of college to, 158–65 *passim*, 169, 311, 314; students from, 43, 358; mentioned, 17, 102, 223, 230, 260. *See also* Loyola Marymount University
Los Gatos, 98, 117, 127, 136, 166, 264
Lougheed, Victor, 138
Louisiana State University, 253f
Lowe, Edmund, 143
Loyola College (Calif.), *see* Loyola Marymount University
Loyola Corners (Calif.): proposed site for college, 134, 154–57, 160–67 *passim*; sold, 202, 263, 358
Loyola High School (Los Angeles, Calif.), 314
Loyola Marymount University (Calif.): origins, 158–65 *passim*, 180, 311; mentioned, 210, 234, 255, 297, 302, 372
Loyola University (Calif.), *see* Loyola Marymount University
Loyola University (Louisiana), 365
Ludwig, Dr. James B., 303
Lynching, in San Jose: 239–43, 365
Lyons, James, 231–34 *passim*, 243–44, 250–52, 255ff, 314f, 364ff

McClatchy, Charles, 102, 133, 135, 142, 148, 308
McClatchy, Valentine, 102, 308
McClellan, George B., 211
McCoy, Cornelius, 203, 214–21 *passim*, 225–31 *passim*, 255f, 265

McKenzie, Harry, 255
McKinley, Pres. William, 135
McKinnon, Harold, 268
McKinnon, William D., 147
McLaughlin, Edward, 281
McLoughlin, John, 14
McPherson, Aimee Semple, 234
McQuade, Joseph, 147
MacQuarrie, Thomas, 236–37
Madigan, Edward P. "Slip," 190
Maher, Zacheus, 188–89 *passim*, 194–213 *passim*, 224f, 231, 265, 268, 316; later career of, 213, 232–34, 238, 251f, 312, 314f, 364f, 367
Malley, George P., 290
Malone, John T., 103
Maloney, Daniel, 138ff
Maloney, Emile, 255
Management: study of, 216, 261
Mann, Horace, 37
Mao Tse-tung, 293
Maraschi, Anthony, 47
Marconi, Guglielmo, 136, 244
Marquette University (Wisc.), 253
Martín, Luis, 133–34
Marx, Karl, 305. *See also* Communism
Maryland Province (Jesuit), 55, 65f, 102
Masnata, Aloysius, 47, 93
Mason, Col. Robert B., 11
Mathematics: study of, 28, 53, 92, 108, 113, 215, 222, 261
Mayer, Louis B., 303
Mayer Theater, 303
Men, deans of: listed, 332
Mengarini, Gregory, 61, 63
Mercantile Course, *see* Commercial Course
Merle, Martin, 143, 197, 216
Merriam, Gov. Frank M., 236, 252
Messea, Charles, 47, 72, 121 (illus.), 135
Meteorology, *see* Ricard, Jerome S.
Methodists: in Calif., 28, 38, 135, 206, 222
Mexican-Americans, 300
Mexicans: attend Santa Clara, 39, 115. *See also* Latin America: students from
Mexican War, 11–14 *passim*, 49
Mexico, 9–13 *passim*, 39, 64, 115, 217ff
Meyer, Rudolph, 124–25
Miami, University of (Fla.), 275
Michigan State University, 254
Military training, 67, 74–75, 92, 181–84, 238, 259, 262f, 264 (illus.); protests about, 237, 300. *See also* ROTC
Miller, Henry, 143
Miller, Mr. (architect), 203
Mills College (Calif.), 268
Mineralogy: study of, 70–71, 92, 307
Mission Church, 10, 15f, 26, 33, 44, 62, 184, 304; remodeled and restored, 69f, 115–17, 217–21, 318; illustrations of (exterior), 10, 26, 44, 70, 91, 100, 126, 221, 318; illustrations of (interior), 16, 116
Mission Dolores (San Francisco), 8, 35
Mission gardens, 44f, 68; illustrations of, 101, 121, 126, 139, 156, 159
Mission Play of Santa Clara, The, 103, 143, 197
Mission San Jose (Calif.), 22
Mission Santa Clara, 8f, 11f, 17, 26, 33, 44, 62, 69;

transferred to Jesuits, 7, 15–27 *passim*, 66, 342, 363; property disputes, 11f, 23–27 *passim*, 31–36 *passim*; vineyard, 11f, 26, 34, 97; orchard, 12, 26, 32–34, 61, 63, 144; adobe buildings remodeled, 25–27, 31, 49, 68–69, 159; bells of, 217–21 *passim*; mentioned, 62, 105, 303f, 361

Missouri Province (Jesuit), 55, 124

Mitty, John J., 285

Monitor (San Francisco), 147

Monterey, California, 11, 19, 22–23, 37

Montgomery, George, 148

Montgomery, John J., 135–40 *passim*, 139 (illus.), 141 (illus.), 143, 211

Montgomery laboratories, 203, 282–83

Montgomery, Zachariah, 106

Monthly Santa Claran, The, 267

Morrissey, James P., 157–76 *passim*, 178 (illus.), 180, 194, 212, 309–16 *passim*, 357–60 *passim*

Moulder, Andrew J., 57

Mountain View, California, 134, 146, 154–58, 202, 316, 358. *See also* Loyola Corners

Mount St. Michael's (Spokane), 233

Mount Wilson Observatory (Calif.), 225

Murphy, Dr. James D., 290

Murphy, John, 33–34

Murphy, Bernard, 308

Murphy, Martin, Jr., 19, 39f, 49

Murphy, Timothy; presidency of, 185–89 *passim*, 195

Mush, You Malemutes!, 248

Music: at mission, 26f; at college, 27, 58, 62–63, 67, 92, 103, 110, 135

Nash, John Henry, 212

Nation, The, 144

National Geographic, 246

Nativism, 53, 98, 105–6, 147, 200. *See also* Immigration; Jesuits, opposition to

Nazareth (Santa Clara Passion Play), 133, 244, 274

Negroes, 300, 371

Neri, Joseph, 71f, 135

Nevada, 69, 71, 75, 127, 273

New Deal, 231, 234

Newlin, Albert, 227–28

Newman, John Henry, 293

New Orleans, Louisiana, 253f

New York, N. Y., 145, 248f, 364

New York Times, The, 144

New Zealand, 186

Nisei, 260

Nobili, John: background, 7f, 18–23 *passim*, 53, 55, 59, 67; presidency of, 3, 24–49 *passim*, 82, 95–96, 343; death of, 44, 49f, 61ff; mentioned, 110, 117, 120, 173, 312

Nobili Hall, 100, 156, 214, 216, 244, 257f, 260, 265

Nobili Medal: winners, 335–36

"Normalcy" of 1920's, 184–93 *passsim*

Northwestern Association, 278

Norton, Thomas, 83 (illus.)

Noticias de la Nueva California, 107

Notre Dame: sisters of, 17

Notre Dame College (Calif.), *see* College of Notre Dame

Notre Dame University (Indiana), 29, 51, 190, 192f

Nurses: training program of, 285

Oakland, 227, 308

Oberammergau, Germany, 220

O'Brien, Joseph D., 276–77

Observatories, *see* Ricard Observatory

O'Connor Hall, 169, 182, 185 (illus.), 358

O'Connor Hospital (San Jose), 285

Olivier, Louis, 98

Olivieri, Umberto, 271

Olympic Games, 187

O'Malley, Martha P., 287

O'Neill, Paloma, 289

Orange Bowl, 275f

Oregon Province (Jesuit), 7, 14–20 *passim*, 25, 29, 52, 61, 232

Orradre, Michel, 291

Orradre Library, 211, 281, 291, 315

Osio, Antonio, 33

Our Lady of Sorrows (Santa Barbara), 158

Owens, Edwin J., 278

Owens Valley Project (Calif.), 223

Owl, The (student magazine), 104–5, 142, 244

Oxford University (England), 237

Pacifism: on U.S. campuses, 237, 299–301

"Padre of the Rains," *see* Ricard, Jerome S.

Palóu, Francisco, 8, 107

Panelli, Edward A., 295

Panic of 1893, 115, 129ff, 132

Parden, Robert J., 279 (illus.), 290, 302

Paris, France, 53, 71, 181, 187

Passion Play of Santa Clara, The, 103

Patrick, Stan, 249

Pershing, Gen. John J., 181

Phelan, Sen. James D., 135, 142, 154, 198 (illus.), 200ff

Phi Beta Kappa, 291

Philalethic Debating Society, 31 (illus.), 99

Philhistorian Debating Society, 103, 113

Philippine Islands, 147–48, 260

Philosophy: study of, 3, 53, 56, 59, 92, 104, 117, 273f, 305; teachers of, 111–13, 150–51, 212, 222, 272, 294, 372; requirements in, 123–24, 172, 210, 215–16, 280, 294

Photography: study of, 92. *See also* Hubbard, Bernard R.

Physics: study of, 53, 71, 92, 112–13, 124

Pico, Andrés, 12, 34

Pico, Gov. Pío, 32–33

Picpus Fathers (Congregation of Sacred Hearts of Jesus and Mary), 23, 35

Piet, Joseph, 207

Pike, James, 245, 366

Pinasco, John, 111–15 *passim*, 121, 124f, 128f, 131

Pinero, Jose, 39

Pinyero, José María, 19, 22, 341

Pious Fund, 12

Pitt, Leonard: quoted, 39

Poison Drops in the Federal Senate, 106

Political Science: study of, 108, 215, 238

Pomona College (Calif.), 268

Pontifical Gregorian University (Rome), 271, 363

Posey, Addison C., 360

Pound, Roscoe, 274

Powell, John Wesley, 61
Power, Edward J.: quoted, 28, 51, 193, 311
Prefects of Discipline, 166, 177; listed, 332
Prefects of Studies, 166; listed, 331
Premedicine: study of, 152, 171, 210, 261
President, of university: term of office, 63, 65, 95, 128;
    authority of, 65–66, 125, 232–34, 251–52, 267, 276f,
    315; first American, 114; office-holders listed, 331;
    qualifications of, 243, 263–65, 274–75, 284, 297,
    303–4, 316. See also names of specific persons
President's Day, 91 (illus.), 138, 244
Presidents of the Alumni Council: listed, 334
Presidents of student body: listed, 333
Press, of the college. See Santa Clara College Press
Priests: effects of early California on, 11f, 18
Princeton University (N.J.), 1, 150
Printing: study of, 92
Prizes: student, 59, 350; medal winners, 60 (illus.);
    Nobili medal winners listed, 335–36; St. Clare medal
    winners listed, 336
Professions: education for, 3–4, 171–72
Progressivism: in California, 135
Prohibition: Jesuit opposition to, 212, 215, 224, 244
Properties: early disputes over, 11f, 23–27 passim, 31–36
    passim, 62–63, 105. See also Grounds; Loyola
    Corners; Vineyards
Prosperity: of 1880's, 115; of 1920's, 197, 200
Prostitution: near college, 62
Protestants, in California: clergy, 20, 37; attend Santa
    Clara, 41–43, 90, 93, 146–47, 162; mentioned, 22, 40.
    See also Catholic-Protestant tension; Colleges, Pro-
    testant
Publications, of university, 267. See also Santa Clara
    College Press
Publicity: office of, 316
Public Relations: vice-presidents for, 332 (listed)

Radio: and college, 135–37, 240, 246, 248, 261, 355
Raffo, Paul, 53
Railroads, 67, 68–69, 72–73, 96, 102, 154, 167f, 185
Ramer, Edward, 83 (illus.)
Ratio Studiorum, 56f, 111, 118–19, 120, 122, 124,
    353, 356
Reagan, Gov. Ronald, 299
Real, Padre, see Suarez del Real
Realis Philosophiae, 112
Rector: of Jesuit community, 66, 297
Redman, Joshua, 33
Redwoods, see Big Basin Park
Redwood, The, 142–43, 144, 183
Regents, Board of, 288–89, 290, 294–95
Regis High School (N.Y.), 348
Registrar: of university, 257, 259
Reglamento para el gobierno de la Provincia de Californias,
    104, 107
Regulations, for students, see Discipline; Students
Reid, Alfred D., Jr., 352
Reid, Bernard J., 40, 62, 95–96, 110, 352
Religion: place in curriculum, 1–5, 89–91, 148–51 pas-
    sim, 213–16 passim, 272–73, 294, 298f, 304–7 passim,
    320–21; disputes about, 40–43, 200, 224, 292–93, 366;
    study of, 56, 92, 172, 280, 294; compulsory Mass
    attendance, 43, 46, 82, 90, 119–20, 125, 177, 272;
    teachers of, 53, 111–13, 211f, 224, 294

Religious studies, see Religion
Residence halls, see under Buildings
Reuf, Abraham, 135
Rewak, William, 303, 304–5, 320–21
Rhodes scholarship, 282
Ricard, Jerome S., 211, 221–29, 226 (illus.), 363–64
Ricard Observatory, 100, 216, 221–29 passim, 363–64
Rickert, Jim, 249
Río Guadalupe, see Guadalupe River
Riordan, Joseph, 35, 118, 130ff, 133, 144, 161
Riordan, Patrick W., 133, 148, 151, 154, 164, 175, 313
Rock, Leo P., 297
Rockhurst College (Mo.), 345
Rockliff, James A., 160–65 passim, 175, 357
Rockne, Knute, 192
Rodés, Luis, 220
Rolph, Gov. James, 242–43
Roman church authorities, influence on college: and
    Jesuit ministry in California, 17, 20–22, 29–30, 47;
    and academic issues, 57, 113, 120, 352; and admin-
    istration, 65f, 174–77 passim; and Jesuit training,
    179–80, 312, 359; and finances, 207–8, 231, 232–33,
    357, 364–65; and football, 277, 367; mentioned, 108,
    133–34, 213, 275, 285, 290, 297, 309, 315. See also
    Vatican Council II
Roman College (Rome), 53, 111
Rome, University of, 271
Rooney, Edward B., 256, 272
Roosevelt, Pres. Franklin D., 153, 244, 259
Roosevelt, Pres. T. R., 135
Roothan, John, 17, 20, 22, 29–30
Rose Bowl, 253
Rosso, Augusto, 244
ROTC, 181–83 passim, 237f, 259, 280, 298–300, 301
    (illus.), 360, 365, 371
Rudolph, Louis, 232, 234, 256–57
Rudy, Willis: quoted, 4, 285
Rugby, 145, 186–87, 191
Runyan, Damon, 253
Ryan, Edmund, 192, 195, 265
Ryan Field, 34, 63, 192

Sacramento, 43, 134
Sacramento Bee, 102, 135, 142
Sacred Heart Novitiate (Los Gatos), 98, 117, 136,
    166, 264
Salvatierra, Juan, 14
San Diego, 137, 140
San Francisco: during gold rush, 7, 18f, 23, 27, 33, 50;
    schools in, 37f, 42; students from, 43; and college, 58,
    72, 107, 143, 154f, 212, 218, 222, 238; earthquake
    (1906), 154–56; and college football, 154–56, 190,
    249–51 passim, 276; mentioned, 67f, 136, 184, 223,
    234, 240, 266. See also Mission Dolores; University of
    San Francisco
San Francisco, Archbishop of: transfers Santa Clara to
    Jesuits, 23f; properties at college, 32, 34; influence at
    college, 65, 75, 77, 154, 164, 191, 251, 285–86, 363f;
    mentioned, 77, 148–51, 206, 313. See also names of
    specific Archbishops
San Francisco Call, 187, 189f
San Francisco Chronicle, 237
San Francisco Examiner, 138, 242
San Jose: early history of, 9, 19, 24, 39; Jesuits in, 22,

127, 147f, 163; students and, 43, 119, 177; growth of, 68, 258, 266; and college, 75, 131, 136, 140f, 143, 148, 197, 200, 253–57 passim, 282; lynching in (1933), 236, 239–43; mentioned, 68, 133, 135, 148, 155, 184, 206, 260
San Jose Mercury-News, 371
San Jose News, 262
San Jose State College, 236
San Mateo, 127
San Pedro, 102
Sandino, Leo, 83 (illus.)
Santa Barbara, 17, 19, 43, 158f
Santa Clara (town of): and mission, 11, 32, 68; and college, 43, 105, 131–34 passim, 163, 167, 196f, 200, 282; supports college football, 187, 257; photograph of, 235; mentioned, 28, 184, 258, 260
Santa Clara, The (glider), 138, 139 (illus.)
Santa Clara, The (student newspaper), 237, 240–45 passim, 265, 285–86, 287 (illus.)
Santa Clara Cadet Corps, 74
Santa Clara College, see University of Santa Clara
Santa Clara College Press, 92, 98, 103–5, 107, 110
Santa Clara Journal, 187
Santa Clara Plan, 291
"Santa Clara Tree" (Big Basin Park, Calif.), 149 (illus.)
Santa Clara Valley: and mission, 8f, 11, 23, 218; development of, 67, 73, 258, 282; and college, 97, 127, 134, 147, 200, 212, 253ff, 282; mentioned, 95, 234, 235 (illus.)
Santa Clara Valley Youth Center, 282
Santa Cruz, 131, 135, 144, 166, 245, 280
Santa Monica, 102
Santiago (play), 143
Sasia, Joseph, 211
Saturday Evening Post, The, 246
Schiechl, John, 250
Schmidt, Frank C., 355
Schmidt, Walter, 282
Scholarships: number of, 75, 170, 215, 231, 256, 286, 300ff, 309; G.I. Bill, 263, 266; mentioned, 244, 275, 282, 358, 360
Scholz, Rudy, photo, 191
School of Law; see Law School
Science: Study of, 45, 47, 56ff, 69, 71ff, 123–24, 215, 307. See also Bayma, J.; Hubbard, B., Montgomery, J. J.; Ricard, J. S.
Science Hall, 69, 101 (illus.), 108, 156 (illus.), 195
Sciences, College of: Deans, 279 (illus.), 302, 331 (listed)
Seattle University (Wash.), 51
Secularism, in American higher education, see under Colleges, Catholic; Colleges, Protestant; University of Santa Clara
Sedgley, George, 173 (illus.)
Seeliger, Francis, 256
Seifert, George, 202
Seifert Gymnasium, 197, 202–3, 259
Seismology: study of, 224, 228, 363–64. See also Earthquakes
Selective Service Act, 259
Sempervirens Club, 140, 142
Senior Hall, see O'Connor Hall
Serra, Junípero, 9
Shafer, Arthur, 145

Shakespeare, William, 103
Shallo, Michael, 212
Shaw, George Bernard, 293
Shaw, Lawrence "Buck," 235
Sherman, William Tecumseh, 74
Ship, The (theater), 94–96, 102, 143, 182, 203, 303, 350; illustrations of, 91, 100, 216
Shipsey, Edward, 214
Simon, Yves, 274
Sinclair, Upton, 236
Sinn Fein: and college, 186
Smith, James F., 102, 147–48
Smith, Lewis, 364
Smith, Maurice "Clipper," 253
Smithsonian Institution (Washington, D.C.), 140, 228
Social Sciences, 291
Society of Jesus, see Jesuits
Sociology, 294
Sonora, 19
South, Charles D., 143
Southern Pacific Railroad, 68, 102, 167
Spain (and Spaniards), 8–9, 22, 29–30, 62, 220, 341
Spanish, study of, 27, 92, 108
Spanish-American War: Catholic role in, 147–48
Spearman, Arthur, 140
Spokane (Wash.), 161, 233
Spring Hill College (Ala.), 51
S. S. Santa Clara, 263
St. Clare of Assisi, 8, 220
St. Clare's Church (Santa Clara), 363
St. Clare Medal: winners listed, 335–36
St. Francis of Assisi, 8, 220
St. Ignatius, 16
St. Ignatius College, see University of San Francisco
St. John the Baptist, 220
St. Joseph's Church (San Jose), 127, 147
St. Joseph's Hall, 63, 167ff, 211, 264, 357f
St. Louis (Mo.), 14, 20
St. Louis University (Mo.), 29, 51, 57, 124, 284
St. Mary's College (Calif.): founding of, 77, 348; and athletics, 144ff, 189–93 passim, 250–53, 255, 276, 364, 367
St. Patrick, 16
St. Vincent's College (Calif.), 158–65, 180, 357, 350. See also Loyola Marymount University; Loyola High School
Staff: of university, 99, 176, 214, 291, 300
Stanford, Gov. Leland, 74
Stanford Daily, The, 236, 242, 367
Stanford University: and Santa Clara, 93, 129, 142, 146, 160, 162, 242, 268; athletic competition with Santa Clara, 144f, 186f, 191ff, 253f; mentioned, 236, 262, 280, 312, 369
Stanton, Col. Charles, 181, 360
Stanton Field, 360
Starr, Kevin: quoted, 67
Stearns, Abel, 39
Stephens, Gov. William, 197
Stockton, 43, 197, 206
Stoddard, Charles Warren, 103
Stonyhurst College (England), 111
Strub, Charles, 145
Strub, Vera, 289
Student Body presidents, 333

Student refectory, *see under* Buildings
Student Services: Vice Presidents for, 332
Student Union, *see under* Buildings
Students: ages of, 28f, 45, 62, 80ff, 85, 261; antiwar activities of, 237, 298–301 *passim*; and coeducation, 285–86; competition among, 59; confinement of, 62, 85–87, 119–20, 131, 169–170, 273–74; day commuters, 27, 82, 170, 281; diversions of, 45, 61–62, 84–85, 91 (illus.), 188, 191–92, 243–45, 248ff, 273–74; during Depression, 230–50 *passim*; economic background of, 39f, 75–77, 215, 231, 244, 300–301, 314, 366; ethnic groups among, 300; fees, 39, 43, 75, 215; living accommodations, 27, 43–46, 61, 169, 265, 273, 298, 300; married, 265; student body presidents, 286, 333 (listed); prostitution and, 62; publications, 104f, 182–83, 232–44 *passim*; rebellion of, 86–89, 176f, 236–38, 298–301 *passim*; regimen of, 45f, 81–85, 119–20, 169–70, 182–84, 273–77, 307, 353; religion of, 40–43, 90, 93, 146–47, 162, 215; surveys of attitudes of, 259, 371. *See also* Coeducation
Students' Chapel, 117, 132, 217
Suarez del Real, José María del Refugio, 11–13, 23f, 26, 32–33, 49, 62, 340
Sugar Bowl, 253f
Suicide: debated by students, 59
Sullivan Engineering Center, 281, 290
Sullivan, George L., 175, 179, 290
Summer session, 265
Suñol, Dolores, 39
Sunspot, The, 211, 223f
Surveying: study of, 92
Swett, John, 5, 38, 42, 67, 78
Swig, Benjamin H., 288–89, 296 (illus.), 302ff
Swig, Mae, 289
Swig Hall, 289
Swimming pools, 61, 63 (illus.), 202f, 303

Teacher-training, 280
Technocracy Movement, 234
Telegraphy: study of, 92, 110, 136–37
Temple, John, 75
Terra, Stan, 273
Terry, Thomas D., 284, 291, 295–99 *passim*, 302ff
Texas A & M University, 254
Texas Christian University, 253
Textbooks, 27, 113, 211
Tewksbury, Donald G.: quoted, 1, 130, 155
Thámien (Indian name for region), 8
Thaw, Harry K., 102
Theaters, *see under* Buildings. *See also* Dramatics
Theology, *see* Alma College; Religion
Thompson, Alpheus, 39
Thornton, Walter, 176–77, 181, 185, 311
Thurmond, Thomas, 239
Time (magazine), 238, 274
Tobacco: use of, 82–87 *passim*, 120, 124, 173
Tocqueville, Alexis de, 1, 4
Tortore, Bartholomew, 99
Toso, Harold J., 303
Towell, Mr. (San Francisco teacher), 46
Townsend Plan, 234
Treasurer: of college, 61, 163, 313
Trustees, 65f, 329–30 (listed); lay participation, 110, 288, 295, 294–99 *passim*, 302, 304, 317–20 *passim*;

chairman of, 288, 296, 304; mentioned, 40, 231, 261, 271, 280f, 285, 297, 299, 302f
Tuition, 75, 77, 130, 231f, 268f, 282, 286, 313, 348; increases, 215, 271, 280, 288, 317, 369; affects enrollments, 57, 75, 77, 300, 314
Turel, George L., 290
Turin, Italy (Jesuit province of), mission in California: 47, 52–58 *passim*, 66, 110, 117–18, 345
Twohy, James F., 152–53, 356

Union Pacific Railroad, 67
Unionism: in California, 143, 196, 212, 234, 236–37, 239, 272, 274
United States Bureau of Education, 84
United States Coast and Geodetic Survey, 246
United States Land Commission, 23, 25, 32
U.S.S. Akron, 244
United States War Dept., 181
United States Weather Bureau, 222f
University of California, Berkeley, 93, 128–29, 236–39 *passim*; competition with, 144ff, 160, 162, 186f, 249f, 252, 255; Newman Center at, 151, 313; and Santa Clara, 103–7 *passim*, 128–29, 150, 210, 215, 354, 363, 365; mentioned, 1, 38, 107, 130, 142, 224, 268, 313, 372
University of California, Davis, 297
University of California, Los Angeles, 236–37, 239, 245
University of Detroit (Mich.), 193, 255
University of Kentucky, 275
University of Michigan, 128
University of Minnesota, 304
University of Nashville (Tenn.), 130
University of Nevada, 187, 276
University of Pennsylvania, 144
University of Portland (Ore.), 276
University of Redlands (Calif.), 268
University of San Francisco, 1, 38, 47, 111ff, 114, 117, 128, 130, 365; and Santa Clara, 72, 102, 137, 160, 192, 245, 249, 251ff, 276; difficulties of, 97, 123–27 *passim*, 155, 165, 180
University of Southern California, 186, 302
University of the Pacific (Calif.): early history of, 1, 28, 38, 41, 58; relocation of, 93, 129, 197, 206, 208; mentioned, 130, 135, 192, 212, 252, 369
University of Toronto, 372

Vallejo, Napoleon, 39, 308
Vanderbilt, Cornelius, 68
Varsi, Aloysius, 52f, 72, 88, 93–97 *passim*, 94 (illus.), 102, 106–8 *passim*, 352
Varsi Library, 100, 203, 216, 283, 291
Vásquez del Mercado, Jesús María, 12
Vatican Council, Second, 4, 284, 292–95 *passim*, 299, 309, 319
Veterans' Village, 265
Veyret, Francis, 87
Veysey, Laurence: quoted, 79, 122
Viader, José, 9
Vice-Presidents, University, *see under specific titles*
Vietnam War: protests against, 299–300, 301 (illus.), 371
Villa Maria, 97–98, 136, 244, 263
Villiger, Burchard, 52, 65–68 *passim*, 72–78 *passim*, 92, 100, 105, 194, 284

Vincentians (Congregation of the Missions), 158–60
  passim, 165
Vineyards, of Santa Clara, 11f, 26, 34, 97–98, 100,
  114–15, 121–26 passim. See also Villa Maria; Wine
Vocational training: attitudes toward, 3–6 passim, 108,
  120–24, 171–72, 306–7, 310; during World War II,
  262–63
Volstead Act. See Prohibition

Walsh, Adam, 192
Walsh, Charles J., 260–64 passim, 268, 272–73, 293, 314
Walsh, Delia L., 269
Walsh, Henry L., 260
Walsh, James E., 269
Warburton, Dr. H. H., 99
Warner, Glenn "Pop," 192
Warren, Gov. Earl, 275
Weber, Francis, J., 158
Welch, Andrew J., 154
Welch, Bertha, 154
Welch, Robert, 293
Wernz, Franz, 174–79 passim, 311
West Point Military Academy (N.Y.), 80, 181
Western Association of Schools and Colleges, 275, 278
Western Gear Corporation, 290
Westlake, Elmer, 83 (illus.)

Whelan, Edward, 251
Wheeler, Benjamin Ide, 150
White, Sen. Stephen M., 102
White, Stanford, 102
Williams College (Mass.), 150
Wilson, Woodrow, 181
Wine: produced by college, 97–98, 114–15, 313. See also
  Vineyards
Winston, James, 191 (illus.)
Wolff, Al, 250
Wolter, Henry, 145
Women: students, 188, 214, 261, 265, 284–89 passim,
  292; faculty, 188, 214, 282, 317; deans of, 332; men-
  tioned, 85, 196, 249, 303f, 315, 370. See also Coedu-
  cation
Woods, Henry, 212
World War I, 181–84
World War II, 249f, 255–66 passim, 314ff
Wright, Orville and Wilbur, 137–40 passim
Wright, Louis B.: quoted, 41

Yale University, 1, 102, 143–44, 274
Yeats, William Butler, 135
Yellow Book, The, 143
Young, Edmund, 55, 86 (illus.), 102
Yorke, Peter, 186

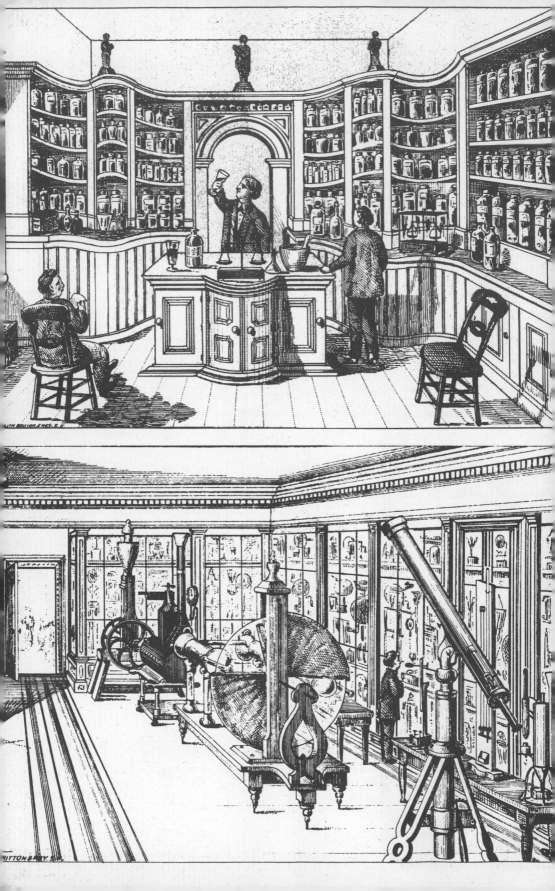